Rural Geography

Rural Geography

Michael Pacione MA PhD
Senior Lecturer in Geography
University of Strathclyde

Harper & Row, Publishers
London

Cambridge
Hagerstown
Philadelphia
New York

San Francisco
Mexico City
São Paulo
Sydney

First published 1984
Harper & Row Ltd
28 Tavistock Street
London WC2E 7PN

British Library Cataloguing in Publication Data
Pacione, Michael
   Rural geography.
   1. Rural geography   2. Human settlements
   I. Title
   307.7'2   GF127
   ISBN 0-06-318-290-4

Typeset by BookEns, Saffron Walden, Essex
Printed and bound by Butler & Tanner Ltd, Frome and London

The front cover map extract is reproduced from 1965 Ordnance Survey 1:50000 map 183 with the permission of the Controller of Her Majesty's Stationery Office, Crown Copyright Reserved. This map has now been superceded by the Ordnance Survey Second Series Landranger sheet No. 183.

Front cover photograph/A F Kersting

*To Christine, Michael John, and
Emma Victoria*

Contents

Chapter Four

Chapter Five

Chapter Six

Chapter Seven

Chapter Eight

Chapter Nine

Chapter Ten

Chapter Eleven

Chapter Twelve

Chapter Thirteen

Chapter Fourteen

Chapter Fifteen

Chapter Sixteen

Chapter Seventeen

Chapter Eighteen

Chapter Nineteen

Chapter Twenty

Preface

The study of the rural environment is a major growth area in contemporary human geography. This trend is reflected both in the amount of space devoted to rural issues in academic and professional publications, and in the expansion of undergraduate courses in the field.

A number of books have been produced dealing with specific aspects of the rural environment, for example agriculture, housing, transport, employment, land use, recreation, conservation, settlement planning and social conditions. To date, however, teachers and students engaged in university, polytechnic and college courses have not had the advantage of a basic textbook which offers a more comprehensive coverage of the wide range of themes of relevance to contemporary rural geography.

Several years of teaching an undergraduate course in rural geography unaided by such a text provided the motivation to write the present volume which is intended to provide an introduction to this important branch of geography. The spatial and temporal focus of the book is the developed world in the postwar era and an applied or problem-oriented viewpoint underlies many of the arguments presented. The book is structured into 20 chapters each of which is designed to form the basis of a lecture or block of lectures depending on the depth of treatment required and the study time available. An international perspective is employed in the selection of case studies and illustrations, and each chapter is accompanied by a lengthy bibliography as a guide to further independent investigation.

The character of contemporary rural geography owes much to the work of a host of academic geographers and others with an interest in the rural environment. I am grateful for the stimuli provided by contact with this particular 'rural community'. I would also like to record my appreciation of the technical assistance provided in the Department of Geography, University of Strathclyde, by Ms R. Spence, cartographer; Mr B. Reeves, photographer; and by Mrs M. McLeod and Mrs J. Simpson who typed the manuscript. My wife, Christine, acted as an invaluable sounding board for ideas as well as unpaid proof-reader, while Michael, aged 3, and Emma, aged 1, contributed to the progress of the work in ways only they could.

Michael Pacione,

University of Strathclyde,
Glasgow.
April, 1984

1   Introduction

The status of rural geography within the broader discipline has undergone significant change in recent decades. As Clout (1972) observed, from being at the core of studies in human geography prior to World War II, by the early 1970s the countryside as a field of geographical investigation had been relegated to an inferior position. This decline in interest in the rural environment contrasted with a growing academic and professional interest in various aspects and problems of the urban environment. By the early 1980s, however, a revival in the academic fortunes of rural geography was apparent, and Wood and Smith (1982) were able to conclude that rural geography is 'coming of age' and that its position as 'a poor relation' is no longer acceptable. Most certainly, the range and volume of work carried out under the umbrella of rural geography during the 1970s generated considerable enthusiasm for the subject and the momentum built up has ensured a central position for this branch of the discipline in the 1980s.

Significant changes have also occurred in the scope and content of rural geography. Until recently rural geography traditionally referred to studies concerned with agriculture or comprised historical analyses and descriptions of the settlement or land use patterns of the countryside. While these areas of investigation retain their importance, the subject has expanded over the last decade to encompass other lines of enquiry including, for example, the systematic study of rural transportation and accessibility, employment, housing and service provision; the assessment of planning and development policy in rural areas; investigation of conflict, power and decision-making processes; as well as attempts to develop relevant theory and methodology for rural studies. Contemporary rural geography is a multifaceted phenomenon. As Figure 1.1 indicates, the subject interacts with a host of other subdisciplines within geography, and has strong linkages with related fields of interest in economics, sociology, politics and planning. Rural geography is concerned with the operation and effects on the countryside of a wide range of economic, social and political processes, each of which has generated a field of systematic inquiry in its own right. But it is important to appreciate that rural-based investigations are not simply regional applications of some wider perspective; the rural environment poses new conceptual and methodological questions, and presents unique problems for investigation.

The rural area

Definition of the study area is an essential first step to the study of rural geography. The terms urban and rural, however, are akin to the descriptions nucleated and dispersed in that while most people recognize the characteristics of the polar types, between the two extremes there exists a high degree of uncertainty and ambiguity. Precise definition of what is meant by the term 'rural' has proved to be an elusive goal. National population censuses normally resolve the problem by employing a

1

Figure 1.1 The character of rural geography.

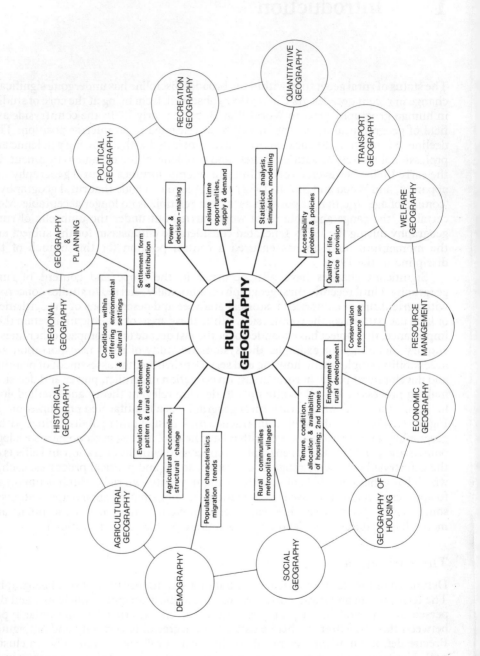

legal definition based on administrative areas that have been delineated as rural or urban on the basis of population size or population density. Another widely used criterion relates to the lower population limit to define a town. This measure is clearly culturally dependent and varies widely, from a population of 200 in some Scandinavian countries to 10,000 in Greece. Some authors, such as Cherry (1976) and Dower (1980), have employed land use as the major criterion, defining rural areas as those parts of the country which have a relatively low population density and in which agriculture, forestry or upland grazing are the predominant activities. For Volgyes (1980) rurality is characterized by four factors: (1) a landscape or habitat commonly recognized by its visual elements as countryside; (2) a relatively low population density; (3) predominance of labour-intensive, usually agricultural occupations; and (4) traditional attitudes and lifestyle. Wibberley (1972, p. 2) also employed a definition based on the dominance of extensive land uses but, significantly, added that 'it is important to emphasise that these extensive uses might have had a domination over an area which has now gone because this allows us to look at settlements which to the eye still appear to be rural but which, in practice, are merely an extension of the city resulting from the development of the commuter train and the private motor car'. Others, such as Whitby and Willis (1978), have underlined the highly general nature of land use criteria, which cannot represent the complex social structure of contemporary rural areas. Thus, an area which is defined as rural in physical/land use terms may house large numbers of people who have no connection with these activities, and the interests and needs of such residents may not coincide with those of the workers engaged in the primary sector.

By the 1970s the need to replace subjective and nebulous expressions of rurality with a more objective statistically based view was widely recognized (Cloke 1977). An early attempt to define rurality based on a selection of relevant objective measures was made by the Department of the Environment (1971) which employed 3 variables to calculate an index by which degrees of rurality could be gauged. This study pioneered the inductive approach subsequently extended by Cloke (1977) who derived an index of rurality by applying principal components analysis to 16 variables measuring population, housing, occupation and migration characteristics as well as distance from urban centres for rural districts in England and Wales. Scores on the index were mapped to display the spatial incidence of rurality and four categories of rural area were identified (Figure 1.2). An analysis of temporal changes in the rurality index over the period 1961–1971 (Cloke 1978) suggested two summary categories of 'pressured' and 'remoter' rural areas, each characterized by particular types of rural problem. The former are areas affected by the spread of urban influences into the countryside, while the latter are generally areas of outmigration. The intensity of urban influence in pressured rural areas normally falls with increasing distance from the urban centre, but specific local factors, such as restrictive planning policies in green belt areas or the personal residential preferences of migrants can operate to modify this pattern. The precise nature of urban influence can take a variety of forms ranging from physical pressure created by the movement of newcomers into rural areas and, in particular, their effect on local housing submarkets and on the demand for services, to pressure on the traditional rural social system as typified by the socio-spatial divisions within many metropolitan villages. By con-

Figure 1.2 Degrees of rurality in England and Wales, 1971.

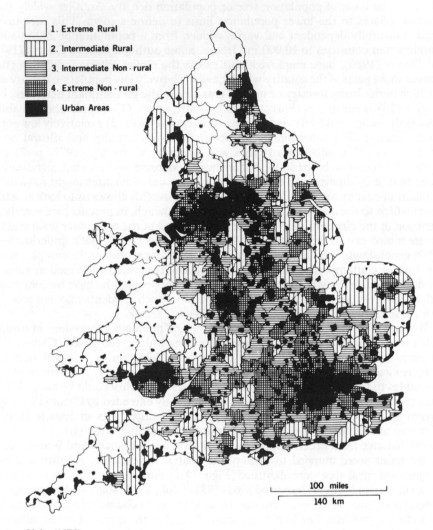

Source: Cloke (1978)

trast, in remoter rural areas urban influence is seen mainly in pressure for leisure and recreation opportunities, including second-home development in some places; and the principal problems stem from the declining economic base and resulting depopulation, loss of village service facilities, growing inaccessibility and unbalanced age-sex structure. Table 1.1 suggests some of the major problems confronting contemporary rural communities. The fact that the particular balance of concerns varies

Table 1.1   *Some major problems confronting rural areas*

1   Declining job prospects, accentuated by the loss of jobs from agriculture and rural services.
2   Below-average incomes, shortage of part-time jobs and low 'female activity rates'.
3   Deteriorating accessibility to many services and lack of mobility for those without personal transport.
4   Decline in key village services like schools, shops and post offices, and the threat of further cuts.
5   Increasing pressure on rural housing stock, with inmigration of commuters, retired people and others, high house prices, a shortage of rented housing in the private and public sectors, and severe housing problems for people with low incomes.
6   An imbalance in population, with a high proportion of elderly people in many rural communities.
7   Limited opportunities for leisure and cultural activity, felt particularly by young people.
8   Overdependence on supply of energy, jobs and services from outside the rural areas.
9   Particularly acute problems experienced by those who live in remote and small communities.
10   In many fields of policy and provision, a failure to adjust to the specific needs of rural communities.
11   Inflexible planning controls in many areas, particularly affecting smaller villages and inhibiting the development which is needed for the vitality of communities.
12   Limited ability of local residents to exercise control over decisions affecting their lives.

Source: Rural Voice (1981)

greatly between rural areas underlines the fact that the countryside is a complex and dynamic environment. Neither should the recognition of such problems disguise the fact that many rural areas are relatively problem-free and offer attractive residential environments with significant advantages and opportunities. It is also important to emphasize that the rural environment is not a closed system. Consideration must always be given to the interactions between the rural zone and urban areas (as, for example, in the case of urban fringe agriculture), as well as with national (e.g. development policies) and international (e.g. the Common Agricultural Policy) economic, social and political systems. In short, the study of rural geography requires an appreciation of the linkages among a wide variety of themes both within and outwith the immediate rural environment.

Contents overview

It is not the intention of these few paragraphs to provide a detailed account of the contents of the book, but rather to offer the reader an insight into the organization of the work.

The introductory statement on the changing status and nature of rural geography and the definition of the study area is followed by a set of three chapters dealing with the general theme of rural settlement. Chapter 2 analyses village morphology and the historical evolution of the contemporary settlement pattern. The principal theories postulated to explain the spatial organization of settlement are critically examined in Chapter 3, while Chapter 4 considers both the planned and unplanned changes affecting rural settlement as a result of postwar social and economic trends. Particular attention is given to key settlement policy, which has been a cornerstone of British rural planning, and to possible alternative strategies.

Agriculture has been a ubiquitous rural land use for millenia and this activity forms the focus of a second major theme. Chapter 5 discusses different types of farmers and farming enterprises and provides an overview of agricultural systems in the developed world. Most governments intervene in the agricultural sectors of their economies to some extent, and the varying types and degrees of public involvement along the capitalist–socialist socio-political spectrum are analysed. Farm structure is a fundamental factor in agricultural production and in Chapter 6 the issue of structural change is examined at various scales ranging from land fragmentation and plot consolidation to farm enlargement, settlement remodelling and land reform schemes. The real and potential conflicts between agriculture and urban development form the central theme of Chapter 7 in which the debate over the loss of agricultural land is considered and a range of possible strategies to protect valuable agricultural land evaluated.

In Chapter 12 the concept of quality of life is introduced and spatial variations in life quality at different geographic scales are examined. Prime components of life quality include satisfactory housing; employment; a reasonable level of personal mobility; and the availability of basic services such as health, education and shopping facilities. These welfare-related topics form the basis of Chapters 13–16. In Chapter 13 the issue of rural housing is examined first in terms of housing conditions, and then by analysing housing and household types, and by addressing the important equity question of the relationship between housing supply and demand. In Chapter 14 the prospects for rural employment generation in the private sector are examined before attention is given to the role of public development agencies in regenerating rural economies. In the postwar period, the number and range of services and facilities available to rural dwellers have shown a marked and steady decline. In Chapter 15 the scale of the problem is identified and the difficulties of and prospects for the provision of rural health care, education and retail facilities assessed. Transport is a main agent in enabling rural residents to satisfy their basic service needs and in Chapter 16 the related issues of transport and accessibility are considered. The decline in the various forms of public transport is traced and major policy responses examined, before a range of transport- and non-transport-based options to alleviate the problem are evaluated.

The resources of the natural environment form the theme which underlies the topics considered in Chapters 17–19. The exploitation and management of four environmental resources of particular significance in rural areas – minerals, water, woodlands and landscape – are discussed in Chapter 17. Conservation is clearly related to the notion of resource management and in Chapter 18 the growth of the conservation ethic is described. Attention is then afforded to the various organizations involved and powers available to pursue conservation goals. The conflict between agricultural and conservation interests is analysed and the main kinds of conservation strategies are discussed. Chapter 19 acknowledges the increasing significance of rural-based leisure activities in the modern world. Several methods of assessing demand for recreation facilities, via concepts such as potential surface analysis, demand curves and carrying capacity, are examined. Various types of recreation management procedures are considered, prior to a discussion of the role of leisure and recreation in two widely differing rural zones – national park areas and the urban fringe.

The final chapter in the book is concerned with the fundamental concept of power. The differential powers of individual property owners, pressure groups, and the State are examined at both national and local levels. The revealed redistributive effects of rural decision-making processes underlines the conclusion that to comprehend contemporary rural society fully it is essential to understand the locus and exercise of power.

References

CHERRY, G. (1976) *Rural Planning Problems.* London: Leonard Hill.

CLOKE, P. J. (1977) An index of rurality for England and Wales, *Regional Studies* 11, 31–46.

CLOKE, P. J. (1978) Changing patterns of urbanisation in the rural areas of England and Wales 1961–71, *Regional Studies* 12, 603–17.

CLOUT, H. (1972) *Rural Geography: an introductory survey.* Oxford: Pergamon.

DEPARTMENT OF THE ENVIRONMENT (1971) *The Nature of Rural Areas of England and Wales* Internal Working Paper. London: The Author.

DOWER, M. (1980) *Jobs in the Countryside.* London: National Council for Voluntary Organisations.

RURAL VOICE (1981) *A Rural Strategy.* London: The Author.

VOLGYES, I. (1980) Rural transformation. *In* I. Volgyes, R. Lonsdale and W. Avery *The Process of Rural Transformation: E. Europe, Latin America and Australia.* New York: Pergamon, 3–18.

WHITBY, M. and WILLIS, K. (1978) *Rural Resource Development.* London: Methuen.

WIBBERLEY, G. P. (1972) *Rural Activities and Rural Settlements* Paper presented to the Town and Country Planning Association Conference, London.

WOOD, A. P. and SMITH, W. (1982) *Review and Directory of Rural Geography in the Commonwealth* Discussion Paper No. 30, Department of Geography, University of Toronto.

References

2 Evolution of the settlement pattern

Rural settlements are the most significant element of the human geography of the countryside. In the world as a whole it is estimated that there are 14 million rural settlements of less than 2000 persons (Doxiadis 1968) and that 2 out of every 3 people still live in villages, hamlets or isolated rural dwellings. England with an urban:rural population ratio of 4:1 still has nearly 1500 *green villages* as well as thousands of others (Best and Rogers 1973) while, in the developing world, a country such as India has well over 600,000 villages most with populations of less than 500 (Hudson 1976). As Bunce (1982, p. 13) points out, however, 'simply because of their size it is logical to expect rural settlements to be more numerous than urban ones. A more realistic measure of the significance of rural settlements is that of the proportion of population that lives in them.' According to Doxiadis (1968), in 1960 53.0 percent of the world population lived in rural settlements (of less than 2500 persons) and nearly 6.0 percent in semi-urban settlements (up to 5000). In 1970 the United Nations (1974) estimated that 60.0 percent of the world population was rural (based on national and therefore widely varying definitions). Regional differences within these averages (e.g. between the Developed and Developing regimes) fail to undermine the importance of smaller settlements in the hierarchy.

The form of dwellings and their arrangement on the land are basic components of the rural landscape and an understanding of the morphology and genesis of villages, hamlets and farmsteads is essential for a proper appreciation of the rural environment. The study of rural settlement to date has focused on three aspects of the landscape: (1) the settlement pattern or distribution of farmsteads and dwellings; (2) the field pattern resulting from man's division of the land for productive use; (3) house and farmstead types including building materials used and folk architecture.

The geographical investigation of rural settlements has moved from an early broad base dealing with all three aspects (Houston 1953; Jones 1964) and defined generally as a study of the visual imprint made by man on the countryside in the process of occupancy to a more restricted focus in which the chief purpose is to describe and analyse the distribution of *buildings* by which people attach themselves to the land for the purposes of primary production (Stone 1965). While this narrower view may be challenged on the grounds that it excludes both important complementary features of the rural landscape, such as the form and distribution of agricultural holdings, and 'non-agricultural' settlements, the concentration on the built environment does offer a clearly definable core for a part of geography which has, until recently, been poorly understood.

The spatial distribution of dwellings

The key to the settlement pattern is the distribution of individual dwellings, and this aspect of the cultural landscape varies between nations and regions. It is generally

9

agreed that most American farmers live on their own land in dispersed or isolated farmsteads although agricultural villages have been established in New England, in Mormon areas, and in the Spanish-American southwest. In contrast dispersed settlement is the exception and agricultural villages the rule in many other parts of the world including Europe, parts of Latin America, in the densely farmed regions of Asia, and among the sedentary farming peoples of Africa and the Middle East. Marked contrasts can be observed, however, even within a country as small as Britain. Thorpe (1964) identified 28 different rural settlement zones in the British Isles each with several subtypes. This high degree of complexity may be reduced if we accept that basically there are only two types of rural settlement – dwellings can be either clustered together or dispersed across the countryside. In reality, of course, these types form the poles of a continuum, with rural hamlets possessing features of both types intermediate between the two extremes. The nucleated–dispersed settlement dichotomy 'is based more upon general statements about grouping and non-grouping of buildings than upon any rigorous definitions. There is, therefore, no agreement on the minimum spacing of dispersed settlements, nor on the number of buildings required for a nucleation' (Bunce 1982, p. 23). Nevertheless this simple division serves as a useful starting point for the morphogenetic analysis of rural settlement.

Factors favouring nucleated settlement

Numerous causal factors, primarily historic rather than modern, led to the nucleation of the rural population. Most writers identify six main influences.

Most obvious, perhaps, is the need for defence against external threat. This was certainly relevant in the past; at a time when outlaw bands roamed freely throughout Europe farmers could better defend themselves by grouping together in villages and travelling out to the fields daily. In more recent times the Kenyan Mau Mau emergency saw the 'villagization' of over 1 million inhabitants (Apthorpe and MacArthur 1968). A significant part of Israel's current agricultural labour force lives in concentrated settlements and commutes to the fields as a response to guerrilla incursions by Palestinian forces (Berler 1970). Both in the past and present there are many instances of villages which have grown larger during periods of insecurity or war only to shrink or disappear when peace has been restored. In Malaya, for example, of the 438 new villages which existed in 1954 following a villagization programme, 38 were abandoned six years later (Chisholm 1979).

Even more important as a cohesive force in the primary settlement of an area were family and clan ties, for the initial sedentary settlements were often made by people who were blood relatives. Such settlements can readily be identified from place name evidence. The common western European suffixes -ingen, -inge, -ing, and -ange, for example, are all derived from the Germanic tongue and mean literally 'the people of'. The accompanying prefix was typically the name of the family or clan leader. Thus Sigmaringen, a settlement in southwestern Germany, was founded by 'the people of Sigmar'. Such social ties were often associated with a degree of communalism in which agricultural land was not privately owned. Cropland was typically allotted so that each villager had equal acreage, equal soil fertility and equal distance to travel. The resultant fragmentation and periodic redistribution of land holdings retarded dispersal of people from the village since individual plots were generally too small to accommodate a house.

The relative abundance or scarcity of water can also influence village formation. Areas of permeable rock such as limestone encouraged clusters of farmsteads where water was available either from deep wells or springs, as on the South Wiltshire Downs in England. Superabundance of water in marshy areas and flood zones can stimulate clustering on available 'dry points', for example the village of Haddenham in the English Fens or the 'wurt' settlements developed on man-made mounds (terpen) in the coastal Netherlands. One must, of course, caution against simple environmental determinism by recalling that there are many areas where wells must be sunk but farms are scattered as in parts of the Chilterns or in the limestone Causses of France. Equally, many areas of abundant surface water are also regions of grouped settlement as in the English Midlands or on the boulder clays of the north German plain.

The presence of villages may also be related to the practice of divided inheritance. Under these conditions an original isolated farmhouse will over the years become a clustered settlement as successive generations of descendants of the original settler build houses on the same site. Examples of this type of settlement can be found in the areas of Europe which came under Roman law. Conversely, in areas where inheritance was traditionally by the law of primogeniture the dispersed settlement pattern persists as in northwestern Germany and parts of Norway.

There is also a correlation between nucleation and crop-based economies, as opposed to those based on the raising of livestock. This is because livestock rearing requires large farms and the larger the farm the less likely is the farmer to live in a village because of the increased travel time between house and farm. Since, in general, lowland areas have been dominated by crop agriculture and upland areas used for pastoral activities, there is a related correlation between level terrain and village settlement in Europe. But, as the physical environment does not absolutely govern man's behaviour, exceptions to this rule do exist as in the dispersed settlements of the plains of Flanders and northwestern Germany and the large clustered villages of mountainous southern Italy (King and Strachan 1978).

Political, religious or ideological considerations may lead to the clustering of the rural population. In USSR from 1959 there was forcible concentration of population into villages of 1000 or more partly to facilitate service provision but partly also as a means of maintaining ideological control of the peasantry, and in the conviction that collective forms of agriculture were both desirable and a suitable means of ensuring the delivery of prescribed quotas (Pallot 1977). The rural settlement structure today is radically different from that of 50 years ago, being a creation of modern Soviet planning and ideology (Burmantov 1968; Voskresensky 1976). Similarly the main aims in the creation of the Chinese village commune were the establishment of communist society in rural areas and the transformation of the agricultural economy to produce food as efficiently as possible for a growing urban-industrial population. Other examples of villagization can be seen in sixteenth-century Mexico (West and Augelli 1966), the Mormon colonization of the USA (Broek and Webb 1973; Jackson 1978) and in many twentieth-century agricultural resettlement schemes. In Tanzania, for example, the principal of the Ujamaa villages and the villagization programme in general is the encouragement of communal and cooperative activity and local participatory democracy. The aim is to reduce the fragmentation of rural settlement by bringing population into these new nucleated settlements in which peasant agricultural productivity and public facilities can be improved (Hirst 1978). Similar trends can be identified in other African states such as Nigeria (Fogg 1971), Kenya (MacArthur 1968; Taylor 1969), and Zambia (Siddle 1971), as well as in some European countries (Bunce 1982; Mayhew 1970).

Factors favouring dispersed settlement

The factors which encourage the dispersed form of rural settlement most common in Anglo-America, Australia, New Zealand and South Africa are precisely the opposite of those favouring the village development characteristic of Europe. They include:

(a)   An absence of the need for defence, prompted by peace and security.
(b)   Colonization by individual pioneer families rather than by groups bound together by the ties of blood-relationship or religion.
(c)   Domination by private-enterprise agriculture rather than communalism.
(d)   Unit block farms rather than scattered holdings.
(e)   A rural economy dominated by livestock-rearing or ranching.
(f)   Hilly or mountainous terrain.
(g)   Readily available water supplies.
(h)   Deliberate governmental action to break up villages, piece together fragmented holdings and thereby produce a more efficient agriculture.

All of these factors are significant but monocausal explanations will in all but the most localized instances provide only partial insight into the reasons behind the distribution of grouped and scattered settlement. Defence, water supply, terrain, and degree of collective organization may play their part but they do so in the general context of the social framework of rural society and in the particular context of the relationship of settlement to agriculture. Consequently geographers are increasingly endeavouring to interpret rural settlement forms as a function of agrarian, social and economic relationships in a particular environment at any given time period (Smith 1965, 1967).

The morphology of rural settlements

Settlement classification

A first step in interpreting rural-settlement morphology is the classification of types and forms to reduce a considerable variety to some form of order. Modern attempts to classify rural settlements date from 1895 when Meitzen produced his classic four-volume work on the settlements and agriculture of Germany. In this he suggested that contemporary patterns of farmstead distribution were an indicator of the cultural group that had first permanently settled an agricultural area; Celtic peoples in isolated farmsteads, Slavs in round and street villages, and Germans in irregular cluster villages. According to this ethnic viewpoint village settlement was associated with Teutonic expansion after the fall of the Roman Empire. The fact that grouped village settlement was characteristic of western Germany, Alsace-Lorraine and northeast France tended to support the validity of this explanation. Similarly in England the difference between village settlement in the Midlands and the scattered farmsteads of western Britain might be thought to confirm this interpretation. On closer analysis, however, the equivalence of German influence with village settlement and of scattered settlement with other ethnic groups cannot be seriously maintained. Northwest Germany and much of Flanders, parts of East Anglia and Kent, parts of Denmark and much of Sweden are regions of scattered settlement but are obviously within the area of Teutonic occupation. The same is true in southern Germany and Austria. Village settlement also occurs widely in areas in which German influence cannot easily be traced in any way, such as parts of western France in the basins of Rennes or Caen.

Demangeon (1928, 1939) divided settlement into agglomerated and dispersed and subdivided each of these broad categories as shown in Table 2.1.

Table 2.1 *Settlement types according to Demangeon*

Agglomerated villages	Dispersed farmsteads
1. with champion or open-field systems	1. primary dispersion of ancient origin (e.g. western France or highland Britain)
2. with contiguous fields (e.g. marsh and forest villages of the Low Countries and central Europe)	2. intercalated dispersion (e.g. scattered farmsteads of medieval foundation between earlier villages as in the English Midlands)
3. with disassociated fields (e.g. in Mediterranean areas)	3. secondary dispersion (e.g. post-enclosure Sweden)
	4. primary dispersion of recent origin (e.g. nineteenth-century settlement of the USA)

Source: Demangeon (1928)

This classification has considerable merit from a European point of view in that it stresses the association of settlement with field systems and a sequential order of dispersion in relation to clustered settlement. A methodological anomaly is that a different basis is used to categorize each of the two major divisions, one functional the other genetic.

Most subsequent attempts to classify rural settlement types have employed morphological criteria. Demangeon (1939) used this criterion to subdivide grouped settlements in France recognizing linear, massed and star-shaped villages but the explanatory power of such a typology is low. Most other work on rural settlement types has been carried out by German scholars. Schwartz (1949) classified grouped settlements on the basis of size (small being 3–10 houses, medium 10–25, and large with over 25 houses), compactness (tight and loose), shape and regularity. Clearly the number of possible combinations of these factors produces a large variety of village

Table 2.2   *Classification of village types according to Christaller*

Village Form	Type Name	Location
(a) Irregular clustered villages	Haufendorfer	Rhineland
(b) Regular clustered villages		
(i) place villages with greens	Platadorfer/Rundlinge	Sorbenland
(ii) linear and compact grouped about an elongated green	Angerdorfer	East Germany
(iii) street villages, compact	Strassendorfer	East Germany
(iv) linear villages:		
marsh	Marschhufendorfer	Schleamig
forest	Waldhufendorfer	Silesia
heath	Hagenhufendorfer	Northwest Germany
fen	Moorkolonien/Fehnkolonien	Northwest Germany
(v) estate settlements	Gutskolonien	

Source: Christaller (1966)

types. More significantly the point at which a division is made between regular and irregular or tight and loose is an arbitrary and subjective one. One of the most satisfactory classifications of German rural settlement was produced by Christaller (1961) but the more general applicability of his typology outside Europe is limited. His classification of village types is shown on Table 2.2.

Roberts (1979) has proposed a classification of village plans on the basis of their shape, degree of regularity, and presence or absence of open space. A set of symbols is designed to facilitate mapping of the village types identified. Figure 2.1 illustrates the application of the scheme with reference to a selection of village plans from northern England. Roberts (1979, p. 123) suggests that although constructed for use in the north of England the classification appears to have more general applicability, but he also cautions that it is 'a working tool to be used flexibly and to be abandoned when no longer useful'. A number of qualifications must be kept in mind when using the system. First, the classification is based entirely on morphology. Function is not considered being regarded as 'an entirely different dimension of reality'. Thus the fact that two settlements have virtually identical forms need not mean that they have a common origin. A second point is that no village ever accords completely with the most regular ideal type although in the USA and Israel perfectly regular settlements can be found. Third, village plans are frequently composites of two or more basic types. Finally, while the three variables which form the basis of the classification system are the principal plan variables, additionally important factors are size, complexity, building density and degree of fragmentation.

Figure 2.1 Village forms; principles of classification and mapping symbols.

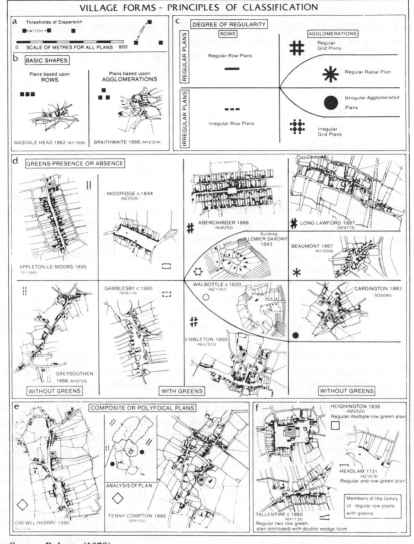

Source: Roberts (1979)

Weaknesses of classification systems

All of the systems produced to date share some of the following weaknesses.

(1)   Degree of subjectivity involved: Hart (1975, p. 159) observed that 'distinctions between village types, especially between types which are quite similar, are some-

times based upon differences so extremely subtle that the classification of individual villages becomes more an act of faith than an objective exercise'. Clearly the subjective element of many classification schemes limits their utility for comparative purposes. Attempts to employ statistical indices to describe degrees of population nucleation or dispersion, such as Demangeon's index of agglomeration (shown below), have not been widely adopted (Houston 1953);

$$K = \frac{E.N.}{T}$$

where K is the index of agglomeration
   E is the population of the commune excluding that of the chief nucleated settlement
   N is the number of settlements excluding the chief centre
   T is the total population of the commune

(2)   Lack of general applicability: most classification systems having been devised within a particular regional context (e.g. Christaller in Germany, Demangeon in France, and Thorpe in Britain) are only accurately calibrated for a particular cultural realm. None of these cited are applicable outside Europe.

(3)   Morphological emphasis: a basic weakness is the emphasis on settlement morphology and the insufficient attention given to the functional bases of modern rural settlement. The fact that villages may be similar in physical form but different in origin and function renders these classifications largely descriptive.

(4)   Temporal validity: they are essentially historical, being classifications of agricultural settlements set in the context of nineteenth-century and early-twentieth-century land use patterns.

(5)   Scale: the usefulness of settlement form classifications depends to a great extent on the scale of application whether local, regional or national. Even within an area as small as Britain many possible settlement classifications may be applied.

An attempt has been made by the International Geographical Union (IGU) to overcome these difficulties by producing a general typology of rural settlement according to which all rural settlements can be registered and classified, and existing terminology uniformly arranged and defined (Uhlig 1972). Four basic criteria related to function, morphology and location, genesis, and future development are divided into 66 subcriteria 'which appears to permit the categorization of virtually any type of settlement' (Bunce 1982, p. 25). In principle the IGU classification system permits the identification of the whole range of rural settlement types. The taxonomic approach, however, is highly technical and abstract and far removed from the reality of rural settlements as human habitations. Nevertheless, provided these limitations are kept in mind classification schemes based on explicitly stated criteria do offer a means of reducing the complexity of the real world and imposing some order on the confused palimpsest that is the built countryside.

Distribution of settlement types

For a full understanding of rural settlement types one must consider morphology, function and the factors influencing each within a particular cultural setting at a particular time. Such a multivariate perspective can now be employed to examine the distribution of rural settlements in Europe and North America.

Europe

Since German writers have been most active in such research much of their terminology has been accepted to describe the different types of rural settlement identified. As Figure 2.2 shows, one of the common types of nucleated settlement is the 'irregular clustered village' or *Haufendorf* found in parts of western Germany, northern France, lowland Britain and much of southern Europe. As the name implies, the irregular clustered village presents a haphazard appearance lacking any trace of planning with winding streets and randomly bunched farmsteads. The village church is usually found somewhere toward the centre of the cluster surrounded by the farmhouses, barns and kitchen gardens of the villagers. The size varies greatly ranging from 400–1,000 population in the Germanic lands to 10,000 or more in the hilltop agricultural villages of southern Italy, and even as many as 20,000–30,000 inhabitants in the farming settlements (kertes varos) of the Hungarian basin. The key

Figure 2.2 Forms of rural settlement in Europe.

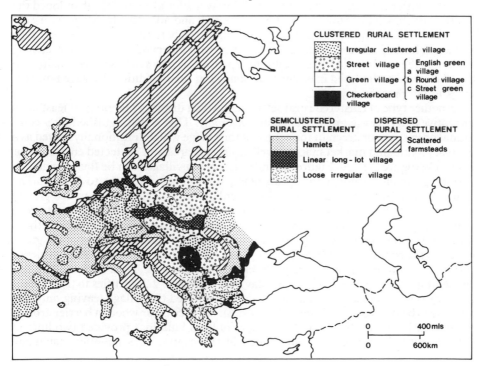

to the origin of the haufendorf lies in the obvious lack of formal planning. These irregular clustered villages probably began either as a loose grouping of a few farmsteads of related families forming a clan hamlet with enlargement consequent upon population growth; or, in some cases, as a single isolated farmstead with the practice of divided inheritance causing the multiplication of houses. The irregular clustered village is the dominant form of settlement west of the ancient German-Slav border of AD 800 which ran from Lubeck on the Baltic to Bohemia via the rivers Elbe and Saale.

By contrast in much of eastern Europe, in the traditional Slavic domain, most village types exhibit in their present form a high degree of planning. The most typical of these regular forms is the 'street village' or *Strassendorf*. Instead of the disorderly maze of streets found in the haufendorf only one straight street is present with the farmhouses lined up along the street and the kitchen gardens lying out behind (Figure 2.3). Street villages range in size from small farms usually found on side roads or on dead-end lanes to long settlements of several hundred people on the main rural highways. Almost certainly, the street village is of Slavic origin with many of the village names, even in eastern Germany, bearing the characteristic suffixes of -ow, -in, -itz, and -zig. What particular aspect of the northern Slav culture led them to choose the strassendorf as their most common form of rural settlement is less clear. The outer wooden fence around the kitchen garden perimeter and the rear walls of the farm buildings would have provided two lines of defence, but there are other superior defensive forms of settlement. Equally intriguing is the fact that groups of German settlers moving eastward beyond the river Elbe after AD 800 abandoned the haufendorf they had known in western Germany and adopted the Slavic strassendorf. An explanation may lie in the close relationship between rural settlement type and agricultural practices. A linear street village with independent holdings stretching back from the road would better facilitate expansion as new settlers moved in. In time the Slavs were assimilated in eastern Germany but their traditional village type survives to the present day.

Another type of clustered rural settlement which displays planning, at least in its formative stage, is the green village or *Angerdorf*. This is distinguished by a communal open space or green in the centre of the village which traditionally served as a festival ground and market place as well as grazing area and protected enclosure for livestock (Figure 2.3). As Figure 2.2 indicates, green villages can be found widely in various parts of the north European plain, from lowland Britain to Poland. The shape of the green which determined the configuration of the village varied greatly and several subtypes can be recognized on this basis. One of these is the street-green village or *Strassenangerdorf* found mixed in with the street villages of the northern Slavs and eastern Germans. One of the visually most striking subtypes of the green village is the round village or *Runddorf* (Figure 2.3). Place name and other evidence suggest that round villages were probably of Slavic origin. Their morphology and concentration along the old German-Slav border (Figure 2.2) testifies to their defensive function. A single dead-end street usually entered the village leaving only one opening to be blocked off in times of attack. An outer circular wooden barrier around the garden land and the inner tight cluster of farm buildings provided two lines of defence with the village well and green in the centre. It is possible that many

Figure 2.3 Top – Strassendorf: the farm village of Eicha in the East German province of Sachsen.
Middle – Angerdorf of the East German type.
Bottom – Runddorf: the village of Lichtentanne in the province of Sachsen.

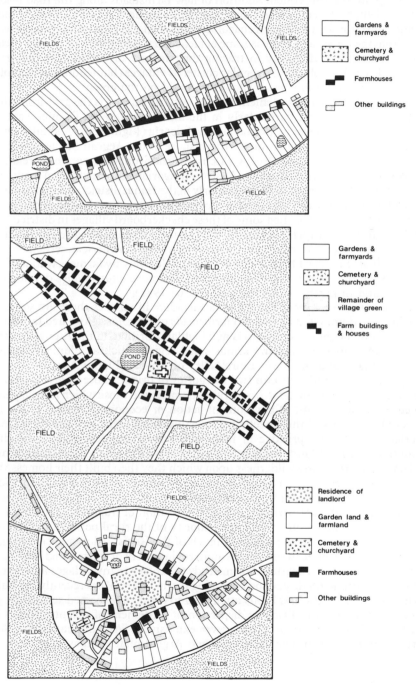

strassenangerdörfer may be simply elongated round villages deprived of their charac-teristic shape by the subsequent addition of new farmsteads along the road leading into the settlement. Green villages may represent a modern survival of one of man's most ancient settlement forms. Archaeologists have discovered green villages as far back as Iron Age times, and there is some evidence that they might be of even greater antiquity. Part of the difficulty in tracing their former distribution is that green villages could easily evolve into irregular clustered villages (haufendörfer) if, as often happened, later generations were allowed to build on the green.

Another planned rural settlement form of eastern Europe is the grid-iron village or *Schachbrettdorf*, found particularly in the middle and lower Danube valley in parts of Hungary, Yugoslavia, Romania and Bulgaria (Figure 2.2). A similar type is found in some areas bordering the northern shore of the Aegean Sea in Greece. In contrast to the village types already discussed grid-iron villages are of relatively recent origin. The government of the Austro-Hungarian empire founded many such settlements beginning about 1750 particularly in the Banat district of Yugoslavia and southern Hungary as part of a project to repopulate areas which had been ravaged by warfare. The Greeks established some of these checkerboard villages in districts from which the Turks were expelled in the 1920s. The trade mark of the grid-iron village is the rectangular street pattern, similar to the layout of most American settlements but differing in that the schachbrettdorf is peopled exclusively by farmers who work the surrounding lands. Some of the best examples of *planned estate village* development are to be found in northeast Scotland (Lockhart 1981).

While it is true that most European farmers live in villages there are some dis-tricts which are dominated by isolated farmsteads of *Einzelhöfe*. Isolated farmsteads are dominant throughout Scandinavia and highland Britain, in the Alps and certain other mountain districts, and in various small regions such as Flanders, parts of western Germany and the lower Loire valley of France (Figure 2.2).

Dispersed farmsteads fall into two categories of origin: those of great antiquity which represent a traditional form of rural settlement and those which have appeared in recent times as a result of government action or economic change. In the first group would be many of the einzelhöfe of northwestern Germany and the adjacent Netherlands where the practice of undivided inheritance left many individuals without property rights and thus forced them to leave the village to reclaim farming land from the surrounding wilderness upon which they then built their homes. More commonly, however, dispersed farmsteads are of more recent origin. In the Scan-dinavian countries, for example, governmental decrees issued in the late eighteenth and early nineteenth centuries led in time to abolition of fragmented holdings and brought about the dispersal of the large majority of the rural population. The con-version from arable to sheep pasture in much of the British Isles, associated with a drastic population decline in rural areas and a replacement of fragmented holdings by unit-block farms, caused scattered farmsteads to replace many villages and hamlets in a process of secondary dispersion beginning in the 1400s. More recently the Italian government in the 1920s and 1930s attempted to create a dispersed settlement pat-tern in the Mezzogiorno. Primary dispersion of settlement of recent origin is less characteristic of Europe than of the newer extensively farmed areas of the North American prairies, Australian grasslands and Argentinian pampas.

North America

Early European colonists of America brought knowledge of agriculture and settlement forms from their homelands, but the challenge of organizing a new territory led to modification of traditional ways and eventually to a distinct American imprint on the landscape. According to Broek and Webb (1973), four separate settlement patterns evolved along the Atlantic seaboard:

(1)   the French in Nova Scotia and along the St Lawrence river;
(2)   the English in New England;
(3)   the ethnically mixed Middle Atlantic States from lower New York to southeastern Pennsylvania;
(4)   the English south from Maryland to Georgia.

Although traditional practices were greatly altered by the new problems, agricultural methods and building materials which were encountered as the wave of occupation moved westward, modern North American rural settlement forms can only be understood as descendants of the earlier colonial activity.

French influence dates from the seventeenth century when the kings of France made land grants to noblemen and the Church to stimulate colonization along the St Lawrence river. Each tract had frontage of a mile or more on the river or its tributaries and stretched inland for several miles (Figure 2.4). The landowners parcelled out their properties in parallel strips to settlers in such a manner that each would have access to the river. Equal inheritance rights among sons, in the French tradition, led in a few generations to the subdivision of each farm. In this way were developed the long-lot farms that still characterize the zone between Montreal and Quebec. Instead of the clustered manor village typical of large parts of feudal France, and initially promoted by officials in Lower Canada, each settler built his farmstead on his own land. A similar linear settlement pattern was also produced for the same reasons by French settlers in Louisiana.

By contrast, village life was characteristic of seventeenth-century New England. Several factors have been suggested to explain this compact form of agricultural settlement in the 'new world'. Some see the New England village as an obvious transfer of the rural tradition of lowland England, others stress the need for defence against Indian attack, and a third view refers to the social organization of close-knit religious groups, such as the Puritans, as the main reason why the early colonists built their dwellings in clusters (Brown 1948; Scofield 1938; Trewartha 1946). There is evidence for the operation of all three. The early agrarian colonies in New England were *group* efforts in land development. The Crown had granted extensive lands to trading companies which in turn gave out tracts or 'townships' of 4 to 10 miles square to groups of men called proprietors for the purpose of establishing a plantation (i.e. a planting or colony of immigrants). Each settler received a home lot in the village ranging from 0.5 acres in some places to 5 acres in others. The degree of village compactness depended on the size of home lots. At the centre was the village green flanked by the meeting-house or church, cemetery, school and homes of distinguished residents. Each family received several strips of land within each of two or three planting blocks which were located around the village in the most favourable places for crops.

Figure 2.4 Long lots in the seigneury of Boucherville, Quebec. Beyond the first range of lots parallel roads were the starting lines for new ranges of lots as settlement proceeded. A road at right angles to the river, called the 'back road' linked the successive ranges with the waterway.

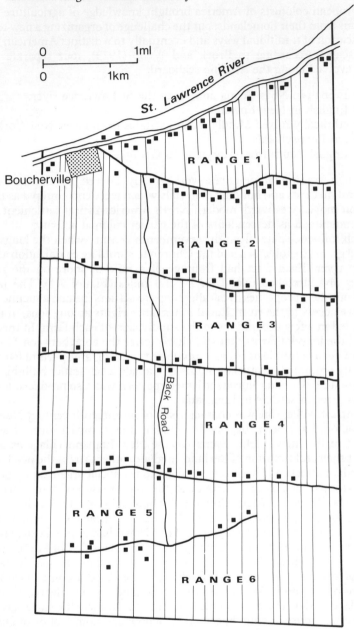

Source: Broek and Webb (1973)

The open-field system of agriculture and the green-village form of settlement were reflections of lowland Britain. Newer colonists tended to locate their farmsteads along the main road entering or leaving the village resulting in a linear row settlement reminiscent of the strassendorf of eastern Europe. Where there was little planning control farmsteads were dispersed throughout the township area. The rural landscape of modern New England still reflects the difference between the layout of the old seventeenth-century villages and the later settlements on individual farms (Scofield 1938). The correlation between degree of central control and the nucleated-village form of settlement is also well illustrated by the nineteenth-century colonization of Utah by Mormon settlers (Figure 2.5).

Figure 2.5 The Mormon village of Escalante, Utah typically laid out in square blocks each divided into four home lots.

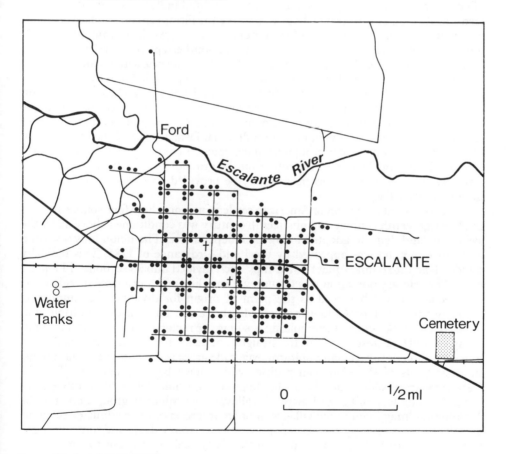

Source: Broek and Webb (1973)

The settlement pattern in the Middle Atlantic area differed markedly from that in New England. Here the village was the exception rather than the rule. Two reasons are usually advanced for the early prevalence of dispersed settlement. First, land development in this area always had a more pronounced commercial character. The vast tracts awarded to land companies or individuals were sold to settlers in compact freeholds. Second, the colonists came singly or in small family groups from many countries, including Holland, Sweden, Scotland, Ireland and Germany, and so lacked the homogeneity characteristic of early New England. In addition, the immigrants found land prices low enough to buy good-sized farms of 100–300 acres and under these conditions dispersed dwellings were the obvious choice.

A fourth major source area for North American settlement forms was the South. Early colonists in Virginia and Georgia lived initially in fortified villages but the dispersed pattern of occupancy soon prevailed. The peculiar agriculture of the region had a marked influence on the form of settlement. From a very early date production of commercial export crops, such as tobacco, rice and indigo, dominated Southern farming. As long as European labour was scarce the farms remained relatively modest in size, but the importation of large numbers of Negro slaves from about 1700 onward allowed many to develop into the classic Southern plantation (Prunty 1955). The later abolition of slavery also influenced the form of rural settlement, leading to the break up of the large plantation estate into sharecropping subunits of 30–40 acres and the dispersal of houses from the cluster around the plantation headquarters onto individual plots. Since the 1940s, however, another change in agricultural methods has affected the settlement pattern. Farm mechanization and plot consolidation have resulted in a decrease in the number of individual farmsteads and the relocation of those remaining into linear groupings along roads. Looking ahead, Prunty (1955) foresaw greater nucleation in the future on the grounds that amenities sufficiently attractive to agricultural workers can only be provided economically by grouping houses into a village.

The westward extension of American settlement from these four source areas in the late eighteenth century and nineteenth century was conditioned above all by the system of land division adopted following independence. The ubiquitous township and range method was approved by the Land Ordinance of 1785. This basically divided land into 6 mile square 'townships' each divided into 36 sections of 1 square mile. The primary operation was to survey a base line and a principal meridian the intersection of which served as the point of origin for dividing and numbering townships and sections. Colonists obtained either a quarter section or multiple of it. Consequently the typical farm holding is square or rectangular, the farm buildings being established close to one of the straight boundary roads. The rural landscape, however, though superficially uniform over wide areas is not without its variations. In those parts of the Canadian prairies which have been occupied by French-Canadian farmers, for example, the holdings are unusually long and narrow resembling the 'long lots' of the St Lawrence valley. Other minority groups, notably the Mennonites, may live in true villages in order to preserve their ethnic or religious identity but, increasingly, farmers are moving away from villages and contributing to the overall dispersed-settlement pattern that is typical of rural North America.

References

APTHORPE, R. and MacARTHUR, J. (1968) Land settlement policies in Kenya. *In* R. Apthorpe *Land Settlement and Rural Development in Eastern Africa*. London: Transition Books, 29–32.

BERLER, A. (1970) *Urban-Rural Relations in Israel: Social and Economic Aspects*. Rlhovet: Settlement Study Centre.

BEST, R. H. and ROGERS, A. W. (1973) *The Urban Countryside*. London: Faber and Faber.

BROEK, J. and WEBB, J. (1973) *A Geography of Mankind*. New York: McGraw Hill.

BROWN, R. H. (1948) *Historical Geography of the United States*. New York: Harcourt, Brace.

BUNCE, M. (1982) *Rural Settlement in an Urban World*. London: Croom Helm.

BURMANTOV, G. G. (1968) The formation of functional types of settlements in the southern Taiga, *Soviet Geography Review and Translation* 9, 112–19.

CHISHOLM, M. (1979) *Rural Settlement and Land Use* 3rd edition. London: Hutchinson.

CHRISTALLER, W. (1961) Reproduced in R. W. Dickenson *Germany*. London: Methuen, 144–8.

CHRISTALLER, W. (1966) *Central Places in Southern Germany* translated by C. W. Baskin. New Jersey: Prentice Hall.

DEMANGEON, A. (1928) La Géographie de l'Habitat Rurale, *Report of the Commission on Types of Rural Settlement*. Newtown, Montgomeryshire: International Geographical Union.

DEMANGEON, A. (1939) Types de villages en France, *Annales de Géographie* 48, 1–21.

DOXIADIS, C. A. (1968) *Ekistics*. London: Hutchinson.

FOGG, C. D. (1971) Smallholder agriculture in eastern Nigeria. *In* G. Dalton *Economic Development and Social Change*. New York: Natural History Press, 575–96.

HART, J. F. (1975) *The Look of the Land*. New Jersey: Prentice Hall.

HIRST, M. A. (1978) Recent villagization in Tanzania, *Geography* 43, 122–5.

HOUSTON, J. H. (1953) *A Social Geography of Europe*. London: Duckworth.

HUDSON, F. S. (1976) *Geography of Settlements* 2nd edition. Plymouth: Macdonald and Evans.

JACKSON, R. H. (1978) Mormon perception and settlement, *Annals of the Association of American Geographers* 68, 317–34.

JONES, E. (1964) *Human Geography*. London: Chatto and Windus.

KING, R. and STRACHAN, A. (1978) Sicilian agro towns, *Erdkunde* 32, 110–23.

LOCKHART, D. G. (1981) The planned villages. *In* M. L. Parry and T. L. Slater *The Making of the Scottish Countryside*. London: Croom Helm, 249–70.

MacARTHUR, J. D. (1968) Agricultural settlement in Kenya. *In* G. K. Helleiner *Agricultural Planning in East Africa*. Nairobi: East African Publishing House, 117–35.

MAYHEW, A. (1970) Structural reform and the future of West German agriculture, *Geographical Review* 60, 54–68.

PALLOT, J. (1977) *Some preliminary thoughts on Soviet rural settlement planning* Working Paper No. 206. Leeds: University Department of Geography.

PRUNTY, M. (1955) The renaissance of the Southern plantation, *Geographical Review* 45, 459–91.

ROBERTS, B. K. (1982) The anatomy of the village, *Landscape History*, 4, 11–20.

ROBERTS, B. K. (1979) *Rural Settlement in Britain*. London: Hutchinson.

SCHWARTZ, G. (1949) *Allgemeine Sedlungsgeographie*. Hannover: Technische Hochschule.

SCOFIELD, E. (1938) The origin of settlement patterns in rural New England, *Geographical Review* 28, 652–63.

SIDDLE, D. J. (1971) Rural development schemes. *In* D. H. Davies *Zambia in Maps*. London: The University Press, 70.

SMITH, C. T. (1965) Historical geography: current trends and prospects. *In* R. J. Chorley and P. Haggett *Frontiers in Geographical Teaching*. London: Methuen, 118–43.

SMITH, C. T. (1967) *An Historical Geography of Western Europe Before 1800*. London: Longman.

STONE, K. H. (1965) The development of a focus for the geography of settlement, *Economic Geography* 41, 346–55.

TAYLOR, D. (1969) Agricultural change in Kikuyuland. *In* M. F. Thomas and G. W. Whittington *Environment and Land Use in Africa*. London: Methuen, 463–93.

THORPE, H. (1964) Rural settlement. *In* J. W. Watson and J. B. Sissons *The British Isles: A Systematic Geography*. London: Nelson, 358–79.

TREWARTHA, G. T. (1946) Types of rural settlement in colonial America, *Geographical Review* 36, 568–96.

UHLIG, H. (1972) Rural Settlements *International Working Group for the Geographical Terminology of the Agricultural Landscape*. Giesson: International Geographical Union.

UNITED NATIONS (1974) *Human Settlement: The Environmental Challenge*. New York: Macmillan.

VOSKRESENSKY, L. (1976) Soviet village resettlement, *Town and Country Planning* 44(12), 535–7.

WEST, R. C. and AUGELLI, J. P. (1966) *Middle America: Its Lands and Peoples*. New Jersey: Prentice Hall.

3   Spatial organization of settlement

Spatial equilibrium theories

Early investigations of rural settlement were carried out as part of a broadly defined interest in the rural environment. Preference was given to the study of house types, village morphology, the historical and cultural origins of settlements, and the relationship between settlement and field patterns. In 1899 a German geographer, Schluter, building on earlier work (Stone 1965), proposed a 'geography of settlement' which would consider topics such as the location, size and growth of settlements, their areal arrangement and relationship to their surroundings, in addition to the traditional elements of internal structure, external form and appearance and related economic and historical-cultural influences (Schluter 1899). Later, Schluter (1906) stressed that *settlement geography* focuses on the residential relationships of man to the land; that groups of houses in villages and towns are important (not the individual houses); and that the overall settlement network is of greater significance than the form and location of single towns or villages. These sentiments defined a more sharply focused subject area and paved the way for subsequent work by others, such as Christaller, on the spatial arrangement of rural settlement.

Before attempting to explain the location, size and spacing of rural settlements, however, it is first necessary to comment briefly on the nature of the village in Europe and North America. Man is a gregarious animal. He also normally attempts to accomplish tasks with the least possible effort. Given this, the nucleated village or hamlet was the most efficient form of settlement for the semicommunal life of early modern man. As we have seen, even after the disappearance of the feudal system, and the consequent loosening of man's ties to the land the nucleated village continued to be a significant feature of the European rural landscape. The importance of the modern European village, however, owes less to its traditional influence over the land and local community than to the diversification of social and economic structure since the Middle Ages (Thirsk 1961). By the mid nineteenth century most villages in England contained a wide range of services and other commercial activities. As Bunce (1982, p. 52) points out, 'from its agricultural peasant beginning the village in industrialised Europe has evolved into a small-scale residential, social and commercial community'. The organizational separation of village settlement from agricultural land use is most apparent in the rural regions of the New World. In most of these areas rural settlement began with a dispersed farm population, and nucleated settlements grew up primarily as trade centres to serve the economic and social needs of the dispersed population. Berry (1967) has described the development of trade centres in southwest Iowa over the period 1851 to 1956. Such a case study is useful because a similar process will have occurred in many other areas of North America as the frontier moved westward. Similarly, in New Zealand Anderson and Franklin (1955, p. 56) describe villages which are 'rural but non-farm, urban but not fully urban' and which 'act principally as servicing and trading, distribution and collecting centres'.

One result of the geneological differences between rural settlements in the Old and New Worlds is that even the use of the word village to describe the latter is problematical. Anderson and Franklin (1955, p. 56), for example, emphasize that while in the English language the word village inevitably carries with it a number of associations 'when applied to New Zealand these associations must be disregarded'. North American terminology for these settlements is confused; for example, in independent studies of small trade centres in Wisconsin, Hart and Salisbury (1965) describe them as villages, and Fuguitt and Deeley (1966) employ the term small town, while Fuguitt later refers to the same places as villages (Johansen and Fuguitt 1973).

Historical differences and terminological difficulties notwithstanding, it is clear that most modern villages possess a wider range of functions than their agricultural antecedents, and that they serve the surrounding territory to some degree. Settlements which interact with and provide goods and services to an adjacent geographical area (as well as to their resident population) have been termed central places.

By definition, the location of central places is closely connected with the general distribution of population. If the population of an area is evenly spread then the settlements which serve it will also be evenly distributed. If the distribution of population is uneven, central places will be concentrated in the most accessible locations. Some central places in favourable locations cater for more people and can offer more specialized services; these centres tend to grow progressively larger. Such differential growth produces various grades of central places characterized by different population sizes and zones of influence. The fact that this arrangement of large and small places has often suggested a degree of regularity encouraged efforts to form generalizations about the size and distribution of central places. Although several earlier writers considered individual aspects of settlement location (Dawson 1969) the best developed of the theories to explain the spatial organization of settlements derives from Christaller's (1933) work in southern Germany. Following Christaller's original statement there have been numerous attempts to test his propositions (Berry and Pred 1961; Berry 1967) and to modify and refine his ideas (Losch 1943; Isard 1956; Beavon 1977). Christaller's spatial equilibrium theory is fundamentally economic in approach and sets out to predict how, through competition for space, an optimal pattern of settlement will emerge.

The assumptions underlying Christaller's model

Like all models central place theory represents a simplification of reality and is predicated on a number of assumptions, as described by Bradford and Kent (1977):

(1)   There is an unbounded uniform plain on which there is equal ease of transport in all directions. Transport costs are proportional to distance and there is only one type of transport.
(2)   Population is evenly distributed over the plain.
(3)   Central places are located on the plain to provide goods, services, and administrative functions to their hinterlands.
(4)   Consumers minimize the distance to be travelled by visiting the nearest central place that provides the function which they demand.

(5)   The suppliers of these functions act as 'economic men', i.e. they attempt to maximize their profits by locating on the plain to obtain the largest possible market. Since people visit the nearest centre, suppliers will locate as far away from one another as possible so as to maximize their market areas.

(6)   They will do this only to the extent that no one on the plain is further from a function than he is prepared to travel to obtain it. Central places offering many functions are called higher order centres, others providing fewer functions are lower order centres.

(7)   Higher order centres supply certain functions which are not offered by lower order centres. They also provide all the functions that are provided in lower order centres.

(8)   All consumers have the same income and same demand for goods and services.

Economic principles and geometry

Christaller's theory applied to those settlements predominantly concerned with serving the needs of the surrounding area. The significance of this service role cannot be measured simply by the population of the place. While population might be a measure of absolute importance it is not a measure of a settlement's *centrality*. Centrality is the degree to which a place serves its surrounding area and this can only be gauged in terms of the goods and services offered. Clearly, there are different orders of goods and services – some are costly, bought infrequently, and need large populations to support them (e.g. furniture, jewellery); others are everyday needs and require small populations (e.g. groceries). From this two concepts emerge:

(1)   The Threshold Population: the threshold is defined as the minimum population required for a good or service to be provided, that is the minimum demand to make the good or service viable.

(2)   The Range of a Good: this is the maximum distance which people will travel to purchase a good or service. At some range from the central place the inconvenience of travel as measured in time, cost and effort will outweigh the value of or need for the good.

From these two concepts an upper and a lower limit can be identified for each good or service – the lower limit is determined by the threshold, the upper limit by the range (Figure 3.1).

Ideally each central place would have a circular trade area. It is obvious, however, that if three or more tangent circles are placed in an area, unserved spaces will exist. In order to eliminate any unserved areas the circular market areas must overlap and, since people in these overlap zones will choose to visit their nearest centre in keeping with the assumption of minimum movement, the final market areas must be hexagonal (Figure 3.1). The resulting hexagonal pattern is the most efficient way of packing market areas onto the plain to ensure that every resident is served.

Christaller started by identifying typical settlements of different sizes in southern Germany. He then measured their average population, distance apart, and extent of their hexagonal tributary areas. Christaller also stated that the number of central

Figure 3.1 Deriving the hexagonal pattern of market areas.

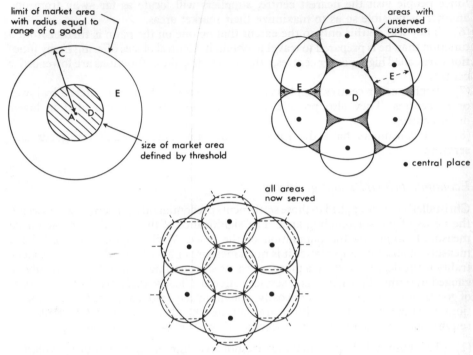

Source: Human Geography: Theories and their implications by M. G. Bradford and W. A. Kent © Oxford University Press.

places at each level of the settlement hierarchy follows a fixed ratio (the K value) from the largest *Landeshauptstadt* (Regional Capital) to the smallest *Marktort* (hamlet) (Table 3.1).

In its simplest terms, therefore, Christaller's model proposed that settlements with the lowest level of specialization (marktort/hamlet) would be equally spaced and surrounded by hexagonally shaped hinterlands. For every 6 hamlets there would be a larger more specialized central place (amtsort/township centre) which would be located equidistant from other township centres. The amtsort would have a larger market area for specialized services not available in the hamlet. Further up the hierarchy even more specialized settlements would also have their own hinterlands and would be located an equal distance from each other.

In the basic model the smallest centres would be spaced 7 km apart. The next higher centres would serve three times the area (and therefore three times the population) of the lower order centres, and would be located $\sqrt{3} \times 7 = 12$ km apart. Similarly, the trade area of centres at the next higher level of specialization would again be three times larger (Table 3.1). This kind of arrangement is called a K-3 hierarchy; in this the number of central places in the settlement hierarchy follows a

Table 3.1 *Characteristics of central places in southern Germany*

	Number of Places	Distance Apart (km)	Number of Complementary Regions	Range of Region (sq km)	Area of Region (sq km)	Number of Types of Goods Offered	Typical Population of Places	Typical Population of Region
Marktort	486	7	729	4.0	44	40	1,000	3,500
Amtsort	162	12	243	6.9	133	90	2,000	11,000
Kreisstadt	54	21	81	12.0	400	180	4,000	35,000
Bezirksstadt	18	36	27	20.7	1,200	330	10,000	100,000
Gaustadt	6	62	9	36.0	3,600	600	30,000	350,000
Provinzhauptstadt	2	108	3	62.1	10,800	1,000	100,000	1,000,000
Landeshauptstadt	1	186	1	108.0	32,400	2,000	500,000	3,500,000

Source: Christaller (1933)

geometric progression: 1, 3, 9, 27 etc. Thus lower order centres in order to be provided with higher order goods and services nest within the tributary areas of higher
order places according to a definite rule (the K-value).

A settlement pattern with these features exhibits what Christaller has called the
Marketing Principle. In this the major factor influencing settlement distribution is
the need for central places to be as near as possible to the population they serve. Thus
the K-3 hierarchy and nesting pattern produces the maximum number of central
places in accordance with the notion of movement-minimization (Figure 3.2).

Figure 3.2 Orders of centres and associated market areas (K = 3).

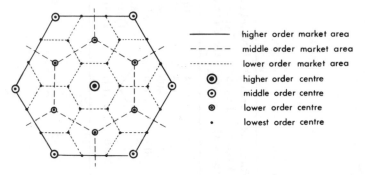

Source: Human Geography: Theories and their implications by M. G. Bradford and W. A. Kent © Oxford
University Press.

The K-value refers to the number of settlements at a given level in the hierarchy
served by the central place at the next highest level. For example, in Figure 3.3 each
higher order centre (village) serves the equivalent of 3 lower order centres (markets).
This is made up of (i) the hamlet part of the functional structure of the village *plus*
(ii) a one-third share of the 6 border hamlets, since each of these is shared between 3
villages. Similarly, the next higher level centres (towns) will provide 'town' level
goods to 3 villages: and it follows from the geometry that they will serve 9 hamlets.
This regular system exists because Christaller assumed that once the K-value was
adopted in a region it would be fixed.

Although Christaller's K-3 model has received most attention in empirical
studies he did postulate two other arrangements to take account of deviations from
the marketing principle (Figure 3.3). These were:

(1)   A K-4 network organized according to the Traffic Principle. This was suggested
to account for situations in which transport costs were significant. This arrangement
eases travel between central places by locating the maximum number of places on the
shortest traffic route between larger settlements. Compared to the K-3 network the
hexagon in this system is slightly larger and reoriented. A lower order centre is
equidistant from only 2 higher order centres. The higher order centre thus serves
one-half of the population in the 6 lower order places (6 × ½) plus its own population
(1) giving a K-4 network.

Figure 3.3 Relationship between the K value and settlement patterns.

K = *3 network, explanation*

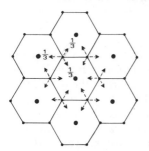

	market areas	central places		
highest order	1	1		
	3	2	9	27
	9*	6		
	27	18		
lowest order	81	54		

*The nine market areas of this order contain nine central places which sell the associated order of goods. Six are considered centres of this order because they do not sell anything of any higher order. Three of the nine sell higher order goods too, one being the highest order central place and the other two being the next highest order central places.

- ● higher order centre
- · lower order centre
- --→ direction and proportion of custom from lower order centres to higher order ones

K = *4 network, explanation*

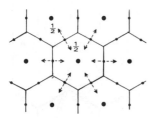

- ● higher order centre
- · lower order centre
- --→ direction and proportion of custom from lower order centres to higher order centres

K = *7 network, explanation*

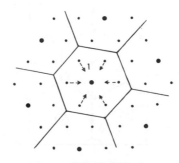

- ● higher order centre
- · lower order centre
- -→ direction of custom from lower order centre

Source: Human Geography: Theories and their implications by M. G. Bradford and W. A. Kent © Oxford University Press.

(2)   A K-7 network organized according to the Administrative Principle. In this a larger and reoriented hexagon now *encloses* 6 lower order centres plus the higher order place (Figure 3.3). The reasoning behind this arrangement is that it is more efficient to administer whole centres than parts of places as would result from a K-3 or K-4 network. In this case nesting follows a K-7 rule and the resultant hierarchy of settlements is 1, 7, 49 etc.

By applying the economic principles, in conjunction with the geometric properties of the theory plus the simplifying assumption of an isotropic surface Christaller derived his general model of the location, size and spacing of settlements.

Modifications of Christaller's system

Following Christaller's original work there have been various attempts to refine his ideas, one of the most impressive being the scheme proposed by Losch (1943). The major difference between the two approaches is that Losch regarded the K-value as being free to vary and not fixed as in Christaller's model. In Losch's system each good has its own threshold and size of market area, which is represented by a different K function. The lowest order good is represented by a K-3 network with the smallest market areas. The next order is represented by K-4, and so on until there are 150 networks of different K values representing the market areas of 150 goods. These hexagonal networks are superimposed and reoriented in such a way that the number of and distances between central places is minimized. This results in an irregular distribution of centres of the same order (Figure 3.4).

Figure 3.4 The hierarchy of central places in a relaxed K network: top – the relaxed K; bottom – the number of functions in each settlement.

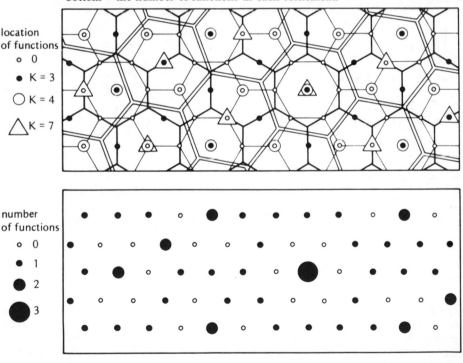

Source: P. Toyne and P. T. Newby (1971) *Techniques in Human Geography.* Macmillan, London and Basingstoke.

Figure 3.5 Loschian landscape with (A) alternating city-rich and city-poor sectors; (B) distribution of large cities; and (C) distribution of all centres within one sector.

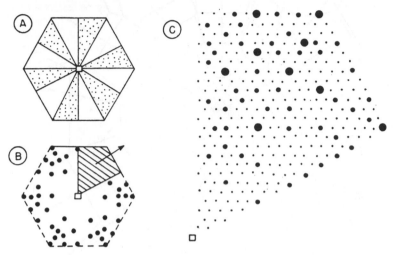

Source: Haggett (1965)

A number of characteristics of Losch's economic landscape (Figure 3.5) should be noted.

(1)   There are concentrations of settlement into sectors separated by areas of less dense settlement.

(2)   Higher order centres do not necessarily provide all the functions of lower order places; thus permitting the occurrence of some centres specializing in certain services.

(3)   Places providing the same number of functions (i.e. of a given order) do not necessarily provide the same kinds of functions. Because of this the populations of places in a given order vary and a continuous rather than discrete hierarchical stepped distribution of places results.

(4)   Within the 'city-rich' sectors central places increase in size with distance from the metropolis.

Isard (1956) modified the Loschian system of market areas to accommodate his suggestion that in reality population density declines with distance from the metropolis. In this modified structure the neat hexagonal pattern is replaced by polygons of varying size but with similar population (Figure 3.6).

Assessment of central place theory

(1)   The theory is not applicable to all settlements being limited to service centres. It does not therefore include some of the functions, such as manufacturing industry, that create employment and population. While Losch's notion of specialist centres is

Figure 3.6 Loschian system of hexagonal trade areas modified by agglomeration.

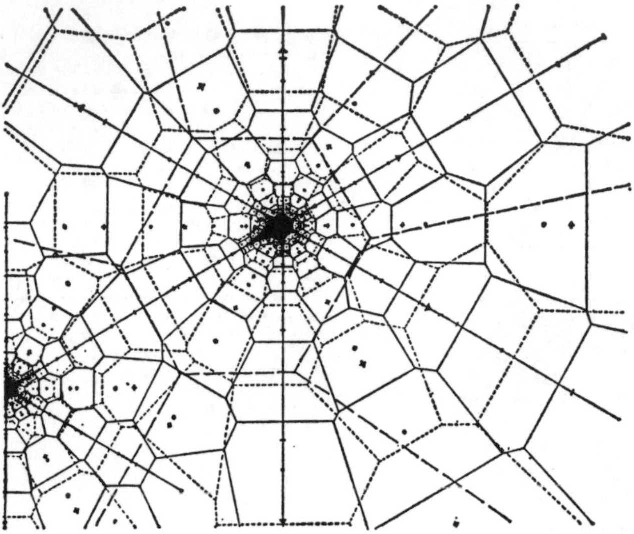

Source: Garner (1967)   *In* R. J. Chorley and P. Haggett (1967) *Socio-economic Models in Geography.* Methuen and Co.

more realistic for the location of industry neither theory includes the effect of the location of raw materials, both assuming an isotropic plain.

(2)   The 'economic man' assumption concerning suppliers and consumers is unrealistic. Human decision-making is more complex. For example, consumers do not always visit their nearest store (Johnston and Rimmer 1967; Clark 1968) and multipurpose shopping often results in low order centres being by passed for low order goods, thus leading to their decline.

(3)   Christaller's theory is static in the sense that it is set in the 1930s and does not take account of recent social and economic changes including increasing population mobility, urban sprawl, the emergence of hypermarkets, and the intervention of government and planning departments in the location of service activities such as office and shopping developments.

(4)   The economic determinism of central place theory takes no account of random historical factors which affect the modern settlement pattern.

(5)   Finally, empirical evidence for such a regular settlement system is ambiguous. The literature on central place theory is voluminous; for example, the presence of hexagonal lattices has been considered by Haggett (1965); the regular distribution of central places has been examined by Dacey (1962), Brush and Bracey (1955) and King (1962); and the presence of a hierarchy of places by Vining (1955), Berry and Garrison (1958) and Stafford (1963). In general it has been suggested that 'Christaller-type settlement patterns are more likely to be found in non-industrial or rural regions like much of Iowa, while elements of the Loschian landscape are more likely to be observed in industrialised areas' (Bradford and Kent 1977, p. 25).

Recognition of the limitations of central place theory is not the same as rejecting it. Skinner's (1964) work on periodic markets in rural China reveals a hierarchical structure which corresponds in some places to a K-3 system and elsewhere to a K-4 (Figure 3.7) and suggests that CPT may have a wider application than Christaller envisaged. Even as an ideal the theory is useful. Study of where theory and reality diverge can lead to explanation. Indeed Kolars and Nystuen (1974, p. 73) suggest that the main contributions of both Christaller and Losch 'have been as much to stimulate further geographic thought as to give us any absolute explanations of the real world'. While there is little evidence of the entire central place settlement structure emerging in the modern world the theory has stimulated much work in the fields of retailing and consumer behaviour, regional science, and physical and social planning; and elements of the theory, particularly the ideas of a settlement hierarchy and complementary area, have been applied at several scales in the real world in the postwar era.

Application of central place theory

The principles of central place theory can be recognized in the policies and plans adopted by rural planning authorities in the United Kingdom, although Woodruffe (1976) suggests that the fundamental classifications of settlements employed have been much closer to the central place work of Dickenson (1947) and Bracey (1953, 1956) than to that of Christaller. The Lindsey district of Lincolnshire, for example, recognized five levels of service centre which were not radically different from those proposed by Dickenson:

(1)   A regional centre (250,000+ population) with specialized services such as a university, theatres and central government administration – e.g. Nottingham.
(2)   A provincial centre (60,000–100,000) serving a radius of 20–40 miles with services such as further education, cinemas and local government – e.g. Lincoln.
(3)   The district centre (5,000–60,000) serving a radius of 10–15 miles with less specialized services – e.g. Louth.
(4)   The local centre (1,000–5,000), being the urban village or small market town with a variety of shops and a secondary school and often catering for weekly needs in shopping and entertainment over a radius of 5–8 miles.
(5)   The rural centre (300–1,200), being a medium or large village self-sufficient in everyday necessities and acting as a service centre for a group of 4–6 villages.

The ultimate aim of the policy was to identify some 90 settlements as suitable for expansion of services, facilities and housing. As Woodruffe (1976, p. 20) points out, 'this type of policy was very largely a static one: it did not take account of the fact that services and facilities had capacities, that the quality and nature of services were changing, that population was becoming more mobile and that the structure of village populations differed widely and altered with time'. The policy for Lindsey applied for over two decades until, in 1973, it was found to be in need of revision because of changes in living standards and expectations and, above all, in the distribution of population – whereas the 1952 development plan had envisaged an increase of only 15,000 in the rural districts by 1971 the actual increase had been around 40,000.

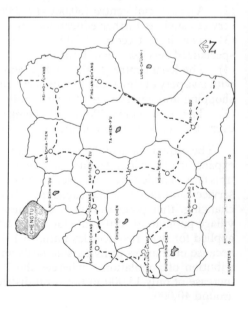

Figure 3.7 Market structures in parts of Szechwan province, China: top left – depicts an area southeast of Chengtu in which there are two levels of centres: standard markets such as Hsin-Tien-Tzu and larger intermediate markets such as Chung-Ho-Chen. Straightening out market area boundaries (middle left) and reducing the resulting abstraction to diagrammatic form (bottom left) reveals a K-3 network. A similar sequence in an area northeast of Chengtu (right) produces a K-4 network.

Source: Skinner (1964)

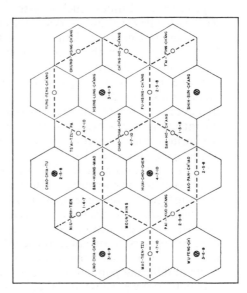

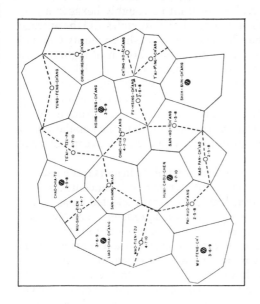

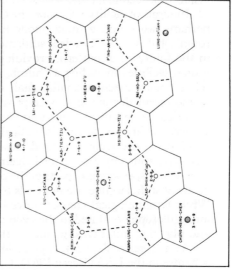

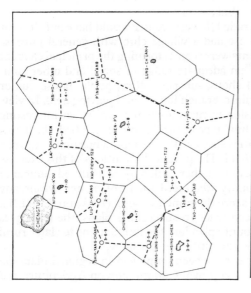

An early plan for the county of Cheshire prepared in 1946 attempted to apply the principles of central place theory to define a hierarchy of rural centres which should be developed to improve the provision of facilities and to discourage development on good agricultural land. The plan found that in Cheshire the basic settlement pattern was 'determined by the distribution of small villages or hamlets at intervals of approximately 2 miles. Such a system resolves itself into a roughly hexagonal pattern, each village having a service area of approximately 3½ sq. miles and the average settlement having a population of less than 200 persons' (Cheshire County Council 1946, p. 115). From this basic pattern the theoretical distribution of higher order settlements was determined using the principles of the central place model. Thus, for example, if the distance separating Grade I places is 2 miles, settlements of the next highest rank should be $2 \times \sqrt{3} = 3\frac{1}{2}$ miles apart (Table 3.2). It is significant to note that even at this early date the deviation from a purely rural economic structure, with the intrusion of industrial or dormitory development, meant that 'the populations of the various grades of settlement no longer correspond with their relative importance in the scale' (ibid., p. 116).

The main aims were to retain the basic pattern of small villages (Grade I settlements) but also to encourage in the longer term a greater degree of concentration 'by limiting future development, as far as is practicable, to certain selected villages, and also by arranging social provision as nearly as possible on a predetermined scale and pattern designed to achieve the most effective distribution of services and at the same time to foster concentration in the villages selected as distribution centres' (Ibid., p. 112). The ideal settlement pattern according to a K-3 arrangement for three districts of differing population density is shown in Table 3.2. On the basis of these calculations it was concluded that 'in most rural areas of the county a service area of approximately 31 square miles centred about one of the larger villages would embrace a population of about 4/5,000 persons, a number sufficient to justify the provision of a secondary modern school' (Ibid., p. 119).

In terms of facility provision the Grade I (lowest) centre would have only 'one or perhaps two shops, a small public house and a village club with general purpose room' (Ibid., p. 120). Grade II settlements were seen as forming the principal element in the future rural pattern, providing an adequate range of social and other communal facilities including a church, 4 shops, sub post office, public house, junior school, motor mechanic, village hall, clinic, branch library and playing field. In view of the recent decline of service provision in rural areas it provides an interesting historical perspective to note that the final type of rural centre identified, the urban village, would provide additional facilities such as 10–18 shops, a bus link to town, a hotel, bank, and secondary modern school. The practical intentions of this exercise were underlined by the acknowledgement that 'there will only be a limited number of such villages, as in many parts of the county urban settlements of greater size already occur at sufficiently close intervals to serve the same purpose' (Ibid., pp. 120–121). While terminological changes have been made in succeeding plans, the principles and philosophy outlined in the 1946 county plan laid the foundations for later rural and planning initiatives, including the key settlement strategy.

At a larger scale, central place ideas have been employed in regional planning schemes in the USA (Berry 1967), Canada (Royal Commission on Agriculture and

Table 3.2 *Theoretical distribution of settlement in Cheshire Rural Districts according to a K-3 network, and varying population densities*

Type of Settlement	Distance Apart (ml)	Service Area (sq ml)	Malpas Rural District (Av. Pop. Density = 134 pp sq ml)		Tarvin Rural District (Av. Pop. Density = 150 pp sq ml)		Nantwich Rural District (Av. Pop. Density = 162 pp sq ml)	
			Centre Population	Total Pop. of Settlement and Service Area	Centre Population	Total Pop. of Settlement and Service Area	Centre Population	Total Pop. of Settlement and Service Area
Small Village (Grade I)	2	3.46	207	376	242	412	270	438
Village (Grade II)	3.5	10.38	399	1286	470	1428	524	1535
Urban Village (Grade III)	6	31.14	728	4173	870	4671	977	5045

Source: Cheshire County Council (1946)

Rural Life, Saskatchewan 1957), Africa (Grove and Huszar 1964), India (Johnson 1965), Europe and the Middle East. Israeli settlement on the Laklish plains to the east of the Gaza strip, for example, was based on a three-level hierarchy of:

(1) 'A' settlements, of various types (including protective border kibbutzim) housing immigrant settlers and serving as agricultural centres containing facilities used daily.
(2) 'B' settlements (rural community centres), each planned to serve 4–6 'A' settlements and to supply facilities and buildings used by them once or twice a week.
(3) 'C' settlements (regional centres), a town roughly at the geographical centre of the region, providing administrative, educational, medical and cultural facilities, and with factories for crop processing.

Perhaps the most clearly articulated application of central place principles has occurred in the Dutch polderlands (Van Hulton 1969; Constandse 1978). The increasing importance attached to a planned settlement pattern can be seen by tracing the development of the Wieringermeer, drained in 1930, and the North East and East Flevoland polders, drained in 1942 and 1957 respectively (Figure 3.8).

In the first polder the location of villages (service centres) was not successful. The settlement pattern did not conform to any model distribution with the planners expecting that a spontaneous process of settling would lead to certain clusters at road intersections (Constandse 1978). As a result the three regional villages of Slootdorp, Middenmeer and Wieringerwerf were clustered in the middle of the polder which meant they had overlapping trade areas and that people living well away from the villages were inconvenienced by long journeys. The lower than expected population growth on the polder exacerbated the problems with small villages incapable of providing a satisfactory level of service.

In the second polder (North East) a settlement pattern was carefully planned in an attempt to avoid the mistakes of the Wieringermeer. Since it was one of the few places in the world where no historic or physical obstacles frustrated the realization of a theoretical spatial model Christaller's hierarchical system was applied with some modifications. In the middle of the area a regional centre, Emmeloord, was founded (with a target population of 10,000), with ten surrounding villages as local service centres each with target populations of 1,000–2,000 (Figure 3.9). Despite this careful planning, however, the settlement pattern quickly demonstrated a number of shortcomings. Because of agricultural mechanization and the reduced demand for labour the populations of most villages did not reach the target figure and this made it difficult to keep the services feasible and the community viable. Paradoxically Emmeloord has grown more rapidly than anticipated. This is due to the increased accessibility of the rural population to the varied services in the regional centre, largely a result of the general increase in mobility engendered by the spread of the motor car in the 1960s.

Experience gained in the first two polders was applied to the settlement of East Flevoland. The initial settlement plan had been similar to that of the North East polder, with ten 'A' centres having a local service function surrounding a single 'B' or district centre, Dronten. A 'C' centre, Lelystad, the capital of the polders province, was planned at the junction of the four polders but in the western corner of East

Figure 3.8 The Zuider Zee Polders.

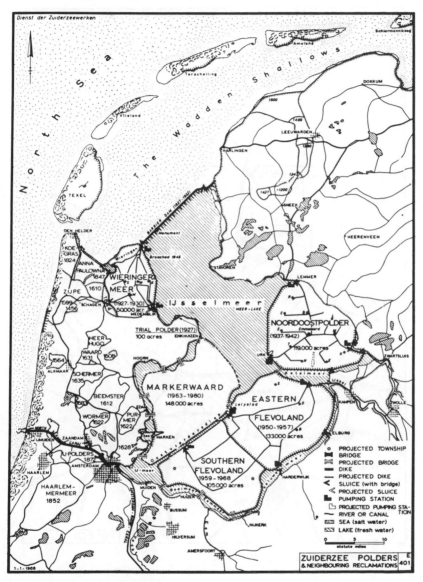

Figure 3.9 The North East Polder

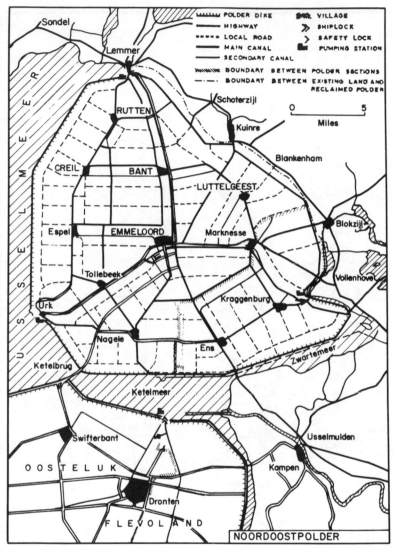

Source: Meyer and Huggett (1979)

Flevoland (Figure 3.10). Because of the diminishing importance of farm employment and the increasing affluence, aspirations and mobility of the population this pattern was reduced to only four villages in 1959 and eventually to two by 1965 (Figure 3.10).

The declining significance of agricultural employment over the course of the development of the first three polders influenced the location and population composition of settlement in the later Southern Flevoland and Markerwaard polders, with less emphasis on placing villages to serve the needs of farming, and the introduction of commuters and other nonagricultural workers from Randstad Holland. The fact that in Southern Flevoland, an area within the sphere of influence of Randstad Holland, no thought is given to a system of service-centres set up according to a hierarchically arranged pattern of villages suggests that in such pressured rural areas classical central place theory is of limited relevance today.

Figure 3.10 East Flevoland: changes in the number of villages planned, 1954–1965.

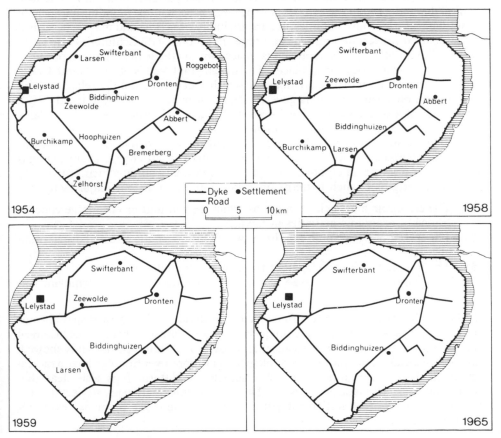

Source: Adams and Dunlop (1976)

Diffusion theories

One of the most serious disadvantages of Christaller's theory is its static nature which does not enable it to respond easily to changing social and economic conditions. This has led some writers to suggest that attempts to understand 'natural' as opposed to planned rural settlement patterns in terms of spatial equilibrium theory are of limited value. An alternative, which explicitly acknowledges the importance of the time dimension and historical perspective, is to examine the processes by which settlement spreads across a region from the initial point of colonization.

Bylund (1960) has proposed, within a deterministic framework, six hypothetical models of settlement diffusion based upon his study of early colonization in central Lappland. His four basic models are shown in Figure 3.11; each differs in the number and location of 'mother settlements'. The process of clone-colonization (model B) appears to imitate the actual pattern of colonization most closely, and this concept is developed in two further models to replicate the known settlement history of the area. The principles underlying these models have also been developed by Morrill (1962) in a probabilistic simulation of central place patterns over time. The idea behind the model is that the behaviour of persons, as seen in the founding and growth of settlements and transport lines, occurs gradually over time and may be described as random within certain limiting conditions. In keeping with Schluter's early views (1906) the aim of Morrill's approach is to account for the general pattern of settlement, not the exact location of places. The model employed is of the 'Monte Carlo' type (a stochastic growth process model) in which a set of probabilities related to both human and physical conditions governs choice of behaviour (Hagerstrand 1952). The mechanics of the method have been well illustrated elsewhere (Abler, Adams and Gould 1972; Saare 1974; Chapman 1979).

Morrill (1963) examined the spread of settlement in Sweden using this historical-predictive approach. As the number, size and location of settlements in any region is the result of a long and complex interplay of forces, any study which proposes to explain the origins of such patterns must take into account four major factors:

(1)   The economic and social conditions which permit and/or encourage concentration of economic activities in towns.
(2)   The spatial or geographic conditions which influence the size and distribution of towns.
(3)   The fact that such development takes place gradually over time.
(4)   Recognition that there is an element of uncertainty or indeterminancy in all behaviour.

While the first two factors are also explicit considerations in classical spatial equilibrium theories, the latter two are uniquely central to diffusion theory. The historical dimension is crucial not least because, as study of the Dutch polderlands showed, changes in social, economic and technological conditions over time can have a radical effect on the efficient functioning of a settlement pattern. It is also clear that locational decisions made on the basis of incomplete information are subject to error and consequently real settlement patterns are the outcome of many less-than-perfect decisions.

Figure 3.11 Bylund's model of settlement diffusion.

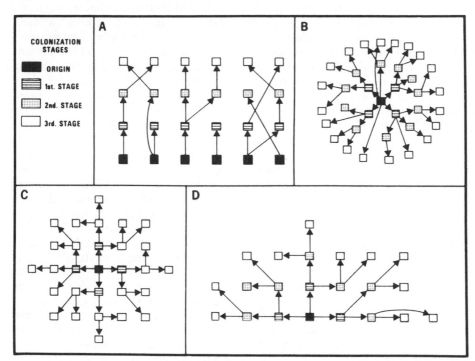

Morrill (1963, p. 9) attempted to simulate the development of the settlement pattern in southern Sweden over the period 1860–1960 in order to discover the major locational forces channelling urban development and migration. He was able to conclude that 'in sum, the model results can be considered realistic from the point of view of distribution, that is similarity in spatial structure; and from the point of view of process, as a reasonable recognition and treatment of the pertinent forces. Deviations resulted in the main from oversimplified assumptions rather than from a mistaken approach.'

The construction of a theory to explain the spread of rural settlement also forms the basis of Hudson's (1969) work in Iowa, in which he attempts to integrate diffusion theory with central place theory. Drawing on the work of plant and animal ecologists he identifies three phases of settlement diffusion:

(1) Colonization which involves the dispersal of settlement into new territory.
(2) Spread in which increasing population density creates settlement clusters and eventually pressure on the physical and social environment.
(3) Competition which produces regularity in the settlement pattern in the way suggested by central place theory.

Empirical testing of these hypotheses using settlement data from six areas of eastern Iowa at three different times between 1870 and 1960 found that the suggested increase in settlement regularity over time did occur. In the study area 'the early twentieth century was a period of transition between the higher-density more clustered agriculture and the large-size more widely spaced forms of the present' (Hudson 1969, p. 380). The results led Hudson to suggest that his theory is appropriate to parts of the world where regular spacing of settlements occurs without external planning 'as the predictable result of several spatial processes where interactions produce the distinctive geometry of regular forms' (Ibid., p. 381). Grossman (1971) and Birch (1970) offer critical reactions to the theory. Birch points out that in analysing the spatial development of the settlement pattern in Iowa it is necessary to appreciate the distinction between patterns created by farmholdings and those resulting from farmhouse distributions (the basis of Hudson's analysis). Since there is evidence that the location of farmhouses on holdings in the Mid West has altered over time in response to changes in the settlers' domestic and operational needs Birch (1970, p. 612) argues that one must analyse 'the farmholding pattern and its process of change, as well as that of the farmsteads whose locations are partly conditioned by the farms, in a theory for rural settlement'. Grossman suggests that Hudson's theory is of limited relevance largely because of the uniqueness of the Iowa study area, and the fact that the theory's biologically derived principles only rarely apply to patterns of human mobility. He maintains that where regular patterns of rural settlement have developed it has frequently been the result of central planning rather than of automatic adjustments towards optimality of location. According to Grossman (1971, p. 202) Hudson's model 'is limited to societies which lack communal control and encourage individualism rather than conformity to central authority. Even in such limited cases, however, his model should not be taken to provide an ultimate *law* of settlement location.'

It is difficult to avoid the conclusion that a general theory to explain the location of rural settlement is unattainable. The great variety of rural settlement forms and distributions lends support to Grossman's (1971, p. 192) view that 'general laws are meaningless outside the specific cultural and technological context', and Bunce's (1982, p. 96) contention that 'settlement patterns are the product of the area which they occupy'. This suggests a return to the traditional ideographic or case-study approach. Clearly, the main value of the theoretical propositions examined lies in the ability to suggest the basic variables which may influence the spatial arrangement of settlement. Progress towards a fuller understanding of the spatial organization of rural settlement will best be gained by pursuing both ideographic and normative studies.

References

ABLER, R., ADAMS, J. S. and GOULD, P. (1972) *Spatial Organisation*. New York: Prentice Hall.

ADAMS, A., and DUNLOP, S. (1976) *Village, Town and City*. London: Heinemann.

ANDERSON, G. and FRANKLIN, H. (1955) The villages of the Manawatu, *New Zealand Geographer* 11, 53–71.

BEAVON, K. (1977) *Central Place Theory: a reinterpretation*. London: Longman.

BERRY, B. J. L. (1967) *Geography of Market Centres and Retail Distribution*. New Jersey: Prentice Hall.

BERRY, B. J. L. and GARRISON, W. L. (1958) Functional bases of the central place hierarchy, *Economic Geography* 34, 145–54.

BERRY, B. J. L. and PRED, A. (1961) *Central Place Studies: a bibliography of theory and applications*. Philadelphia: Regional Science Institute.

BIRCH, B. P. (1970) On a theory for rural settlement, *Annals of the Association of American Geographers* 60, 610–13.

BRACEY, H. E. (1953) Towns as rural service centres—an index of centrality with special reference to Somerset, *Transactions of the Institute of British Geographers* 19, 95–105.

BRACEY, H. E. (1956) A rural component of centrality applied to six southern counties in the United Kingdom, *Economic Geography* 32, 38–50.

BRADFORD, M. and KENT, W. (1977) *Human Geography: theories and their implications*. Oxford: The University Press.

BRUSH, J. E. and BRACEY, H. E. (1955) Functional bases of the central place hierarchy, *Economic Geography* 34, 145–54.

BUNCE, M. (1982) *Rural Settlement in an Urban World*. London: Croom Helm.

BYLUND, E. (1960) Theoretical considerations regarding the distribution of settlement in Inner North Sweden, *Geografiska Annaler* 42, 225–31.

CHAPMAN, K. (1979) *People Pattern and Process*. London: Arnold.

CHESHIRE COUNTY COUNCIL (1946) *County Palatine: a plan for Cheshire*. London: Country Life.

CHRISTALLER, W. (1933) *Die Zentralen Orte Suddeutschland*. Jena: Fischer. English edition translated by C. W. Baskin (1966) *Central Places in Southern Germany*. New Jersey: Prentice Hall.

CLARK, W. A. V. (1968) Consumer travel patterns and the concept of range, *Annals of the Association of American Geographers* 58, 386–96.

CONSTANDSE, A. K. (1978) New towns on the bottom of the sea. *In* G. Golany *International Urban Growth Policies*. Chichester: Wiley, 53–74.

DACEY, M. (1962) Analysis of central place and point patterns by nearest neighbour method, *Lund Studies in Geography Series B* 24, 55–75.

DAWSON, J. A. (1969) Some early theories of settlement location and size, *Journal of the Royal Town Planning Institute* 53, 444–8.

DICKENSON, R. E. (1947) *City Region and Regionalism*. London: Routledge and Kegan Paul.

FUGUITT, G. V. and DEELEY, N. A. (1966) Retail service patterns and small town population change, *Rural Sociology* 3, 53–63.

GARNER, B. J. (1967) Models of urban geography and settlement location. *In* R. J. Chorley and P. Haggett *Socio-economic Models in Geography*. London: Methuen, 303–60.

GROSSMAN, D. (1971) Do we have a theory for settlement geography? *Professional Geographer* 23, 197–203.

GROVE, D. and HUSZAR, L. (1964) *The Towns of Ghana*. Accra: Ghana University.

HAGGETT, P. (1965) *Locational Analysis in Human Geography*. London: Arnold.

HART, J. F. and SALISBURY, N. E. (1965) Population change in middle western villages, *Annals of the Association of American Geographers* 55, 140–60.

HAGERSTRAND, T. (1952) The propogation of innovation waves, *Lund Studies in Geography Series B* 4, 3–19.

HUDSON, J. C. (1969) A location theory for rural settlement, *Annals of the Association of American Geographers* 59, 365–81.

ISARD, W. (1956) *Location and Space Economy*. Cambridge, Massachusetts: MIT Press.

JOHANSEN, H. E. and FUGUITT, G. V. (1973) Changing retail activity in Wisconsin villages, *Rural Sociology* 38, 207–218.

JOHNSON, E. (1965) *Market Towns and Spatial Development of India*. New Delhi: National Council of Applied Economic Research.

JOHNSTON, R. J. and RIMMER, P. (1967) A note on consumer behaviour in an urban hierarchy, *Journal of Regional Science* 7, 161–6.

KING, L. J. (1962) A quantitative expression of the pattern of urban settlements in selected areas of the USA, *Tijdschrift voor Economische en Social Geografie* 53, 1–7.

KOLARS, J. and NYSTUEN, J. (1974) *Geography: The Study of Location Culture Environment*. New York: McGraw Hill.

LOSCH, A. (1943) *Die Raumiche Ordnung der Wirtschaft*. Jena: Fischer. English translation by W. H. Woglom (1954) *The Economics of Location*. New Haven: Yale University Press.

MEYER, I. R. and HUGGETT, R. J. (1979) *Settlements*. London: Harper and Row.

MORRILL, R. L. (1962) Simulation of central place patterns over time, *Lund Studies in Geography Series B* 24, 109–20.

MORRILL, R. L. (1963) The development of spatial distributions of towns in Sweden, *Annals of the Association of American Geographers* 53, 1–14.

ROYAL COMMISSION ON AGRICULTURE AND RURAL LIFE, SASKATCHEWAN (1957) *Service Centres*. Regina: Queen Printer.

SAARE, P. (1974) Channels of synthesis, *New Trends in Geography V*. Milton Keynes: Open University.

SCHLUTER, O. (1899) Bemerkungen zur Siedlungsgeographie, *Geographische Zeitschrift 5*, 65–84.

SCHLUTER, O. (1906) *Die Zeile der Geographie des Menschen*. Munich: Oldenbourg.

STAFFORD, H. A. (1963) The functional bases of small towns, *Economic Geography* 39, 165–75.

THRISK, J. (1961) Industries in the countryside. *In* F. J. Fisher *Essays on the Economic and*

Social History of Tudor and Stuart England in Honour of R. H. Tawney. Cambridge: The University Press, 70–88.

TOYNE, P. and NEWBY, P. (1971) *Techniques in Human Geography.* London: Macmillan.

VAN HULTON, M. (1969) Plan and reality in the Ijsselmeerpolders, *Tijdschrift voor Economische en Sociale Geografie* 60, 67–76.

VINING, R. (1955) A description of certain spatial aspects of an economic system, *Economic Development and Cultural Change* 3, 147–95.

WOODRUFFE, B. (1976) *Rural Settlement Policies and Plans.* Oxford: The University Press.

4   Settlement planning and change

An inherent assumption in settlement theory is the tendency for settlement to evolve towards some optimum pattern within contemporary economic and social conditions. But, since the existing settlement pattern adjusts only slowly to the changing social and economic needs of society significant imbalances may prevail (Lewis 1979).

In most parts of the world the rural settlement pattern has been inherited from a time when rural population was greater than it is now and when the needs of country people could normally be served by local tradesmen found in nearly every village. The rural settlement pattern of the United States, for example, evolved to suit a 'horse and buggy' society (Clawson 1966) while that in many parts of Europe still reflects its medieval origins. Since then, however, the decline in agricultural employment, the increased mobility of many rural residents, and generally higher expectations of life quality have reduced demand for local village services and have undermined the viability of smaller settlements, particularly those in the remoter rural regions (Rikkinen 1968; Hart and Salisbury 1965; Fuguitt 1981).

Unplanned change

Evidence of 'automatic' or natural change in the rural settlement pattern is provided by several North American studies. In the USA in particular, centrally directed rural planning has been slow to evolve, partly because of the relative availability of land but more importantly because of a strong ideological bias against public infringement of private property rights and a preoccupation with local control and autonomy (Lassey 1977). Lamb (1975) has noted that between 1900 and 1930 the population and functions of small places generally declined in response to the increasing use of motor vehicles and the tendency for population and activities to centralize in few higher order places. After 1940, however, he detected selective population growth, especially in small places within commuting range of major employment centres. By the 1960s some of the larger places, those in amenity-rich locations, and those within urban fields had remained viable, whereas outlying centres continued to lose functions and population. As Dahms (1980, p. 296) observes, 'the same mobility that had destroyed local service centres in the 1930s had enabled many to survive and even grow as dormitory communities or recreational centres after 1940'. Similar findings have been reported from Canada (Hodge and Qadeer 1976; Stabler 1978).

In addition to the general decline of smaller rural centres several researchers (Anderson 1950; Fuguitt 1963) found a tendency for some rural trade centres to specialize and develop functional linkages. Hodge (1966, p. 185) observed that 'there are emerging two general types of trade centers: a large group of small centers serving local needs, and a small group of centers serving specialised shopping needs over large areas'. Studies of Canadian prairie communities by Zimmerman and Moneo

(1971) and by Meredith (1975) have also identified a specialization of services and growing interdependence between small hamlets and rural service areas. As Meredith (1975, p. 20) explained, 'the rural settlement system is much like a city as a type of human settlement. The major difference is that its parts – downtown, community centres, and neighbourhood centres – are dispersed over the countryside, separated by open country farms that must also be seen as part of the system.'

Hart et al. (1968) adopted the term 'dispersed city' to describe a similar spatial organization of rural trade centres in the American Mid West. They provided evidence to show that 'while most villages make a rather poor showing when one merely tabulates the number and variety of their central place functions ... over large parts of the Middle West nearly every village has at least one enterprise which has not only survived but has survived quite handsomely' (Ibid., p. 345). This successful economic activity was termed an 'outsized function'. Based on an analysis of sales tax data for nine categories of business in villages within a two-hour drive of Kankakee, Illinois, Hart et al. found that 50.0 percent of villages derived at least one-third of receipts from a single kind of business. Eating and drinking establishments provided the outsized functions for two-fifths of the villages, while lumber and hardwear dealers and filling stations ranked next. Food stores, automobile dealers and general merchandise stores were outsized functions in at least one village, and only apparel stores, furniture stores, and wholesaling establishments were not represented at all. Thus, 'just as city residents once thought nothing of boarding a streetcar and travelling to other parts of the city in search of various goods and services, so the modern village dweller and farmer may hop into his car and drive to many other villages to obtain the goods and services provided by their outsized functions' (Ibid., p. 346). These findings have been supported by more recent evidence from Wellington County, Ontario (Dahms 1980). For shopping activities, depending on their specific needs, between 12.0 and 47.0 percent of households regularly utilized local outsized functions rather than travelling to larger places higher in the hierarchy, as postulated by central place research.

These studies from the USA and Canada all describe areas where some 'urban' functions are scattered about the rural countryside. 'Shopping, residential areas and employment opportunities existed in rural communities linked by the car, creating a form of spatial organisation completely compatible with the mobile life style of North Americans in the 1980s' (Dahms 1980, p. 297). In many other rural areas of the Developed World, however, the major 'natural' trends in the settlement pattern remain the decline of the smaller centres and the concentration of facilities in a number of well-distributed larger places.

Planned change

In marked contrast to the situation in North America governments in the redistributive welfare states of Western Europe (Berry 1973) and in the Socialist bloc of Eastern Europe (Pallot 1977) have shown greater willingness and ability to intervene in an effort to accelerate or modify the evolution of the rural settlement pattern.

The United Kingdom has one of the most highly developed planning systems of any industrial democracy. In the context of rural settlement planning in the postwar era the major issues have centred on the 'concentration–dispersal' debate, and the related key settlement strategy. The conceptual development of key settlement policy from its roots in growth centre and central place theory has been discussed by Cloke (1979). In essence, the principle behind the concept is one of concentration of limited financial resources upon a few selected centres rather than dispersal throughout the settlement hierarchy. Specifically, the various objectives of key settlement policy may be summarized as: (1) the promotion of growth in remote rural areas; (2) the reduction or reversal of rural depopulation through the creation of locations of intervening opportunity; (3) the achievement of the most efficient pattern of rural services; and (4) the concentration of resources in centres of greatest need. It is important to note that while the key settlement itself is planned for comprehensive growth in terms of housing, services and often employment, the policy also incorporates an overview of the settlement pattern as a whole and lays special emphasis on the relationship between the key settlement and other settlements served by it.

Key settlement policy has been a cornerstone of British rural planning for the past 30 years, having been adopted by most local authorities in development plans prepared in the 1950s, in informal or interim rural policy statements in the 1960s, as well as in the Structure Plans of the 1970s. The policy has been applied in all types of rural area. In pressured rural areas the key settlement strategy has generally been used as an efficient method of controlling residential development, the chief objectives being (a) to concentrate infrastructure and services into the optimum economic pattern, and (b) to protect the environmental quality of settlements where growth is deemed inappropriate. Key settlement policies in remote rural areas aim to promote growth and stem rural depopulation. It can also be argued that this type of policy is the most efficient and economic means of servicing a scattered settlement pattern. A detailed review of UK County planning documents identified 22 reasons given to justify policies of resource concentration (Martin and Voorhees 1981), the most frequently mentioned of which are shown in Table 4.1.

Selection of key settlements

With limited theoretical work available to assist them to decide which settlements should be selected for investment, rural planners throughout the UK have employed various types of classification procedure to rank settlements in terms of their potential as service centres; the assumption being that the permitted level of development will decrease down through the hierarchy to the lowest level where in some cases a policy of no-growth or even phasing-out may be adopted. The planning surveys carried out in the course of Development Plan preparation, as required by the 1947 Town and Country Planning Act, enabled authorities to identify settlements with particular service deficiencies; and conversely, to recognize areas where services were not being fully utilized. The latter situation was a factor favouring population growth. These surveys led to a series of settlement classifications initially based on status of services or functions but later on potential for residential development. Woodruffe (1976) and Cloke (1979) provide reviews of the different methods of settlement classification employed. In Devon, for example, key settlements were selected on the basis of existing

Table 4.1   *Principal reasons for adopting concentration policies, 1945–1980*

Physical

(i)   Concentrate residential development to prevent sporadic/ribbon development or development inappropriate in scale or character to the smaller rural settlements.

(ii)   Locate new residential development in certain settlements, so that accessibility to work is improved.

(iii)   Maintain the quality of the environment; in particular, protect heritage areas and Green Belts.

(iv)   Create or restore a hierarchy of central places.

(v)   'Tidy up' the settlement pattern; hasten the process of decline in small, sporadic settlements so that only the large and compact settlements remain.

Agricultural

(vi)   Assist increased production in agriculture by restraining demand for development land in the countryside.

(vii)   Assist the supply of agricultural labour by stemming the drift to the towns.

Economic

(viii)   Concentrate in order to reduce the costs of providing engineering infrastructure and services.

(ix)   Reduce the costs of, and increase the catchment for, social services, i.e. for schools, health centres, playing fields, village halls etc.

Socio-Economic

(x)   Maintain population numbers in the countryside and stop the drift to the towns.

(xi)   Encourage the diversification of economic activity in rural areas; build up the larger settlements so that they are attractive to industry.

(xii)   Improve the quality of rural life/'resuscitate' it as recommended in the Scott Report.

(xiii)   Foster community spirit, friendliness by promoting more compact settlements.

(xiv)*   Meet constraints imposed by natural drainage on the dispersal of settlement.

(xv)*   Promote road safety by limiting isolated and sporadic development.

(xvi)*   Direct overspill population to rural areas to increase the catchment population for services.

(xvii)   Facilitate development control and administrative procedures related to implementation.

(xviii)   Confine housing development to the satisfaction of local needs.

(xix)   Limit growth because previous policies have led to the overcommitment of land for development purposes.

(xx)   Halt the decline in rural facilities and the rationalization of services.

(xxi)*   Preserve the Welsh language and culture.

(xxii)*   Concentrate new development in order to safeguard open land for recreational and leisure purposes.

* Cited only in isolated cases.
Source: Martin and Voorhees (1981)

social facilities and sources of employment; location in relation to principal routes, urban centres and dependent villages; availability of land; public utility capacity; and the effect of development on the visual environment (Table 4.2). Some authorities such as Huntingdonshire (in 1962) and West Suffolk (in 1968) based their settlement policy on an assessment of each village's growth potential in view of the factors for and against residential development; while others, such as Wiltshire (in 1976), first considered the anticipated amount of growth at a subregional level and then searched for suitable villages. A minority of authorities gave explicit attention to the overall spatial relationship of selected growth centres. In the pressured rural area of Warwickshire, for example, the selection of key settlements depended on an analysis of development potential (measured by 14 variables representing various attributes of services and infrastructure), land constraints, and existing building commitments; plus the intention to disperse them throughout the County (Figure 4.1).

Settlement rationalization through selective growth implies that some settlements will remain static or decay. While it is relatively simple to select the settlements for planned expansion it is much more difficult to condemn villages to decline. Most parish councils hope for some measure of growth in their village and, as Green (1971, p. 43) has pointed out, 'there is a tradition in this country that every existing settlement large or small has the right to grow in size. Planning policy in rural regions is very much concerned with denying that deeply felt right.' Clearly, this operation is difficult both socially and politically and, in practice, little has been done deliberately to accelerate the decline of small rural settlements. The settlement rationalization

Table 4.2 *Criteria for key settlement selection in Devon*

(a)	Existing social facilities, including primary (and in some cases, secondary) schools, shops, village hall and doctor's surgery; and public utilities (gas, water, electricity, sewerage).
(b)	Existing sources of employment (excluding agriculture) in, or in the vicinity of, a village.
(c)	Their location in relation to principal traffic roads and the possibility that new development may create a need for a by-pass.
(d)	Their location in relation to omnibus routes or railways providing adequate services.
(e)	Their location in relation to urban centres providing employment, secondary schools (where not provided in the key settlement itself), medical facilities, shops and specialized facilities or services. A town will provide all services and facilities which one would expect to find in a key settlement. Key settlements are not appropriate near main urban centres.
(f)	Their location in relation to other villages which will rely on them for some services.
(g)	The availability of public utilities capable of extension for new development.
(h)	The availability and agricultural value of land capable of development.
(i)	The effect of visual amenities.

Source: Cloke (1979)

Figure 4.1 Warwickshire: key settlements and sub areas, 1973. The 11 first category key settlements were considered suitable for 'moderate expansion' of more than 1000 population by 1986; the 8 second tier settlements for 'modest expansion' of 100–500.

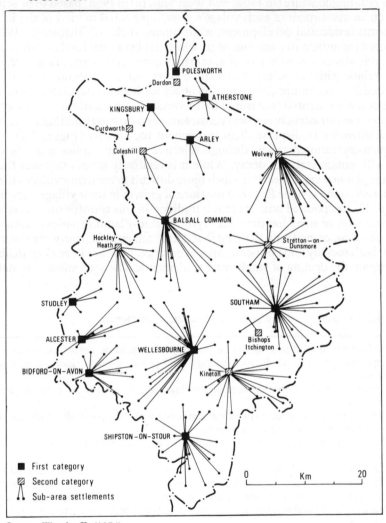

Source: Woodruffe (1976)

policy of Durham County Council did involve the planned decline of nonviable mining villages. Each of the 370 settlements in the County was classified according to its physical condition, siting, and predicted population change based on their employment prospects. Four categories were devised and a policy recommendation made for each (Table 4.3). Naturally the greatest controversy centred on the villages 'condemned to die', with nearly one-third of the 370 coalfield settlements considered to

Table 4.3 *Classification of settlements in County Durham, 1951*

Category A:	Villages in which further large-scale capital investment is envisaged because of an expected future rise in population either through migration or by natural increase.
Category B:	Villages in which the population is likely to remain at about the present level for many years to come. Sufficient capital should only be invested in these communities to cater for a stable population.
Category C:	Villages from which population is likely to emigrate. Sufficient capital should be invested only to cater for the needs of a reduced population.
Category D:	Villages from which a considerable loss of population may be expected. In these cases there should be no further capital investment. When existing houses become uninhabitable they should be replaced elsewhere. Long-term investment on public services would be carefully related to the estimated life of the existing community.

have no long-term future (Barr 1969; Blowers 1972). Even where such a clear statement of intent exists, putting the policy into effect is far from straightforward, and by 1970 only 8 villages had been completely cleared. Among the reasons for this limited success were that the long life of buildings and infrastructure was not appreciated, the attachment of people to seemingly isolated, redundant and unattractive villages was not realized, and the time which people took to move, voluntarily or involuntarily, to larger settlements was underestimated.

An equally controversial resettlement scheme was introduced in Newfoundland where financial incentives were offered to families to relocate to larger centres in order to reduce the costs to the government of maintaining services to outlying fishing communities. Relocation assistance was granted only to those living in designated settlements (i.e. those in which at least 80.0 percent of the population applied to move) in order to ensure the complete evacuation of settlements and so produce the desired cost savings. The scheme encountered similar social difficulties to the Durham plan, and divided opinion over the economic benefits of the resettlement programme led to its discontinuation.

Assessment of key settlement policy

Attempts by planners to influence the broad pattern of resource distribution via a key settlement policy were undertaken first using the mechanism of development planning (Woodruffe 1976) and then structure planning at the county council level (Derounian 1979). During the 1970s several writers began to argue against the key settlement approach, mainly because of its impact on nondesignated settlements, and to advocate alternative dispersal-oriented strategies (Ash 1976; Hancock 1976; McLoughlin 1976; Martin 1976). The debate may be examined from three viewpoints: economic, social and political.

1 An economic perspective In general, public service provision costs per head are higher for rural than for urban areas (HM Treasury 1976). A major principle upon which the key settlement policy has been founded is that significant savings in public sector costs may be made if new development in rural areas is concentrated in a limited number of larger settlements rather than dispersed throughout the country-side. Whitby and Willis (1978) have demonstrated how such scale economies may arise, both for individual services and when unit costs of a range of services are aggregated. Three local studies by Warford (1969), Norfolk County Council (1976) and Gilder (1979) directly examined the cost of providing rural public services.

Warford (1969) used a cost–benefit approach to examine various settlement strategies in the South Atcham area of Shropshire. The work was prompted by the realization that the level of cost involved in providing piped water to remote unserved dwellings might be obviated by rationalizing the settlement pattern into a more con-centrated form. This study, which supported a strategy based on relocation of popu-lation, represented a major contribution to the economic analysis of rural settlement strategies. It also illustrated the difficulties of translating a raw cost–benefit analysis into policy. Several policy options were considered ranging from retention of the existing settlement pattern to relocation of population at various levels. When these options were ranked in terms of net social benefit they displayed an almost perfect inverse relationship with a ranking based on decreasing budgetary costs. In other words, adopting a least cost policy would entail suboptimum social benefits. Thus, the degree to which a 'best' option can be isolated within this process is almost entirely dependent upon the criteria adopted by decision-makers. As Whitby and Willis (1978, p. 243) point out, 'the importance of this distinction between budgetary cost and social cost cannot be overemphasised'.

Rather than studying the costs and benefits of a fixed population under various relocation strategies, Norfolk County Council (1976) predicted a level of population growth for the North Walsham area and then attempted to assess the relative costs and benefits associated with the accommodation of this population within different settlement patterns. Thus, this study set out explicit policy-making guidelines prior to the commencement of option evaluation; 'the strategy which achieved the highest return on public spending, by producing the most effective provision of services in relation to their cost, was judged to be the "optimum" strategy' (Norfolk County Council 1976, p. 4). Four possible settlement options were analysed:

(1)   Concentration – concentrating growth in the largest settlements
(2)   Dispersal 1 – allowing a standard rate of growth in all villages
(3)   Dispersal 2 – making use of spare capacity in services taking account of physical constraints
(4)   Dispersal 3 – developing villages of 500–1,000 population

For each of these options the capital and revenue costs of various public utility and community services were considered. Other social costs and benefits were assessed in nonmonetary terms. The general conclusion reached was that policies of concen-tration were superior in both capital and revenue cost terms than policies of dispersal, but that strong social arguments existed in favour of accepting the higher cost of dispersal.

The economic basis of the study has been criticized, notably by Gilder (1979) who points out that in assessing future costs of servicing the various settlement pattern options the study omits those costs incurred in maintaining services for the present population tied to existing locations. Gilder (1979) also points out that the study assumes the continuation both of existing levels of service provision and of the current balance of public and private sector contributions towards the costs of these services, both of which may prove invalid. Clearly, as Cloke (1983, p. 205) concludes, 'in view of these deficiencies, the apparent evidence offered by the North Walsham study in favour of resource concentration policies is of reduced impact in the general context of resource evaluation methodology'.

Another important milestone in the analysis of rural settlement strategies is Gilder's (1979) study in the Bury St Edmunds area of Suffolk. He employed a 'full-costing' rather than a 'relocation of present population' (Warford 1969) or 'additional costs of future growth' (Norfolk County Council 1976) approach. His conclusions that 'the accommodation of future growth will be less costly if that growth is dispersed widely throughout the area, than if it is concentrated in Bury St Edmunds and the larger villages' (1979, p. 264), are in sharp contrast to those from South Atcham and North Walsham, and effectively challenge the resource concentration ethic. Clearly, a crucial factor in any analysis of this kind is the basis of the measurement of cost employed. Gilder (Ibid., p. 47) defends his use of public sector budgetary costs, rather than the broader notion of economic cost, on the pragmatic grounds that 'public authorities are, regrettably, most influenced in any decision by the costs that will actually fall on the public purse'. Similarly, he rejects the measurement of economic cost as this 'would inevitably require a series of assumptions to be made about the distribution of costs and benefits. Questioning each of these assumptions would have provided a convenient refuge for all those who cling to the conventional wisdom'. As Cloke and Woodward (1981) remark, if further use of the full-costing technique confirms Gilder's pro-dispersal conclusions the economic basis of key settlement policies will have been undermined, and the need to consider alternative rural settlement strategies will be even stronger.

A fundamental distinction affecting the assessment of rural settlement strategies is that between social costs and economic costs. As Gruer (1971) has demonstrated with reference to hospital outpatient care, if all costs acruing to both the supplier and beneficiary of a particular service are taken into account, it may be less expensive for a travelling service to visit a scattered population than for the people to travel to a centralized resource. If the economics of rural settlement planning are calculated in this way a dispersed pattern of village investment becomes a possible alternative to the key settlement system. As Cloke (1979, p. 205) observes, however, 'the stumbling block to this metamorphosis of policy is that this type of equation would take account of personal expenditure by rural dwellers, whereas present financial assessments by local authorities are based upon costs to the exchequer'. Clearly, should social costs become part of the official planning balance-sheet, the economic justification for key settlements would be greatly reduced.

2   A social perspective   Key settlements are intended to raise rural living standards at a minimum cost to the community, and to act as viable service centres for the surrounding area. But, as critics like MacGregor (1976) claim, the concentration of facilities in key settlements without concern for hinterland transport links has merely exacerbated the plight of the nonmobile population in small villages. In addition, planners have often been reluctant to allow small-scale workshop enterprises to locate in nonkey settlements. Moreover, the failure to provide low-cost housing in small villages has coincided in many places with processes of gentrification and geriatrification each with their attendant problems. In short, it may be argued that the positive social contributions of key settlement policies, such as the retardment of depopulation in some areas, have been counteracted by an apparent exacerbation of a wide range of social problems in small rural settlements. Although a direct cause and effect relationship between policy and problems is hard to prove, Rawson (1981, p. 8) considered that the key settlement policy has 'generated too many undesirable side-effects' and 'has been powerless to mitigate the social problems which characterise most of the remoter parts of Rural Britain'. As Martin and Voorhees (1981) conclude, key settlement policy is a weak instrument of social change. It, alone, cannot be expected to reverse rural depopulation, raise the quality of rural life or ensure that rural dwellers can meet their needs for housing because it lacks the statutory powers to fulfil these objectives. Key settlement policy has greater relevance in the physical planning field, and is more able to halt development than to initiate it. This implies that it is a more appropriate tool to use in areas of growth and development, than in areas of rural depopulation where the main priorities are for social and economic regeneration.

3   A political perspective   Politics and planning are inextricably linked; and as Jenkins (1978, p. 23) observes, 'there is really no such thing as an apolitical arena'. Cloke (1979) has argued that the ineffectiveness of key settlement policies in both social and economic terms has been due, in part at least, to deficiencies in policy implementation and coordination. Reasons suggested to explain the less than hoped for success include: (a) lack of experience and the inevitable learning from mistakes in the early stages, and (b) the fact that initial procedures for selecting growth settlements in many counties were at best suboptional (e.g. based on little more than the population of the settlement, itself partly a reflection of past planning decisions) and at worst subject to political pressures both from influential groups and from individuals. Most importantly, however, the implementation of resource distribution strategies within the planning system has been ineffective because the scope of rural planning is too narrow to deal effectively with the social and economic problems of rural communities. As Moss (1978, p. 123) comments, 'few planning departments are able to coordinate, for example, the social, economic and physical aspects of village planning without exceeding their terms of reference'. There are many instances where growth of some key settlements has been halted by lack of adequate sewage-disposal or education facilities (Glyn-Jones 1979). Moreover, the reliance on restrictive rather than positive planning in rural areas has meant that vital stages in the development of key settlements and in the spread of opportunities to their hinterlands are outwith the capabilities of the present planning system.

Cloke and Shaw (1983), in a survey of rural structure plans, found that planners themselves identified four major problems associated with previous resource concentration policies:

(1)   The assumption that hinterland villages will benefit from investment in key settlements has been undermined by the decline in rural accessibility.

(2)   The key settlement concept has granted respectability to market trends of service rationalization and has positively discouraged beneficial development in non-selected villages.

(3)   The scale of new public investment is often too small to realize any scale economy benefits.

(4)   Planning authorities have limited control over the provision and disposition of rural resources so policies often do not have their desired effect.

Given the volume of opinion expressed against a continuation of a resource concentration strategy, attention has been given to possible alternatives.

Alternative settlement policies

The village unit (Venner 1976), the village constellation (Hancock 1976), cluster–dispersal (Department of the Environment 1974) and functional interdependence (McLoughlin 1976) are all examples of schemes where the idea of single growth centres in rural areas is replaced by a collective interaction of smaller settlements each receiving part of the rural resource base (Figure 4.2).

Particular attention has been given to the concept of functional or lateral interdependence among rural settlements. This argues that a key settlement policy fails to recognize the complex interrelationships between adjacent villages which often do not fall into the simple pattern generated by dominant and subordinate (key and non-key) settlements. Obvious parallels can be drawn between this model and the kind of functional interrelationships which have evolved 'naturally' in some rural areas of North America. The key element in an interdependent lateral system of service and employment provision is transport. Basically, an absence of effective transport will promote segregated service provision identifiable in the extreme case as community self-sufficiency; a hierarchical transport network as is classically provided by public buses will tend to generate hierarchical service provision; while the availability of the private car encourages the lateral as well as hierarchical provision of services. Weekly (1977) found evidence of integrated lateral interdependence among villages in Northamptonshire. His findings suggested that these rural areas do not function within a rigid hierarchical structure; that a concept which considers the area as a functionally interdependent system seeking centrifugally for unsatisfied services is more useful; and that although services will often be provided in the towns they do not dominate the service and employment provision of the rural area but are integrated within it and complementary to it. Such an arrangement would dispute that village services are necessarily disadvantageously located and would instead emphasize their local monopoly of provision. Evidence of a similar territorial organization of rural functions is cited by Lewis (1979) with reference to Lincolnshire, and Martin (1976) in the Peak District.

Figure 4.2 *Alternative rural settlement strategies*

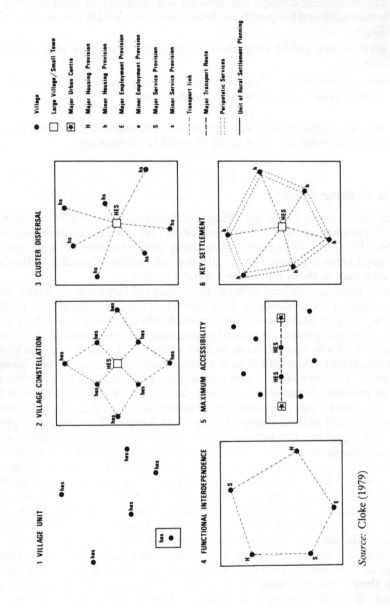

Village
Large Village / Small Town
Major Urban Centre
Major Housing Provision
Minor Housing Provision
Major Employment Provision
Minor Employment Provision
Major Service Provision
Minor Service Provision
Transport link
Major Transport Route
Peripatetic Services
Unit of Rural Settlement Planning

1 VILLAGE UNIT
2 VILLAGE CONSTELLATION
3 CLUSTER DISPERSAL
4 FUNCTIONAL INTERDEPENDENCE
5 MAXIMUM ACCESSIBILITY
6 KEY SETTLEMENT

Source: Cloke (1979)

Future settlement strategies

In a review of postwar rural settlement strategies in the UK Martin and Voorhees (1981, p. 177) concluded that 'there is no conclusive evidence that settlement policies of concentration have achieved the most economical pattern of infrastructure and service provision'. Equally, however, 'no real evidence has been advanced to demonstrate that alternative planning frameworks would provide a more practical or successful approach to rural planning than would the key settlement system' (Cloke 1979, p. 233). These conclusions serve to illustrate the need to advance from debate over the relative merits of polar opposites and to acknowledge that there is no single strategy that will suit all types of rural area. Martin and Voorhees (1981), for example, subdivided rural Britain into three categories entitled 'agricultural areas of population stability or moderate growth', 'green belt areas of population growth' and 'areas of remoteness and population decline', and recommended different settlement policies for each type of area. Clearly more detailed consideration would be necessary at the local level within these broad regimes.

With few exceptions settlement strategies have tended to adopt comprehensive policies of concentration and have overlooked the different levels of demand, potential and locational requirements for the development and maintenance of housing, services and industry. In order to achieve rural settlement strategies which are closely attuned to local needs the three aspects of settlement which are covered by settlement policy, namely, new housing development, the provision and maintenance of community facilities and services, and the attraction of industry and employment, need to be planned separately though in a coordinated fashion. A settlement which is suitable to receive new housing development need not be appropriate to function as a rural service centre, or employment centre. Conversely, rural service centres or villages with industry present are not necessarily the best or only settlements in which new housing should be built (Martin and Voorhees 1981). Equally the needs of different population groups must be considered and incorporated into the planning process.

Planning should be, above all, a problem-solving activity and the ideal settlement policy would be one which is responsive to local conditions and opinion, and which considers all settlements regardless of their size. An approach is required which is capable of generating alternative solutions and evaluating them against a wide range of social and economic criteria relevant to the study area, and then implementing the most favoured policy. While in reality there are legislative and financial constraints which will always hamper progress towards this goal, greater flexibility and integration of the various agencies involved in rural planning is more readily attainable, for example, through an extension of the principles of corporate management to rural areas. Corporate planning or PPBS (planning, programming, budgeting systems) seeks to eliminate the gulf between local government plan-making and budget-preparation. The comprehensive approach of PPBS brings together (1) physical planning – comprising land use and physical environment, (2) social planning – development of local services and their impact on the local community, and (3) resource planning – which includes both financial and manpower planning – in an attempt to ensure that the choice of priorities and policy options employs all available relevant information. This approach has antecedents in basic cost–benefit analysis and in variants such as the goals achievement matrix (Hill 1972), systems evaluation by community goals and objectives (Schimpeler and Grecco 1972), and the planning balance sheet (Lichfield et al. 1975). In PPBS, analysis has been interpreted more liberally than a strict definition of cost–benefit analysis would allow. It is conceded that a combination of criteria including monetary measures, other quantitative data, and qualitative discussion could, if properly prepared and presented, be perfectly satisfactory as a basis for policy judgement. This is because making judgements and taking decisions are recognized as the vital concluding stages of analysis in which the final result is hardly ever capable of a straight numeric computation (Rose 1970).

Clearly this widening of the concept of rural planning means that planners must extend their interests and expertise to encompass social and economic planning as well as their traditional concern with land-use strategies.

References

ANDERSON, A. M. (1950) Space as a social cost, *Journal of Farm Economics* 52, 411–30.

ASH, M. (1976) Time for change in rural settlement policy, *Town and Country Planning* 44(12), 528–31.

BARR, J. (1969) Durham's murdered villages, *New Society* 340, 523–5.

BERRY, B. J. L. (1973) *The Human Consequences of Urbanisation*. London: Macmillan.

BLOWERS, A. (1972) *The declining villages of County Durham* D281 Block III Unit 12 Part 2. Bletchley: Open University Press.

BUNCE, M. (1982) *Rural Settlement in an Urban World*. London: Croom Helm.

CLAWSON, M. (1966) Factors and forces affecting the optimum future rural settlement pattern in the United States, *Economic Geography* 42, 283–93.

CLOKE, P. J. (1979) *Key Settlements in Rural Areas*. London: Methuen.

CLOKE, P. J. (1983) Rural resource evaluation and management. *In* M. Pacione *Progress in Rural Geography*. London: Croom Helm, 198–225.

CLOKE, P. J. and SHAW, D. P. (1983) Rural settlement policies in structure plans, *Town Planning Review* 54(3), 338–54.

CLOKE, P. J. and WOODWARD, N. (1981) Methodological problems in the economic evaluation of rural planning strategies. *In* N. Curry *Rural Settlement Policy and Economics*, Gloucestershire Papers in Local and Rural Planning 12, 34–45.

DAHMS, F. A. (1980) The evolving spatial organisation of small settlements in the country-side – an Ontario example, *Tijdschrift voor Economische en Sociale Geografie* 71(5), 295–306.

DEPARTMENT OF THE ENVIRONMENT (1974) *Study of the Cambridge Sub-Region*. London: HMSO.

DEROUNIAN, J. (1979) *Structure Plans and Rural Communities*. London: National Council of Social Service.

FUGUITT, G. V. (1963) The city and the countryside, *Rural Sociology* 28, 246–61.

FUGUITT, G. V. (1981) Population trends in sparsely settled areas of the U.S.: the case of the Great Plains. *In* R. E. Lonsdale and J. H. Holmes (eds) *Settlement Systems in Sparsely Populated Regions*. Oxford: Pergamon, 125–47.

GILDER, I. (1979) Rural planning policies: an economic appraisal, *Progress in Planning* 11(3), 213–71.

GLYN-JONES, A. (1979) *Rural Recovery: Has it Begun?* Exeter: Devon C.C. and University of Exeter.

GREEN, R. J. (1971) *Country Planning*. Manchester: The University Press.

GRUER, R. (1971) Economics of outpatient care, *The Lancet* 20th Feb, 390–4.

HANCOCK, T. (1976) Planning in rural settlements, *Town and Country Planning* 44(12), 520–3.

HART, J. F. and SALISBURY, N. E. (1965) Population change in middle Western villages: a statistical approach, *Annals of the Association of American Geographers* 55, 140–60.

HART, J. F., SALISBURY, N. E. and SMITH, E. G. (1968) The dying village and some notions about urban growth, *Economic Geography* 44, 343–49.

HILL, M. (1972) A goals achievement matrix for evaluating alternative plans. *In* I. M. Robinson (ed) *Decision-making in Urban Planning*. London: Sage, 185–207.

HM TREASURY (1976) *Rural Depopulation*. London: HMSO.

HODGE, G. (1966) Do villages grow? – some perspectives and predictions, *Rural Sociology* 31(2), 183–96.

HODGE, G. and QADEER, M. (1976) *Towns and Villages in Urban Canada*. Ottawa: Ministry of State for Urban Affairs.

JENKINS, W. I. (1978) *Policy Analysis: A Political and Organisational Perspective*. London: Robertson.

LAMB, R. (1975) *Metropolitan Impacts on Rural America* Research Paper No. 162. Chicago: University Department of Geography.

LASSEY, W. R. (1977) *Planning in Rural Environments*. New York: McGraw-Hill.

LEWIS, G. J. (1979) *Rural Communities*. Newton Abbot: David and Charles.

LICHFIELD, N., KETTLE, P. and WHITEHEAD, M. (1975) *Evaluation in the Planning Process*. Oxford: Pergamon.

MacGREGOR, M. (1976) Village life: facts and myths, *Town and Country Planning* 44, 524–7.

MARTIN, I. (1976) Rural Communities. *In* G. E. Cherry (ed) *Rural Planning Problems*. London: Leonard Hill.

MARTIN AND VOORHEES ASSOCIATES (1981) *Review of Rural Settlement Policies 1945–1980*. Bristol: HMSO.

McLOUGHLIN, B. P. (1976) Rural settlement planning: a new approach, *Town and Country Planning* 44(3), 156–60.

MEREDITH, M. L. (1975) The prairie community system, *Canadian Farm Economics* 10, 19–27.

MOSS, G. (1978) Rural settlements, *Architects Journal* 18th January, 100–39.

NORFOLK COUNTY COUNCIL (1976) *The North Walsham Area.* Norwich: The Author.

PALLOT, J. (1977) *Some Preliminary Thoughts on Soviet Rural Settlement Planning* Working Paper No. 206, Leeds University, School of Geography.

RAWSON, J. (1981) *The impact of rural settlement policies of concentration and dispersal in Rural Britain* Paper presented to the PTRC Summer Annual Meeting, University of Warwick.

RIKKINEN, K. (1968) Change in village and rural population with distance from Duluth, *Economic Geography* 44, 312–35.

ROSE, K. E. (1970) Planning and P.P.B.S. with particular reference to local government, *Environment and Planning* 2, 203–10.

SCHIMPELER, C. G. and GRECCO, W. L. (1972) Systems evaluation: an approach based on community structure and value. *In* I. M. Robinson (ed) *Decision-Making in Urban Planning.* London: Sage, 241–68.

STABLER, J. C. (1978) Regional economic change and regional spatial structure: the evolving form of the urban hierarchy in the Prairie region. *In* B. S. Wellar (ed) *The Future of Small and Medium Sized Communities in the Prairie Region.* Ottawa: Ministry of State for Urban Affairs, 1–26.

VENNER, D. G. (1976) The village has a future, *The Village* 31, 39–41.

WARFORD, J. J. (1969) *The South Atcham Scheme.* London: HMSO.

WEEKLY, I. G. (1977) Lateral interdependence as an aspect of rural service provision: a Northamptonshire case study, *East Midland Geographer* 6, 361–74.

WHITBY, M. C. and WILLIS, K. G. (1978) *Rural Resource Development.* London: Methuen.

WOODRUFFE, B. J. (1976) *Rural Settlement Policies and Plans.* Oxford: Oxford University Press.

ZIMMERMAN, C. C. and MONEO, G. W. (1971) *The Prairie Community System.* Ottawa: Agricultural Economics Research Council of Canada.

5   Agriculture in the modern world

Agriculture is a ubiquitous rural activity which has formed the basis of Man's economic life for over ten thousand years (Sauer 1952; Grigg 1974). In Grigg's (1982, p. 15) view, 'the history of agriculture was the history of mankind until the nineteenth century'. On a global scale, as late as 1970 agriculture employed 51.0 percent of the world's economically active population and remained, as it had done since the Neolithic age, the single most important form of employment (Grigg 1975). Regionally, however, there are marked contrasts in the numbers engaged in agriculture. In the developing countries there has been an uninterrupted increase so that the agricultural labour force is now twice what it was at the beginning of the century. By contrast, in most of the developed world there has been an absolute decrease in the numbers employed in agriculture as a direct result of the industrialization-modernization process; and in many parts of the Western world this decline has been in progress for over a century (Figure 5.1).

During the process of economic development the proportion employed in agriculture continuously declines but the absolute numbers typically increase, stagnate

Figure 5.1 Date at which permanent decline in the agricultural labour force commenced.

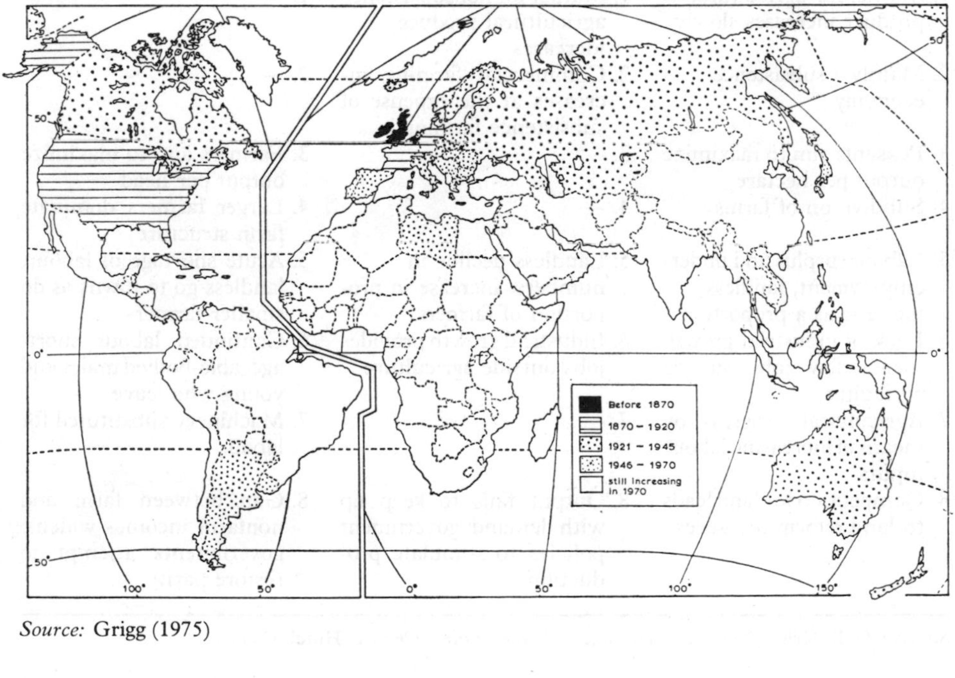

Source: Grigg (1975)

and then decline. Bicanic (1972) has argued that characteristic agricultural changes accompany each of these three periods (Table 5.1). The Stage 3 features are typical of most Western European countries since 1945 where rapid industrial growth between the end of the war and the late 1960s prompted an exodus from the land of both farm labourers and, for the first time, farmers. This led to some increase in the size of farms and to greater mechanization. A large number of farms, however, are still too small to provide an income comparable with that obtainable in industry.

Industrialization, combined with the spread of scientific research in agronomy, has transformed the productivity of modern agriculture. This is reflected in the increasing proportion of inputs purchased off the farm. Farm inputs may be divided into (a) those that increase yield per unit area, i.e. land saving, and (b) those that increase output per manhour, i.e. labour-saving. Before industrialization few innovations were overtly labour-saving, most aiming to increase output per hectare. Since the early twentieth century the level of mechanization has increased dramatically

Table 5.1 *Turning points and agrarian consequences according to Bicanic*

Stage 1: Agricultural population increases absolutely and decreases relatively	Stage 2: Stagnates absolutely and decreases relatively	Stage 3: Decreases absolutely and relatively
1. Market for agricultural produce increases slowly	1. Market for nonsubsistence agricultural produce increases	1. —
2. Mainly a subsistence economy	2. Commercial farming increases at the expense of subsistence farming	2. —
3. Peasants aim to maximize output per hectare	3. —	3. Farmers aim to maximize output per head
4. Subdivision of farms	4. —	4. Larger farmers dominate farm structure
5. Labour surplus and underemployment; landless increase as a proportion	5. Landless decline in numbers; increase in proportion of farmers	5. Acute shortage of labour; landless go to towns as do smaller farmers
6. Lack of industrial growth means few jobs outside agriculture	6. Industrial growth provides jobs outside agriculture	6. Continued labour shortage: able-bodied males and young who leave
7. Agricultural progress by means of increasing labour inputs	7. —	7. Machinery substituted for labour
8. Competition for land leads to land reform measures	8. Output fails to keep up with demand: government policies to stimulate production	8. Gap between farm and nonfarm incomes widens: governments attempt to restore parity

Source: D. B. Grigg (1982) *The Dynamics of Agricultural Change.* Hutchinson.

resulting in massive increases in productivity. A particularly significant event, regarded by some as heralding the beginning of modern farming, was the introduction of the general-purpose tractor in the USA in the late 1920s. The impact of this inanimate power source can be gauged from the fact that in 1920, the peak year for workstock in the USA, there were almost 26 million horses and mules and 246,000 tractors (a ratio of 106:1). Only 10 years later the number of work animals had fallen to 19 million while the tractor population had grown to 920,000 (21:1). By 1978 farmers in the United States employed tractors supplying the equivalent of 212 million horsepower. Most strikingly, the time taken to produce 2,700 kg of wheat fell from 383 manhours in 1800 to 10 manhours in the 1960s.

There is ample evidence of the spread of industrial farming techniques in the USA. Under the feedlot system, for example, cattle are kept in regularly shaped pens and instead of being grazed are fed from a central feed store, the aim being to maximize output by maintaining maximum feedlot capacity throughout the year and fattening cattle to optimum weight as rapidly as possible (Gregor 1974). One man using modern systems can now handle up to 5,000 head of cattle, operate a dairy enterprise of 50 cows, or take care of 75,000 chickens (Bertrand 1978). The development of industrialized farming systems has also influenced cash-crop agriculture. Hart and Chestang (1978) describe the industrialization of tobacco farming in east Carolina, while Bunce (1982) discusses the industrial crop farms producing fruit, vegetables and cotton in California. Similarly, in the UK arable farming has benefited most from mechanization while certain types of horticulture and the poultry industry have been extensively automated. In general, modern commercial agriculture is demanding a smaller but more skilled workforce.

The intensification and mechanization of agriculture has been a feature of the postwar industry throughout the Developed World. However, in some areas, such as California, where technological innovation has had a significant impact on agriculture and in particular on the labour requirements of modern farming, some concern has been expressed over the social consequences of such advances. In the view of Martin and Hall (1978, p. 208) 'the current agricultural mechanization debate centers on the extent of public and private responsibility for farm workers displaced by labor-saving agricultural innovations'. It has even been argued that some of the savings stemming from technological innovation should go to compensate farm workers unable to find other employment, and that the developers of new machinery should have to prepare *social-impact statements* to anticipate the effect on humans (Bradshaw and Blakeley 1979, p. 51). In California, investigations into the viability of small farms (The Small Farm Viability Project 1978) underlined the important difference between farms which are *optimal* and those which are merely profitable. As a result the state has attempted to direct resources to encourage small farms and rural communities.

Types of agriculture

Attempts to define agricultural regions are fraught with difficulty (Tarrant 1974) but classifications are normally based on land capability, land use or farming type. Whichever criterion is selected the choice of basic land unit depends primarily on the level at which data are available and the scale of operation that it is intended to depict.

On a world scale the most widely accepted classification of agriculture is that adopted by Whittlesey (1936) who identified the following 13 types of world agriculture: (1) nomadic hunting, (2) livestock ranching, (3) shifting cultivation, (4) rudimentary sedentary tillage, (5) intensive subsistence tillage with rice dominant, (6) intensive subsistence tillage without paddy rice, (7) commercial plantation crop tillage, (8) mediterranean agriculture, (9) commercial grain farming, (10) commercial livestock and crop farming (mixed farming), (11) subsistence crop and stock farming, (12) commercial dairy farming, (13) specialized horticulture. At a regional scale Buchanan (1959) has discussed pioneer work on defining agricultural regions of the USA; Scott (1957) employed crop and livestock combinations to produce a regional breakdown of Tasmanian agriculture; while Birch (1954), Napoletan and Brown (1963) and Church (1968) have produced maps of farming types in the UK on the basis of the predominant farming enterprise measured by the proportion of standard manday units devoted to different farm activities. As Weaver (1954) in the USA and Coppock (1964) in the UK have shown, however, maps depicting only the leading enterprise fail to consider the importance of the crops and livestock which are found in combination with the major activity. Coppock (1964) has produced a map of enterprise combinations which affords a more detailed description of the farming landscape in England and Wales (Figure 5.2). This also underlines the relevance of the traditional distinction between the predominantly arable south and eastern England and the pastoral agriculture of the north and west, first noted by Caird (1851). The boundary between the zones generally follows the Tees-Exe line separating highland and lowland Britain. The structure and nature of the farming industry in the UK has been the subject of detailed examination elsewhere (Coppock 1971; Edwards and Rogers 1974).

Types of farmers

Just as there are many kinds of farming enterprise so there are many types of farmers. Newby (1980) offers a four-fold 'ideal-type' categorization of farmers based on the degree of market orientation which they exhibit, and the extent to which they are manually involved in the husbandry operations on the farm (Table 5.2). Cell 1 com-

Table 5.2 *A typology of farmers*

		Market orientation		
		Low		*High*
Degree of direct involvement in husbandry	*Low*	1 Gentleman farmer		2 Agribusinessman
	High	3 Family farmer		4 Active managerial farmer

Source: Newby (1980)

Figure 5.2 Enterprise combinations for the National Agricultural Advisory Districts of England and Wales, 1958. The leading enterprises are shown by the shading and the others in the combination systems by the overprinted letters.

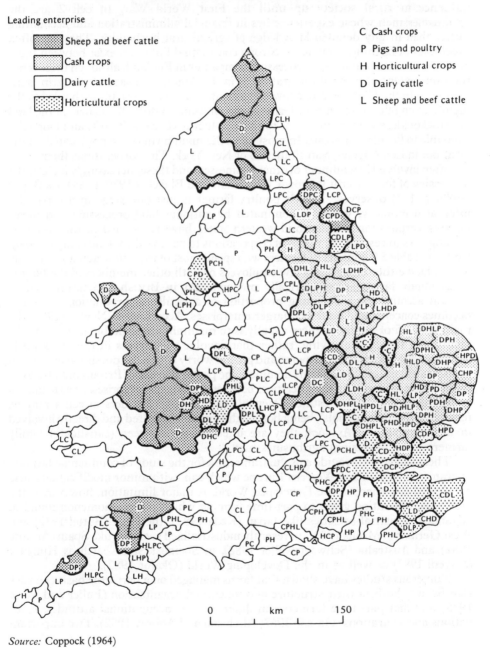

Leading enterprise

Sheep and beef cattle

Cash crops

Dairy cattle

Horticultural crops

C Cash crops
P Pigs and poultry
H Horticultural crops
D Dairy cattle
L Sheep and beef cattle

0   km   150

Source: Coppock (1964)

prises farmers whose orientation to the market is low and who take little part in the actual farming operations of their enterprises. In many cases such 'gentlemen farmers' represent the residue of the landed estate owners who wielded considerable influence in rural society up until the First World War. In cell 2 are the agribusinessmen whose experience lies in financial administration and accounting rather than in any detailed knowledge of agricultural husbandry. They are often executives of farming companies. Strong contractual links can exist between these businessmen and major food-processing companies in England, although there is not the same extent of vertical integration as in the American usage of the term 'agribusiness'. In the USA the move towards a capital-intensive agriculture has led to the organization of certain types of farms as corporations. 'Often the owners of the land are stockholders whose purpose is to share in lucrative tax write-offs and loopholes available to farming interests. In most cases the main owners are not located on the farm but in Los Angeles, San Francisco or New York. The corporations themselves are often involved in a number of other businesses, and these increasingly include the processing of food after it is grown' (Bradshaw and Blakeley 1979, p. 49). As Bunce (1982, p. 147) observes, 'today's poultry farmer is just one stage in a vertically-integrated industry, which is dominated by national food-processing and meat-packing corporations'. Some mid-western states have responded to this trend by passing laws to restrict the rights of corporations to control farm land (Harris 1980). Cell 3 in Table 5.2 consists of farmers who spend most of their time actually working on the land either alongside a few employees or with other members of the family. Such family farms are numerically preponderant in British agriculture, but in general account for a declining proportion of agricultural production as output becomes concentrated on fewer, larger enterprises. According to Newby (1980) the main concern of family farmers usually is to maintain an equitable level of profitability and standard of living, rather than involve themselves in the extra work, increased risk, extended borrowing and greater worry which the pursuit of maximum profits might entail. Such farms dominate the pastoral areas of Britain but also exist in the arable lowlands 'in the interstices between the larger enterprises, or as tenancies to the remaining landed estates' (Newby 1980, p. 106). Farmers in cell 4 may be termed 'active managerials', being both highly market-oriented and directly involved in farm husbandry. As such they are intermediate between (satisficing) family farmers and (optimizing) agribusinessmen.

These categories provide a useful framework for the study of commercial farming operators in Britain and Western Europe which can, with minor modifications, also be applied elsewhere in the Developed World. A major limitation, however, is the lack of consideration given to part-time farming which is a phenomenon found in advanced industrial societies like Japan (Kada 1982), the USA (Buttel 1982) and West Germany (Mrohs 1982); in recently industrialized societies like Spain (Arnalte 1982) and Australia (Schwartzweller 1982), in Socialist States such as Hungary (Enyedi 1982) as well as in the Developing World (Okafor 1982).

Numerous studies have shown that farms managed on a part-time basis can vary significantly both in their structure and functional organization (Fuller and Mage 1975) and that part-time farmers can differ in their occupational attitudes, motivations and aspirations (Gasson 1967; Aitchison and Aubrey 1982). Two important subtypes of part-time farming can be distinguished. First, that in which the farmer and his family seek nonfarm employment to supplement their farm incomes. Second, hobby farming where 'farmers' are involved for essentially nonagricultural reasons (e.g. tax and investment purposes, or for the recreational or amenity value) and the farm provides only a nominal source of income.

In the UK part-time farming is important in the southeast particularly around London (Blair 1980) and in areas of small farms or marginal farming. In Europe during the postwar period concentrations of part-time 'worker-peasants' have grown up around the urban-industrial areas, with many rural dwellers commuting to factory jobs each day and working on their farms during their free time. A similar situation occurs in Eastern Europe. Clearly this dual economy provides the worker-peasant with the material advantage of a higher income than could be derived either from farming or industrial work alone. For society in general however this can have several disadvantages. Farms operated by part-time farmers are small, often fragmented and usually of low productivity. As a result of the limited time and labour available sections of farmland may fall out of cultivation. This phenomenon of 'social fallow' is widespread in southern Germany (Kunnecke 1974) where up to 50.0 percent of the agricultural land surface may be abandoned around villages with large numbers of worker-peasants. Ruralites who secure full-time employment in the city may continue to live in their farmhouse and commute to work or may move to accommodation in town. Whichever action is followed many retain ownership of their land for sentimental or family reasons. Weeds and pests from these patches of under- or unused land can invade surrounding properties, and the existence of such holdings may hinder farm enlargement schemes which would benefit full-time farmers.

For some practitioners part-time farming is an end in itself; for some it is a transition stage prior to entering agriculture (Mage 1982; Bollman 1982); while for others it is a means of gradually leaving the industry. In the latter case if the farmhouse is not occupied by the owner, leased out, or abandoned completely it may be used as a weekend cottage or second home. The surrounding land may even be run as a hobby farm. Hobby farming is of increasing importance in Britain and Australia and is especially evident in North America where a highly mobile population with a strong demand for exurban development is helped by a relatively ready supply of land due to nonrestrictive planning controls (Layton 1979; Healy and Short 1979). During the past three decades the proportion of farms operated on a part-time basis has been stable in Canada, moderately increasing in England, growing at a steady rate in Germany and the USA, or has reached a maximum level as in the case of Japan. Part-time farming is now an established feature of both marginal agricultural areas, such as the crofting counties of Scotland or mountain regions of Norway, and areas within commuting distance of the larger urban places.

Government intervention in agriculture

Most governments intervene in the agricultural sectors of their economies to some degree, with the level of involvement increasing along the socio-political spectrum from the capitalist economies of North America, through the redistributive welfare states in Western Europe, to the centrally planned economies of Eastern Europe and the USSR. The objectives of intervention have been divided by Self and Storing (1962) into equity goals (i.e. those that seek an equitable treatment for the agricultural sector) and utility goals (i.e. those that require a useful contribution by this sector to the national economy) as illustrated in Figure 5.3. The actions of governments in pursuit of different combinations of goals have been a feature of postwar agriculture in the Developed World.

USA

Historically, public policy to benefit farmers in the USA has been justified in terms of (a) improving the farming community's share in national economic prosperity, (b) the belief that a plentiful supply of food should be provided to everyone at reasonable prices, (c) the importance of agriculture to the balance of payments, and (d) the general view that agriculture and the family farm are components of American life worth protecting.

Two different kinds of policy have been used to benefit farmers. Introduced first were public programmes to provide farmers with resources and skills in order to increase efficiency and reduce costs per unit of farm output. These measures have included establishment of a farm credit system; cost-sharing soil conservation programmes; the development of a railway system to facilitate the distribution of farm products; the setting up of land-grant agricultural colleges and research stations; and programmes to provide farmers with irrigation water and to allow them to graze livestock on public lands (Schaller 1978).

The second set of policy measures has dealt more directly with the prices and incomes received by farmers for their products. Of particular importance have been the price support and production control programmes initiated with the passage of the Agricultural Adjustment Act 1933. Though subsequently amended, the Act remained the basic price and income legislation for decades (Rasmussen et al. 1976). The primary purpose of the Act was to restore the farmers' purchasing power to the more favourable levels which had prevailed in the period 1910–1914. Initially farmers were paid to dispose of surplus crops and livestock. Various price support measures were effected later to raise the price of individual commodities in the market place. These were followed by acreage allotments or production quotas since the increased production stimulated by higher prices had tended to offset the intended gains in farm income. During the 1970s as a result of food shortages acreage controls were withdrawn, and following the Agriculture and Consumer Protection Act 1973 target prices were substituted for support prices. By the 1980s after nearly a decade of rapid growth American farmers experienced declining revenues due in part to a series of bumper harvests, inflation, high interest rates, a slow-down in consumption due to the world recession, and competition from the EEC and Japan in world markets. The fluctuating fortunes of agriculture were underlined when, in 1983, the US government introduced a 'crop-swap' plan aimed to boost prices and reduce the production of further commodity surpluses. Under this scheme farmers would agree not to plant some of their land, and in return would receive from government storage crops equal to between 80.0 and 90.0 percent of their normal output.

Figure 5.3 Agricultural policy goals.

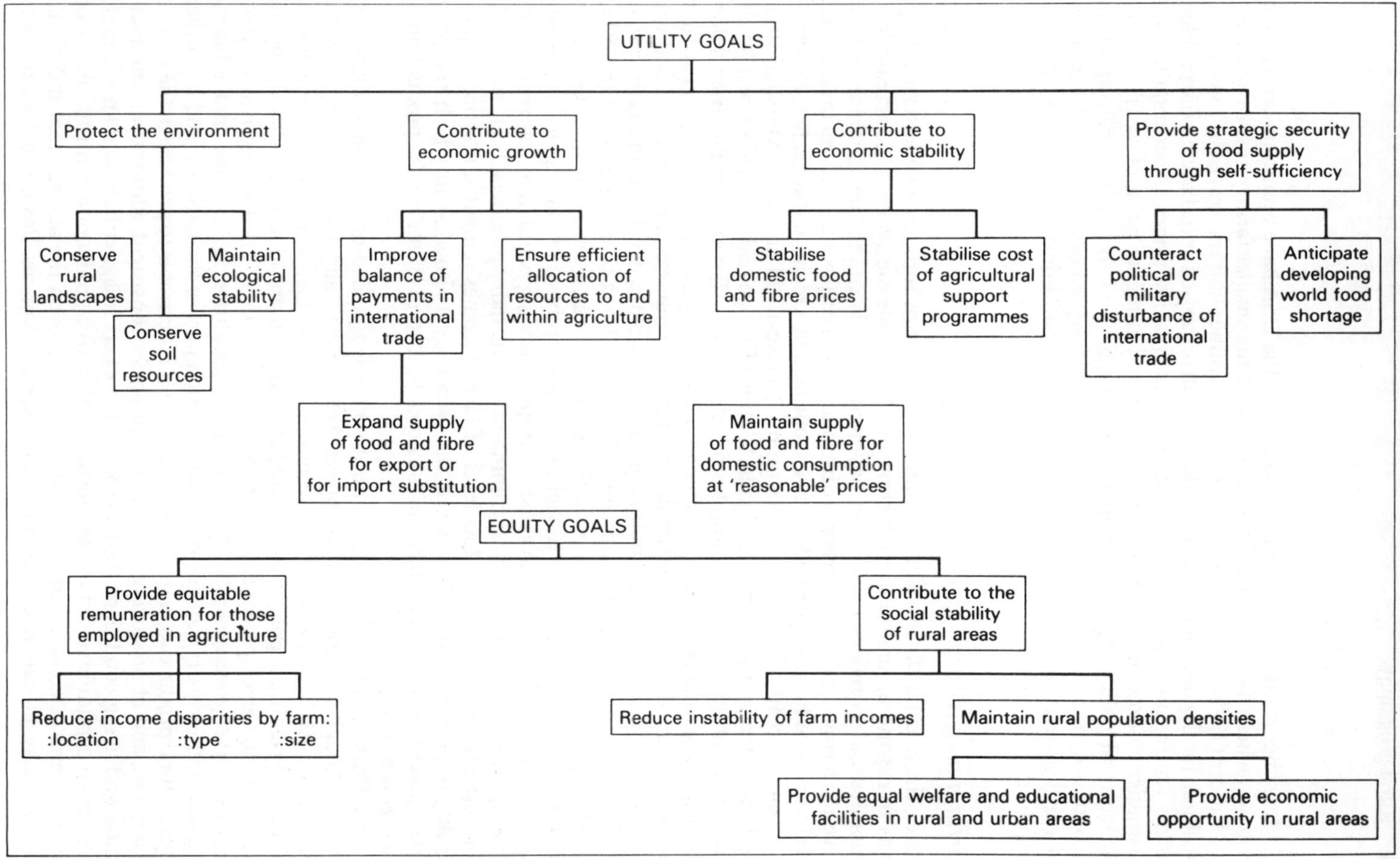

UTILITY GOALS

Protect the environment
- Conserve rural landscapes
- Maintain ecological stability
- Conserve soil resources

Contribute to economic growth
- Improve balance of payments in international trade
- Ensure efficient allocation of resources to and within agriculture
- Expand supply of food and fibre for export or for import substitution

Contribute to economic stability
- Stabilise domestic food and fibre prices
- Stabilise cost of agricultural support programmes
- Maintain supply of food and fibre for domestic consumption at 'reasonable' prices

Provide strategic security of food supply through self-sufficiency
- Counteract political or military disturbance of international trade
- Anticipate developing world food shortage

EQUITY GOALS

Provide equitable remuneration for those employed in agriculture
- Reduce income disparities by farm: location :type :size

Contribute to the social stability of rural areas
- Reduce instability of farm incomes
- Maintain rural population densities
- Provide equal welfare and educational facilities in rural and urban areas
- Provide economic opportunity in rural areas

Source: Bowler (1979)

It is important to note that farm policies in the USA have been commercial farm policies, which have not solved the problems of the smaller farmer or the rural poor. As Kalder (1975, p. 144) concludes, the programmes 'did not solve the low-returns problem for the large majority of small, less well organised units because the problem of low returns on these farms involved more than just low prices. In general they sold a smaller volume of output, which was produced at higher per unit costs'. Clearly, agricultural policy can help ameliorate the vagaries of free market pricing to the benefit of commercial farmers but it alone is not designed to solve the wider problem of rural poverty for which more comprehensive rural development strategies are required.

Britain and Western Europe

After the Second World War the immediate concern throughout Western Europe was to expand agricultural production by all possible means both to increase food supplies and to relieve balances of payment. To this end income guarantees were given to farmers, price supports were introduced or reinforced, and farm investments and improved farming methods were encouraged by credits and subsidies. Recovery was rapid, greatly helped from 1948 on by American aid under the Marshall Plan; and by 1950 agricultural production in Western Europe had regained prewar levels. By the end of the 1950s agricultural production was 50.0 percent higher than before the war for a total population which had increased by 20.0 percent. This growth in output occurred despite a steady fall in numbers employed in agriculture and was achieved as a result of technological and agronomic developments rather than through an extension of the agricultural acreage. Food consumption, on the other hand, grew relatively slowly once the shortages had been overcome. Gradually therefore from the mid 1950s the initial postwar problem of making up lost ground and producing enough food to satisfy Europe's growing population was replaced by that of overproduction of several commodities (e.g. dairy products, beef, wheat). At the same time the relatively low level of farm incomes remained a serious equity problem. Governments, thus, faced the paradoxical situation in which the price guarantees offered to raise farmers' incomes tended to stimulate the production of excess commodities.

In Britain, government agricultural policy is founded on the Agricultural Act 1947 although modified by subsequent Acts in 1957 and 1963 and, since Britain joined the EEC in 1973, by the provisions of the Common Agricultural Policy (CAP). Agricultural policies are devised centrally but are administered locally by the Agricultural Development and Advisory Service (ADAS). The 1947 Agricultural Act identifies the government's objectives for agriculture as 'a stable and efficient agricultural industry capable of producing such part of the nation's food and other agricultural produce as in the nation's interest it is desirable to produce in the United Kingdom, and of producing it at minimum prices consistent with proper remuneration and living conditions for farmers and workers in agriculture and an adequate return on capital invested in the industry'. Negative production controls employed by government consist mainly of systems of quotas on the acreage that individual farmers may allocate to certain crops and maximum prices. Positive inducements to agricultural production are of two main types: (1) the price support system and (2) direct payment of production grants and subsidies.

Price support was an essential ingredient of the 1947 Agricultural Act. Between 1947 and 1973 this operated by means of a deficiency payments scheme. The system worked by fixing a guaranteed price each year and if the market price fell below this level the farmer received a 'deficiency payment' from the government to make up the difference. Under this arrangement the direct relationship with market forces meant that food prices could fall to the advantage of the consumer without the farmer suffering uneconomic returns. It also prevented the creation of unsaleable surpluses and excessive support bills for the government. Britain's entry into the EEC agricultural structure was phased over the period 1973–1977, since when, price support policy has followed the intervention payments system of the CAP.

Most West European countries provided income and price guarantees to their farmers in the early postwar years and later had to grapple with problems of surpluses while still trying to ensure adequate incomes for farmers. Within the agricultural sector large disparities persisted between large farms and small, and between prosperous regions and less-favoured ones. Small farms, producing relatively little for the market, gained limited benefit from price support. Detailed consideration of the changing agricultural situation in a selection of European countries is provided by Tracy (1982).

The Common Agricultural Policy   The objectives of the CAP, set out in Article 39 of the Treaty of Rome 1957, are typical of agricultural policy in Developed countries. These are (1) to increase agricultural productivity, (2) to ensure, thereby, a fair standard of living for the agricultural population, (3) to stabilize markets, (4) to guarantee regular supplies, and (5) to ensure reasonable prices for consumers. In practice, the dominant objective has been the achievement of reasonable living standards for the agricultural population.

The CAP accounts for about 75.0 percent of the EEC budget and has been a central part of the organization since the formation of the Common Market. The CAP consists of two parts: a guidance section and a guarantee section, with the latter dominating expenditure patterns (Table 5.3). The European Agricultural Guidance and Guarantee Fund (EAGGF/FEOGA) finances (a) measures to regularize agricultural prices throughout the Community as well as (b) the refunds payable on exports to nonmember countries to enable EEC produce to find an outlet on world markets (i.e. by covering any differences between Community market prices and world market prices). Price support is an integral part of the CAP guarantee policy but is based not on the deficiency payment system as in Britain prior to 1973, but on a system of intervention prices. Under this arrangement when open market prices fall below the intervention price the Community must buy all produce offered to it at the fixed intervention price. This provides a floor to the market but also a guaranteed sale for producers with the result that overproduction and large surpluses have accrued. The problem has been compounded by the high levels set for intervention prices as a result of pressure from the powerful farming lobby, and by the exclusion, through import levies and quotas, of cheaper supplies of food on the world market.

Different rates of inflation and fluctuating exchange rates for national currencies,

Table 5.3   *The EEC budget 1980/1981*

	1980	1981
	million EUA/ECU	
Appropriations*		
Agricultural policy	11,803	13,338
Guarantee Section	11,486	12,870
Guidance Section	317	468
Fisheries policy	64	48
Regional Fund	403	619
Social Fund	701	620
Food aid	396	369
Other development aid	246	239
Repayments to UK	848	1,388
Other expenditure	1,721	2,707
Total appropriations	16,182	19,328
Revenue†		
Agricultural import levies	1,520	1,902
Sugar and isoglucose levies	504	571
Customs duties	6,000	6,274
Other	902	330
Total above revenue	8,926	9,077
Revenue required from VAT	7,256	10,251
Total revenue	16,182	19,328
Yield from max. 1% VAT†	9,910	11,510
as % of revenue required	0.73%	0.89%

* Appropriations for payments as finally adopted by the European Parliament at the end of 1980.
† Preliminary estimates.
Source: Tracy (1982)

particularly since the 'energy crisis' of 1973, also have had a serious impact on the operation of the CAP. The assumption of fixed exchange rates upon which the Common Market organization has been based was seriously undermined, necessitating the introduction of compensatory measures at national frontiers, contrary to the ideal of free movement of goods within the Community. These are based on special exchange rates (green rates) which have been negotiated to meet the needs of particular countries instead of basing market and consumer prices upon current rates of exchange. The Community makes up the difference between the green currency and the national currency. Thus when 'green currencies' are either lower or higher than the real currencies this can be compensated for by 'monetary compensation amounts' (MCAs) which take the form of either border levies (charges) or subsidies (payments) as food crosses a national boundary. Maintaining these 'green rates' imposes considerable financial strain on the EEC. Detailed accounts of the working of the CAP are offered by Fennell (1979), Marsh and Swanney (1980) and Buckwell et al. (1982).

The main emphasis of the CAP has been on the support of product prices in order to ensure a reasonable standard of living for producers. However, since price supports to farmers are in proportion to output, the larger producers and the richer regions benefit correspondingly more than the smaller farmers located mainly in the poorer regions. This has led Cuddy (1980) to argue that although guaranteeing a minimum income for producers the CAP has resulted in a widening of the income gap between farmers in the different regions of the EEC.

Eastern Europe

Postwar recovery of agricultural production levels took much longer in Eastern Europe than in the West. As a result of war action and the enforced movement of the resident population much of the land had been poorly farmed and there had been heavy losses of livestock. In Yugoslavia, for example, 80.0 percent of farm equipment, 60.0 percent of draught animals and 40.0 percent of rural housing had been destroyed during hostilities. Conditions throughout Eastern Europe were worsened by a drought in 1946–47 which led to further slaughter of animals due to a shortage of feedstuffs. In addition the wartime shortage of fertilizers and manpower incurred long-lasting damage to the soil. Later upheavals in the agricultural system associated with land reform and collectivization meant that as late as 1950 agricultural production in Eastern Europe remained below its 1935 level (Clout 1971).

The preeminent change in Eastern Europe following the Second World War was the spreading influence of the Communist ideology. By 1948 most of the socialist regimes had solidified their power base in the countries of Eastern Europe, and had begun to make plans for the economic and social transformation of their societies in keeping with the Communist manifesto (Marx and Engels 1961). These plans placed particular emphasis on industrialization; a process requiring (a) a rural–urban transfer of manpower and (b) maintenance of an agricultural surplus sufficient to meet growing internal needs and to retain foreign markets (Enyedi 1967).

The establishment of totalitarian regimes in Eastern Europe permitted radical State intervention in agriculture. The collectivization of farmland following the Soviet model was begun in all of the East European States by 1949 and was largely completed by 1962, with the exception of Poland and Yugoslavia where the family farm has survived. Two chief types of enterprise were established – State and collective farms. The former are owned and financed by the State with the employees receiving a wage and any profits accruing to the national budget. By contrast on collective farms land, while theoretically owned by the State, is leased to the collective in perpetuity. Profits are distributed among members on the basis of the number of hours worked. Since they are both part of the planned State economy the volume and type of crops to be produced is determined either entirely (as on State farms) or partly (on collectives) by central planners. In practice, the degree of collectivization varies from country to country in Eastern Europe. At one end of the scale is the most integrated collective farm akin to the Soviet kolkhozes in which decisions are made by the collective (in effect, by the local party secretary, the collective farm chairman, and the agronomist), every implement is owned in common, and members receive equal remuneration for their work. At the other, are specialized cooperatives where although everything is theoretically owned and accomplished in common, in reality members farm their 'own' land (i.e. land that was originally allocated to them), and collective work and collective rewards are kept to a minimum.

The initial hostile reaction of landowning peasants to forced collectivization had a deleterious effect on production levels. As Sanders (1958, p. 1) reasoned, 'the peasant who for centuries has longed for land of his own or else has been attached to actual holdings passed down from his forefathers, has little relish for the regimented way of life represented in the collective farm. As a result, he works under protest and with little enthusiasm. Production is low and the regimes are forced to import foodstuffs into agricultural countries which exported these same commodities before the Second World War.' Insufficient financial investment by the State compounded the problem so that by the early 1950s the demand for foodstuffs had increased more rapidly than supplies. In some countries such as Hungary, Czechoslovakia, Yugoslavia and in particular Poland this led to some decollectivization of land. In most cases however this redirection was only temporary and the State policy was reinforced throughout Eastern Europe following the Moscow Conference of 1957. By 1962–63 the present structure of the East European agricultural region was firmly established. Collectives are now the basic form of land occupation in most East European countries, with State farms covering smaller areas.

Private landownership, however, has not been abolished entirely. Members of collective farms are allotted small patches of land, usually less than 0.5 ha, to cultivate for themselves. While the long-term aim of governments is to improve the output of the collective farms and the income of the farmer so that the personal plot becomes unwanted, 'it continues to have lavished on it the maximum amount of attention and fertiliser that the farmer and his family can manage' (Symons 1978, p. 147). As a result in the three year period 1972–74 one-third of the meat and milk, 67.0 percent of the potatoes and 44.0 percent of the eggs produced in the USSR came from personal plots which accounted for only 3.0 percent of the land in cultivation. The produce of the personal plots is consumed mainly by the producers but surpluses are sold in kolkhoz markets located in the towns. In Poland and Yugoslavia where cooperative and State farms are weak, over 85.0 percent of agricultural land remains in private hands (Volgyes 1980). The small size of plots, however, means that the productive potential of this private agricultural land is less than in commercial farming regions of the West.

The drive for urban-industrial-led modernization in the Communist States of Eastern Europe had a marked impact on the rural population. Among the most significant changes were (a) the gradual ageing of the agricultural labour force; (b) the progressive feminization of farm labour; (c) the increasing shortage of labour in some countries, such as Czechoslovakia and Hungary; and (d) the growth of the worker-peasant class which has been a distinctive addition to the rural landscape of Eastern Europe since the last war. Each of these trends influenced agricultural output. The first three factors had a similar effect by reducing the input of a key factor of production that could not be readily replaced. For example, in Bulgaria, the median age of the rural population in 1973 was 40 years compared with 28 years for urban dwellers; the proportion of females in the agricultural labour force rose from 19.7 percent in 1957 to 48.5 percent in 1972; and the proportion of population employed in agriculture fell from 80.0 percent in 1938 to 45.0 percent in 1970. The continued growth of the peasant-worker class also had a negative impact on total output since land was underutilized by these part-time farmers (Korbonski 1980). In 1973 peasant-workers comprised 40.0 percent of the nonagricultural labour force in Czechoslovakia, 33.0 percent in East Germany, 30.0 percent in Hungary and in Yugoslavia, 25.0 percent in Bulgaria and 20.0 percent in Poland. A related phenomenon which mainly affects Yugoslavia is that of the foreign- or guest-worker. Foreign employment of Yugoslavs reached its height in 1973 when almost 5.0 percent of the total population found temporary employment abroad, mostly as gastarbeiters in West Germany. Only when an economic slow-down forced a reduction in the employment of foreign workers in the Western industrialized countries did this migration diminish. Those who returned home had normally accumulated sufficient savings with which to improve their dwellings and agricultural holdings (Hoffman 1980).

One way of alleviating the negative effects of a farm labour shortage is to increase the amount of capital inputs. Some governments, such as Czechoslovakia and East Germany, have progressed with mechanization and have increased the average size of State and collective farms. In other countries, such as Poland, agriculture's share of total State investment has lagged well behind that devoted to industry. In order to increase agricultural productivity and retain the workforce on the land, East European governments must overcome the fundamental problem related to (a) farm–nonfarm income differentials and (b) differences in living and working conditions between urban and rural areas. Two methods to make farming more profitable for those involved, which have been favoured by most of the East European governments, are (1) expansion of the social security programmes both to cooperative farmers and to 'independent' peasants; and (2) increases in the wages or levels of prices paid to peasants.

In Poland, for example, the rural peasantry have been included in the national health system since 1972. Independent farmers delivering produce to the State and retired producers giving over land parcels of more than 2.0 ha are eligible for old-age pensions and other privileges. Hungary maintains, for all workers, the pension eligibility age at 60 years for men and 55 years for women. In order to overcome any resulting labour shortage retirees are encouraged, through payments in kind, to work during the harvest season. The second set of material incentives is designed to raise incomes either through increased wages, tax incentives to cooperatives (Albania) or private farmers (Poland), and/or legislation favouring production on private plots (Hungary, Poland). Increasing the prices paid to peasants without raising wholesale and retail food prices cannot be sustained in the long run in most East European countries, where food subsidies already absorb a significant part of the State budget. As riots and strikes in Poland (1956, 1970, 1976 and 1980) testify, a rise in the price of such a basic commodity as food can threaten the stability even of one-party states. According to Rosenblum-Cale (1980, p. 240) 'only in Albania, East Germany and Czechoslovakia, the least flexible regimes, is the workforce still urged to increase its efforts in the rhetoric of "socialist competition". Elsewhere, the exhortatory messages and rewards have been softened, brightened, concretized, and rendered more reassuring to agriculturalists as an occupational group.' Both sets of measures, as well as increasing the costs of East European agriculture, pose significant idealogical questions for Communist states.

It is futile to attempt to construct a useful single model of East European agriculture from national components which range from industrialized East Germany to still-agrarian Albania. Generally, however, agriculture in Eastern Europe has advanced significantly from its precarious position after the Second World War. An industrial base has been built up which should be able to provide most of the necessary farm inputs. The exodus from rural areas eliminated the traditional agricultural over-population. In most countries the 'socialist transformation' of the countryside resulted in an improved farm structure more conducive to mechanization and modern agricultural methods, and the general modernization process has altered, in part, the traditional attitudes and values of the peasants, making them more receptive to innovation and experimentation. Nevertheless, difficulties remain. The food industry can still be plunged into a state of chaos by the weather, human error, bureaucratic inertia or international economic trends. General consumption standards have risen but shortages of key commodities persist. Self-sufficiency in basic products, the aim of all East European countries, is still a problematic yearly goal. Almost all states suffer a lack of machinery, spare parts, and a deficiency of skilled technical personnel; and coordination between producers and food-processors has been difficult to achieve (Rosenblum-Cale 1980). The crucial factor underlying all of these questions is the priority attached to agriculture within the Communist development programme.

References

ADEEMY, A. S. (1968) Types of farming in North Wales, *Journal of Agricultural Economics* 19, 301–16.

AITCHISON, J. W. and AUBREY, P. (1982) Part-time farming in Wales: a typological study, *Transactions of the Institute of British Geographers* N.S. 7, 88–97.

ARNALTE, E. (1982) Part-time farming in Spain, *Geojournal* 6(4), 337–42.

BERTRAND, A. L. (1978) Rural social organizational implications of technology and industry. *In* T. R. Ford *Rural USA: Persistence and Change*. Ames: Iowa State University Press, 75–88.

BICANIC, R. (1972) *Turning Points in Economic Development*. The Hague: Mouton.

BIRCH, J. W. (1954) Observations on the delimitation of farming-type regions, *Transactions of the Institute of British Geographers* 20, 141–58.

BLAIR, A. M. (1980) Urban influences on farming in Essex, *Geoforum* 11, 371–84.

BOLLMAN, R. (1982) Part-time farming in Canada, *Geojournal* 6(4), 313–22.

BOWLER, I. (1979) *Government and Agriculture: a spatial perspective*. London: Longman.

BRADSHAW, T. K. and BLAKELEY, E. J. (1979) *Rural Communities in Advanced Industrial Society*. New York: Praeger.

BUCHANAN, R. O. (1959) Some reflections on agricultural geography, *Geography* 44, 1–13.

BUCKWELL, A., HARVEY, D., THOMSON, K. and PARTON, K. (1982) *The Costs of the Common Agricultural Policy*. London: Croom Helm.

BUNCE, M. (1982) *Rural Settlement in an Urban World*. London: Croom Helm.

BUTTEL, F. (1982) The political economy of part-time farming, *Geojournal* 6(4), 293–300.

CAIRD, J. (1851) *English Agriculture 1850–51*. London: Cass.

CHURCH, B. M. (1968) A type of farming map based on agricultural census returns, *Outlook on Agriculture* 5, 191–6.

CLOUT, H. (1971) *Agriculture*. London: Macmillan.

COPPOCK, J. T. (1964) *An Agricultural Atlas of England and Wales*. London: Faber.

COPPOCK, J. T. (1971) *An Agricultural Geography of Great Britain*. London: Bell.

CUDDY, M. (1980) European agricultural policy: the regional dimension, *Built Environment* 7, 200–10.

EDWARDS, A. and ROGERS, A. (1974) *Agricultural Resources: an introduction to the farming industry of the United Kingdom*. London: Faber.

ENYEDI, G. (1967) The changing face of agriculture in Eastern Europe, *Geographical Review* 57, 358–72.

ENYEDI, G. (1982) Part-time farming in Hungary, *Geojournal* 6(4), 323–6.

FENNELL, R. (1979) *The Common Agricultural Policy of the European Community*. London: Granada.

FULLER, A. M. and MAGE, J. A. (1975) *Part-time Farming: Problem or Resource in Rural Development*. Norwich: Geo Books.

GASSON, R. (1967) Some economic characteristics of part-time farming in Britain, *Journal of Agricultural Economics* 18, 111–20.

GREGOR, H. F. (1974) *An Agricultural Typology of California*. Budapest: Akademiai Kiado.

GRIGG, D. B. (1974) *The Agricultural Systems of the World: an evolutionary approach*. Cambridge: The University Press.

GRIGG, D. B. (1975) The world's agricultural labour force 1800–1970, *Geography* 60(3) 194–202.

GRIGG, D. B. (1982) *The Dynamics of Agricultural Change*. London: Hutchinson.

HARRIS, P. E. (1980) Land ownership restrictions of the Midwestern States: influence on farm structure, *American Journal of Agricultural Economics* 62, 940–5.

HART, J. F. and CHESTANG, E. L. (1978) Rural revolution in East Carolina, *Geographical Review* 68, 435–58.

HEALY, R. and SHORT, J. (1979) Rural land: market trends and planning implications, *Journal of the American Planning Association* 45(3), 305–17.

HOFFMAN, G. (1980) Rural transformation in eastern Europe since World War II. *In*

I. Volgyes, R. E. Lonsdale and W. Avery *The Process of Rural Transformation*. New York: Pergamon, 21–41.

KADA, R. (1982) Trends and characteristics of part-time farming in post-war Japan, *Geojournal* 6(4), 367–72.

KALDER, D. (1975) Rural income policy in the United States. *In* E. O. Heady and L. R. Whiting *Externalities in the Transformation of Agriculture*. Ames: Iowa State University Press, 143–63.

KORBONSKI, A. (1980) Political management of rural change in eastern Europe. *In* W. Avery, R. E. Lonsdale and I. Volgyes *Rural Change and Public Policy*. New York: Pergamon, 21–35.

KUNNECKE, B. H. (1974) Sozialbrache – a phenomenon in the rural landscape of Germany, *Professional Geographer* 4, 412–5.

LAYTON, R. L. (1979) The hobby farming issue, *Town and Country Planning* 48, 53–4.

MAGE, J. (1982) The geography of part-time farming, *Geojournal* 6(4), 301–12.

MARSH, J. S. and SWANNEY, P. J. (1980) *Agriculture and The European Community*. London: Allen and Unwin.

MARTIN, P. and HALL, C. (1978) Labour displacement and public policy. *In* Division of Agricultural Services, *Technological Change, Farm Mechanization and Agricultural Employment*. University of California, Davies: The Authors, 200–43.

MARX, K. and ENGELS, F. (1961) *The Essential Left: Manifesto of the Communist Party*. New York: Barnes and Noble.

MROHS, E. (1982) Part-time farming in the Federal Republic of Germany, *Geojournal* 6(4), 327–30.

NAPOLETAN, L. and BROWN, C. J. (1963) A type of farming classification of agricultural holdings in England and Wales according to enterprise patterns, *Journal of Agricultural Economics* 15, 596–616.

NEWBY, H. (1980) *Green and Pleasant Land*. Harmondsworth: Penguin.

NEWBY, H., BELL, C., ROSE, D. and SAUNDERS, P. (1978) *Property Paternalism and Power*. London: Hutchinson.

OKAFOR, F. (1982) Environmental constraints and part-time farming in southeastern Nigeria, *Geojournal* 6(4), 359–66.

RASMUSSEN, W., BAKER, G., and WARD, J. (1976) *A Short History of Agricultural Adjustment, 1933–75* Agriculture Information Bulletin 391. Economic Research Service Washington: US Dept. of Agriculture.

ROSENBLUM-CALE, K. (1980) The search for economic viability in east European agriculture. *In* W. Avery, R. E. Lonsdale and I. Volgyes *Rural Change and Public Policy*. New York: Pergamon, 231–52.

SANDERS, I. T. (1958) *Collectivism of Agriculture in Eastern Europe*. Lexington: University of Kentucky Press.

SAUER, C. (1952) *Agricultural Origins and Dispersals*. New York: American Geographical Society.

SCHALLER, W. N. (1978) Public policy and rural social change. *In* T. R. Ford *Rural USA: Persistence and Change*. Ames: Iowa State University Press, 199–210.

SCHWARTZWELLER, H. (1982) Part-time farming in Australia, *Geojournal* 6(4), 381–2.

SCOTT, P. (1957) Agricultural regions of Tasmania, *Economic Geography* 33, 109–21.

SELF, P. and STORING, P. (1962) *The State and the Farmer*. London: Allen and Unwin.

SYMONS, L. J. (1978) *Agricultural Geography*. London: Bell and Hyman.

TARRANT, J. R. (1974) *Agricultural Geography*. Newton Abbot: David and Charles.

THE SMALL FARM VIABILITY PROJECT (1978) *Technology Task Force Final Report*. Sacramento: Dept. of Economic Development.

TRACY, M. (1982) *Agriculture in Western Europe*. London: Granada.

VOLGYES, I. (1980) Economic aspects of rural transformation in eastern Europe. *In* I. Volgyes, R. E. Lonsdale and W. Avery *The Process of Rural Transformation*. New York: Pergamon, 89–127.

WEAVER, J. C. (1954) Crop combination regions in the Middle West, *Geographical Review* 44, 175–200.

WHITTLESEY, D. (1936) Major agricultural regions of the earth, *Annals of the Association of American Geographers* 26, 199–240.

6   Structural change in agriculture

Farm structure – the size and spatial disposition of land holdings – is an integral part of the rural landscape and a fundamental factor in agricultural production. Above all farm structure is a major determinant of farm income (Bowler 1983). Clearly, 'even if average incomes could theoretically be improved through price policy to the satisfactory level, the basic structural inadequacies could still remain' (OECD 1975, p. 50). High prices may enable large farmers to earn big profits but the small or structurally disadvantaged farmer will never acquire adequate income or capital through price policy alone.

Structural change can take place at different scales. At the smallest scale it refers to the spatial arrangement of fields comprising individual farms. Farms may consist of tiny fragmented parcels of land which may be time-consuming to reach and uneconomic to work. This situation can be improved by plot consolidation. At the next scale the issue concerns the number and size of individual farms. Farms may be physically too small to provide full-time profitable employment, in which case enlargement is required or suitable alternative part-time employment must be found. Structural changes above the individual farm level may involve remodelling of the settlement pattern to improve the efficiency of agricultural practice in an area; land reform; or some form of comprehensive regional management and development policy. Structural change in agriculture should not be viewed as an event but rather as an ongoing process. The need for continuous structural change arises mainly from the necessity of adjusting to new techniques, adapting to changing economies of scale, and to changes in the commodity composition of consumers' demand.

Land fragmentation

On a world scale the Census of Agriculture 1960 reported that fragmentation was most severe in Europe (with an average of 6.7 plots per holding), followed by Asia (4.0 plots per holding). Within Western Europe the extent of the problem varies between countries, being of little significance in the UK (as a legacy of the Enclosure Movement) and in Denmark and Sweden (due to reforms dating from the late eighteenth century) but is of serious proportions in southern European countries like Spain and Portugal. Although significant progress towards consolidation has been made since 1960 in countries like France, West Germany, Spain and the Netherlands (Lambert 1963) the overall situation has not altered greatly. Indeed, it may even have worsened 'for since 1950 the technical requirements for rational farm layout have become more stringent with the advent of machines and increased labour costs' (King and Burton 1982, p. 480).

The causes of land fragmentation may be related to socio-cultural, economic, physical and political influences (King and Burton 1981). Socio-cultural causes appear to predominate, with inheritance laws which facilitate or demand equal division of land among heirs being of particular importance (OECD 1972). This principle is enshrined in the Napoleonic Code in France and in the Islamic inheritance laws. Clearly, once the process of fragmentation has commenced it continues at a geometric rate with each succeeding generation. A rapidly growing population and absence of alternative sources of work contribute to land fragmentation. In the Netherlands Vanderpole (1956) showed that fragmentation was more severe in the southwest where the Catholic religion prevails and families are larger on average than in the rest of the country. Economic causes of land fragmentation include the piecemeal reclamation of moor or marshland; the fossilization of open-field patterns inherited from earlier systems of communal farming; and the gift, sale, purchase or renting of plots of farmland. Fragmentation may also be underlain by physical factors such as high or broken relief with an extreme example being the transhumance economy of Alpine farms. Finally, fragmentation may result from government action as in the land distribution programmes carried out in Turkey (Busch et al. 1979) and Greece (Thompson 1963). In the latter case between 4 and 18 tiny plots of land were assigned to each recipient rather than one parcel in an attempt to produce an equitable distribution of all land types.

As Johnson (1970) points out, at low levels of economic development land fragmentation has certain advantages. It may, for example, be an ecologically adaptive strategy reflecting variations in land quality; the intermixed pattern of land use produced by the multiplicity of plot ownership can check the diffusion of crop and animal diseases; and it spreads the risk of climatic or other environmental hazards. Galt's (1979) study of viticulture on the Mediterranean island of Pantellaria exemplifies a situation where land fragmentation is a highly rational response to local environmental conditions. Such fragmented agricultural systems are geared primarily towards stability rather than towards productivity.

Once a commercially oriented agriculture develops, fragmentation increasingly imposes economic costs on farming. These include the value of the time wasted in moving labour or livestock between scattered plots (Chisholm 1979); the high cost of fencing; the difficulty of mechanization; and the high cost of cultivating awkward corners manually. Social-psychological problems include disputes over access to plots and litigation over contested ownership. In Greece, for example, 47.0 percent of plots and 33.0 percent of farmland are accessible only by trespass on another property (Thompson 1963; Herzfeld 1980).

Plot consolidation

Consolidation is concerned with the rearrangement and reallocation of scattered parcels of land to produce a compact holding around the owner's farmstead. This can take place through a voluntary exchange or purchase of plots on the initiative of individual owners (Thompson 1961; White 1966). More often, however, government intervention is necessary to accelerate what is otherwise a slow process.

Land consolidation schemes exist in nearly all countries of Western Europe. Most of the consolidation authorities have the power to undertake compulsory consolidation if necessary but many acknowledge the importance of voluntary and active participation by farmers and landowners. Thus in some countries consolidation schemes are contingent upon approval by a certain majority of landowners. In several countries there must be not only a majority of owners but of area involved as well. Spain, for example, requires 60.0 percent of the owners possessing at least 60.0 percent of the land as a minimum rate. In other countries, such as West Germany, central government can initiate consolidation without recourse to public opinion. Detailed discussion of the various phases of a land consolidation project is provided by King and Burton (1981). The completion of a programme of land consolidation in an area does not in itself ensure that refragmentation will not occur. Lamartine Yates in 1960, for example, described how land around an Austrian village which had been consolidated at the turn of the century was as fragmented as before. A consolidation programme must be supported by legislation to prevent the land reverting to its previous condition. Measures include legislation establishing minimum farm and plot sizes (as in Denmark, Spain, Switzerland and the Netherlands) and controlling subdivision of newly established holdings, as in West Germany (Muller 1964) but difficulties of implementation are compounded by the need to take into account local physical conditions, type of land use, and, if local hardship is to be avoided, alternative employment opportunities.

Within Western Europe plot consolidation and farm enlargement is a basic objective of national and EEC agricultural policy but it is occurring much more slowly than desired (Rickard 1970). In France, remembrement took 28 years to consolidate 43.0 percent of the land in need of treatment while the general conclusion is that it will take most countries about 30 years to treat the areas currently suffering from fragmentation. The monetary cost of schemes is also high (OECD 1972). In order to speed the process and cut costs some countries, such as Sweden, Switzerland and West Germany, introduced 'accelerated' schemes which rely more on the initiative of farmers, with public support limited to advisory services and coverage of some of the costs involved. A major problem, however, is that consolidation does not necessarily reduce the number of holdings or increase farm size. As Bowler (1983, p. 55) observes, 'from a social point of view plot consolidation without farm enlargement maintains the rural population on the land while increasing the economic viability of each farm. But from an economic viewpoint the amount of land per farm still remains too small to provide a reasonable income.' Land consolidation therefore cannot be isolated from the larger issues of farm enlargement and regional rural development, the latter being necessary to provide nonfarm employment for those farmers losing land.

Farm enlargement

Central to the process of farm enlargement is the balance between the supply of and the demand for farm land. It has been suggested that land comes onto the market for sale in four main ways: (a) a farmer moving to another farm, (b) a farmer selling some land to raise capital for investment, (c) a farmer leaving agriculture either through death, age retirement or alternative employment, and (d) the creation of new land by reclamation (Bowler 1983). Although exact proportions vary from country to country and between regions, most farm surveys reveal that death and age retirement are the main ways by which land is made available for purchase, with retirement becoming increasingly important (Gasson 1969). Parson (1977), in Gatineau county Quebec, found that age and ill-health together accounted for 37.3 percent of retirements with a further 20.3 percent attributable to low farm incomes. Positive reasons, such as taking up alternative employment, tend to be in a minority.

Under normal market f rces land is made available for farm enlargement at a very slow rate due to the low occupational mobility of farm people. Reasons suggested for this include the 'psychic' attractions of farming as a way of life, and the loss of status and apparent admission of failure attached to leaving agriculture (Hill 1962); the relative unattractiveness of industrial employment (Weerdenburg 1973); a wish to pass the farm on to an interested son or daughter; government financial support which reduces the disparity between farm and nonfarm incomes; the fixity of farm assets (Kingman and Samuel 1977); the lack of education or industrial skills in the farm population for off-farm employment; the high average age of farmers; the direct cash costs of moving to an urban area; and uncertainty about the future in an urban occupation.

In many parts of North America and Australia farm enlargement has become increasingly difficult to achieve through the addition of land which is contiguous to the original holding. Consequently a common method of expanding acreage is the acquisition of noncontiguous parcels of land either purchased or rented from farmers leaving agriculture. The operation of discontinuous agricultural units was recognized by Diller in Nebraska as early as 1941, while the large crop farms of the Great Plains tend to be highly fragmented reflecting the long-established practice of suitcase or sidewalk farming (Kollmorgen and Jenks 1958a, 1958b). Williams (1972) for Australia, Edwards (1978) for the UK, Bunce (1982) for Canada, and Smith (1975) and Van Otten (1980) in the USA all demonstrate how farm enlargement can lead to a fragmented pattern of farm ownership (Figure 6.1).

Governments have attempted to accelerate the 'natural' process of farm enlargement using three broad measures: (1) retirement pensions, (2) farm amalgamation grants, and (3) retraining schemes.

(1)   Retirement pensions, annuities and lump sum payments are available to farmers who retire voluntarily from agriculture and allow their land to be used to enlarge neighbouring farms. Sweden has had a Retirement Compensation Scheme since 1967, France has provided termination payments (Indemnité Viagère de Départ) since 1962, and the EEC contributes to all such schemes in member states under Directive 72/160.
(2)   For those who remain in agriculture credit facilities and grant aid are provided to assist with the costs of farm amalgamation. West Germany, for example, gives low-interest loans for purchasing land to applicants who must demonstrate that after enlargement their holdings will be economically viable.
(3)   Retraining schemes, especially for the sons of farmers, operate in several countries including Japan, France and the USA.

The method of administering these various measures differs between countries. In the UK, for example, the Ministry of Agriculture, Fisheries and Food (MAFF) controls the schemes but the sale and purchase of farmland is left to market forces. In other countries, such as Japan, West Germany and Denmark, government agencies intervene directly in the land market. Sweden has had a network of County

Figure 6.1 Holdings comprising more than two sections in South Australia, 1969.

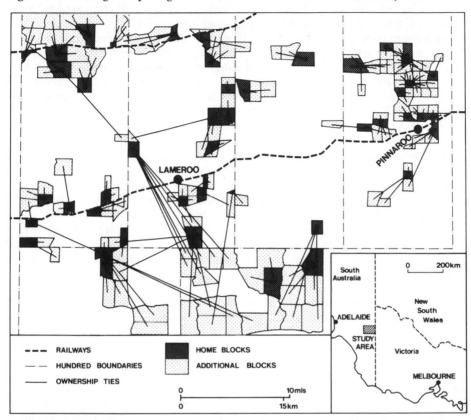

Source: Williams (1972)

Agricultural Boards since 1957 (Whitby 1968) which authorize land transactions and also buy and sell land in an attempt to produce a more rational pattern of land allocation than achieved by market forces. In France, under the terms of the Loi d'Orientation of 1960 and particularly the Loi Complémentaire of 1962, 29 regional authorities (Sociétés d'Aménagement Foncier et d'Établissement Rural) were established to buy and resell farmland with the aim of improving farm structures (Butterwick and Neville-Rolfe 1965). A similar Farm Consolidation and Enlargement programme operates in Canada (Bunce 1973).

Most evaluations of structural measures, however, emphasize the limited results that have been achieved. The response of farmers to voluntary retirement schemes has been generally poor. The financial incentives of most pension and lump sum payments have not been sufficient to overcome the reasons for remaining in agriculture, and payments appear to have been made mainly to those who would have retired from farming in any event (Hine 1973; Naylor 1982). The impact of farm amalgamation schemes has also been less than hoped for. The volume of land handled by government intervention authorities has been relatively small compared with the number of farms in need of enlargement and the total amount of land passing through the market. A major problem is that the market price of land tends to exceed the maximum at which intervention agencies are permitted to purchase. This does mean, however, that as in France (Clout 1968) their operations tend to be limited to regions with the poorest farming and the greatest social and economic problems. A further issue identified by Hirsch and Maunder (1978) is that in many countries a relatively small proportion of the land freed for amalgamation has been added to the holdings most in need of enlargement. As Bowler (1983) explains, although it may be socially desirable to assist farmers with the lowest incomes, the very nature of their position militates against their making the best use of the available land. Consequently intervention authorities tend to discriminate in favour of middle- rather than low-income farmers in an area.

An indication of the farming structure of Western Europe is given in Figure 6.2. The need for structural change to deal with the basic causes of maladjustment in the farm sector of the EEC formed the core of the 1968 Mansholt Plan. The aim was to create 'modern production units' through selective investment aids. It was suggested that a suitable arable farm for the 1980s would have 80–120 ha of cropland, and that a livestock farm would raise 40–80 dairy cows (or 150–200 beef cattle, or 450–600 pigs, or 100,000 head of poultry) each year. The magnitude of these targets is underlined by the fact that at that time two-thirds of all farms in the EEC were of less than 10 ha and two-thirds of dairy farmers had fewer than 5 cows each. The plan also envisaged a reduction in the agricultural labour force of 5 million people, in the agricultural area of 5 million hectares, and in the Community dairy herd of 3 million cows. Violent opposition to these proposals from agricultural interests throughout the EEC ensured that only a much modified version of the plan emerged in 1972. In this, provision was made for 'common measures' for investment aids for farm modernization (Directive 72/159); for payments to outgoers (Directive 72/160); and for promotion of socio-economic guidance and training (Directive 72/161). Subsequently other common socio-structural programmes were adopted. Directive 75/268 provided income aids or 'compensatory allowances' (based usually on the number of livestock units per farm) to farmers in mountain, hill and other less favoured areas. A significant new development in structural policy was the introduction from 1978 onwards of a series of measures for designated regions. Thus the 'Mediterranean package' (which also included measures for Ireland and Greenland) was intended to support specific types of improvement corresponding to the needs of the regions concerned (e.g. irrigation in the Mezzogiorno; sheep rearing in Greenland; and reafforestation and development of rural infrastructures in the south of France).

Settlement remodelling

In addition to plot consolidation and farm enlargement, in many European countries resettlement of farm families is regarded as an essential part of structural change, the general aim being to resite dwellings that are too distant from fields, or located on a

Figure 6.2 Distribution of farms by size group in 1975.

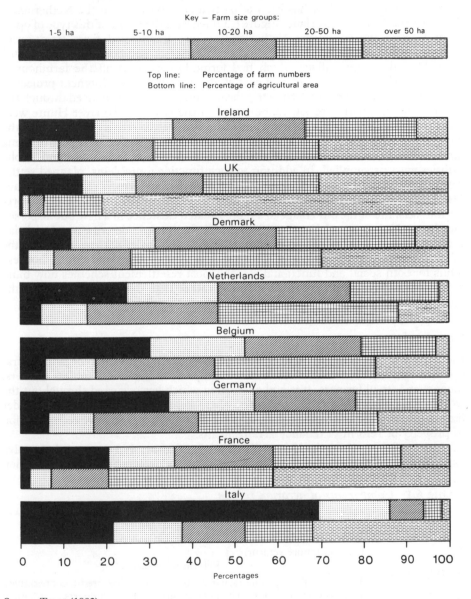

Source: Tracy (1982)

congested site, or where existing farm buildings are inadequate. Chisholm (1979) has explored the economic rationale behind the siting of new holdings.

Settlement remodelling has been of particular importance in the Netherlands, West Germany and Switzerland. Figure 6.3 illustrates the result of this type of operation at Vriezenveen in the Netherlands where fragmented farm strips were regrouped into consolidated holdings and new farmsteads and field roads constructed away from the street village which had formerly contained all the farmhouses. Mayhew (1971) provides a detailed case study of a similar development project at Mooriem in West Germany. Long-strip farms which had been produced through the progressive reclamation of low marshy land in the valley of the river Hunte were replaced by rectangular-block farms, and some farmsteads were resettled outside the village. This kind of settlement remodelling process is costly since, besides constructing farm buildings, roads have to be made to each dispersed farmhouse and public utilities must be supplied. In addition to such functional problems, planned settlement dispersal must also overcome social resistance from farmers reluctant to leave property which may have been in their family for generations, and those who prefer the social life of the old village to a more isolated existence in a new but dispersed farmhouse. McEntire and Agostini (1970, p. 198), for example, describe how Calabrian peasants preferred to live in a poor, unsanitary village crowded with people 'while the adjoining countryside was dotted with modern, commodious and empty houses'. Thus for both social and functional reasons most resettlement schemes now build new farmsteads in small groups or hamlets rather than dispersing them over the countryside.

Land reform

Land reform represents a radical attempt by governments to reorganize rural economies, normally via a redistribution of property in favour of landless workers, tenants and small farmers. It is a phenomenon which has occurred throughout the world (King 1977). Table 6.1 indicates where land reform fits into the broader framework of agrarian change – thus, land tenure reform may involve redistribution of property or reform of tenancy arrangements.

Land reforms which include redistribution of ownership necessarily involve expropriation of part or all of the land of the large landowners and its redistribution

Table 6.1   *Components of agrarian reform*

Agrarian Reform	Land reform (Land tenure reform)	Land redistribution (also including consolidation and collectivization)
		Reform of tenancy
	Reform of complementary institutions (including: credit, cooperatives, marketing, taxation, labour legislation, price supports, settlement schemes, extension services, etc.)	

Source: King (1973)

Figure 6.3 Field and settlement structure in Vriezenveen commune in the Netherlands before and after integrated land management.

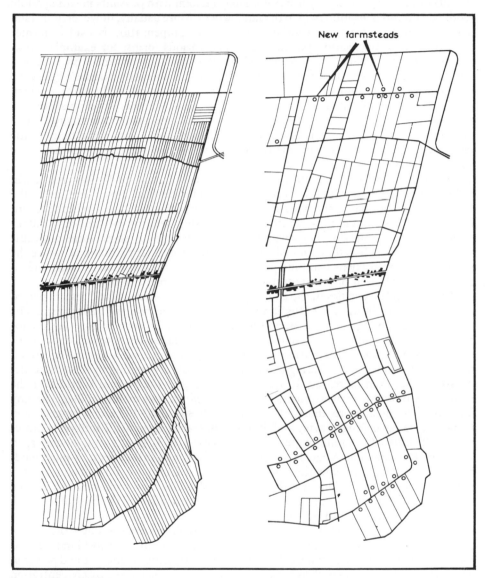

Source: Clout (1972)

to landless peasants, usually in the form of individually owned small farms but some-times communally as in the Mexican ejidos. In the case of revolutionary reforms like the 1953 Bolivian uprising, expropriation may be total with peasants invading estate lands and no compensation paid to the landowners. More usually, however, only land over a permitted area is expropriated, and some compensation is paid to former owners. This compensation payment can take various forms; for example, (a) in exceptional circumstances as in Venezuela in 1958 (due to government oil revenues) land may be purchased at market prices; (b) more usual is a cash settlement below the market value of the land; or (c) there may be a payment based on the value at which the land has been returned for tax purposes (thus those who have previously under-estimated the value of their land for tax reasons are paid accordingly). Most authorities require the beneficiaries of land redistribution to pay something for the land they receive but this is normally well below the real value, and payments are spread over 20–30 years.

Tenancy reform has been most common in Asia. In Japan and Taiwan, reforms in 1953 largely replaced tenancy with outright landownership. Elsewhere, as in the Philippines, policy has been concerned with strengthening the position of the tenant by securing rent reductions or through increasing security of tenure. Another alternative to transferring landownership to the peasant is some form of profit-sharing scheme such as that applied on the Puerto Rico sugar plantations, where the proportional profit farms combine public ownership, efficient management and an equitable distribution of profits to labour and management (King 1973).

Sharp social disparities in the countryside and the promise of land reform played a significant part in the 1917 Russian revolution and the rise of Communism. The major reforms in the interwar period were enacted in Eastern Europe largely for political considerations rather than for reasons of social and economic policy. Thus they involved land redistribution but no supporting measures regarding credit, technical assistance or marketing facilities. As a result production in some areas de-creased rather than increased. In Eastern Europe after the Second World War the incoming Communist governments passed land reform laws making it illegal for any individual to hold more than 50 ha in Czechoslovakia, Poland, Hungary and Rumania; 35 ha in Yugoslavia; and 20 ha in Bulgaria. In total 12 million hectares were distributed to 3 million peasants. As King (1973) points out, however, in Bulgaria, Rumania and Yugoslavia the land reform had little effect, as most land-holdings were already below the ceilings set; in East Germany, Poland and Albania about 25.0 percent of the land was distributed, and in Czechoslovakia about half. The most radical impact was in Hungary where land reform affected the bulk of the land, instigating a switch from large estates to small farms.

The specific objectives of land reform policies differ between countries but in general motives can be classified as social, economic or political. Most land reforms have occurred in situations where there were great disparities in income and power in agriculture. This rigid two-class social structure was characterized by concentration of landownership in the hands of a few, accompanied by a high proportion of landless agricultural workers and insecure tenancy arrangements. In prereform Bolivia, for example, the 1950 Census revealed that 4.5 percent of the rural landowners possessed 70.0 percent of all private landed property. In such circumstances the landowners' control over land and capital means that the peasants' possibilities for self-improvement and social mobility are remote. Gadalla (1962) has described how in Egypt in 1947 the capital required to buy 5 acres of land was equivalent to an agricultural labourer's wages for 60 years.

The political motive can also be a decisive force for land reform. Many governments have used land reform or the promise of it to gain or retain power. Land reform was used as a means to power in the peasant revolutions in Mexico and Bolivia, and the Communist uprisings in Russia and China. The more recent land reforms in Italy (1950) and Taiwan (1953) were also, in part, a political response to increasing Communist activity in rural areas. In such cases the motive of social equality was strongly tinged by motives of political self-preservation.

The economic motive is based on the belief that land reform is necessary to maximize the productivity of the agricultural sector, to provide a surplus to serve as capital to build up industry. Johnston and Mellor (1961) list five ways in which agricultural improvements can aid general economic development:

(1) By satisfying an increased demand for food supplies.
(2) By exporting agricultural products and earning foreign currency.
(3) By providing labour for manufacturing and other expanding sectors of the economy.
(4) By investing profits in industry.
(5) By raising agricultural incomes which increases demand for consumer goods thus stimulating industrial expansion.

The major land reform in the postwar capitalist world took place in Italy in 1950. Since the problems of a backward agricultural structure were most severe in the Mezzogiorno the land reform was essentially a southern measure with most of the region designated as a reform area (Figure 6.4). The harsh physical environment, semifeudal rural social structure, polarized landownership (Table 6.2), and problems of overpopulation, underemployment and poverty all help to explain the background to the Italian land reform (King 1973). The land reform was concerned essentially

Table 6.2   *Distribution of private property in prereform Italy, 1946*

Size classes (ha.)	Number of properties '000	Number of properties %	Area of properties '000 ha.	Area of properties %	Average area (ha.)
0–2	7,926	83.4	3,758	17.5	0.5
2–10	1,283	13.5	5,233	24.2	4.1
10–50	254	2.6	5,050	23.5	19.9
50–100	28	0.3	1,956	9.1	68.9
100–500	19	0.2	3,728	17.3	191.7
over 500	2		1,847	8.6	951.0
Totals	9,512	100	21,572	100	2.3

Source: King (1973)

Figure 6.4 Areas affected by Italian land reform laws, 1950.

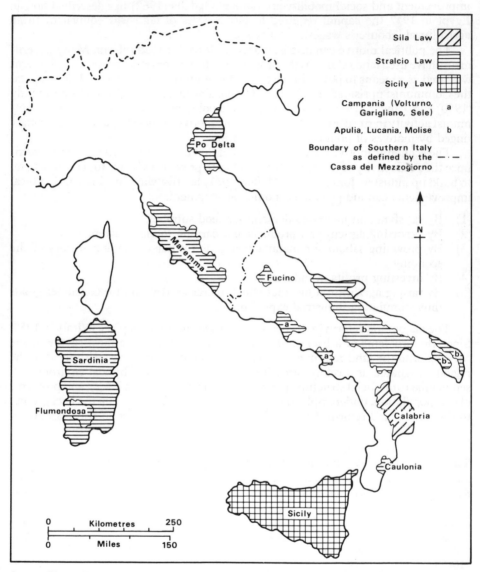

Source: King (1973)

with taking land from the large estates (latifundia) and redistributing it among the peasantry. The demand for land became apparent during the 1930s, gained momentum after the war fuelled by the rise of the Italian Communist Party (PCI), and culminated in the passage of three reform laws in 1950. The provisions of the Stralcio Law may be taken as illustrative of the general format. The main features were:

(1)   The creation of Comprensori di Riforma consisting of large tracts of latifondo land to be administered by a public agency (Ente di Riforma) under the direct supervision of the Ministry of Agriculture.

(2)   The amount of land to be expropriated from a landowner was based on the total area owned and the average per hectare income. Property owners were allowed to retain one-third of the land liable for expropriation provided they agreed to develop it according to the plans of the Ente di Riforma. Also excluded were 'model' farms, i.e. well-organized and efficient farms run in cooperation with the agricultural workers, and certain livestock farms. Compensation to landowners was based on the taxable value of the expropriated lands as of 1947.

(3)   The expropriated territory was to be improved by the State and assigned within three years to landless labourers, sharecroppers and other peasants. The choice of assignees from the large number requesting land was left to the individual Ente to resolve. The beneficiaries were to pay back some of the cost of expropriation and transformation in 30 annual instalments during which time the land could not be sold or rented out. Assignees were obliged to join the reform cooperatives. Land assignments took two forms: (a) the podere or self-sufficient farm usually with a farmhouse on the holding, and (b) a quota or smaller plot designed to 'top-up' income derived from another source.

(4)   The Ente di Riforma was responsible for land improvements, construction of buildings, farms and service villages, roads, and irrigation works; as well as for giving technical assistance, education and establishing cooperatives.

A detailed assessment of the Italian land reform is provided by King (1973). Criticisms levelled at the programme include:

(1)   Although the reform was a step in the right direction it was a small step and one that did not basically affect the socio-economic structure of much of rural Italy. The reform directly affected only 3.0 percent of the national territory and benefited slightly more than 1.0 percent of the total agricultural population.

(2)   Many of the braccianti (landless labourers) who became small owner-occupiers were not equipped to cope with the responsibilities of landownership. As King (1973, p. 225) remarks, 'their only credential was poverty'.

(3)   In 1950 the reform of agricultural tenancy was as necessary as the break up of the large estates yet nothing on these lines was done.

(4)   The cost of the land reform has been criticized, with accusations of inefficiency and maladministration.

It must be recognized, however, that any land reform is 'a response to a political situation within the confines of a given political structure' (King 1973, p. 225). Before 1950 the southern Italian peasant lived in a hopeless state of poverty. Immediate industrialization was impossible because of lack of capital, skilled labour and local demand. What were available were large expanses of underused, monopolistically controlled land. The peasants were hungry for that land and the land reform allowed some of them access to it. As King (1973) concludes, given the characteristics of poverty, unemployment and exploitation in southern Italy in 1950, a reform-based approach was undoubtedly the correct one at the time.

Regional management

The regional management approach to agricultural rationalization is based on the view that, since agriculture is only one component of the regional economy, its problems cannot be treated in isolation; and that the most effective means of raising farm incomes is through the general economic development of regions. Cuddy (1980, p. 207) underlines the inadequacy of a sectoral approach to regional development and concludes that 'coordination of sectoral policies at the regional level is imperative for efficient regional agricultural development'. With reference to the EEC he maintains that a more effective approach than the Common Agricultural Policy would be to articulate regional objectives consistent with overall regional needs and to formulate a strategy embracing all sectors, including agriculture, which can come closest to meeting those objectives within the overall budget available. To date, regional policy in the EEC has been left almost exclusively to national governments with only 2.6 percent of the community budget going to the regional fund in 1980. The proposal to finance experimental Integrated Regional Development Programmes (Commission of the European Communities 1981) represents a small step in the right direction.

References

BOWLER, I. (1983) Structural change in agriculture. *In* M. Pacione *Progress in Rural Geography*. London: Croom Helm, 46–73.

BUNCE, M. (1973) Farm consolidation and enlargement in Ontario and its relevance to rural development, *Area* 5(1), 13–16.

BUNCE, M. (1982) *Rural Settlement in an Urban World*. London: Croom Helm.

BUSCH, R., BUSCH, C. and UNER, N. (1979) Field fragmentation on an irrigated plain in Turkey, *Human Organisation* 38(1), 32–43.

BUTTERWICK, M. and NEVILLE-ROLFE, E. (1965) Structural reform in French agriculture: the work of the SAFERS, *Journal of Agricultural Economics* 16, 548–54.

CHISHOLM, M. (1979) *Rural Settlement and Land Use*. London: Hutchinson.

CLOUT, H. D. (1968) Planned and unplanned change in French farm structures, *Geography* 53, 11–15.

CLOUT, H. D. (1972) *Rural Geography: an introductory survey*. Oxford: Pergamon.

COMMISSION OF THE EUROPEAN COMMUNITIES (1981) *Proposal for a Council Regulation (EEC) Amending Regulation (EEC) No. 724/75 Establishing a Regional Development Fund* Com. (81) 589. Brussels: The Author.

CUDDY, M. (1980) European agricultural policy: the regional dimension, *Built Environment* 7, 200–10.

DILLER, R. (1941) *Farm Ownership, Tenancy and Land Use in a Nebraska Community.* Chicago: University of Chicago Press.

EDWARDS, C. (1978) The effects of changing farm size upon levels of farm fragmentation, *Journal of Agricultural Economics* 29, 143–54.

GADALLA, S. (1962) *Land Reform in Relation to Social Development in Egypt.* Columbia: University of Missouri Press.

GALT, A. (1979) Exploring the cultural ecology of field fragmentation and scattering in the island of Pantellaria, *Journal of Anthropological Research* 35(1), 93–108.

GASSON, R. (1969) *Occupational Immobility of Small Farmers* Occasional Paper 13, Department of Land Economy, University of Cambridge.

HERZFELD, M. (1980) Social tension and inheritance by lot in three Greek villages, *Anthropological Quarterly* 53, 91–100.

HILL, L. D. (1962) Characteristics of the farmers leaving agriculture in an Iowa county, *Journal of Farm Economics* 44, 419–26.

HILL, R. and SMITH, D. (1977) Farm fragmentation on Western Eyre peninsula, South Australia, *Australian Geographical Studies* 15, 158–73.

HINE, R. (1973) Structural policies and British agriculture, *Journal of Agricultural Economics* 24, 321–29.

HIRSCH, G. P. and MAUNDER, A. H. (1978) *Farm Amalgamation in Western Europe.* Farnborough: Saxon House.

JOHNSON, B. and MELLOR, J. (1961) The role of agriculture in economic development, *American Economic Review* 51(4), 566–93.

JOHNSON, O. (1970) A note on the economics of fragmentation, *Nigerian Journal of Economic and Social Studies* 12(2), 175–84.

KING, R. (1973) *Land Reform: the Italian experience.* London: Bell.

KING, R. (1977) *Land Reform: a world survey.* London: Butterworth.

KING, R. and BURTON, S. (1981) *An Introduction to the Geography of Land Fragmentation and Consolidation* Occasional Paper 8. Leicester: University Geography Department.

KING, R. and BURTON, S. (1982) Land fragmentation, *Progress in Human Geography* 6(4), 475–94.

KINGMAN, O. T. and SAMUEL, S. N. (1977) An economic perspective of structural adjustment in the rural sector, *Quarterly Review of Agricultural Economics* 30, 201–15.

KOLLMORGEN, W. and JENKS, G. (1958a) Suitcase farming in Sully county, South Dakota, *Annals of the Association of American Geographers* 48, 27–40.

KOLLMORGEN, W. and JENKS, G. (1958b) Sidewalk farming in Toole county, Montana and Trail county, North Dakota, *Annals of the Association of American Geographers* 48, 209–31.

LAMARTINE YATES, P. (1960) *Food Land and Manpower in Europe.* London: Macmillan.

LAMBERT, A. (1963) Farm consolidation in western Europe, *Geography* 48(1), 31–48.

MAYHEW, A. (1971) Agrarian reform in West Germany, *Transactions of the Institute of British Geographers* 52, 61–76.

McENTIRE, D. and AGOSTINI, D. (1970) *Towards Modern Land Policies*. Padua: University of Padua Press.

MULLER, P. (1964) Recent developments in land tenure and land policy in Germany, *Land Economics* 40, 267–75.

NAYLOR, E. (1982) Retirement policy in French agriculture, *Journal of Agricultural Economics* 33, 25–36.

OECD (1972) *Structural Reform Measures in Agriculture*. Paris: The Author.

OECD (1975) *Review of Agricultural Policies*. Paris: The Author.

PARSON, H. (1977) An investigation of the changing rural economy of Gatineau County, Quebec, *Canadian Geographer* 21, 22–31.

RICKARD, R. (1970) Structural policies for agriculture in the EEC, *Journal of Agricultural Economics* 21, 407–33.

SWEET, E. (1975) Fragmented farms in the U.S., *Annals of the Association of American Geographers* 65, 58–70.

THOMPSON, I. B. (1961) Le remembrement rural en France, *Geography* 46, 240–2.

THOMPSON, K. (1963) *Farm Fragmentation in Greece* Research Monograph Series 5. Athens: Centre of Economic Research.

TRACY, M. (1982) *Agriculture in Western Europe*. London: Granada.

VANDERPOLE, P. (1956) Reallocation of land in the Netherlands. *In* K. H. Parsons, R. Penn and P. Roup *Land Tenure*. Madison: University of Wisconsin Press, 548–58.

VAN OTTEN, G. (1980) Changing spatial characteristics of Willamette Valley farms, *Professional Geographer* 33, 63–71.

WEERDENBURG, L. J. M. (1973) Farmers and occupational change, *Rural Sociology*, 13, 27–38.

WHITBY, M. (1968) Lessons from Swedish farm structure policy, *Journal of Agricultural Economics* 19, 279–99.

WHITE, J. (1966) Kerastren Bras, a private remembrement rural, *Geography* 51, 246–8.

WILLIAMS, M. (1972) Stability and simplicity in rural areas, *Geografiska Annaler* 54B, 117–35.

7 Agriculture and urban development

Agriculture represents the most extensive land use in most metropolitan regions of North America and Western Europe. Despite this seeming abundance serious debate has ensued over the magnitude and effects of the loss of agricultural land in the face of urban development. The protagonists either take the view that there is no serious threat to future food supplies or open space, or conversely, demand controls over the transfer of land out of agricultural use, often within the context of a national land use plan. In the UK, for example, differing interpretations of agricultural and urban land use statistics have provoked debate between authorities like Coleman (1978, p. 32), who contends that 'we are taking land unnecessarily, wastefully, blindly and much faster than we realise', and Best (1978, p. 13), who considers that 'there is no real land problem in Britain at the moment. Most of the problem is simply in the mind; it is not out there on the ground.' Equally polarized assessments of the land situation are evident in North America. Hart (1976, p. 15), for example, finds it 'reasonable to conclude that little more than 4.0 percent of the nation's land area will be urbanized by the year 2000 and that urban encroachment will not remove significant acreages of land from agricultural production within the foreseeable future'. By contrast Lapping (1974, p. 394) considers that since the 1960s 'the transfer of huge amounts of productive farm lands to residential, industrial and speculative uses (has) approached ominous proportions'.

In addition to the physical demand for land, other urban-related pressures on the agricultural sector stem from the increased employment opportunities in towns. This factor has contributed to rural depopulation, provided opportunities for farm amalgamation, and encouraged the substitution of capital for labour in agriculture. Urban employment opportunities can also result in land abandonment in harsher agricultural environments, as well as hobby farming (Layton 1979) and part-time farming (Fuller and Mage 1976) in areas within commuting distance of the towns. Finally, some urban regions offer significant market potential for surrounding agricultural areas and can affect the nature of agricultural production (Shakow 1981).

As Figure 7.1 shows, these urbanization forces operate in conjunction with other forces which are largely independent of urban development (such as technological change and political decisions) to affect the character of agriculture in the 'city's countryside' (Bryant et al. 1982). The urban impact on the countryside is thus both direct (e.g. physical take-up of land, or fragmentation of farms by transport and utility lines) and indirect (e.g. land speculation).

Patterns of land use change

Figure 7.2 indicates the pattern of land use in 1971 and trends over the preceding decade for selected countries. In all cases rural land uses predominate even though many of the countries are among the most urbanized in the world. In the EEC, group

Figure 7.1 External forces of change affecting agriculture in the urban fringe.

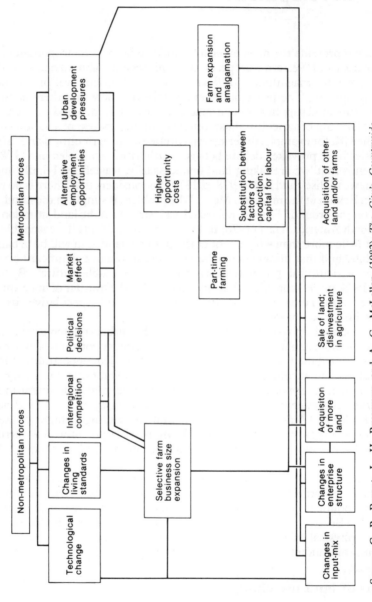

Source: C. R. Bryant, L. H. Russwurm and A. G. McLellan (1982) *The City's Countryside.* Longman.

Figure 7.2 Land use competition and change in selected countries: countries arranged according to extent of urban coverage.

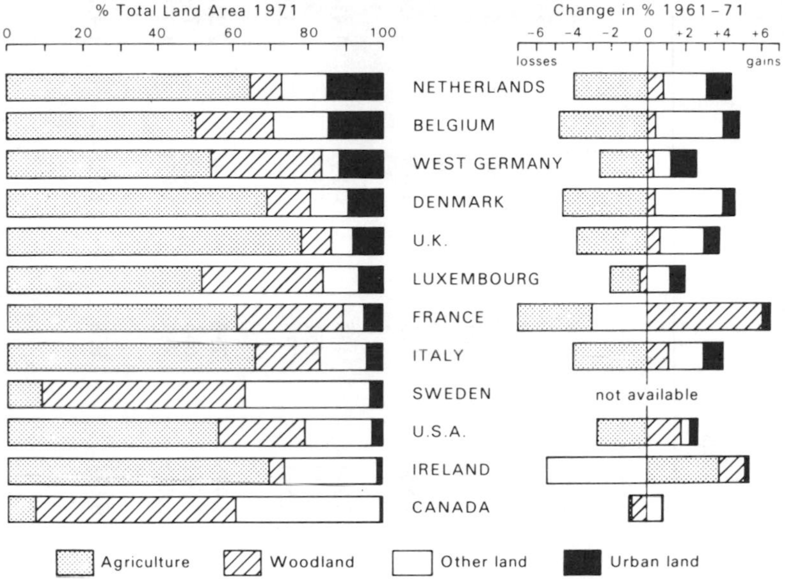

Source: Champion (1983)

agriculture took up 64.0 percent of the land surface and urban uses only 7.0 percent, and even in densely settled Belgium and the Netherlands the urban coverage did not exceed 15.0 percent. The area recorded as agriculture and forestry represented over four-fifths of the total land area in most countries and fell below two-thirds only in Sweden and Canada where the statistics reflect the vast wastes of mountain regions and more northerly latitudes (Best 1981, Hansen 1982). Over the 10-year period most countries exhibited a loss of land from the agricultural area. In six of the EEC member states the decline was around 4.0 percent of the total land area although, as Best (1979) points out, an unknown part of this loss may be explained by statistical irregularities representing 'corrections, reclassification and unexplained differences'. Only in Ireland is a net gain of agricultural land recorded with a large area of formerly unused territory being brought into cultivation. While farmland was transferred into several different uses, in all countries a consistent net gain was recorded by urban development, with the rate of increase ranging from 1.5 percent of the land surface in West Germany to 0.1 percent in Canada.

Within the framework of this broad international perspective, more detailed consideration can be given to the situation in Britain, where until the nineteenth century the changing pattern of land use had been dominated for hundreds of years by the decline of woodland and wasteland and the extension of agriculture. 'This long-continued trend has only been arrested and re-directed in any significant way in the last few decades' (Best 1981, p. 45). As Table 7.1 shows, the emphasis has now shifted

Table 7.1 *The structure of land use in Britain, 1901–1971*

Year	Population (millions)	Agriculture[a]	Cropland[b]	Permanent grass	Rough grazings[c]	Woodland	Urban land[d]	Other land[e]	Total land area
				'000 ha.					
England and Wales									
1901	32.5	12,576	4,904	6,232	1,440	748	674	1,027	15,025
1921	37.9	12,496	4,702	5,879	1,915	730	854	949	15,029
1931	40.0	12,383	3,878	6,354	2,151	840	1,005	800	15,028
1939	41.5	12,215	3,616	6,357	2,242	927	1,206	680	15,028
1951	43.8	12,104	5,536	4,365	2,203	971	1,339	614	15,028
1961	46.1	11,880	5,522	4,350	2,008	1,034	1,490	623	15,027
1971	48.8	11,515	5,666	3,965	1,884	1,115	1,646	750	15,026
Scotland									
1931	4.8	5,718	1,235	639	3,844	443	141	1,416	7,718
1961	5.2	6,776	1,387	356	5,033	651	199	91	7,717
1971	5.2	6,226	1,258	417	4,541	738	225	529	7,718
Great Britain									
1931	44.8	18,101	5,113	6,993	5, 995	1,283	1,146	2,216	22,746
1961	51.3	18,656	6,909	4,706	7,041	1,685	1,689	714	22,744
1971	54.0	17,741	6,934	4,382	6,425	1,853	1,871	1,279	22,744
United Kingdom									
1971	55.6	18,831	7,227	4,926	6,678	1,908	1,918	1,436	24,093

percent

England and Wales								
1901	32.5	83.7	32.6	41.5	9.6	5.0	4.5	6.8	100.0
1921	37.9	83.1	31.3	39.1	12.7	4.9	5.7	6.3	100.0
1931	40.0	82.4	25.8	42.3	14.3	5.6	6.7	5.3	100.0
1939	41.5	81.3	24.1	42.3	14.9	6.2	8.0	4.5	100.0
1951	43.8	80.5	36.8	29.0	14.7	6.5	8.9	4.1	100.0
1961	46.1	79.1	36.7	29.0	13.4	6.9	9.9	4.1	100.0
1971	48.8	76.6	37.7	26.4	12.5	7.4	11.0	5.0	100.0
Scotland								
1931	4.8	74.1	16.0	8.3	49.8	5.7	1.8	18.4	100.0
1961	5.2	87.8	18.0	4.6	65.2	8.4	2.6	1.2	100.0
1971	5.2	80.7	16.4	5.4	58.9	9.6	2.9	6.8	100.0
Great Britain								
1931	44.8	79.6	22.5	30.7	26.4	5.6	5.0	9.8	100.0
1961	51.3	82.0	30.4	20.7	30.9	7.4	7.4	3.2	100.0
1971	54.0	78.0	30.5	19.3	28.2	8.2	8.2	5.6	100.0
United Kingdom								
1971	55.6	78.2	30.0	20.5	27.7	7.9	8.0	5.9	100.0

Slight discrepancies in some totals result from rounding of figures and conversions from acres to hectares

[a] In the first part of this century, the agricultural area was seriously underestimated in the official statistics because of the underrecording of rough grazings, especially those held in common, and cultivated land which escaped enumeration.

[b] Woodland and other land (buildings, yards, roads, etc.) on farms are recorded under other headings in this table. Arable land, including fallow, temporary grass and orchards.

[c] Specifically including common rough grazings in 1921 and later, and also the area of all deer forests in Scotland after 1931.

[d] Including villages, isolated dwellings and farmsteads, and all transport land.

[e] Includes land unaccounted for, many mineral workings and defence areas in the open countryside, and unutilized rural areas not recorded under other uses.

Source: Best (1981)

to a situation in which the major changes in land use structure are related to growth in urban and forest areas rather than agricultural extension. The rate of conversion of agricultural land to urban use in the UK can be readily seen in Figure 7.3. Apart from the dramatic effect of the Second World War the pattern exhibits three notable features. First, the scale of urban growth and agricultural displacement was at its greatest in the 1930s. This was a period of suburban expansion at more liberal space standards, cheap building sites on open farmland, improved public and private transportation, and a virtual absence of planning control prior to the 1947 Town and Country Planning Act. Secondly, there has been no sustained increase in the loss of farmland to urban use in the postwar years. This has been due partly to the improved economic position of farming since the 1930s, rising land and property prices during the 1970s, the increased difficulty of obtaining mortgages, the sharp fall in the birth rate up to the end of the 1970s, the growth of rural preservation groups, and most of all is a result of the conservation-protectionist ethic which has dominated postwar rural planning. Thirdly, in Britain as a whole the annual extension of forest and woodland now often outpaces that of urban growth (Best 1981).

Direct urban impacts on agriculture

Statistical description of land use changes at the national scale provide a useful background picture on which to base more detailed analyses of the relationship between different land uses. Although, nationally in Britain, the annual extension in forest cover often exceeds that of land lost to urban development, the greatest gains in forest area are taking place in Scotland on land of lower quality (Table 7.1). Measurement at a regional scale would reveal above-average levels of agricultural land taken for urban development in certain parts of the country, particularly around the urban

Figure 7.3 Transfers of agricultural land to urban use.

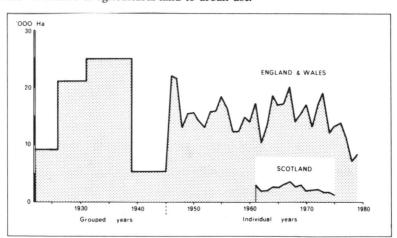

Source: Best (1981)

zone stretching from the London region northwest towards Merseyside. Similarly in the USA, though long-term predictions of agricultural land availability suggest that nationally there is no immediate threat to the production of food and fibre, these statistics 'mask major changes in the individual states or multi-county regions' and overlook the loss of land in urbanized regions such as New York, Florida and California which produce important vegetables and fruit (Vlasin 1975). The importance of considering the intranational location of urban development is highlighted by the fact that in most countries, since many cities developed in the richest agricultural areas, urban encroachment on rural areas often involves prime agricultural land. Thus Best (1981, p. 146) provides evidence to suggest that nationally 'the present urban areas of England and Wales are constructed mainly on medium quality and poor land (Grade 4) . . . and not more than a quarter was good land (Grades 1 and 2)'. In Scotland, however (where good quality land is more spatially restricted than in England, with a high proportion around the major urban areas), while less than 3.0 percent of the farmland is classed as Grade 1 or 2 some 26.0 percent of the area transformed to urban development between 1973 and 1975 was taken from these grades. Within Scotland, Smith (1981) has shown that in the Grampian Region and Moray Firth subregion nearly 70.0 percent of the land taken between 1966 and 1980 consisted of the three highest classes of agricultural land. More generally, Vining et al. (1977, p. 144) note that 'in most of the major industrial nations of Europe as well as Japan, the best agricultural land does seem to be mainly concentrated around the large urban centers'. A tendency for certain North American cities to expand disproportionately at the expense of the best soils has been noted in California (Gregor 1963), southern Florida (Psulty and Salter 1969) and the Niagara Fruit Belt (Krueger 1959; Gayler 1982), while Berry and Plaut (1978, p. 156) calculate that in terms of potential cropland (i.e. land not presently being farmed but readily available for agricultural production) 'at the present rate of loss the conversion of cropland and prime land to urban and built up uses could equal 7.0–14.0 percent of the potential cropland and 11.0–31.0 percent of the potential prime cropland in the next 25 years'.

It is clear, therefore, that the effects of urban pressures on agricultural activities are quite different at the national, regional and local levels, and that the focus of concern over the physical encroachment of urban land on farmland is on prime agricultural land. Jackson (1981) cites four reasons for preserving prime agricultural land in the USA. The first refers to the necessity of maintaining world food supplies. On a world scale demand for food continues to increase faster than increases in production and the USA is currently the world's largest net surplus producer of food. Secondly, to contain the waste and cost associated with urban sprawl. Thirdly, to maintain open space and environmental quality. The final reason is related to local, national and international economics. Nationally, export of agricultural surpluses is an important method of offsetting balance of trade deficits associated with energy imports. At the local scale, the economies of many American towns are highly reliant on their agricultural hinterlands and continued loss of prime agricultural land could undermine their economic base and lead to a cycle of cumulative decline in many communities. Other factors which must be considered in evaluating the importance of prime agricultural land include: (a) the possibility of future shortages of fertilizer and the need for less energy-intensive forms of agriculture, and (b) the indication that application of advanced technology in the agricultural sector may have reached a stage of diminishing marginal returns. As Platt (1981, p. 114) observes, 'growth of farm productivity cannot continue to provide ever increasing harvests in a shrinking land base'.

In recent decades the food shortage argument has been tempered by overproduction in many Western countries, for example as witnessed in the Canadian cereal economy in the 1950s and 1960s, in the payments by the US government to farmers in some areas not to produce certain crops, and in the surpluses of dairy produce in the EEC since the 1960s. A factor of continuing relevance, however, refers to the costs associated with the conversion of prime agricultural land to urban use. According to Jackson (1981) these costs are two-fold relating to (1) the value of crop production forgone and the actual cost of replacing the lost farmland, and (2) the cost of the sub-urbanization process itself. Although more land is reclaimed each year in the USA than is lost to urban sprawl this land normally comes through subsidy from the general public via projects initiated by the Bureau of Reclamation. The cost of such public works is substantial. In addition to these direct costs associated with large-scale reclamation projects, other Federal subsidies are paid to encourage farmers to undertake irrigation, drainage or other modifications to reclaim land. The costs associated with suburbanization include the provision of public utilities to new sub-urban developments, Federal programmes to lend money for purchase of private housing, and income tax deductions for interest associated with mortgage payments.

In North America, where planning restrictions on urban development are less developed than in the UK, the effects of urban sprawl on the rural landscape are readily apparent. Urban development proceeds by scatteration and some infilling rather than by accretion contiguous to past development. Figure 7.4 shows the process of urban spread by means of noncontiguous leapfrog development during the period 1967–1975 in part of Dakota county, Minnesota, south of Minneapolis-St Paul, and illustrates how a relatively small amount of rural land converted to urban uses by this scatteration process can drastically alter the appearance of the landscape. In addition to the largely irreversible physical loss of land, such sprawl can provoke farm fragmentation by its demand for roads, power lines, reservoirs, and other components of urban infrastructure. Severance of previously unified agricultural holdings goes against the general trend towards larger farm sizes and may undermine the viability of an enterprise.

Indirect urban impacts on agriculture

The inpacts referred to here are those of urban development on the continuing agricultural structure (the urban shadow effect) as opposed to the physical conversion of land. Urban growth may have both positive and negative impacts on agriculture in the urban fringe (Rettig 1976; Blair 1980; Thomson 1981). On the one hand proximity to the urban area provides opportunities for direct sale of produce to the public, nearby towns may supply casual labour for seasonal activities such as fruit picking, and farmers can augment their income via 'horsiculture' or other recreational activities. Beneficial interaction can also occur through the rental back

Figure 7.4 Built-up land in Dakota county.

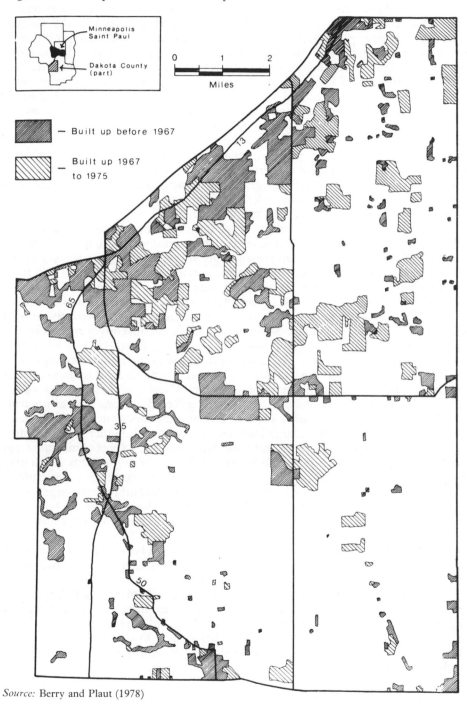

Source: Berry and Plaut (1978)

to farmers of farmland which has been purchased by nonfarm interests. Provided that lease conditions are not onerous, from a purely economic perspective, it may be more attractive for a farmer to rent land than to purchase and encumber the business with a heavy mortgage, thus releasing more of the farmer's capital for improvements. Bryant and Fielding (1980) indicate that close to North American cities nonfarm ownership of land is often high and rental back to farmers is common; while Munton (1982) describes a similar situation in the green belt around London where property developers' land interests extend to several thousand hectares. On the other hand, urban forces may impose additional problems for farmers, including incidents of trespass, theft and vandalism; the extra risk of moving stock along busy roads; possible pollution from nearby urban-industrial activities; restrictions imposed on normal farming activities by pressure from residents who may object to the sight, sound and smell of farming or conservation groups who want to preserve trees and hedgerows on the farmer's land; rising land prices and land speculation making farm enlargement costly; and where tax is levied on land values, as in the USA, increased burdens on potential development sites near the city.

The effects of land speculation constitute one of the most important impacts on agriculture in the urban fringe. This is, in effect, concerned with the impact of *potential* urban development. Where urban pressures are strong, farmers may become active speculators, disinvesting in their farms while anticipating a large capital gain from the sale of their land in the near future. Some farmers may 'farm to quit' (Wibberley 1959) or attempt to 'mine' the soil fertility while others may 'idle' their farmland. In the absence of effective land market regulation idle land may be a perfectly rational land use response by individual owners to the economic incentives created by the urban fringe property market (Harrison 1977). Berry and Plaut (1978), for example, estimated that for every acre converted to urban uses in the northeastern USA another was idled due to urban pressures. Farmers living under less intense urban pressures may be involved in a more passive form of land speculation, watching the appreciation of land values with a view to selling for a large profit on retirement. Another form of response to urban pressure is seen in the slow switchover from those types of agriculture requiring large long-term investments to other types of enterprise. For such farmers the uncertainty over land uses in the short to medium term may be sufficient to dissuade them from undertaking large investments which may not pay off for 20 years. Dairying is an agricultural activity which is particularly sensitive to urban pressures. Dairy farmers often are reluctant to make large investments in immobile capital equipment (barns, milking parlours, bulk tanks) that they are unlikely to be able to recover should they sell their land to a speculator or developer. As Berry (1979, p. 175) found in a study of dairy farming in northeastern Illinois, 'with increasing uncertainty over the future use of farmland subject to urban pressure there is a shift toward "safer" agricultural investments and consequently a change in land use'.

In general, as Sinclair (1967, p. 28) explains, 'as the urbanized area is approached from a distance, the degree of anticipation of urbanization increases. As this happens, the ratio of urban to rural land value increases. Hence, although the absolute value of the land increases, the relative value for agricultural utilization decreases.' Bryant (1981) has attempted to model the adaptive behaviour of farmers in the Paris region to these urbanizing forces.

Protective policies

United Kingdom

In Britain the major planning instrument exercised to limit and control the spread of urban development into the countryside is the *green belt*. Green belt policies have been applied to London since 1938 (Thomas 1970; Munton 1983) and were encouraged around provincial cities by a government circular in 1955 (Ministry of Housing and Local Government 1955) so that they now cover 4800 km² of England and Wales, including the 2260 km² of the metropolitan green belt. The objectives of green belts are both negative (e.g. checking further growth of large urban areas, preventing the merging of neighbouring towns, providing agriculture with a more stable urban frontier, and preserving the special character of certain towns) and positive (e.g. providing relatively close scenic and recreational areas for city dwellers). Until recently, however, the positive aspects of the concept have been pursued with less vigour than the protectionist element. Despite its widespread recognition and acceptance, green belt designation carries with it no extra planning powers. It is, in effect, a statement of principle by planning authorities that certain clearly enunciated guidelines will be followed in considering development applications in these areas.

In addition to the green belt legislation two further means of protecting open countryside from widespread development are available. First, there is a suite of statutory controls upon land use and changes in land use. These powers are often operated by local planning authorities through their normal development control procedures, but sometimes deal with subject areas which are also overseen by other statutory bodies concerned specifically with amenity and recreation (e.g. the Countryside Commission), research in the natural sciences (Nature Conservancy) or timber production (Forestry Commission). Parts of London's green belt, for example, are also designated as Sites of Special Scientific Interest or Areas of Outstanding Natural Beauty, or are subject to Tree Preservation Orders. Secondly, publicly owned land can act as a buffer against unwanted urban and industrial expansion, being more resistant to market forces than land in private ownership. Mention should also be made of the Land Commission (1967–1970) and the Community Land Scheme (1976–1980) which were legislative attempts to ensure that the development of land proceeded in accordance with public needs and priorities, and that a substantial part of the development value of the land returned to the community in general. Both, however, were short-lived creations being killed off by incoming Conservative governments (Ratcliffe 1981).

There is no doubt that green belts have been successful in achieving their protective aims, and without them much greater amounts of agricultural land would have been lost under suburbia. Munton (1981), for example, cites the growth of nonconforming land uses in the approved metropolitan green belt at a comparitively slow rate of 2.0 percent per decade or 600 ha per annum. The green belt is not, however, an impenetrable barrier, rather it acts 'like a more or less leaky dyke: there is the occasional break, and there is constant seepage through land speculation and blight, but for the most part it holds back a flood' (Hebbert 1981, p. 22).

The fact that some development has leapfrogged the green belt around most large towns has prompted the criticism that the policy is spreading urban influences and the pressures of 'fringe farming' further into the countryside than would otherwise have been the case. Furthermore, even within the green belt 'urban anticipation' still affects the behaviour of landowners. By reducing the supply of housing land in a desirable residential area, green belts have the effect of raising the value of the small amount of land that is released for development. In a situation of strong demand for development land, as in London's green belt, for the planning system to be *largely successful* in preventing development is not sufficient. The *possibility* of planning permission is kept alive in the minds of property owners within the restricted zone, who are well aware of the enormous price differences between land with planning permission for residential development and land valued for agricultural purposes, and whose ultimate goal is to realize this 'hope value' of their land. In the West Midlands, JURUE (1977) noted a very high level of applications for development within the green belt despite a clear awareness by the applicants of the planning authorities' stated green belt principles. As Munton (1982) points out, what green belt restraint does is to increase the risk of planning refusal and in spatial terms to concentrate the prospects of development close to existing settlements located within or just beyond the green belt boundary. A further consideration is that the green belts are not uniformly 'green'. The presence of idle or underused farmland, the intrusion of often unsightly urban-type facilities such as hospitals and sewage works, the operation of activities outwith the scope of planning control, and the low level of positive provision for recreation all indicate a need for greater attention being afforded to the changes taking place within the protected area, especially in those parts nearest to the cities.

Davidson and Wibberley (1977, p. 127) identify a basic dilemma of green belt policy in asking 'how is it possible to be less rigidly protective, and accommodate the changing demands of a city, but at the same time prevent the misuse and neglect of land in the face of the uncertainty which may follow such a policy?'. Their suggested solution is based on 'extensive public acquisition of open land which is managed in a positive and dynamic way for local and regional benefit'. West Midlands County Council (1978) have developed the green belt concept at its inner edge into 'green wedges' and 'linear open space systems and associated walkways' which will require stronger and more positive policies than outer green belt areas. The idea of green wedges separated by axial development corridors has also been suggested for Ottawa, and can be identified in the *zones naturelles d'équilibre* (ZNE) for Paris. An important feature of the latter is that a *chargé de mission* (project leader) is appointed for each ZNE with the task of promoting continuing dialogue and concensus among the various regional administration, local elected officials, and countryside interests, in order to achieve an integrated policy.

North America

In the USA and Canada the 'taste for space' (Raup 1975, p. 374) and national philosophy against government intervention in the actions of individual property owners has meant that a centrally developed set of planning guidelines to protect agricultural land from urban pressures does not exist. As Gayler (1982, p. 321) observes, 'in the past a society imbued with the growth ethic, the perception of a limitless supply of land for development, the weakness or nonexistence of land-use planning and the belief in the right of the individual owner to decide on property matters has been responsible for a relative neglect of issues relating to the physical nature of urban growth'. Recent concern over locally significant losses of prime agricultural land has provoked action by state and provincial governments who are responsible for land use decisions. With 50 US states and 10 Canadian provinces there exists, consequently, a wide variety of measures aimed at protecting the best farmland around expanding urban areas (Bryant and Russwurm 1982). In general the major land use controls may be classified as direct or indirect corresponding to the types of urban pressures they address. Direct land use controls attempt to restrict use of land to agriculture, open-space or low-density residential purposes; while indirect controls offer incentives to owners to retain land as farmland or open space in an attempt to mitigate influences such as rising property taxes which may force owners to sell land to non-agricultural interests.

The main types of direct approach to retaining agricultural land include:

(1) Agricultural zoning Since its approval by the United States Supreme Court in 1926, land use zoning has been largely an urban phenomenon and zoning regulations in rural areas were not employed extensively until the 1970s. Although most states now have legislation allowing local governing bodies to enact regulations that could be used to protect prime agricultural land, in practice, zoning has been ineffective not least because 'in areas where zoning ordinances have been enacted, too frequently they are permissive, arbitrary, or not enforced' (Jackson 1981, p. 180). As Platt (1981, p. 117) remarks 'although agricultural zones are often included in county zoning ordinances, this is regarded as an "everything else" category with an apparent expectation that a zoning change or variance will be granted upon application for a non-agricultural use'. A second problem undermining the effectiveness of agricultural zoning is that it may result in a diminution of value to the extent that it constitutes a de facto public confiscation of land without compensation; something which is alien to the North American land ethic.

(2) Public purchase of development rights The idea behind PPDR is to allow the owner of land to sell the development rights to the land (a resource) separate from the land itself (a commodity). A state or local public agency may buy from a farm owner the right to subdivide or develop his property. Once the purchase price is paid a permanent restriction upon the use of the land is recorded and this is binding on subsequent purchasers. The farmer benefits because he receives the development value of the land and thus recaptures his equity and the inflated value of his property, while maintaining the agricultural rights. He also pays reduced real estate taxes since the land is permanently designated nondevelopment land. In 1974 Suffolk County in New York State was one of the first to enact a PPDR programme (Bryant and Conklin 1975). Weaknesses of the approach are that (a) the cost to the public may be considerable where development rights account for a major part of the value of the property; (b) there is no guarantee that the land subject to an easement (i.e. PPDR) will be actively farmed; and (c) public acquisition of a portion of the development rights associated with land will eliminate that value for tax purposes and represent a loss to the general community.

(3)   Land banking   A government agency may obtain land either through the power of eminent domain (compulsory purchase) or by means of a voluntary arrangement under which the public has the first right of refusal when property becomes available for sale. Land acquired can then be sold or leased back to genuine commercial farmers while the state retains the development rights. In theory land banking encourages orderly growth and development and minimizes the adverse effects of sprawl, reduces the price of land by controlling the land market and eliminating speculation, and preserves prime agricultural lands. In practice it has been used only sparingly, its weaknesses being similar to those of PPDR, namely (a) the cost of acquiring large quantities of land in advance of development, (b) public ownership of large areas of land would eliminate the property tax revenue they generate (because the government and service structure of the USA is heavily tied to the property tax, loss of revenue is a serious consideration in programme assessment), and (c) the incompatibility of such a programme with the general American tradition of private landownership.

The most widely implemented indirect land use controls are of two types:

(1)   Preferential taxation   Although details differ from one local jurisdiction to another, under this approach the farmer is offered an incentive to keep his land in agriculture through current use value assessment rather than market value assessment of his land. If there are strong urban pressures on the land, the tax savings can be substantial since the market value contains considerable speculative development value. Eligibility is normally based on a minimum parcel size and minimum annual sale of farm products. In the event of the land being converted to nonagricultural purposes while preferential assessment is in effect, the owner or his successor is liable for the taxes that would otherwise have been paid, plus interest. Since 1957 when Maryland enacted the first differential assessment in favour of agricultural land another 45 states have followed suit.

California's programme for preferential assessment based on the Land Conservation Act 1965 has been the subject of detailed examination (Gustafson and Wallace 1975; Goodenough 1978; Jackson 1981; Pryde 1982). Critics of the California scheme point out that most of the land enrolled in the scheme is that farther from urban centres. Farmers closer to the metropolitan edge have been reluctant to enter into restrictive agreements on land conversion, preferring to remain under existing taxation in anticipation of realizing large capital gains from the sale of their land for urban development. A second criticism refers to the tendency for developers to use the Act as a means of purchasing land in advance of use at lower prices and then holding it under the preferential assessment scheme for a number of years until inflation allows them to make even greater windfall profits. Clearly the basic difficulty relates to the voluntary nature of the Act which is inadequate to influence the allocation of land between agricultural and nonagricultural uses.

(2)   Agricultural districts   New York's Agricultural Districting Programme (Lapping 1974; Bryant and Conklin 1975) is the best example of this multiple incentive type of approach although features of the districting idea are reproduced in

Oregon, Maryland and California (Gustafson and Wallace 1975; Jackson 1981; Pease 1982). In New York, since 1971, farmers may collectively apply to have their area designated an Agricultural District. Within the district farmers benefit from preferential taxation and are protected to some extent from local zoning ordinances (which must not infringe upon farming activities), from local use of eminent domain to acquire farmland without adequate consideration of alternative sites for urban infrastructure, and from special taxation assessments for nonagricultural purposes. Like preferential taxation alone, however, agricultural districts do not appear to be the answer to the problem of farmland preservation in semisuburban areas where urban pressures are more intense. Under these circumstances farmers are not willing to voluntarily form an agricultural district and possibly sacrifice the chance of a lucrative nonfarm sale.

A further point to note is that many of the developments that have extended the urban area have been the result of public investment. The expansion of infrastructure (e.g. roads, sewage works) increases the potential for land conversion. Clearly, limiting public activities in this area would slow down the loss of agricultural land. The weakness of this strategy is that 'the farmer is outvoted by suburbanites who demand greater services in the rural-urban fringe, and developers too often have actively and effectively lobbied for such improvements' (Jackson 1981, p. 190). In situations where development is inevitable, Pryde (1976) has suggested the use of planned urban development and the concept of a 'residential landscape conservation zone' which aims to concentrate development within a land parcel and avoid the excesses of scatteration.

Direct controls are potentially more effective than indirect controls in areas under strong urban pressure by removing the right to develop land in a manner not in keeping with the public good. In such areas the incentives offered by indirect controls are overwhelmed by land speculation and development pressure. When employed in isolation indirect controls are better suited to protection of agricultural land in more rural areas. Overall, North American programmes to protect prime agricultural lands may be effective in areas removed from urban pressure but are ineffective in the urban fringe where the alternative to farming is most profitable. According to Fuguitt et al. (1979, p. 79) the problem is not lack of expertise or experience but 'the irrelevance of much existing planning literature and legal precedent to small town and rural county conditions as well as the legal and administrative obstacles that prevent connecting planning and performance (i.e. connecting the maps, alternatives, objectives and needs to the zoning ordinance, capital budget, subdivision controls, etc.)'. Further, while voluntary controls may be easier to enact, mandatory programmes can be more effective and greater consideration of such measures may be necessary in some urban fringe areas in spite of the objections of many North Americans to such intervention. While it is difficult to refute Jackson's (1981, p. 192) contention that 'it is doubtful whether any state will adopt regulations that are truly effective in light of the general American tradition of speculative profits and individualism', Oregon's programme to restrict urban growth and zone for exclusive agricultural activities, Wisconsin's income tax credit scheme, and the use of development rights transfer in New York are indicative of an increasing awareness of the limited availability and fragility of certain agricultural and open spaces.

References

BERRY, D. (1979) The sensitivity of dairying to urbanization: a study of northeastern Illinois, *Professional Geographer* 31(2), 170–76.

BERRY, D. and PLAUT, T. (1978) Retaining agricultural activities under urban pressures: a review of land use conflicts and policies, *Policy Sciences* 9, 153–78.

BEST, R. H. (1978) Myth and reality in the growth of urban land. *In* A. Rogers *Urban Growth, Farmland Losses and Planning.* London: Institute of British Geographers, 2–15.

BEST, R. H. (1979) Land use structure and change in the EEC, *Town Planning Review* 50, 395–411.

BEST, R. H. (1981) *Land Use and Living Space.* London: Methuen.

BLAIR, A. M. (1980) Urban influences on farming in Essex, *Geoforum* 11, 371–84.

BRYANT, C. R. (1981) Agriculture in an urbanizing environment: a case study from the Paris region, 1968–76, *Canadian Geographer* 25(1), 27–45.

BRYANT, C. R. and CONKLIN, H. E. (1975) New farmland preservation programmes in New York, *Journal of the American Institute of Planners* 41(6), 390–6.

BRYANT, C. R. and FIELDING, J. A. (1980) Agricultural change and farmland rental in an urbanising environment, *Cahiers de Géographie du Quebec* 24, 277–98.

BRYANT, C. R. and RUSSWURM, L. H. (1982) North American farmland protection strategies in retrospect, *Geojournal* 6(6), 501–11.

BRYANT, C. R., RUSSWURM, L. H. and McLELLAN, A. G. (1982) *The City's Countryside.* London: Longman.

CHAMPION, A. E. (1983) Land use and competition. *In* M. Pacione *Progress in Rural Geography.* London: Croom Helm, 21–45.

COLEMAN, A. (1978) Agricultural land losses: the evidence from maps. *In* A. Rogers *Urban Growth, Farmland Losses and Planning.* London: Institute of British Geographers, 16–36.

DAVIDSON, J. and WIBBERLEY, G. P. (1977) *Planning and the Rural Environment.* London: Pergamon.

FUGUITT, G. V., VOSS, P. R. and DOHERTY, J. C. (1979) *Growth and Change in Rural America.* Washington D.C.: Urban Land Institute.

FULLER, A. M. and MAGE, J. A. (1976) *Part-time Farming: Problem or Resource in Rural Development.* Norwich: Geo Books.

GAYLER, H. J. (1982) Conservation and development in urban growth, *Town Planning Review* 53, 321–41.

GOODENOUGH, R. (1978) An approach to land-use control: the California land conservation act, *Urban Studies* 15, 289–97.

GREGOR, H. F. (1963) Urbanization of southern California agriculture, *Tijdschrift voor Economische en Sociale Geografie* 54, 273–78.

GUSTAFSON, G. C. and WALLACE, L. T. (1975) Differential assessment as land use policy: the California case, *Journal of the American Institute of Planners* 41(6), 379–89.

HANSEN, J. A. G. (1982) *Land Use Structure and Change in North America and the EEC* Occasional Paper No. 6, Department of Environmental Studies and Countryside Planning, Wye College, University of London.

HARRISON, A. J. (1977) *Economics and Land Use Planning.* London: Croom Helm.

HART, J. F. (1976) Urban encroachment on rural areas, *Geographical Review* 66(1), 1–17.

HEBBERT, M. (1981) The land debate and the planning system, *Town and Country Planning* 50(1), 22–3.

JACKSON, R. H. (1981) *Land Use in America.* London: Arnold.

JURUE (1977) *Planning and land availability.* Birmingham: University of Aston, Joint Unit for Research in the Urban Environment.

KRUEGER, R. R. (1959) Changing land use patterns in the Niagara fruit belt, *Transactions of the Royal Canadian Institute* 32, 39–140.

LAPPING, M. B. (1974) Preserving agricultural lands: the New York experience, *Town and Country Planning* 43(a), 394–7.

LAYTON, R. L. (1979) The hobby farming issue, *Town and Country Planning* 49, 53–4.

MINISTRY OF HOUSING AND LOCAL GOVERNMENT (1955) *Green Belts* Circular No. 42/55. London: HMSO.

MUNTON, R. J. (1981) Agricultural land use in the London green belt, *Town and Country Planning* 49, 17–19.

MUNTON, R. J. (1982) *Land speculation and the under-use of urban fringe farmland in the metropolitan green belt* Paper presented to the Anglo-Dutch Symposium on living conditions in Peri-Urban and Remoter Rural Areas in north western Europe. University of East Anglia, Norwich.

MUNTON, R. J. (1983) *London's Green Belt.* London: Allen and Unwin.

PEASE, J. (1982) Commercial farmland preservation in Oregon, *Geojournal* 6(6), 547–53.

PLATT, R. H. (1981) Farmland conversion: national lessons for Iowa, *Professional Geographer* 33(1), 113–121.

PRYDE, P. (1976) The residential landscape conservation zone, *Geographical Review* 66, 200–8.

PRYDE, P. (1982) Is there any hope for agriculture in California's rapid growth areas? *Geojournal* 6(6), 533–8.

PSULTY, N. P. and SALTER, P. S. (1969) Land use competition on a geomorphic surface: the mango in South Florida, *Annals of the Association of American Geographers* 59, 264–79.

RATCLIFFE, J. (1981) *An Introduction to Town and Country Planning.* London: Hutchinson.

RAUP, P. M. (1975) Urban threats to rural lands: background and beginnings, *Journal of the American Institute of Planners* 41(6), 371–8.

RETTIG, S. (1976) An investigation into the problems of urban fringe agriculture in a green-belt situation, *Planning Outlook* 19, 50–74.

SHAKOW, D. (1981) The municipal farmers market as an urban service, *Economic Geography* 57, 68–77.

SINCLAIR, R. J. (1967) Von Thunen and urban sprawl, *Annals of the Association of American Geographers* 57, 72–87.

SMITH, J. S. (1981) Land transfers from farming in Grampian and Highland, 1969–1980, *Scottish Geographical Magazine* 97(3), 169–74.

THOMAS, D. (1970) *London's Green Belt*. London: Faber and Faber.

THOMSON, K. J. (1981) *Farming in the fringe* CCP142. Cheltenham: Countryside Commission.

VINING, D. R., PLAUT, T. and BIERI, K. (1977) Urban encroachment on prime agricultural land in the United States, *International Regional Science Review* 2(2), 143–56.

VLASIN, R. (1975) Food production and its implications for land resource conservation, *Journal of Soil and Water Conservation* 30, 2–3.

WEST MIDLANDS COUNTY COUNCIL (1978) *Green Belt Subject Plan: Report of Survey*. Birmingham: The Author.

WIBBERLEY, G. P. (1959) *Agriculture and Urban Growth: a study of the competition for rural land*. London: Michael Joseph.

8   Population dynamics

Two different migration waves have swept over Western Europe and North America in the course of the last 150 years. For much of the period the dominant direction of population movement was from rural to urban areas in response to the growth of urban-industrial society. With few exceptions rural areas lost population to the burgeoning towns and cities. More recently, since World War II, a reversal of this long-standing form of migration has become apparent with people reoccupying periurban areas on both sides of the Atlantic and in Australia. In addition population growth has been recorded in remoter rural areas beyond metropolitan commuter zones. This reverse movement has been termed 'counterurbanization', the 'rural renaissance', or the 'population turnaround'. Significant though this trend is, it has not affected all rural areas, and many remote regions continue to experience the problems of population decline.

Rural depopulation

In many parts of the developed world net migration has replaced natural change as the principal component of local population dynamics. Britain, being a leader of the Industrial Revolution, was one of the first countries to experience large-scale movement of population from rural to urban locations. The growth of towns in nineteenth-century England was the product of three factors: (1) the high rate of natural increase of the urban population, (2) the continuous inflow from the rural areas, and (3) immigration from Scotland and Ireland. The influx from the rural areas into the rapidly growing urban agglomerations remained of major importance for the whole of the nineteenth century and continued in the twentieth century, although as the towns grew in size the proportionate effect of the rural inflow gradually lessened (Saville 1957). As a result, 'at some point between 1821 and 1851 a considerable proportion of the villages and rural parishes of England and Wales passed their peak of population and entered upon an almost continuous decline of their total populations; for the rest of the rural areas, their curve of peak and decline was set in the second rather than in the first half of the century, but few parts of the country failed to conform to the pattern' (Saville 1957, p. 5). The main areas of attraction for migrants were London and the metropolitan counties, the northern textile counties, Birmingham and the Black Country, the northeastern coalfield, and Glamorgan and the South Wales coalfield. The exodus from the British countryside continued at a slower rate in the twentieth century, and the proportion of the population living in rural districts changed only slightly over the period 1921–1951, reaching a relative stability with an urban–rural ratio of 80:20. But, as Saville underlines, this stability 'conceals the disintegrating factors which are still working within the rural economy and which have been carried over from the nineteenth century' (Ibid., p. 7). The more rural an area the greater the likelihood that it has steadily lost population up to the present day.

Causes of migration

The causes of rural depopulation have not altered in any significant way during the last 150 years. While a change in emphasis has occurred between the various factors involved at different places and times the basic cause is everywhere the same – 'rural depopulation has occurred in the past century and a half and will continue in the future, because of declining employment opportunities in the countryside' (Saville 1957, p. 7). The rural resident forced out of agriculture will have two choices: rural to urban migration or commuting to urban employment. The decision to migrate is a complex mix of 'push' and 'pull' considerations. As Stouffer (1962, pp. 109–110) points out, 'nobody who contemplates the multiplicity of economic, political, social and psychological factors that must enter into the personal contemplation of any prospective migrant would expect any simple model using only two or three variables to account for everything'. Most basic are economic conditions and in particular the labour-shedding structural changes which have taken place in agriculture. In the UK the proportion of the workforce engaged in agriculture, forestry or fishing is at 2.0 percent, the lowest in the world; while in the USA only 4.0 percent of the nation's labourforce is employed in the primary sector. Declining demand for agricultural labour has also been a constant feature of the postwar European economy, although the process has not gone as far as in the UK. According to Clout (1976), in 1950 30 million people were involved in primary activities in the six original member states of the EEC. Within 10 years, this figure had fallen by half and had almost halved again by 1972 when it stood at 8.4 million. From representing 28.9 percent of the workforce in 1950 primary employment declined by almost two-thirds to 11.2 percent in 1972 (Table 8.1). Agriculture remains an important employer in peripheral parts of the EEC and it is from areas such as western France, the Republic of Ireland, and southern Italy that rural–urban migration flows are greatest (Commission of the European Communities 1973). As Table 8.1 indicates, agriculture is also important in other European States, such as Portugal, Spain, Greece, and Turkey. 'These predominantly rural parts of Mediterranean Europe form a series of population reser-

Table 8.1 *Employment in farming, forestry and fishing as percentage of labour force*

	1950	1960	1972		1960	1972		1960	1972
Belgium	12.6	8.7	4.1	Austria	23.0	17.9	Portugal	41.0	31.1
France	27.6	22.4	12.6	Denmark	18.1	9.7	Spain	40.0	29.1
West Germany	22.1	14.0	7.5	Finland	25.0	22.3	Sweden	16.0	8.0
Luxembourg	25.9	16.3	9.3	Greece	54.0	45.8	Switzerland	11.0	6.7
Italy	43.9	32.8	17.5	Republic of Ireland	37.3	24.1	Turkey	79.0	71.5
Netherlands	14.3	10.0	6.9	Norway	16.0	13.8	United Kingdom	4.2	2.7

Source: Clout (1976)

voirs, containing literally millions of potential migrants to be attracted to urban areas in their home countries or abroad' (Clout 1976, p. 36).

Equally fundamental reasons propelling farmworkers from the countryside are the low wages, the arduous nature of farmwork and the lack of alternative job opportunities (McIntosh 1969). Drudy (1978) found that in North Norfolk, between 1960 and 1970, the most important single reason for leaving farm employment was redundancy, mainly due to the substitution of capital for labour especially on large units. Second in importance were the low wages in agriculture (Table 8.2). Since the decline in agricultural employment is not normally matched by an expansion of alternative job opportunities migration is inevitable for much of the labour force leaving agriculture. In North Norfolk, of 477 workers leaving the 153 sample farms 24.7 percent left the area completely, and most of those leaving school and coming on to the job market for the first time face similar prospects. Other material disadvantages of living in rural areas can include poorer housing; absence of piped water supply, electricity and mains drainage; limited social and intellectual contacts; lack of local shopping, education and entertainment facilities; and inadequate public transport (House 1965; Bracey 1970). Mitchell (1950) in a study of rural parishes in southwest England also considered the loss of a 'sense of community' as being of fundamental importance in the decision to migrate.

Age and sex differences are also important variables. With little prospect of inheriting land or managing a farm, and the limited employment opportunities in manufacturing and tertiary activities offered by most rural areas, many young women see their future in the town. Women also tend to move at an earlier age than their male counterparts and to migrate greater distances (Wendel 1953). House (1965) found that female outmigration from the countryside tended to occur at certain key ages such as immediately after leaving school and in the early twenties when the search for an urban marriage partner forms a strong motive for emigration.

Table 8.2 *Reasons for mobility of active workers from North Norfolk farms, 1960–1970**

	Number	%
Dissatisfied with work or conditions	86	18.0
Worker's wife or family dissatisfied	10	2.1
Attracted by other employment	24	5.0
Low wages	111	23.3
Dismissed	35	7.3
Ill-health	18	3.8
Housing problems	18	3.8
Redundancy	154	32.3
Other reasons	21	4.4
Total	477	100.0

*Workers who retired or died not included.
Source: Drudy (1978)

The resulting imbalance in rural communities may in turn provide a stimulus for young men to leave for urban areas.

Variations in education are also important in encouraging migration. The higher the level of education the greater the probability that young people will migrate to urban areas in order to find the kind of work that their schooling has trained them for (Friedlander and Roshier 1966; Jansen 1968; Hannan 1969). The size, and degree of isolation of the home community may also affect the migration decision. Although at a regional scale net outmigration is most pronounced from the agricultural periphery of Western Europe, more detailed examination suggests that young people living within easy access of urban areas leave the countryside more rapidly than those in remote areas where facilities may be poorer and the future viewed more exclusively in terms of agriculture and the rural life (Clout 1976). Also, in remote areas the spread of car ownership is less effective in offering access to new sources of employment. Knowledge of the opportunities and conditions in potential destinations is obviously of great importance to those considering emigration. Formal education, the mass media, contacts with family and friends, and holiday travel all provide images of an alternative urban life-style which may be compared with the countryside. Personal contacts are particularly significant in this respect since many rural–urban migrants find initial accommodation and employment with the help of friends or family members who are already established in the city (Pourcher 1970).

In the general context of rural depopulation the identification of cause and effect is extremely complex since the two may be closely interrelated and what constitutes a cause may easily itself become an effect in a vicious circle of decline (Drudy 1978).

Ravenstein (1885) in a classic analysis that has greatly influenced subsequent work presented seven broad generalizations concerning intercounty population movements in nineteenth-century Britain.

(1)   The great body of our migrants only proceed a short distance. There takes place consequently a universal shifting or displacement of the population, which produces 'currents of migration' setting in the direction of the great centres of commerce and industry which absorb the migrants.

(2)   It is the natural outcome of this movement, limited in range, but universal throughout the country, that the process of absorption would go in the following manner: the inhabitants of the country immediately surrounding a town of rapid growth, flock into it; the gaps thus left in the rural population are filled up by migrants from more remote districts, until the attractive force of one of our rapidly growing cities makes its influence felt, step by step, to the most remote corner of the kingdom. Migrants enumerated in a certain centre of absorption will consequently grow less with the distance proportionately to the native population which furnishes them.

(3)   The process of dispersion is the inverse of that of absorption, and exhibits similar features.

(4)   Each main current of migration produces a compensating countercurrent.

(5)   Migrants proceeding long distances generally go by preference to one of the great centres of commerce and industry.

(6)   The natives of towns are less migratory than those of the country.
(7)   Females are more migratory than males.

These 'laws of migration' have been shown to be generally correct although the 'migration by stage' thesis has yet to be adequately verified.

Measurement considerations

Since the interwar years the volume of migration from rural to urban areas in Britain has been of less significance than movements of population between urban areas. As a result, migration statistics based on UK county boundaries no longer reveal the real currents of internal migration, even in a generalized way. This underlines the critical influence that the scale of enquiry can have on the nature of results. Furthermore, not all national censuses record internal migration. The alternative 'residual method' for calculating net migration involves computing intercensal changes in population for appropriate areas and then subtracting natural increase or decrease in order to determine the migratory balance. This may provide a deceptive picture since it deals with net results rather than with actual volumes of inward and outward flow. Thus it can give an indication of the extent of depopulation but not details of rural–urban migration. The presence of significant urban–rural flows of population in some areas make statistics on migratory balance inadequate indicators of rural–urban flow for all except the most remote areas of countryside in which significant counterflows are absent. Finally the true volume of rural–urban migration may be disguised in many areas by important local flows which redistribute people within the countryside.

Recent trends

Woodruffe (1976) working at the district level analysed population trends in rural Britain for the intercensal periods 1951–61 and 1961–71 thus complementing Saville's (1957) investigation of trends over the preceding century. A six-fold classification of population change was devised:

(1)   Accelerated depopulation: districts which were decreasing in population between 1951 and 1961 and in which the rate of depopulation increased between 1961 and 1971.
(2)   Reduced depopulation: districts which were decreasing in population between 1951 and 1961 and in which the rate of depopulation slackened in the 1961–71 period.
(3)   Reversed depopulation: districts where population was decreasing in the 1951–61 period but in which the trend was reversed in the 1961–71 period.
(4)   Reversed growth: districts which were increasing in population between 1951 and 1961 but in which population decreased in the 1961–71 period.
(5)   Reduced growth: districts in which population was increasing between 1951 and 1961 and in which the rate of population increase dropped over the 1961–71 period.
(6)   Accelerated growth: districts which have increased in population during both periods but in which the rate of increase rose in the 1961–71 period.

The spatial distribution of these population trends is shown in Figure 8.1. Areas of accelerated depopulation are to be found mainly in the upland zones of Scotland and Wales. Two extensive areas of decline are located in northeast Scotland and in the Borders, with other smaller pockets of accelerating depopulation in central Wales and in scattered rural districts most of which are relatively remote from urban areas. Districts which have experienced reduced depopulation tend either to fringe the core areas of depopulation or to be in dispersed and isolated locations where the outmovement of population has slowed down and is stabilizing. At the other end of the scale districts showing growth trends are almost all related to increasing urban influence. Rings of differential growth may be identified around London, the West Midlands conurbation and the West Yorkshire conurbation, and to a lesser extent around cities like Nottingham, Bristol and Gloucester-Cheltenham. Districts displaying trends of reduced growth tend to lie adjacent to the urban edge; those with accelerating growth are slightly further away; and those with reversed depopulation are situated still further out.

Nationally, the trend over the period 1951–71 is one of growth in rural areas (Table 8.3); this general move being accompanied by a similar pattern of growth in small towns and rural market centres of less than 10,000 (Table 8.4). Even in areas of

Table 8.3   *Population in rural and county districts 1951, 1961, 1971*

	1951 (’000s)	1961 (’000s)	Change 1951–61 (%)	1971 (’000s)	Change 1961–71 (%)
England	7,428	8,176	+10.1	9,730	+19.0
Wales	766	778	+ 1.6	838	+ 7.7
Scotland	1,475	1,472	− 0.2	1,527	+ 3.8
Total	9,669	10,426	+ 7.8	12,095	+16.0

Source: Woodruffe (1976)

Table 8.4   *Population in small towns 1951, 1961, 1971*

	1951 (’000s)	1961 (’000s)	Change 1951–61 (%)	1971 (’000s)	Change 1961–71 (%)
England	1,493	1,664	+11.5	2,079	+24.9
Wales	297	304	+ 2.6	334	+ 9.8
Scotland	533	546	+ 2.4	596	+ 9.2
Total	2,323	2,514	+ 8.2	3,009	+19.7

Source: Woodruffe (1976)

Figure 8.1 Population trends in Great Britain 1951–61 and 1961–71.

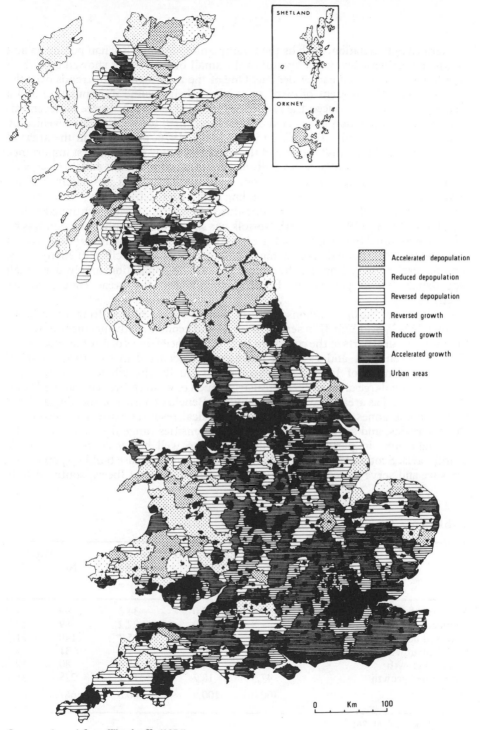

	Accelerated depopulation
	Reduced depopulation
	Reversed depopulation
	Reversed growth
	Reduced growth
	Accelerated growth
	Urban areas

Source: adapted from Woodruffe (1976)

accelerated depopulation, such as the Grampian mountains, Buchan peninsula and Angus in northeast Scotland, several of the small burghs either showed growth in population or stemmed earlier decline. One of the most significant trends over the period is that 21.0 percent of districts reversed their decline in population and a further 13.0 percent reduced the rate of decline (Table 8.5). A degree of decentralization and repopulation of selected districts and small towns was also revealed by Champion (1973, 1976). According to Woodruffe (1976, p. 14) it is in the areas of reversed depopulation that the role of the small town may be of greatest importance in revitalizing the countryside, 'initially as a centre of employment and services, subsequently encouraging commuting from nearby villages, and ultimately perhaps stimulating employment in the surrounding larger rural settlements'. Nevertheless, it is clear from Table 8.5 that nearly one-third of all rural districts continued to lose population. Drudy (1978) in North Norfolk has shown that this phenomenon was by no means confined to the 'marginal' areas of the country. As Commins (1978) points out, national or regional figures mask severe population decline in many more remote rural areas. Although the proportion of the population involved is small (approximately 3.0 percent in England and Wales) the areas concerned are extensive.

In Western Europe millions of rural dwellers have moved from their home regions since World War II in search of social and economic advancement in towns. Virtually all rural parts of the continent have experienced flows of outmigration since 1945. Between 1961 and 1971 net outmigration occurred in the greater part of Scandinavia, most of Ireland and Scotland, virtually the whole of central and southern Italy, large areas of Iberia, Austria, much of western France and the Massif Central, as well as areas in West Germany, the Benelux countries, and England and Wales. These zones vary greatly in their physical resource base, socio-economic characteristics, and spatial extent. Population densities range from more than 100 inhabitants/km^2 in parts of the Italian south to well below 20 persons/km^2 in Scandinavia, Scotland and Spain. High rates of natural increase build up population pressure and serve to accentuate outmigration from parts of Iberia, southern Italy

Table 8.5   *Trends of population change 1951–61–71*

	Rural & County Districts in			Total	
	England (%)	Wales (%)	Scotland (%)	No.	%
Accelerated depopulation	4.4	22.0	34.3	99	14.9
Reduced depopulation	7.8	22.0	22.2	89	13.3
Reversed depopulation	23.2	23.7	15.7	140	21.0
Reversed growth	2.2	6.8	9.1	31	4.6
Reduced growth	14.9	6.8	7.6	80	12.0
Accelerated growth	47.5	18.7	11.1	228	34.2
	100.0	100.0	100.0	667	100.0

Source: Woodruffe (1976)

and the Republic of Ireland, but conversely deaths exceed births in some other areas of serious outmigration. Mean incomes are comparatively low in all the exporting zones, each of which is relatively isolated from major urban-industrial growth areas and from the connecting transportation axes. Finally, although the farming systems they support and the environmental conditions in which they operate are diverse, all outmigration zones are characterized by a predominance of agriculture and a relative lack of services and alternative employment (Clout 1976).

In the USA the concentration of population into metropolitan areas has been one of the most enduring population trends of the twentieth century. Migration from rural areas to urban places outnumbered the reverse flow in every decade from 1900 to 1970. As in Britain and Western Europe, changes in the structure of agriculture were prime determinants of this cityward migration. In about 400 of the nation's 3,100 counties the maximum population was reached as early as 1900 because they were oversettled to begin with or because deteriorating productivity induced loss of farm people even before mechanization. From 1940 to 1970 about 900 counties showed a decline in population in each successive decade, the vast majority declining because the loss of farm jobs was not offset by other forms of employment. For example, in the Great Plains and western Corn Belt regions, stretching from Iowa to Montana and from North Dakota to Texas, the total rural population fell by 27.0 percent between 1940 and 1970 while in the old Cotton Belt of the coastal southern plain from South Carolina to east Texas rural population fell by 36.0 percent during the same period.

At the same time rural population was increasing steadily in the southern Piedmont textile belt, the industrialized and suburbanizing rural areas of the lower Great Lakes region and the northeastern coast, the Florida peninsula recreation and retirement communities, and areas of the far west and southwest. As a result the national level of rural population changed little as these regional changes compensated each other. But 'in the agricultural regions, hundreds of towns declined in population, hundreds of thousands of former farm homes were demolished or abandoned, and many businesses closed. The volume of agricultural output grew, but the proportion of rural people engaged in agriculture fell, either directly or indirectly' (Wardwell and Brown 1980, p. 7). Rural population loss through outmigration accelerated sharply following World War II and from 1950 to 1960 3.0 million people left nonmetropolitan counties for metropolitan destinations. The loss continued from 1960 to 1970 although the amount declined to a net figure of 2.2 million persons for the decade.

In Canada, a similar process of agricultural change and population dislocation has been described for the Manitoba portion of the Prairies (Todd 1980). Of the 114 rural municipalities a mere 8 actually gained in population over the period 1961–71, and the majority of these have benefited from Winnipeg overspill. Conversely, areas of population loss are ubiquitous. The problems associated with depopulation have also been experienced in New Zealand (Cant and O'Neill 1980).

The impact of rural–urban migration

Migration from the countryside affects the migrants, the departure zones, and reception areas. Individuals move in order to obtain better-paid employment; to have access to better social, educational and cultural facilities; and to enjoy better living conditions in the city. In short the goal of most people is to improve their quality of life. Beijer (1963) has studied the reception of rural migrants into the city. Large flows of migrants, for example, into the cities of northern Italy place a strain on the housing, educational and welfare functions of reception areas. A particularly severe European example is provided by the gecekondus or squatter colonies that have proliferated around many Turkish cities as a result of intense rural–urban migration.

Of more immediate concern here is the impact on the exporting communities. A net loss of population from a rural area may have effects which are either beneficial or detrimental to the residual community. For example, by relieving pressure on land rural–urban migration may open the way for farms to be amalgamated and enlarged leading to a more economically viable agricultural system. In the case of Spain and Italy rural migration has acted as a safety valve to stabilize rural social structures and ameliorate population pressure at a time of high natural increase (Franklin 1971). In the USA, however, there remain conflicting views of the implications of out-migration. Some contend that depressed agricultural areas benefit from the removal of excess labour (Okun and Richardson 1961) but others note that the continuing heavy outmigration from such areas has failed to alter appreciably the disadvantaged income position of farm workers in relation to farmers, let alone the on-going disparities between farm and nonfarm workers (Boyne 1965; Hathaway and Perkins 1968).

In general it can be argued that it has been with the onset of the fertility decline in developed nations that rural migration loss has become a problem rather than a cure. This has been the case from the nineteenth century in Britain and France. The demographic effects are basically two-fold; ageing of the population, and the creation of an imbalanced sex structure.

By the end of the nineteenth century the age structure of rural and urban areas of Britain were markedly different due to the selective nature of migration. The most striking demographic consequence of rural depopulation, however, was the changing ratio between the sexes in affected rural areas. At the turn of the century urban areas showed a significantly higher proportion of females to males at all ages than the rural areas; ably demonstrating Ravenstein's seventh law. This may be explained by the fact that within England and Wales the sex ratio was primarily the result of the distribution of employment opportunities, and since in the rural areas the occupations available to women (e.g. in rural industries like lace and glove making, and straw plaiting) declined at a faster rate than those for men (primarily agriculture) the force of expulsion from the countryside was stronger for women than for men. By 1901 the rural areas of England and Wales had a ratio of 101 females to every 100 males, compared with a national average of 106.8 and a figure of 111.8 for London (Saville 1957). These same forces continued to operate during the first half of the present century; thus, in rural Britain the proportion of residents in the 20–50 years age range continued to be below the national average, and the sex structures of town and country remained markedly different. Foeken (1980) has examined the links between an imbalanced sex structure and return migration in northwest Ireland. Strong outward flows of migrants have contributed to the ageing of rural communities in Sweden (Rundblad 1957) and to the recent reduction of birth rates in southern Italy, while in parts of the Massif Central and central Wales the process has gone even further with deaths exceeding the number of births each year (Clout 1976).

Socially, outmigration often results in a loss of the more dynamic and potentially innovative members of the population with the result that the residual community may become attuned to a homogeneous psychological outlook which is dominantly a negative one towards the future of the community. Economically, the reduction in population brought about by emigration reduces the scope for, and viability of, commercial activity, which may lead to further migration. The reduced tax base may make it difficult to maintain even the most elementary public services, especially if the remaining population is disproportionately old or impoverished. Contraction of services operates in a vicious downward spiral which may encourage further outmigration among those able to move. Drudy (1978) has applied the theory of 'cumulative causation' to describe the situation in rural North Norfolk and the Galway Gaeltacht region of Ireland, and Figure 8.2 presents a model of the rural depopulation process. White (1980, p. 201), in a detailed analysis of the impact of migration loss on seven rural communes in Normany, France, concluded that 'in total, the effects of migration loss may be such that demographically, socially, and in terms of economic potential there is little possibility of future stabilization, let alone growth or development'.

The population turnaround

While many rural regions and communities continue to experience outmigration and depopulation, in some industrialized countries the direction of population flow has been reversed in recent years. Vining and Kontuly (1978) examined population dispersal in 18 countries, 11 of which (Japan, Sweden, Norway, Italy, Denmark, New Zealand, Belgium, France, West Germany, East Germany, and the Netherlands) showed either a reversal in the direction of net population flow from their sparsely populated peripheral regions to their densely populated core regions or a drastic reduction in the level of this net inflow. In the first 7 of these 11 countries this reversal or reduction became evident only in the 1970s; in the last 4 its onset was recorded in the 1960s. Figure 8.3 presents evidence from 6 countries where significant net inmigration to their metropolitan regions in the 1950s and early 1960s had disappeared by the mid 1970s, often giving way to net outmigration. It is important to realize that these metropolitan regions were consciously defined to be 'large enough to contain all conceivable spillover of population from their central cities' (Vining and Kontuly 1978, p. 50). That is, these regions were purposefully over-bounded in anticipation of the objection that the decline of migration into the major metropolitan regions is simply an extension of their functional fields beyond their official boundaries. Thus 'in most countries, the core region contains between 20 percent and 30 percent of the territories of those countries, a much larger area than is commonly assigned to them' (Ibid.).

A similar turnaround has been identified in Australia (Australian Government 1977), Canada (Bourne and Simmons 1979) and Western Europe (Fielding 1982), but the most remarkable turnaround in nonmetropolitan population growth has occurred in the United States. Fuguitt (1981) has summarized the long-run trends of

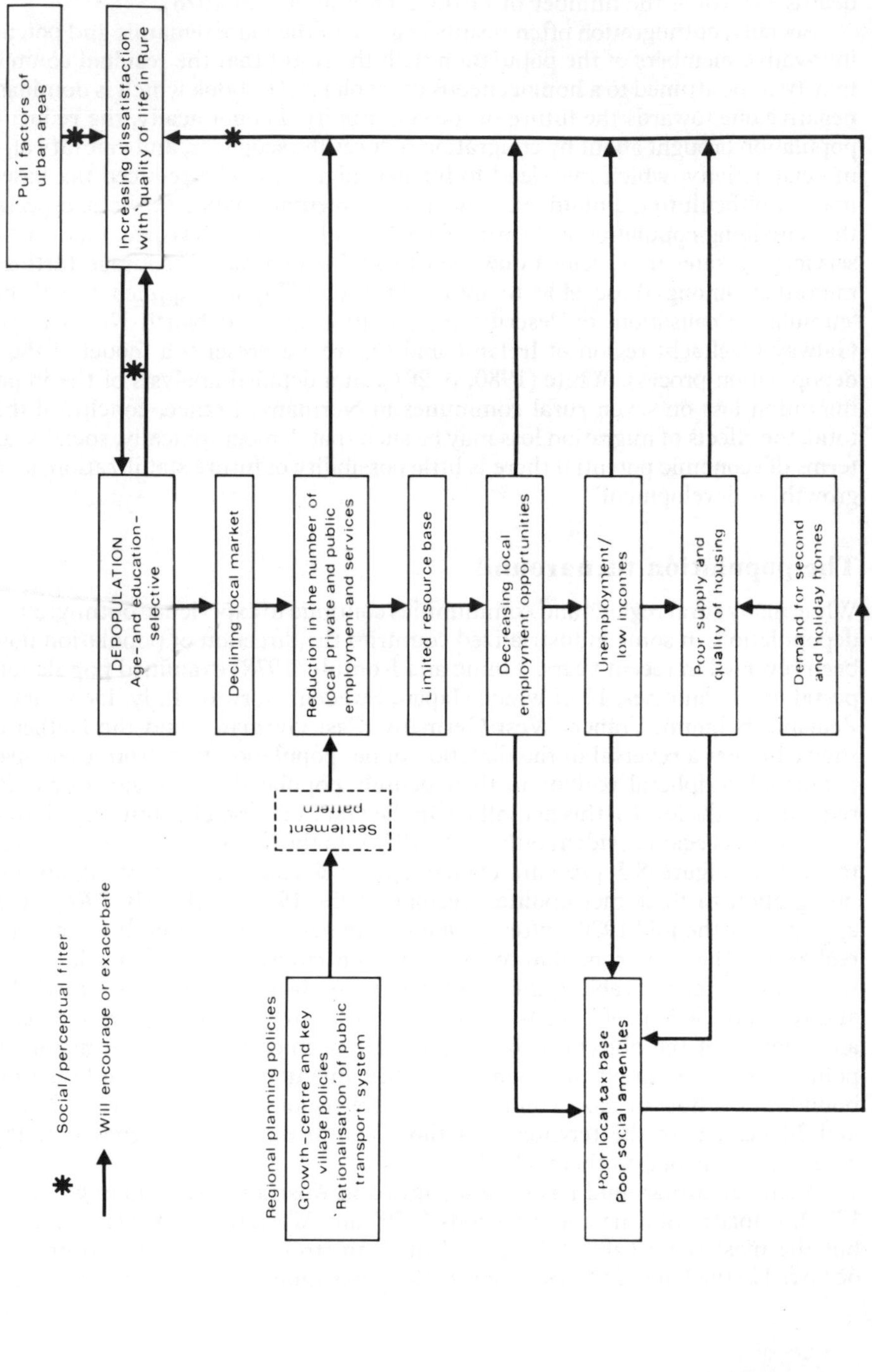

Figure 8.2 A model of rural depopulation.

∗ Social/perceptual filter

↑ Will encourage or exacerbate

Source: Grafton (1980)

Figure 8.3 Annual net internal migration into core regions of selected countries.

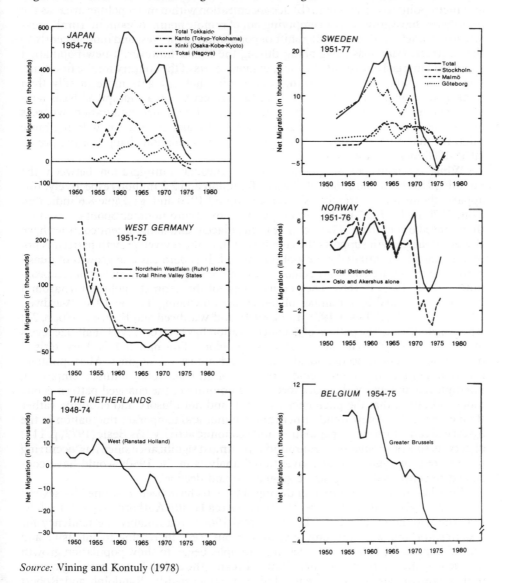

Source: Vining and Kontuly (1978)

population distribution in the United States as: (a) rapid growth with urbanization and metropolitan development, (b) deconcentration within metropolitan areas as the peripheries have grown, (c) an emptying out of remote nonmetropolitan (rural) areas already sparsely settled, and (d) a shift of population to the west and more recently to the southern Gulf coast. Beginning during the 1960s, however, a new population trend has emerged as a result of which, in many parts of the country for the first time, nonmetropolitan areas are growing and gaining net migrants more rapidly than metropolitan areas. As Fuguitt (1981, p. 125) observes, 'on a widespread basis non-metropolitan areas have shifted from net outmigration to net inmigration, whereas overall metropolitan areas and a large number of major cities are now losing more migrants than they are gaining'. Figure 8.4 shows population change for the period 1970–1980 at a county level.

While nonmetropolitan population loss through outmigration between the periods 1950–1960 and 1960–1970 was 3.0 million and 2.2 million respectively, this apparently inexorable trend was reversed around 1970 and, as Table 8.6 indicates, from 1970 to 1977 2.6 million more people moved into nonmetropolitan counties than moved out of them. The fact that both adjacent and nonadjacent counties have shared in the growth supports the conclusion that 'the revived growth pattern is not merely one of accentuated metropolitan sprawl. It is both close-in growth of quasi-metropolitan nature and more remote growth not stimulated by metropolitan proximity' (Beale 1977, p. 166). The pervasiveness of the nonmetropolitan turnaround has been suggested by a number of researchers including Tucker 1976, Wardwell 1977, Beale 1977, Zelinsky 1978, Long 1980, and Wardwell and Brown (1980, p. 23) who conclude that 'the pattern of deconcentration has been observed at all size levels of urban places and in virtually all of the sub-regions of the nation. It is characteristic of most age cohorts, occupational classes, and industry groupings. Metropolitan–nonmetropolitan migration includes persons of all labor-force statuses: employed, unemployed and out of the work force. The ubiquity of the changed pattern is one more indication that the phenomenon is real and not illusory and enduring rather than ephemeral – a new trend rather than a minor and temporary fluctuation in the historical concentration of population and economic activity.' As Beale (1977, p. 118) observed, such a population turnaround is of utmost significance since it is 'occurring in hundreds of counties that conventional analysis in the 1960s would have consigned to continued demographic stagnation and decline'.

Population changes in Britain during the 1970s have been examined by several researchers. Kennett and Spence (1979) used Area Health Authority records to show that the population trends of the 1950s and 1960s, and notably the tendency for deconcentration, were not only continuing but were increasing in intensity and spatial impact. Parts of rural Wales, for example, began to show population growth for the first time in over a century (Powys became the eighth fastest growing county with a growth rate of 6.8 percent). This was supported by Randolph and Robert (1981, p. 228) who found that 'when demographic shifts in the 1950s were compared with those of the 1960s, the major feature was the reversal from centralisation to decentralisation . . . The trends described for 1971 to 1981 do not imply such radical changes, but rather a deepening and extending of the patterns evolving in the late 1960s.' These general trends are displayed in Figure 8.5 for economic planning

Figure 8.4 Population change in the USA by counties, 1970–1980.

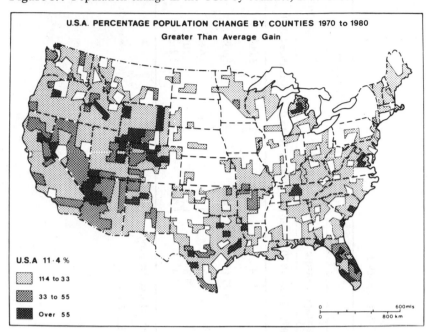

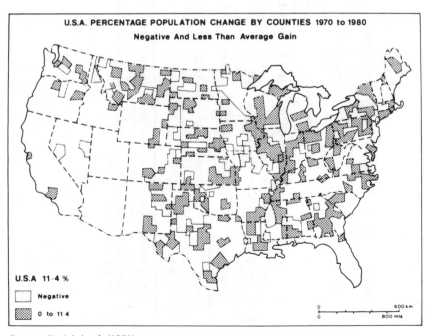

Source: Cruickshank (1981)

Table 8.6 *Population change by metropolitan status in USA, 1960–1977*

Area	Population Number ('000s)			Percentage change		Net migration[a]			
	1977	1970	1960	1970–1977	1960–1970	1970–1977 Number ('000s)	Rate (%)	1960–1970 Number ('000s)	Rate (%)
Total United States	216,350	203,301	179,323	6.4	13.4	3,210	1.8	3,001	1.7
Metropolitan counties[b]	156,984	148,877	127,191	5.4	17.0	617	0.5	5,959	4.7
Nonmetropolitan counties	59,366	54,424	52,132	9.1	4.4	2,593	5.0	−2,958	−5.7
Adjacent counties[c]	30,775	28,033	26,116	9.8	7.3	1,504	5.8	−705	−2.7
Nonadjacent counties	28,591	26,391	26,016	8.3	1.4	1,089	4.2	−2,253	−3.7

[a] Net migration expressed as a percentage of the population at beginning of specified period
[b] Metropolitan status as of 1974
[c] Nonmetropolitan counties adjacent to Standard Metropolitan Statistical Areas

Source: Wardwell and Brown (1980)

Figure 8.5 Population change in Great Britain by economic planning regions, 1971–1981.

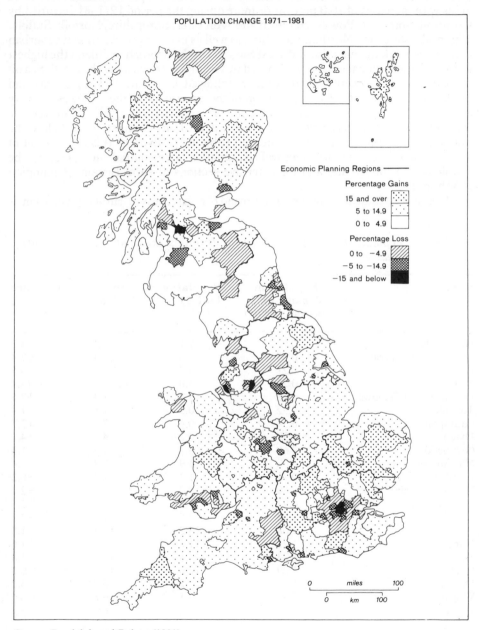

POPULATION CHANGE 1971–1981

Economic Planning Regions ———

Percentage Gains

15 and over

5 to 14.9

0 to 4.9

Percentage Loss

0 to −4.9

−5 to −14.9

−15 and below

Source: Randolph and Robert (1981)

regions. There is a clear correspondence with the OPCS (1981) findings at the county level, which revealed a significant concentration of most rapid growth in more rural areas with increases of 10.0 percent or more during the period 1971–81 recorded by Cornwall, Somerset, Powys, Hereford and Worcester, Shropshire, Norfolk, Suffolk, Cambridgeshire, and Northamptonshire, as well as in the more traditional suburban counties of Buckinghamshire and West Sussex. On the Scottish mainland the highest growth rate at regional level was recorded by Grampian (a centre of the North Sea oil industry) at 7.3 percent for the decade, followed by Central (3.8 percent) and Highland (3.4 percent). An examination of the experience of the 20 lowest-density (most rural) parts of Britain reveals that only one of these areas grew at a slower rate than the national average between 1971 and 1981, in contrast to 10 below the national average in the previous decade (Table 8.7). 'Even at this crude level of analysis, therefore, evidence of a rural rejuvenation is substantial enough for it to be visible over a full decade and for extensive sections of rural Britain' (Champion 1981b, p. 14).

The clearest indication of the strength and pervasiveness of 'rural rejuvenation' is

Table 8.7 *Population change 1961–81 in Britain's areas of lowest population density*

Area*	Population density 1981 (persons per ha)	Population change (%) 1961–71	1971–81	Difference
Highlands	0.07	7.1	3.4	−3.7
Scottish Island areas	0.15	−7.0	20.4	+27.4
Borders	0.21	−3.7	0.8	+4.5
Powys	0.22	−3.0	11.4	+14.4
Dumfries and Galloway	0.23	−2.2	1.3	+3.5
Tayside	0.52	−0.1	−1.5	−1.4
Grampian	0.54	−0.4	7.3	+7.7
Dyfed	0.57	0.2	4.3	+4.1
Gwynedd	0.60	3.2	4.5	+1.3
Northumberland	0.60	1.9	7.3	+5.4
Cumbria	0.71	1.3	1.5	+0.2
North Yorkshire	0.80	9.0	6.3	−2.7
Lincolnshire	0.93	7.4	8.7	+1.3
Central	1.04	7.5	3.8	−3.7
Shropshire	1.08	13.2	11.4	−1.8
Cornwall	1.21	11.2	12.8	+1.6
Somerset	1.23	11.8	10.0	−1.8
Norfolk	1.29	10.6	10.8	+0.2
Devon	1.42	9.2	6.0	−3.2
Wiltshire	1.49	15.1	6.5	−8.6
National average	2.39	5.3	0.3	−5.0

* County (England and Wales), and Region (Scotland)
Source: Champion (1981b)

provided at the district level. Particularly helpful in this context, is an analysis under-taken by OPCS (1981). This compares the experience of the 1960s and 1970s on the basis of a modified version of the district socio-economic classification developed by Webber and Craig (1976), which divided the British population into six family groups each composed of several clusters. As Figure 8.6 shows, clusters 7 and 10 con-tain the most remote rural districts, being concentrated in Wales and Scotland respectively; while clusters 8 and 9 are confined to England and Wales and are broadly differentiated on an east-west basis. Figure 8.6 also includes cluster 2 (termed 'rural growth areas') which consists of those rural areas which grew fastest during the 1960s and which were generally located close to areas of strong metro-politan influence. The 78 districts belonging to clusters 7–10 of the Webber-Craig scheme may be amalgamated to form a separate category of 'remote, largely rural, districts'. As Table 8.8 indicates, for England and Wales this group was the only settlement category showing accelerated growth over the periods 1961–71 and 1971–81. Not only was this positive shift contrary to the national trend towards slower growth, it meant that whereas in the 1960s the less remote rural areas around the major metropolitan centres, the new towns, the resorts, and even the industrial dis-tricts of southern and midland England had all been growing faster than the remoter districts, the 1970s saw the latter growing faster than all of these except the new towns.

Concerning individual clusters, between 1961 and 1971 both clusters 7 and 10 lost population, whereas they grew rapidly during the next ten years. Cluster 10 pro-duced the greatest positive change and in the period 1971–81 had the second fastest growth rate of all five clusters. In clusters 8 and 9 the high growth rates of the 1960s were broadly maintained. Finally the results for cluster 2 showed that the 'rural growth areas' of the 1960s did not maintain their full momentum through the 1970s, having a lower growth rate than all other clusters except for cluster 7 (Table 8.9).

Overall, we can agree with Champion (1981a, p. 22), that 'the preliminary results of the 1981 Census show that in rural local authorities population growth over the last ten years has been considerable and there has been a substantial revival in the population of rural areas in the more peripheral parts of the country'. A note of caution is appropriate however; statistical trends in population do not necessarily equate with 'rural recovery'. Champion (1981a) in a careful analysis of mid-year population estimates has shown that much of the population gain in the remoter rural areas (clusters 7 and 10) occurred during the first few years of the decade since when the rates have dropped back to levels below those of the more accessible areas (clusters 8 and 9), and even in cluster 2 the situation had been stabilized by the mid 1970s. If rural growth rates are intimately tied to cycles of economic prosperity and recession at the national level, it is likely that in any recession the most remote areas may be affected the most severely.

Causes of the population turnaround

The reasons for this reversal of established trends are so multifaceted that any attempt to apply a single explanation to the widely diverse changes under way in dif-ferent regions would be unduly simplistic. Synthesizing the findings from a range of

Figure 8.6 Classification of rural areas in Britain.

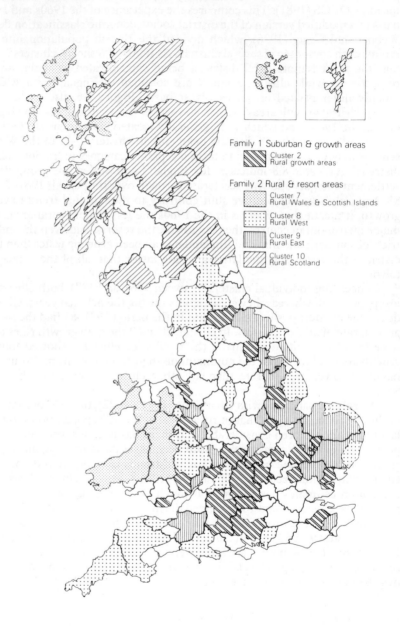

Source: OPCS (1981)

Table 8.8 *Population change for different categories of districts in England and Wales 1961–81*

Category of district	No. of districts	Population present on census night	1971–81 population change ('000s)	(%)	1961–71 population change (%)
England and Wales	403	49,011	262	0.5	5.7
Greater London boroughs	33	6,696	−756	−10.1	−6.8
1. Inner London	14	2,497	−535	−17.7	−13.2
2. Outer London	19	4,199	−221	−5.0	−1.8
Metropolitan districts	36	11,235	−546	−4.6	0.5
3. The principal cities	6	3,486	−386	−10.0	−8.4
4. Others	30	7,749	−160	−2.0	5.5
Nonmetropolitan districts	334	31,080	1,564	5.3	11.8
5. Large cities (over 175,000 population in 1971)	11	2,763	−149	−5.1	−1.4
6. Smaller cities	16	1,687	−55	−3.2	2.2
7. Industrial districts					
(a) Wales and the three northern regions of England	39	3,348	42	1.3	3.7
(b) Rest of England	34	3,320	158	5.0	12.1
8. Districts that include new towns	21	2,165	283	15.1	21.8
9. Resort and seaside retirement districts	36	3,335	156	4.9	12.2
10. Other urban, mixed urban-rural and more accessible rural districts					
(a) Outside South East	42	3,793	307	8.8	21.9
(b) In South East	57	5,656	354	6.7	22.1
11. Remoter, largely rural, districts	78	5,013	468	10.3	9.7

Source: Champion (1981b)

Table 8.9   *Population change in rural local authorities, 1961–1981, by type of district*

Cluster	Number of districts	1981 population ('000s)	Percentage population change		
			1961–71	**1971–81**	**Difference**
7. Rural Wales and Scottish Islands	16	645	−0.2	7.0	7.2
8. Rural, mainly West	32	2,009	7.2	8.8	1.6
9. Rural, mainly East	31	2,411	15.0	12.7	−2.3
10. Rural, mainly Scotland	23	911	−1.9	9.3	11.2
Subtotal	102	6,056	7.5	10.2	2.7
2. Rural growth areas	31	2,872	22.0	8.6	−13.4
Total	133	8,928	11.8	9.7	−2.1

Source: Champion (1981a)   Crown copyright 1981; reproduced with the permission of the Controller of Her Majesty's Stationary Office.

recent investigations (De Jong and Sell 1977; Beale 1977; Wardwell 1977; McCarthy and Morrison 1977; Blackwood and Carpenter 1978; Williams and Sofranko 1979; Dillman 1979; Wardwell and Brown 1980) provides a useful inventory of possible contributory factors. These are:

(a)   continued growth of metropolitan centres and their spillover into adjacent non-metropolitan counties;

(b)   decentralization of manufacturing in pursuit of lower land and wage costs;

(c)   increased employment in service occupations;

(d)   early retirement coupled with higher retirement incomes not tied to a particular location;

(e)   increased per capita disposable real income;

(f)   increased pursuit of leisure activities at all ages, centred on amenity-rich areas outside the daily range of metropolitan commuting;

(g)   increased enrolments in rural colleges and universities in the USA, especially in the late 1960s and early 1970s as a result of the postwar 'baby boom';

(h)   growth of state governments in the USA;

(i)   levelling off of the loss of farm population;

(j)   growth of an antimaterialist perspective among the young;

(k)   narrowing of the traditional gap between urban and rural lifestyles with the extension of electrification, water and sewage systems, telecommunications and access to modern facilities;

(l)   more long-distance commuting;

(m)   growth associated with energy and extractive industries;

(n)   completion of the interstate highway system in the USA;

(o)   lower cost of living in rural areas;

(p)   growth of antiurbanism as characterized by increased fear of crime and concern with urban disamenities such as congestion and pollution;

(q)   the current recession which, as in the 1930s, may encourage people to return to rural home environments to weather personal economic difficulties;

(r)   growth in importance of military establishments in some US counties during the 1960s;

(s)   residential preference for lower-density rural living;

(t)   government decentralization policy in some countries, such as Sweden and France.

Clearly the list of factors is diverse and many are interrelated. The extent to which each contributes to the population turnaround will depend on local conditions. Over the period 1970–1975 in the USA, for example, industrial decentralization was of primary importance in the Ozarks, southern Piedmont and northern Great Plains; energy extraction in Appalachia, northern Great Plains and Rocky Mountains; and recreation and retirement in the upper Great Lakes, the Ozark-Ouachita uplands, northern New England, Florida, the northern Pacific coast and the southwest. The growing complexity of the factors promoting nonmetropolitan population growth and net migration in the 1970s and 1980s is evident. As McCarthy and Morrison (1977, p. 136) observed with reference to the USA, 'of the traditional growth-inducing factors (metropolitan adjacency, intra county urbanization, and an economic base in manufacturing or government) all but metropolitan adjacency have diminished in importance. Other factors (some even associated historically with economic distress) now appear to be growth-related: a low level of urbanization, a Southern non metropolitan location, and specialization in retirement and recreation.' In broad terms, the turnaround 'strongly implies an attraction exceeding mere pecuniary considerations, that has prompted people to stay in or move to areas that will continue to be comparatively small, remote, rural, and low in income even after the migration has occurred' (Beale 1977, p. 118).

Few models have been constructed to explain the population turnaround. Wardwell (1980) has proposed a paradigm based on the premise that the turnaround has occurred largely because of convergent socio-economic change in rural and urban areas as a consequence of the declining constraint of distance on human activities. Vining and Kontuly (1978) suggest a developmental theory to explain the deconcentration phenomenon. They argue that diseconomies of metropolitan scale set in only at an advanced stage in a country's economic development. Even in the presence of these diseconomies, migration out of the metropolitan regions may not occur if undeveloped areas are limited in extent or only exist near to the current areas of concentration. Where development possibilities do exist in regions remote from the capital and other major metropolitan regions, the diseconomies of metropolitan scale eventually express themselves in the outmigration of persons from these core regions. *When* these diseconomies appear is seen as a function of the stage of economic development of the country as a whole.

In prospect, there remains some uncertainty as to whether the population reversal will be temporary or long-term. Some, such as Kain (1975, p. 224), adopt the view that 'during periods of high unemployment large numbers of workers migrate to other areas to find employment or they may return temporarily to their place of birth to wait until labour market conditions improve'. Others, such as Alonso (1977, p. 173) envisage that the current shift to net migration toward nonmetropolitan areas will be an enduring one; 'to be sure, good economic times may reverse the hunkering-down phenomenon, and the passing of the crest of the baby boom will dim the effects of rurally-set colleges; but the number of the aged will continue to grow, environmental and resource investment will likely continue at high levels, recreation seems likely to remain a growing industry, manufacturing shows no signs of curtailing its dispersal; and not least, urban fields are likely to continue their expansion, in spite of the energy crisis'.

References

ALONSO, W. (1977) Surprises and rethinkings of metropolitan growth: a comment, *International Regional Science Review* 2(2), 171–74.

AUSTRALIAN GOVERNMENT (1977) *Trends in Non-Metropolitan Population Growth and Their Relevance to Decentralisation Policy.* Department of the Environment, Decentralisation Policy Branch, Canberra.

BEALE, C. L. (1977) The recent shift of United States population to nonmetropolitan areas 1970–75, *International Regional Science Review* 2(2), 113–22.

BEIJER, G. (1963) *Rural Migrants in Urban Setting.* The Hague: Martinus Nijhoff.

BLACKWOOD, L. G. and CARPENTER, E. H. (1978) The importance of antiurbanism in determining residential preferences and migration patterns, *Rural Sociology* 43, 31–47.

BOURNE, L. S. and SIMMONS, J. W. (1979) *Canadian Settlement Trends: An Examination of the Spatial Pattern of Growth 1971–76* Major Report 15, Centre for Urban and Community Studies, University of Toronto.

BOYNE, D. H. (1965) Changes in the income distribution in agriculture, *Journal of Farm Economics* 47, 1213–24.

BRACEY, H. E. (1970) *People and the Countryside.* London: Routledge and Kegan Paul.

CANT, G. and O'NEILL, A. (1980) *Towards a Land Use Policy for Rural New Zealand* Land Use Series No. 8, Department of Lands and Survey, Wellington.

CHAMPION, A. G. (1973) Population trends in England and Wales, *Town and Country Planning* 41, 504–9.

CHAMPION, A. G. (1976) Evolving patterns of population distribution in England and Wales, *Transactions of the Institute of British Geographers* 1(4), 401–20.

CHAMPION, A. G. (1981a) Population trends in rural Britain, *Population Trends* 26. London: HMSO, 20–3.

CHAMPION, A. G. (1981b) *Counterurbanisation and Rural Rejuvenation in Rural Britain: An Evaluation of Population Trends Since 1971* Seminar Paper No. 38. Department of Geography, University of Newcastle upon Tyne.

CLOUT, H. (1976) Rural-urban migration in Western Europe. *In* J. Salt and H. Clout *Migration in Post War Europe*. London: Oxford University Press, 30–51.

COMMINS, P. (1978) Socio-economic adjustments to rural depopulation, *Regional Studies* 12, 79–94.

COMMISSION OF THE EUROPEAN COMMUNITIES (1973) *Report On the Regional Problem of the Enlarged Community*. Brussels: The Author.

CRUICKSHANK, A. (1981) USA Census '80: a note, *Scottish Geographical Magazine* 97(3), 175–82.

DE JONG, G. F. and SELL, R. R. (1977) Population redistribution, migration and residential preference, *Annals of the American Academy of Political and Social Science* 429, 130–44.

DILLMAN, D. A. (1979) Residential preferences, quality of life and the population turn-around, *American Journal of Agricultural Economics* 61, 960–66.

DRUDY, P. J. (1978) Depopulation in a prosperous agricultural subregion, *Regional Studies* 12, 49–60.

FIELDING, A. J. (1982) Counterurbanisation in Western Europe, *Progress in Planning* 17(1), 1–52.

FOEKEN, D. (1980) Return migration to a marginal rural area in northwestern Ireland, *Tijdschrift voor Economische en Sociale Geografie* 71(2), 114–20.

FRANKLIN, S. H. (1971) *Rural Societies*. London: Macmillan.

FRIEDLANDER, D. and ROSHIER, R. J. (1966) A study of internal migration in England and Wales, *Population Studies* 20, 45–59.

FUGUITT, G. V. (1981) Population trends in sparsely settled areas of the United States: the Case of the Great Plains. *In* R. E. Lonsdale and J. H. Holmes *Settlement Systems in Sparsely Populated Regions*. Oxford: Pergamon, 125–47.

GILG, A. G. (1983) Population and employment. *In* M. Pacione *Progress in Rural Geography*. London: Croom Helm, 74–101.

GRAFTON, D. (1980) *Planning for Remote Rural Areas: the Swiss experience* Discussion Paper No. 5. Southampton: University Department of Geography.

HANNAN, D. F. (1969) Migration motives and migration differentials among Irish rural youth, *Sociologia Ruralis* 9, 195–220.

HATHAWAY, D. E. and PERKINS, B. B. (1968) Farm labour mobility, migration, and income distribution, *American Journal of Agricultural Economics* 50, 342–53.

HM TREASURY (1976) *Rural Depopulation*. London: HMSO.

HOUSE, J. W. (1965) *Rural North East England 1951–61* Papers on Migration and Mobility 1. Department of Geography, University of Newcastle upon Tyne.

JANSEN, C. J. (1968) *Social Aspects of Internal Migration*. Bath: University Press.

KAIN, J. F. (1975) Implications of declining metropolitan population on housing markets. *In* G. Sternlieb and J. W. Hughes *Post-Industrial America: Metropolitan Decline and Inter-Regional Job Shifts* New Jersey: Rutgers Centre for Urban Policy Research, New Brunswick, 221–7.

KENNETT, S. and SPENCE, N. (1979) British population trends in the 1970s, *Town and Country Planning* 48, 220–23.

LONG, J. (1980) *Population Decentralisation in the United States* U.S. Bureau of the Census Monograph, Washington D.C.: U.S. Government Printing Office.

McCARTHY, K. F. and MORRISON, P. A. (1977) The changing demographic and economic structure of non-metropolitan areas in the United States, *International Regional Science Review* 2(2), 123–42.

McINTOSH, F. (1969) A survey of farmworkers leaving Scottish farms, *Scottish Agricultural Economics* 19, 191–7.

MITCHELL, G. D. (1950) Depopulation and rural social structure, *Sociological Review* 42, 69–85.

OKUN, B. and RICHARDSON, R. W. (1961) Regional income inequality and internal population migration, *Economic Development and Cultural Change* 9, 128–43.

OPCS (1981) *Census 1981 Preliminary Report for England and Wales* Series CEN 81 PR (1). London: HMSO.

POURCHER, G. (1970) The growing population of Paris. *In* C. J. Jansen *Readings in the Sociology of Migration.* Oxford: Pergamon, 179–202.

RANDOLPH, W. and ROBERT, S. (1981) Population redistribution in Great Britain 1971–1981, *Town and Country Planning* 49, 227–31.

RAVENSTEIN, E. G. (1885) The laws of migration, *Journal of the Royal Statistical Society* 48, 167–227.

REGISTRAR GENERAL SCOTLAND (1981) *Census 1981 Scotland, Preliminary Report.* Edinburgh: HMSO.

RUNDBLAD, B. G. (1957) Problems of a depopulated rural community. *In* D. Hannerberg et al. *Migration in Sweden: a Symposium* Lund Studies in Geography, Series B, 13, 184–91.

SAVILLE, J. (1957) *Rural Depopulation in England and Wales.* London: Routledge and Kegan Paul.

STOUFFER, S. A. (1962) *Social Research to Test Ideas.* Glencoe: Free Press.

TODD, D. (1980) Rural outmigration and economic standing in a prairie setting, *Transactions of the Institute of British Geographers* 5(4), 446–65.

TUCKER, C. J. (1976) Changing patterns of migration between metropolitan and non-metropolitan areas in the United States: recent evidence, *Demography* 13, 435–43.

VINING, D. R. and KONTULY, T. (1978) Population dispersal from major metropolitan regions: an international comparison, *International Regional Science Review* 3(1), 49–73.

VINING, D. R., PALLONE, R. and PLANE, D. (1981) Recent migration patterns in the developed world, *Environment and Planning A* 13, 243–50.

WARDWELL, J. W. (1977) Equilibrium and change in nonmetropolitan growth, *Rural Sociology* 42, 156–79.

WARDWELL, J. W. (1980) Toward a theory of urban-rural migration in the developed world. *In* D. L. Brown and J. W. Wardwell, *New Directions in Urban-Rural Migration: The Population Turnaround in Rural America*. New York: Academic Press, 71–114.

WARDWELL, J. W. and BROWN, D. L. (1980) Population redistribution in the United *In* D. L. Brown and J. W. Wardwell *New Directions in Urban-Rural Migration: The Population Migration: The Population Turnaround in Rural America*. New York: Academic Press, 5–35.

WEBBER, R. and CRAIG, J. (1976) Which local authorities are alike? *Population Trends 5*, 13–19.

WENDEL, B. (1953) *A Migration Schema: Theories and Observations* Lund Studies in Geography Series B, 9.

WHITE, P. E. (1980) Migration loss and the residual community: a study in rural France 1962–75. *In* P. E. White and R. Woods *The Geographical Impact of Migration*. London: Longman, 198–222.

WILLIAMS, J. D. and SOFRANKO, A. J. (1979) Motivations for the immigration component of population turnaround in nonmetropolitan areas, *Demography* 16(2), 239–55.

WOODRUFFE, R. J. (1976) *Rural Settlement Policies and Plans*. Oxford: Oxford University Press.

ZELINSKY, W. (1978) Is nonmetropolitan America being repopulated? *Demography* 15, 12–39.

9   Rural communities

The British regard themselves as country people despite the fact that, since 1911, at least four-fifths of the population of England and Wales have lived in urban areas (MacGregor 1976). As Williams (1973) points out, there is a long-standing British reverence and nostalgia for the traditional rural way of life. Most people, if asked, would express a belief that rural communities are warm, human, secure, friendly places with a strong spirit of 'togetherness' – quite different from the anonymous way of life in towns. This well-established ideal of a balanced, integrated rural community is closely related to the 'pastoral myth' which has been a persistent feature of English thought since the Romantic poets of the nineteenth century (Williams 1972). A similar popular proclivity for 'the rural life' was detected in the United States by Anderson (1963, p. 8) who stated that 'the American ideal of home, community and work was clearly rural and puritanic. Industrialism and urbanism combined in various ways to shock all established norms.'

Numerous studies have recognized differences between life in towns and life in the countryside. More than 50 years ago Sorokin and Zimmerman (1929) listed eight groups of variables which they considered as characteristically rural:

(1)   a high proportion of the population occupied with work on the land;
(2)   a predominantly 'natural' as opposed to man-made landscape;
(3)   rural settlements are normally smaller than towns;
(4)   population densities are lower in rural areas;
(5)   the populations of rural communities are more homogeneous in their social traits, with less variation in beliefs and social behaviour;
(6)   class differences are less pronounced;
(7)   both spatial and social mobility is less intense in the countryside;
(8)   a close-knit social network, including cooperation in economic life, and a higher degree of mutual aid.

In many traditional societies localism has a particular economic base in the system of agriculture and craft-manufacturing and much of the work in support of the idea of communities as local groups possessing some cohesion and some common institutions has been carried out within traditional rural societies (Lewis 1967; Hauser 1967). Throughout the Developed World, however, the growth of urban industrial capitalism since the end of the eighteenth century has led to the steady dilution of localism as a structural principle of contemporary society, and the continued vitality of many rural communities is seriously in doubt. Consequently many would agree with Wibberley (1960, p. 121) that 'in the middle of the twentieth century we are uncertain as to what is really meant by the term rural community, and whether there are now any significant differences between rural and urban people in the life they lead, in their hopes and aspirations, and in their attitudes and mores'.

Studies of the community concept have generated a vast literature (Bell and Newby 1971) and yet there is still considerable confusion over the precise meaning of the term. There is no need here to extend the pedagogic debate over definition but simply to note that Hillery (1955) found 94 different definitions in the literature up to 1953 and Sutton and Munsen (1976) 125 from 1954 to 1973. A major cause of the lack of consensus is the different emphases which have been placed upon the social and spatial aspects of the concept. The early human ecologists did not distinguish between the spatial and social dimensions underlying community (North 1926; Carpenter 1933). Since this classical position was stated, geographers and sociologists have followed divergent paths in their development of the concept; one maintaining the spatial locus, the other emphasizing the aspatial nature of social networks. Bell and Newby (1976) shed some light when they identify three broad perspectives on community:

(1)   community as a geographical expression, i.e. a finite and bounded physical location;
(2)   community as a sociological expression, i.e. a local social system (Stacey 1969);
(3)   community as a particular kind of human association irrespective of its local focus.

They point out that Tönnies (1887) 'was concerned with the third of these in his concept of gemeinschaft. Subsequent sociologists elided all three, and current urban and rural sociologists have concentrated on the second' (1976, p. 196). A review of the diverse literature suggests that definitions of community tend to include three ingredients – networks of interpersonal ties (outside of the household) which provide sociability and support to members; residence in a common locality; and solidarity sentiments and activities.

Theories of social differentiation and change

The rural–urban continuum

Establishing a model or framework against which reality can be tested is a valuable research methodology. The best known of the typologies used to differentiate rural from urban communities is the rural–urban continuum which has been employed in one form or another by sociologists and anthropologists for over a century (Bell and Newby 1971). In its original form this merely distinguished the extremes, thus stressing the differences and discontinuities between the 'rural' and the 'urban'. More recent interpretations have emphasized the transformation which occurs from one pole to the other, thus offering a theory of social change which can be used to identify the nature and direction of the social processes involved. Different terms have been employed to indicate the two poles (Table 9.1) with perhaps the most influential in social geography being those coined by Tönnies (1887) and by Redfield (1941). The essence of all, whether as a dichotomy or as a continuum between urban and rural, is to typify the rural pole as an idealized, unchanging peasant society organized in small, inward-looking, idyllic communities based on kinship and supported by sub-

Table 9.1   *Typologies and continua analogous to the rural–urban continuum*

Author	'Rural' or 'non-urban' terminology	'Urban' terminology
Sir Henry Maine (1861)	Status	Contract
Herbert Spencer (1862)	Military	Industrial
Ferdinand Tönnies (1887)	*Gemeinschaft*	*Gesellschaft*
Emile Durkheim (1893)	Mechanical solidarity	Organic solidarity
Max Weber (1922)	Traditional	Rational
Robert Redfield (1947)	Folk	Urban
Howard Becker (1950)	Sacred	Secular

Source: Gwyn E. Jones (1973) *Rural Life.* Longman.

sistence agriculture. The urban extreme is the ever-changing life of the large cosmopolitan, commercial cities (Jones 1973), as can be seen in Table 9.2. The existence of such a rural–urban continuum has received considerable support (Rees 1951), particularly from Wirth (1938) who formulated a theory of urbanism which maintained that the size of the aggregated population will affect relations between members, increasing the process of differentiation which ultimately leads to segregation. More recently, Frankenberg (1966, p. 275) has developed a theory of social change by which it is seen as 'a progressive and historical development from rural to urban, mediated by industrialisation, division of labour and role differentiation'. He goes on to list 25 ways in which this urban–rural dichotomy is revealed.

Assessment of the rural–urban continuum model

As Carter (1972, p. 27) remarks, 'criticism of these ideas has been continuous since they were first put forward'.

(1)   It has been argued that Tönnies' ideal types do not offer a realistic description of modern life. There is ample empirical evidence to support the contention that relationships in the city are not always Gesellschaft-like (Young and Willmot 1957) while many rural communities are more influenced by urban forces than by traditional rural ways of life. As Bailey (1975) noted, 'we see villages in our cities and cities in our villages'. The model thus fails to recognize the possibility of a coexistence of different societal elements within the same community.
(2)   Objections to the continuum have been raised over its Western ethnocentrism and particular ideological stance based on the realization that the transformation of social values is not a universal process but is related to a particular cultural context.
(3)   Critics such as Pahl (1966) have argued that the interpretations and uses to which the model has been put have been too simplistic leading to broad and often inaccurate generalizations. Supporters would argue that the major fault lies in the uses made of the continuum rather than in the ideas of the original formulators. As

Table 9.2   *Major characteristics of Gemeinschaft and Gesellschaft*

Social characteristics	Gemeinschaft	Gesellschaft
Dominant social relation-ships based on:	kinship, locality and neighbourliness, fellowship – a sharing of responsibilities and fates, and a furtherance of mutual good through familiarity and under-standing, and the exercise and consensus of 'natural' wills or sentiment in evaluations, assessments and decisions; 'common goods – common evils; common friends – common enemies'	exchange, rational calcu-lation, specific function, – formal and limited responsibilities, and a furtherance of personal good through the exercise of rational wills and validated knowledge; '. . . everybody is by himself and isolated, and there exists a condition of tension against all others'
Ordering of social institutions:	family life, rural village life, town life	city life, national life, cosmopolitan life
Characteristic form of wealth:	land	money
Central institutions and forms of social control:	family law, extended kinship group, concord, customs and mores, religion	the state, convention, contracts, political legislation, public opinion
Status-role:	everyone's role fully integrated in the system, the status of each being ascribed	role based on each specific relationship, the status in each being based on personal achievement

Source: Gwyn E. Jones (1973) *Rural Life.* Longman.

Hauser (1967, p. 504) explains, 'most of the scholars who contributed to the emergence of these concepts regarded them not as generalisations based on research, but rather as ideal-type constructs' but 'the widespread acceptance of these ideal-type constructs as generalisations, without the benefit of adequate research well illus-trates the dangers of catchy neologisms which often get confused with knowledge' (Ibid., p. 514).

(4)   The typology focuses attention on the city as a source of social change and obscures the wide range of values and ways of life of individuals at the folk end of the continuum.

(5)   Frankenberg's (1966) work underlined a major criticism of the rural–urban continuum; namely that a single continuum can describe only a small part of the total relationships in society, and models such as Tönnies' which are very broadly drawn may be dissected into several sub-elements, not all of which will vary to the same degree and in the same direction. In Duncan's (1967, p. 43) words, 'it is highly doubt-ful that the uni-dimensional continuum, in any rigorous mathematical sense, is a suf-

ficiently realistic model for research on inter-community variation'; and as Martin (1976, p. 51) comments, 'instead of one continuum there may well be a hundred, each having some measure of independence'.

(6)   A fundamental problem of particular concern to geographers arises from the contention that the rural–urban dichotomy or continuum 'revolves less around place than around the degree of involvement of the human being' (Bell and Newby 1971, p. 161). For several critics the main disadvantage of the model is that it locates social relationships in a specific locale. Both Gans (1962) and Pahl (1966), for example, doubt the *sociological* relevance of the physical differences between rural and urban in complex industrial societies. For Bell and Newby (1971, p. 51) the basic question here is 'whether the community is a sociological variable at all or merely a geographical expression'. As Gans (1962, p. 643) has observed, 'ways of life do not coincide with settlement patterns'. This view is underlined by Pahl (1966, p. 293) who states that 'whether we call the process acting on the local community "urbanization", "differentiation", "modernization", "mass society" or whatever, it is clear that it is not so much communities that are acted upon as groups and individuals at particular places *in the social structure*. Any attempt to tie patterns of social relationships to specific geographic milieux is a singularly fruitless exercise.'

Perhaps the most fundamental factor undermining the validity and relevance of the continuum model is the extent to which 'in highly developed countries a common culture is arising between town and country' (Wibberley 1960, p. 121). While the folk–urban idea may have relevance in parts of the Developing World where urban–rural contrasts are greatest, in the Developed realm the spreading influence of urban society has done much to lessen this difference and consequently undermine the utility of such a simple typology. The extent to which rural–urban differences are being reduced can be illustrated with reference to a selection of community studies.

In the mid 1960s Pahl (1965, 1966) prompted a major reappraisal of sociological thinking by suggesting that the similarities between social conditions in urban and rural areas were greater than the contrasts. He based his views on a study of two villages in London's green belt which had grown rapidly in the postwar period. The villages of Watton (pop. 278 households) and Tewin (340) were analysed by questionnaire techniques and Pahl (1966) was able to point to fundamental differences in life-style *within* each village between post-1945 incomers and the 'established' villagers. The newcomers differed markedly from the other residents in terms of occupation, commuting, education and shopping behaviour but the most significant difference was in social class. As a result of selective migration into the urban fringe by middle class commuters, two overlapping communities were being created within the villages with the recent arrivals and established population living and working in different social and economic worlds. Such analyses clearly undermined the traditional ideas about the cosiness and homogeneity of village life and led Pahl (1966, p. 299) to conclude that 'in the sociological context, the terms rural and urban are more remarkable for their ability to confuse than for their power to illuminate'.

Pahl's conclusions were drawn from only 2 villages barely 25 miles from London. It did not follow that these conclusions are true of all rural settlements. Around the same time a survey of 75 parishes and 7 villages in Hampshire was undertaken for the County Council in an area removed from the development pressures emanating from London and Southampton. Data from 7 towns were included for the purposes of comparison. Once again the contrasts between town and village life were less than expected with more similarities than differences being encountered. The levels of employment and the proportion of people commuting to work was similar in both villages and towns, as were the distances travelled each day. Nearly one-fifth (19.0 percent) of villagers were born in the villages where they now lived while the corresponding figure for towns was 21.0 percent, thus disputing the commonly held belief that there is a 'core' of established population in rural communities. Finally, when questioned directly about the attractions of village life most of the people who preferred the country to the town did so because it was more peaceful (55.0 percent) or because the countryside was more beautiful, more natural and healthier (53.0 percent). Only 27.0 percent referred to the hypothesized qualities of rural community life (Hampshire County Council 1966).

The results of the Hampshire study and of Pahl's work in Hertfordshire provide scant evidence of the traditional rural community but, clearly, urban influences may be attenuated by distance. Remote communities have been studied as possible representatives of the classical rural lifestyle (Arensberg and Kimball 1940; Rees 1950; Williams 1956, 1962. One such study was carried out by Littlejohn (1963) in the Cheviot parish of Westrigg. 'It is an upland parish with a population of 326 devoted mainly to forestry and to sheep farming. There is no village in the parish, no shop and no pub. It is 15 miles from the nearest town and is remote even by the standards of the Scottish borders' (Martin 1976, p. 54). Remarkably in these circumstances Littlejohn (1963, p. 63) felt compelled to emphasize the similarities between Westrigg and urban centres. His conclusion that 'the term "parish" now refers merely to a population living within a geographically defined boundary which has little sociological importance' reflects the fact that the relationships of the local social organization and network have been replaced by those of the modern industrial economic system. As Martin (1976, p. 55) comments, 'the lesson of these studies is not that rural life is identical with the town but rather that their coincidences over-ride their contrasts to a much greater extent than popular or professional sentiment is prepared to allow. Differences will still remain, a function of the small scale of rural life rather than of rurality per se.' It would clearly not be sensible to expect any British rural community or village to be identical to the ideal type of the rural–urban continuum; nowhere is like this! As the originators of the continuum stress, the ideal type is simply a base against which reality may be tested. Despite support from some writers (Lupri 1967; Richmond 1969; Jones 1973), however, the weight of opinion is firmly against the continued utility of the continuum (Mann 1965; Pahl 1966; Lewis 1979) and according to Newby (1978, p. 5) 'the rural–urban continuum now lies generally discredited'. Yet although the usefulness of the rural–urban continuum as a classificatory device has been questioned it has proved more difficult to replace the model with a new conceptual apparatus. Despite the spreading influence of urbanism, 'at any one time an immense diversity exists among our rural communities' (Jones 1973, p. 19) and there is a clear need for some classificatory structure to impose order on the complexity of the real world.

A social typology of villages

Mitchell (1951) in a study of Devon villages differentiated rural communities on the basis of their attitude to change and degree of integration. The typology, which has since been interpreted within a time perspective by Thorns (1968), is based on two broad sets of factors designed to distinguish between open and closed and integrated and disintegrated communities. A combination of these two sets of criteria produces four general types (open, integrated; closed, integrated; open, lacking integration; closed, lacking integration) and despite the inevitable overlap among categories Mitchell was able to distinguish villages of each type within a relatively small area. Jones (1973) provides a summary of the characteristics of each type:

(1)   The open, integrated rural community is usually relatively large, with a diversity of occupations and displaying in its institutional and organizational framework an adaptability towards changing conditions. It is often the social and economic centre for several surrounding villages. The community is relatively self-sufficient socially but maintains links with the larger society. Although Mitchell sees this type as resembling a suburban society, a large number of villages in areas very distant from the larger towns and cities exhibit these characteristics to a high degree.

(2)   The closed, integrated community is one which is able to remain more or less isolated with a relatively stable population. Although it may be variable in size it is inward-looking, self-contained and traditional, maintaining firm boundaries against outside influences. Roles are well defined and the range of norms of social behaviour is relatively narrow. Despite the inevitable penetration of numerous urban influences via the mass media this type of community persists and is not confined to the remoter areas of the country.

(3)   An open, disintegrating community is invariably affected by change at a rate which it cannot assimilate. In many instances, this arises from a rapidly growing population as in commuter or dormitory villages. Due to the inflow of population and often a high rate of population turnover the common characteristics of such villages are an instability in any organizations and a lack of civic responsibility and leadership. The external linkages are invariably greater than the internal bonds and, internally, tensions and conflicts are common.

(4)   The closed, disintegrating community is generally small and decreasing in size. Loss of population may have been initiated by the declining labour requirements of agriculture or the closure of a local source of employment; the outcome is a remainder population too small to maintain a viable village economy. The result is likely to be a progressive worsening in services, facilities and amenities, often hastened by planning decisions, with a feeling of helplessness among the remaining inhabitants. This type of decaying village community is common in the older industrial areas and remoter rural areas.

Although formulated over 30 years ago, this typology offers a simple classificatory device applicable at a general scale.

A time-space framework for rural social change

The apparent merging of urban and rural lifestyles in the modern world focuses particular attention on the dynamics of social change (as opposed to the identification of 'ideal types'). This requires that social change be viewed as a process which is not 'place-determined' but which involves the whole society whether located in city, fringe, or remote countryside. Lewis and Maund (1976) have proposed an alternative to the continuum model in an effort to identify the processes underlying social change, and in particular the urbanization of the countryside. Building on the work of Pahl (1966) and Burie (1967) they adopt a behavioural approach to the interpretation of the urbanization of rural communities, and conceive social change as a process of diffusion of new ideas and attitudes.

Rural social change is seen as being effected by a series of population movements. First, *depopulation* as a result primarily of net outward migration. At a later stage, the nature of the community may be changed by a growth in *population* as a consequence of a net inmigration of adventitious population at an early stage of the life-cycle. Thirdly, there is *repopulation* which refers to retirement to the countryside by people in a late stage of the life-cycle. 'Of course all such processes operate at one and the same time within each community, and hence the demographic and social character of a community is controlled by the predominant processes' (Lewis and Maund 1976, p. 20).

The social selectivity of such movements initiates significant structural changes within the communities involved. The immediate effect of *population* is not only to increase the number of residents but also to alter the communities' social, demographic and economic structures. Such inmigrants, though acquiring rural residence, still retain urban employment and tend to be relatively young and wealthy, often middle class in lifestyle and usually divorced from rural society. Demographically a rise in the birth rate produces a younger age structure. *Repopulation* is also age-selective, but such movements tend to take place at a late stage in the family life-cycle and contribute to the ageing demographic structure. *Depopulation* involves the younger and better-qualified elements of rural society moving to the cities, leaving behind an ageing demographic structure and a weakly developed, pyramidal social structure. Such population changes are associated with changes in the value system, the traditional values being slowly displaced. *Population* and *repopulation* appear to accentuate the demise of the local value system, whilst *depopulation* contributes to its eventual collapse. 'In any event rural society is increasingly being assimilated into the total society' (Lewis 1979, p. 43). This argument is summarized in Figure 9.1 which portrays the dynamic nature of the system. The energy for the system is provided by value changes which result in structural and behavioural changes each of which is capable of feeding back into the value system and modifying it further. Under the influence of this system local values are steadily eroded to the extent that they either take the form of the national value system or atrophy entirely.

For geographers a key question is whether such a model of social change has a spatial form. According to Martin (1957) the extension of urban influences within the countryside involves two related principles of spatial change:

Figure 9.1 The components of an urbanization system.

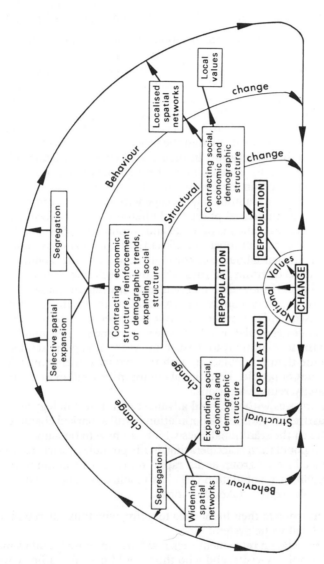

Source: Lewis and Maund (1976)

(1)   first the gradient principle emphasizes the distance-decay effect of cities on their surrounding rural areas;

(2)   secondly the differentiation principle states that 'urbanization' transforms previously undifferentiated areas by the introduction of functional specialization (and an increased interdependence of their differentiated parts).

In other words 'the extent of specialisation of function and differentiation of sub areas in a rural territory varies unevenly with distance to the nearest city and directly with the size of that city' (Ibid., p. 76). Incorporation of a spatial dimension directly contradicts Pahl's (1966) view that the urbanization of the countryside is essentially an aspatial process. Although the general nature of the urbanization process is readily acceptable it is extremely doubtful whether it operates at the same intensity in all locations. As Warntz (1967, p. 7) observed, 'space is a tyrant and distance enforces his rule' and it is much more likely that the process of social change will occur at different rates within the countryside. In Figure 9.2 Lewis and Maund (1976) present a time-space framework to explain how the urbanization process creates intercommunity variation within the countryside. The diagram assumes an isotropic surface. Surface A depicts a traditional landscape with one urban centre surrounded by communities at a preindustrial phase (I). Differentiation between urban and rural functions is marked; circulation is minimal and communities exist in relative isolation. On Surface B, however, a number of differentiating features have appeared. Urban industrialization attracts labour from the more accessible rural communities and this tendency is reinforced within the rural area by a declining demand for labour as a result of technological innovation in agriculture. During this phase migration is on a permanent rather than a commuter basis since transport facilities are poorly developed. Consequently, some communities, especially those nearer the town, begin to experience depopulation (II). At the same time the new middle class start to move out from the town initially for leisure and recreation purposes. Depopulation is greater in volume than repopulation, with the two movements made up of socially discrete categories of people. Traditional communities still exist during this phase, but at increasingly remote locations.

Surface C emerges with the rapid advancement in technology which underpins the urban industrial revolution. Depopulation is still a marked characteristic of most communities, even the traditional ones which are now to be found only in the most remote areas. Repopulation is accelerating, made possible by early retirement among a growing higher-income group and a rapid improvement in the transport system. The spatial extent of repopulation (III) has reached beyond the daily commuting range. Such recolonization takes two forms:

(i)   people returning to their home area to retire, who thus still retain some affinity with the local value system;

(ii) newcomers who on retirement seek residence in those localities made familiar by regular holiday visits, and who thus would have less affinity with the local value system.

Finally the 'population' zone, closest to the town, is characterized by housing estates and expanded dormitory villages. It attracts younger, middle class families who are prepared to commute daily to work.

Figure 9.2 A time-space order of urbanization.

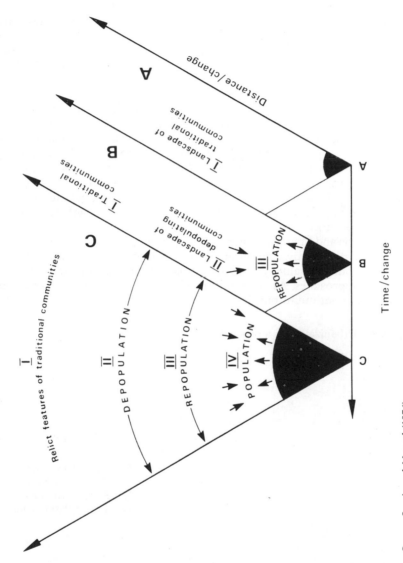

Source: Lewis and Maund (1976)

The landscape envisaged is 'differentiated on social class and life-cycle criteria, and exhibits an order related to distance from an urban centre. The zones marked I to IV are conceived not as discrete categories but rather as tendencies. The processes involved will be present at all locations but it is their relative proportions which vary with distance from an urban centre' (Lewis 1979, p. 146).

The time-space model of rural social change so far discussed has considered a hypothetical rural area surrounding a single urban centre. In reality many urban places of different sizes exist and the processes of socio-spatial differentiation will operate in a much less straightforward manner. Lewis and Maund (1976) speculate on the possible disturbing influences of several towns and cities. For example (Figure 9.3) in a rural area with three urban centres, one of metropolitan size and two of lower order, the greater 'connectiveness' and range of functions of the metropolis will widen the *population* zone and narrow the one experiencing *depopulation*. Within these zones the smaller centres will have their own local influence. In Figure 9.3 settlement 1 appears within the repopulation zone of the conurbation, but simultaneously has its own population, repopulation and depopulation zones. It is suggested that in this case retired people will be found alongside young commuters. In contrast, settlement 2 is located in the metropolitan depopulation zone, and along with its own population zone it can act as a significant growth point in a region of population decline.

The Lewis and Maund (1976) model is an attempt to advance from the traditional rural–urban dichotomy/continuum models. It emphasizes the socio-economic structure, behaviour and value systems in contrast to the more familiar morphological and landscape approaches. As such it acknowledges the 'place-bound' criticisms of the rural–urban continuum but does not reject entirely the spatial dimension.

Figure 9.3 Urbanization at a regional level.

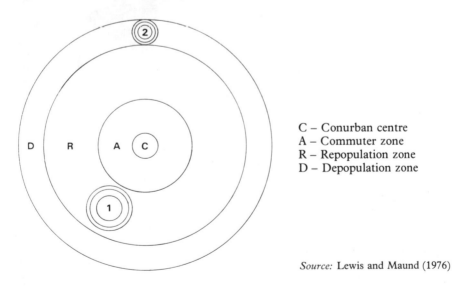

C – Conurban centre
A – Commuter zone
R – Repopulation zone
D – Depopulation zone

Source: Lewis and Maund (1976)

There is general agreement that the processes which activate the urbanization of the countryside are universal (Volgyes et al. 1980) and that such differences that exist from place to place are of degree rather than kind. The extension of urban influences and repopulation of the countryside takes place in a variety of guises. These include the spread of hobby farming and the worker-peasant phenomenon; the development of metropolitan villages via the construction of suburban-type estates; gentrification of existing houses; and the growth of second homes, which for some is the first step towards permanent rural residence.

References

ANDERSON, N. L. (1963) Aspects of rural and urban, *Sociologia Ruralis* 3, 8–22.

ARENSBERG, C. M. and KIMBALL, S. T. (1940) *Family and Community in Ireland*. London: Peter Smith.

BAILEY, J. (1975) *Social Theory for Planning*. London: Routledge and Kegan Paul.

BELL, C. and NEWBY, H. (1971) *Community Studies*. London: Allen and Unwin.

BELL, C. and NEWBY, H. (1976) Community communion class and community action. *In* D. T. Herbert and R. J. Johnson *Social Areas in Cities* Vol. 2. London: Wiley, 189–207.

BURIE, J. (1967) Prolegomena to a theoretical model of intercommunity variation, *Sociologia Ruralis* 7, 347–62.

CARPENTER, N. (1933) *Encyclopaedia of the Social Sciences*. New York: Macmillan.

CARTER, H. (1972) *The Study of Urban Geography*. London: Arnold.

DUNCAN, O. D. Community size and the rural–urban continuum. *In* P. K. Hatt and A. J. Rees *Cities and Society*. Glencoe: Free Press, 35–45.

FRANKENBERG, R. (1966) *Communities in Britain*. Harmondsworth: Penguin.

GANS, H. J. (1962) *The Urban Villagers*. New York: Free Press.

HAMPSHIRE COUNTY COUNCIL (1966) *Village Life in Hampshire*. Winchester: The Author.

HAUSER, P. M. (1967) Observations on the urban–folk and urban–rural dichotomies as forms of western ethnocentrism. *In* P. M. Hauser and L. Schnore *The Study of Urbanisation*. New York: Wiley, 503–17.

HILLERY, G. (1955) Definitions of community: areas of agreement, *Rural Sociology* 20, 111–23.

JONES, Gwyn E. (1973) *Rural Life*. London: Longman.

LEWIS, G. J. (1979) *Rural Communities*. Newton Abbot: David and Charles.

LEWIS, G. J. and MAUND, D. J. (1976) The urbanisation of the countryside: a framework for analysis, *Geografiska Annaler* 58B, 17–27.

LEWIS, O. (1967) Further observations on the folk-urban continuum and urbanization with special reference to Mexico City. *In* P. M. Hauser and L. Schnore *The Study of Urbanization*. New York: Wiley, 491–503.

LITTLEJOHN, J. (1963) *Westrigg: The Sociology of a Cheviot Parish*. London: Routledge and Kegan Paul.

LUPRI, E. (1967) The rural–urban variable reconsidered, *Sociologia Ruralis* 7, 1–20.

MacGREGOR, M. (1976) Village life, *Town and Country Planning* 44(12), 524–7.

MANN, P. (1965) *An Approach to Urban Sociology*. London: Routledge and Kegan Paul.

MARTIN, I. (1976) Rural communities. *In* G. E. Cherry *Rural Planning Problems*. London: Leonard Hill, 49–83.

MARTIN, W. T. (1957) Ecological change in satellite rural areas, *American Sociological Review* 22, 173–83.

MITCHELL, G. (1951) The relevance of group dynamics to rural planning problems, *Sociological Review* O.S. 43, 1–16.

NEWBY, H. (1978) The rural sociology of advanced capitalist societies. *In* H. Newby *International Perspectives in Rural Sociology*. Chichester: Wiley, 3–30.

NORTH, C. (1926) The city as a community. *In* E. W. Burgess *The Urban Community*. Chicago: University of Chicago Press, 233–7.

PAHL, R. (1965) *Urbs in Rure* Geographical Paper No. 2. London: London School of Economics.

PAHL, R. (1966) The rural–urban continuum, *Sociologia Ruralis* 6, 299–329.

REDFIELD, R. (1941) *The Folk Culture of Yucatan*. Chicago: The University Press.

REES, A. D. (1950) *Life in a Welsh Countryside*. Cardiff: University of Wales Press.

RICHMOND, A. (1969) Migration in industrial societies. *In* J. Jackson *Migration*. Cambridge: The University Press, 238–81.

SOROKIN, P. and ZIMMERMAN, C. (1929) *Principles of Rural-Urban Sociology*. New York: Holt, Reinhart.

STACEY, M. (1969) The myth of community studies, *British Journal of Sociology* 20, 134–47.

SUTTON, W. A. and MUNSEN, T. (1976) *Definitions of community 1954 through 1973* Paper presented to the Annual Meeting of the American Sociological Association.

THORNS, D. C. (1968) The changing system of rural stratification, *Sociologia Ruralis* 8, 161–76.

TÖNNIES, F. (1887) *Gemeinschaft en Gesellschaft* translated and supplemented by C. Loomis (1957) *Community and Society*. Ann Arbor: Michigan State University Press.

VOLGYES, I., LONSDALE, R. and AVERY, W. (1980) *The Process of Rural Transformation: Eastern Europe, Latin America and Australia*. New York: Pergamon.

WARNTZ, W. (1967) Global science and the tyranny of space, *Papers and Proceedings of the Regional Science Association* 19, 7–19.

WIBBERLEY, G. (1960) Changes in the structure and functions of the rural community, *Sociologia Ruralis* 1, 118–27.

WILLIAMS, R. (1963) *The Country and the City*. London: Chatto and Windus.

WILLIAMS, W. (1956) *The Sociology of an English Village*. London: Routledge and Kegan Paul.

WILLIAMS, W. (1962) *A West Country Village: Ashworthy*. London: Routledge and Kegan Paul.

WILLIAMS, W. (1972) Sociological criteria for assessing policies. *In* J. Ashton and W. H. Long *The Remoter Rural Areas of Britain*. Edinburgh: Oliver and Boyd, 202–14.

WIRTH, L. (1938) Urbanism as a way of life, *American Journal of Sociology* 44, 3–24.

YOUNG, M. and WILLMOT, P. (1957) *Family and Kinship in East London*. London: Routledge and Kegan Paul.

10   Metropolitan villages

The urbanization of the countryside

The urbanization of the countryside is a process of social change involving the extension of urban ideas and ways of life into rural areas, and is most apparent in the physical movement of population from city to countryside. Despite the resurgence of population growth in some rural areas beyond the periphery of the metropolitan zone, most postwar growth in rural areas has occurred close to the 'urban fringe'. Selective repopulation of periurban areas in Western society has been a major characteristic of the last two decades. This has meant that while the physical land use boundary between urban and rural remains clear, especially in countries with strong planning laws, in social and functional terms the urban–rural distinction has been blurred, producing what Pahl (1965a, p. 5) has called 'mentally urbanised but physically rural parts of the country'.

Urban to rural population movements may be either planned or spontaneous. Planned deconcentration of metropolitan areas has normally been pursued as part of more general attempts to restrain the growth and physical encroachment of the largest cities and to aid rehabilitation of social and economic conditions in inner urban areas (Pacione 1981). Around London, for example, there are several out-country estates beyond the fringes of the conurbation which were constructed largely to combat the immediate postwar housing problem. There are also expanded towns, some over 160 km from the city, which receive overspill under the 1952 Town Development Act. Finally, there is a ring of eight 'Mark I' New Towns up to 50 km from the capital. Spontaneous deconcentration is seen in the spillover of central city populations into the suburbs and then into the rural fringe or exurbia, with a main energizing force being the search for superior residential environments aided by greater affluence and the availability of transport linkages with the central city. In countries like Britain, the application of development controls such as green belts around cities has had the effect of increasing land values in desirable residential areas of the outer suburbs and of diverting new housing demand from the built-up edge of the city so as to leapfrog into the visually rural hinterland.

Bunce (1982) recognizes three major types of residential development effected by spontaneous centrifugal movements of population:

(1)   Rural Estates: this type of exurban development tends to involve the more affluent sections of society being low-density, set on large lots and dispersed in the open countryside. Most rural estate properties have been purchased from farmers who recognize the prospect of significant profits from the sale of portions of their land. Such land transfers tend to stimulate changes in the patterns of agricultural landholding and the types of agricultural enterprise. Frequently, farmers who have sold off portions of their land for residential development are left with an agricultural parcel which is too small to farm efficiently. In this situation some farmers will sell or

rent their remaining land to others who wish to enlarge their operations through fragmented ownership and/or rental.

(2)   Residential Subdivisions: the second main residential development is the subdivision or housing estate. These are located both in the open countryside and in or adjacent to existing rural settlements; and there is considerable variation in the size of lots and style of development. Some of the earlier exurban subdivisions in the USA were the result of the assembly of parcels of farmland by developers who constructed completely new estates (Gans 1969); however most have been on a smaller scale (Hovinen 1977). In Britain this kind of suburban-style development dates from before the Second World War, being a common way of responding to housing demand in the 1920s and 1930s before the practice was curtailed by the Restriction of Ribbon Development Act 1935. Similar types of small subdivisions, however, have continued to appear around North American cities where they exist purely as residential areas often without a full range of services and totally dependent on the mobility conferred by the automobile. Because of the rocketing price of land; the increased cost of living in isolated locations; and the growth of planning restrictions; scattered residential development in rural areas, both in Europe and North America, has tended to diminish in recent years. New housing is now usually located in or adjacent to existing villages. The effects of this kind of estate development on both the social and spatial structure of affected settlements can be pronounced (Pahl 1965b; Walker 1977; Pacione 1980).

(3)   Infilling and Conversion: the influx of urbanites into rural areas can involve a more subtle process of residential change with new homes added to villages through the occupation of individual vacant lots and the conversion of existing buildings to residential use.

The addition of new homes can be facilitated by the relatively large plot sizes of existing village properties, or the existence of vacant lots in villages which, through earlier depopulation or failure to achieve expected growth, have not reached maximum residential density. The latter are characteristic of regions in North America such as the Middle West and Ontario where villages and small towns were laid out and subdivided by private speculators and public authorities. In many cases, the plan for settlement included far more lots than could be occupied in an agricultural economy. Nowadays 'the availability of this type of land within the serviced area of the village and in areas usually designated for residential use has been an important attraction for urbanites seeking a rural residence' (Bunce 1982, p. 165). The conversion of existing buildings to residential use has been made possible by the abandonment of buildings (farms, school-houses, windmills, churches) in many rural areas through depopulation or agricultural change, thus creating a stock of relatively low-cost habitation (Lewis 1972).

The most ubiquitous form of new rural residential development within Great Britain has been the residential subdivision or housing estate, located as an adjunct to an existing rural settlement within commuting distance of an urban workplace. These dormitory settlements, growing almost solely because of outmigration from central cities, have been termed metropolitan villages – tentatively defined by Masser and Stroud (1965) as settlements where more than one in five of the workforce is employed in towns and cities. Completely new villages like New Ash Green in Kent (Bray 1981), Harriston in Cumbria (Hornberry 1980) or Martlesham Heath in Suffolk (Parker 1979) are rare.

Metropolitan villages

As a result of several factors, including early planning restrictions, the massive size of the workforce, and the larger proportion of affluent people for whom travelling costs are less important, there are more metropolitan villages around London, both inside and outside the green belt, than around any other world city. Pahl's (1965b) discussion of such villages in Hertfordshire and the accounts of metropolitan village development around many other major cities, such as Leicester (Elias and Scotson 1965), Reading (Crichton 1965), Nottingham (Thorns 1968), Bristol, (Bracey 1964), Worcester (Radford 1970) and Glasgow (Pacione 1980), allow some general conclusions to be drawn on the social and spatial characteristics of the metropolitan village. These have been summarized by Connell (1974).

Spatially, the key characteristic of the metropolitan village is its accessibility to a centre of urban employment. Villages that were on railway lines, particularly those radiating from London, were in the process of becoming residential dormitories before the war and, except where green belt planning restrictions constrained postwar development, most of these villages (such as East Horsley in Surrey and Radlett in Hertfordshire) are now small towns. The railway remains the most important commuter link with London, with the subregional distribution of house prices often reflecting ease of access to these transport arteries. In the remainder of the country the car is the chief means of commuting and has brought an increasing number of previously remote villages into the daily urban system (Plane 1981).

Differential accessibility is not the sole determinant of whether a place becomes a metropolitan village. Planning restrictions may prohibit residential expansion for a variety of reasons including a wish to preserve the rural landscape or the character of a traditional village; or concern over the absence and cost of providing essential services and infrastructure such as schools, water and sewers. Metropolitan villages are physically distinct from suburbia and this separation is usually maintained by planning restrictions designed to prevent urban sprawl. The potential commuter's image of 'rural life' also affects the demand to settle in particular villages. Those that are bucolic, picturesque and surrounded by pleasant countryside are most sought after whereas villages in less attractive settings such as the mining areas of Northeast England, West Central Scotland or South Wales are avoided by urban commuters. There is generally an absence of industry in metropolitan villages. Finally, spatial variations in property ownership, which condition the release of land for development, also influence whether a village undergoes population growth or not (Kendall 1963).

The social and demographic characteristics of the metropolitan village are, at least partly, determined by the housing situation. There are essentially three tenure types:

(1)   local authority areas where accommodation is owned and allocated by local

government according to such criteria as length of residence, workplace, household size, and present housing situation;

(2)   privately owned housing, often flats, rented to individuals at free market rents;

(3)   privately owned or mortgaged housing.

Within metropolitan villages, however, the second category is rarely present although a parallel category of tied accommodation may exist where housing is rented or given free to an individual and his family as long as he performs a specified job. Of the two basic types of housing present, privately owned housing has always existed but only in the present century has the sale and resale of housing become a major service industry, with the growth of estate agents and building societies. During the depression of the 1930s the real cost of building fell as did building society interest rates with a significant proportion of new housing being built in the earliest metropolitan villages. 'Hence, before the Second World War, almost all railway stations within 30 km of central London, and many stations at lesser distances from provincial cities, were surrounded by growing estates of high quality residential accommodation' (Connell 1974, p. 84). In the postwar era development beyond the green belts has continued steadily. An important consideration for the social structure of metropolitan villages is that the demand for such housing is not confined locally but is both regional (e.g. stemming from a central city) and national (e.g. as a result of job relocation).

The local authority housing system is markedly different. Following the Housing, Town Planning Act 1919, local authorities were empowered to build houses. In the rural areas small estates were built, usually outside the old village, and these became a distinctive part of the village morphology. Local authorities have almost complete autonomy in selecting tenants for their housing; the only statutory provision being that they should give 'reasonable preference to persons who are occupying unsanitary or overcrowded conditions' (Cullingworth 1966, p. 121). In general single persons are usually excluded as are those with annual incomes above a prescribed maximum. These two discrete housing systems operate in parallel and because of the low rate of mobility between them the spatial distribution of housing closely reflects the social differentiation within the settlement.

Characteristically there are three distinctive morphological units in the metropolitan village (Figure 10.1):

(1)   the old village centre sometimes with parish church and a cluster of old houses often, in England, arranged around a green;

(2)   the local authority housing estate built as a distinctive unit usually separate from the old centre;

(3)   the more recent estates of modern postwar housing catering mainly for commuters.

Rarely are the three of equal spatial extent. In the most recent metropolitan villages the first two types will be dominant; in the oldest, where commuting is well established, modern private houses predominate.

Within the metropolitan village the great divider, in both a social and spatial sense,

Figure 10.1 The morphology of a typical metropolitan village, Milton of Campsie, Strathclyde.

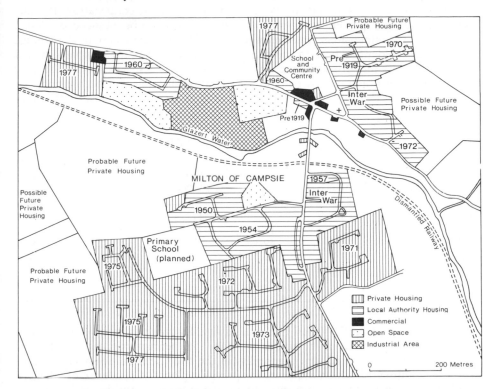

is class. Thus Pahl (1965b, p. 8) contended that 'it is class, rather than commuting characteristics alone, which is the most important factor in promoting change in the social structure of villages in the rural/urban fringe of metropolitan regions'. The main social characteristics which reflect the housing dichotomy are, briefly, that council house tenants tend to work locally, earn wages below the national average, and move house within the geographically constrained local authority system at different stages of their life-cycle. In contrast, owner-occupiers mostly work in the nearest city, earn salaries above the national average, and are free to live in any area within commuting distance of their workplace. Thorns (1968, p. 163) in a study of 11 villages around Nottingham found that for farmworkers 'the village is the centre of their lives. They are often born within a few miles of where they now live. They are restricted in outlook and their involvement outside the village area.' For the middle class residents 'their sphere of associations and contacts is wider than the village community which is seen largely as a dormitory and a place to spend the weekend'.

A detailed discussion of the two communities within a metropolitan village is provided by a study of the differential quality of life in Milton of Campsie, a commuter settlement of 3,000 inhabitants on the edge of the Clydeside conurbation (Pacione 1980). The two groups were readily differentiated along a number of social, economic and behavioural dimensions. In terms of residential history, for example, the average private householder had been in the village for just under 4 years, compared with a mean of 28 years for council house tenants. This greater association with the local area was further illustrated by comparing migration distances for both groups. As Table 10.1 indicates, 85.0 percent of council tenants were either born in Milton of

Table 10.1   *Migration distances of householders in Milton of Campsie*

Place of origin	Private households Number	(%)	Council households Number	(%)	Total Number	(%)
Village-born	0	0	17	37.0	17	14.3
Within 5 miles	13	17.8	22	47.8	35	29.4
Within 20 miles	26	49.3	3	6.5	39	32.8
Scotland	9	12.3	0	0	9	7.6
Great Britain	12	16.4	3	6.5	15	12.6
Other	3	4.2	1	2.2	4	3.3

Campsie or came from less than five miles away. By contrast, none of the private house-owners were born in the village and only 18.0 percent originated within the local area. The differential spatial mobility of the two communities is vividly portrayed in Figure 10.2 which indicates the previous places of residence of villagers. While the majority of local authority tenants came from within five miles, private householders had moved into the village from places as far away as East Anglia, Devon and the south coast of England. The factor of differential mobility was also evident in the daily movements to work. While two-thirds of council house residents worked within two miles of their homes, only 10.0 percent of private householders did so. The great majority commuted to work in Glasgow; with a further 22.0 percent travelling each day to other locations in the Greater Glasgow area. These journey patterns reflected the disproportionate distribution of car ownership in the village – while only one in three council households owned a car (compared with a regional average of 37.0 percent), 95.0 percent of private households had at least one car. The contrast in spatial extent of each community's activity space was also demonstrated by the locations of shopping centres visited, with 82.0 percent of council households shopping only in the village itself or in the town of Kirkintilloch, two miles away. Overall, the council householders cited only four other shopping destinations in addition to the village, while the more mobile private household group visited eleven other shopping centres. These spatial and behavioural differences in both the lifestyle and outlook of the two community groups were clear reflections of the village's socio-economic structure (Table 10.2).

The divisive nature of social class within the village was most clearly underlined

Figure 10.2 Previous places of residence for the population of Milton of Campsie.

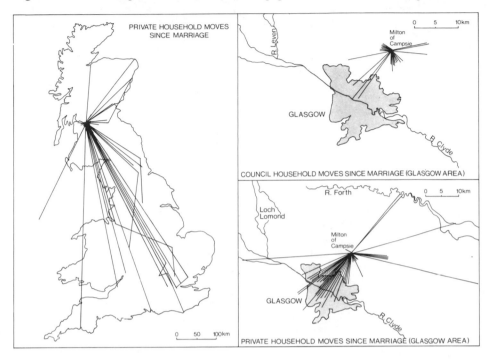

by household activity patterns with respect to the discretionary activity of visiting friends. Figure 10.3 indicates the linkages between households which engaged in social visits. The definite barriers between the two communities are strikingly apparent and, as Table 10.3 shows, only 5.0 percent of private households and 7.0 percent of council households had social activity patterns which transgressed the social class boundaries within the village. This pattern of socio-spatial segregation was also clearly revealed by the distribution of perceived neighbourhoods. As Figure 10.4 indicates, a number of general boundaries emerged from the superimposition of individual perceived neighbourhood areas. The dominant edges were formed by two

Table 10.2 *Socio-economic structure in Milton of Campsie*

Social class	Strathclyde region (1971)	Milton of Campsie (1977)		
		All households	Private	Council
I	10.3	17.3	25.7	0
II	36.1	31.8	39.2	16.7
III	28.2	42.7	32.4	63.9
IV	14.0	4.6	2.7	8.3
V	11.4	3.6	0	11.1

Figure 10.3 Household linkages: social activities in Milton of Campsie.

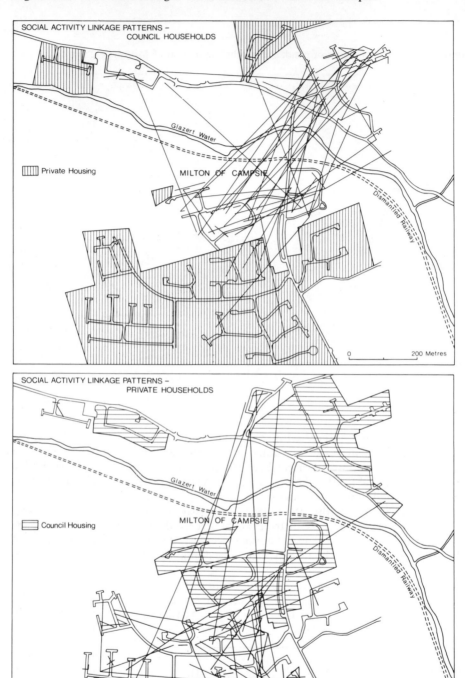

Table 10.3   *Social activity patterns (all residents of households) in Milton of Campsie*

	Private households Number	(%)	Council households Number	(%)	Total Number	(%)
1. Within street	35	32.4	18	24.7	53	29.3
2. Within class	31	28.7	43	58.9	74	40.9
3. Across class groups	5	4.6	5	6.8	10	5.5
4. Outside village	37	34.3	7	9.6	44	24.3

main elements, namely (a) major roads and, most significantly, (b) boundaries between areas of different social status.

Although the social gap within metropolitan villages may close with time, such evidence clearly questions the view of the Countryside Review Committee (1977, p. 9) that 'rural communities have always tended to be close knit; even now villages are places where everyone knows everybody else and individuals count'. Furthermore, in some parts of the country there is evidence for intensification of the process of rural gentrification (defined as an increase in the proportion of settlement population in socio-economic groups I and II; with a figure of 40.0 percent indicative of a significant degree of gentrification). In a study of 12 villages in pressured (South Nottinghamshire) and remote (North Norfolk) rural areas Parsons (1980) found that 7 showed signs of significant gentrification (Table 10.4). As postulated, 4 of the 5 villages with the highest degrees of social imbalance (i.e. more than 50.0 percent of the population in socio-economic groups I and II were in South Nottinghamshire – an area which lies within local commuting distance of a number of large urban areas including Nottingham and Leicester.

Although it may be an exaggeration to describe an atmosphere of 'latent hostility' (Connell 1974, p. 87) between the two main population groups, it is true that while the metropolitan village exists for some people as a rather pleasant and remote suburb, for others it remains a place of work and residence with a conspicuous absence of social services and amenities. Thus in Milton of Campsie, as Figure 10.5 shows, the positive attributes referred to by private householders centred upon the notion of 'the peace and quiet of rural life' (71.0 percent of respondents). Proximity to the city, the major place of work, was mentioned by 13.0 percent of this group. The council house residents also displayed a strong preference for the village lifestyle and the rural surroundings but, significantly, these were closely followed by a well-defined appreciation of the friendly 'community spirit' (26.0 percent). When faced with the task of listing any negative aspects of living in Milton of Campsie, almost one-third of the council house respondents stated that there were none, but only 15.0 percent of newcomers could find no fault with the village. The disadvantages identified by each group closely mirrored their individual outlook and behaviour. Private householders found the lack of facilities such as a doctor or chemist, the rural bus service, and the poor range of shops, a major irritation. Council households also recognized these deficiencies but emphasized the lack of social and recreational opportunities in the

Figure 10.4 The cognitive division of space in Milton of Campsie.

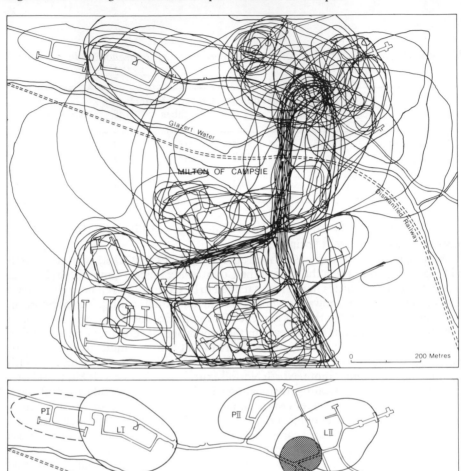

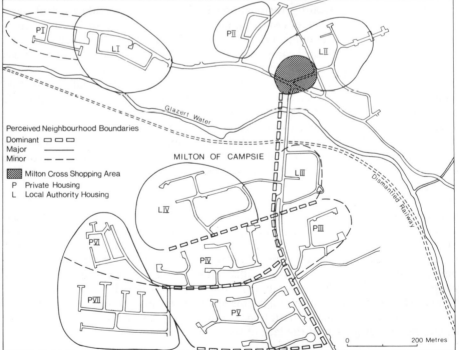

Table 10.4   *Socio-economic structure of selected villages in South Nottinghamshire and North Norfolk*

Village	Socio-economic class (%)							Class
	I	II	III	IV	V	VI	VII	I + II
South Nottinghamshire								
Barton in Fabis	15.0	15.0	0.0	10.0	60.0	0.0	0.0	30.0
East Bridgford	27.3	15.2	24.2	12.1	9.1	9.1	3.1	42.5
East Leake	9.4	25.5	23.6	21.7	16.0	1.9	1.0	34.9
Kinoulton	31.8	22.7	18.2	4.5	22.7	0.0	0.0	54.5
Normanton on Soar	25.0	30.0	5.0	25.0	15.0	0.0	0.0	55.0
Thoroton	19.2	23.1	7.7	23.1	26.9	0.0	0.0	42.3
Wysall	55.0	25.0	5.0	5.0	10.0	0.0	0.0	80.0
North Norfolk								
Brinton	41.2	11.8	0.0	23.5	23.5	0.0	0.0	53.0
Fakenham	12.3	9.2	7.7	35.4	27.6	3.1	4.6	21.5
Great Ryburgh	20.0	20.0	0.0	40.0	20.0	0.0	0.0	40.0
Sharrington	15.4	0.0	15.4	23.1	30.8	15.4	0.0	15.4
Stiffkey	12.5	25.0	6.2	12.5	31.3	12.4	0.0	37.5

Source: Parsons (1980)

village. Clearly, the choice of factors and the differential emphasis each community group placed on the advantages and disadvantages of life in the village provided an overt statement of their subjective views on the general question of what constitutes an acceptable lifestyle.

The residential location decision

The attractions for exurbanites moving to dormitory settlements beyond the urban fringe are well documented (Pryor 1969; Connell 1974; Hovinen 1977; Blackwood and Carpenter 1978; Stevens 1980), with particular importance attached to the superior natural environment (peace, quiet, fresh air, space, recreational opportunities), housing available (cost, style, size, privacy), and ease of access to employment and services (schools, shopping, church, etc.) and to other members of the migrants' social reference group. Clearly, 'noneconomic' factors may be of importance in migration decisions. This raises the question of the extent to which households may actually sacrifice income in order to move out from the city. Although this has not been systematically studied, Ploch (1978) reports that about half of recent inmigrants to Maine did give up income in the migration process. Particular attention has been given to the relative importance of the costs of commuting and the perceived attractions of rural living. The role of each set of factors in the residential location decision process is imperfectly understood. Individual decision-making theories of household location fall broadly into two major groups. In the first

Figure 10.5 Positive and negative characteristics of life in the village of Milton of Campsie, by social group.

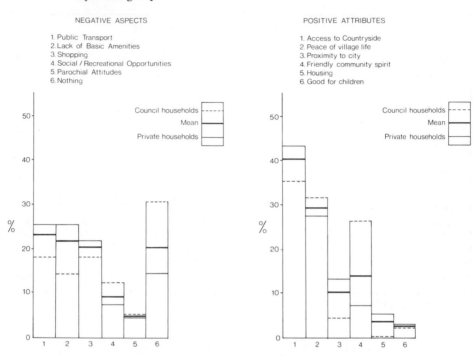

type of model (Alonso 1960; Wingo 1961; Hoover 1968) journey to work costs (measured in money and/or time) are 'traded-off' against housing costs (location rent). The second approach consists of theories which stress choice of house, area and environmental preferences as the principal determinants of residential location; the role of 'journey to work costs' is relegated to that of an outer constraint (Richardson 1971).

In the conventional trade-off theory it is usually assumed that: (a) households substitute travel costs for housing costs and that the rate of substitution is governed by each household's preference for high or low density (urban or rural) living; (b) jobs are centralized; (c) travel costs are an increasing function of distance from the employment centre; (d) site rents (or price per unit of land) decline with distance; and (e) the income elasticity of demand for space is positive. It is argued that the most important aspect of the location decision is the space/access trade-off, and it is here that commuting costs are of relevance (Kain 1962; Winger 1970).

Richardson (1971) contends that even if there is a marked inverse relationship between site costs and travel costs this does not necessarily support trade-off behaviour by households. He rejects the trade-off theory of residential location and proposes an alternative 'behavioural' model. In this he argues that for owner-occupiers housing preferences and financial constraints (e.g. income, mortgage availability) are the primary independent variables and that journey to work costs are at best a secondary factor, and in many cases are determined residually with no explanatory significance. Others supporting this interpretation include Stegman (1969, p. 27) who observes that with the decentralization of work and shopping to the periphery of the American city 'large numbers of suburban families do not have to trade-off accessibility for savings in location rent; they can have both'. Lansing and Barth (1964) found that when costs take the form of a transport input, such as commuting costs, there is evidence that many households are unaware of the total costs of car use or have never considered the cost at all. They concluded that access was relatively unimportant to most people and that location decisions reflect other kinds of preference such as privacy, cost and type of dwelling. O'Farrell and Markham (1975, p. 72) directly investigated people's appreciation of commuting costs in the Dublin conurbation and found that the majority of car-owning commuters had never considered the costs of travelling to work and that 'few, if any, house location decisions are made on the basis of a trade-off, however subjective, between commuting costs and house price. As the majority of car owners are largely indifferent to the magnitude of daily travel costs, this means that within the distances considered in this study (up to 18 miles from the city centre) the friction of space effect is exerting little or no influence upon residential decisions on the periphery of the urban area.' The actual distances involved will, of course, vary from city to city but the general principle is clear. Moreover, there is ample evidence that commuting fields are increasing progressively. Behavioural analyses of this kind, therefore, clearly support the Richardson-type model in preference to the trade-off theory of Alonso and Wingo.

Commuting and the daily urban system

The importance of daily travel from rural residence to central city job, as postulated in the classical studies of the metropolitan village phenomenon, is changing. While such movements remain the most important type of daily journey to work in the UK, in the USA there is evidence to suggest that this 'inward flow' is of decreasing importance, as a consequence of the weakening nodality of many large urban regions (US Department of Commerce 1979). Plane (1981) has identified five types of commuting movement (Figure 10.6):

Figure 10.6 Typology of commuting flows.

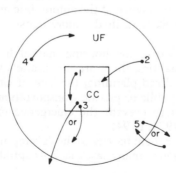

Source: Plane (1981)

Type 1: 'within central city' movements are trips made by workers who both live and work within the city's legal boundaries.
Type 2: 'inward commuting' encompasses both the traditional commuters from suburbs and metropolitan villages to central cities, plus those workers living in one central city who commute to another.
Type 3: 'reverse commuting' is composed of workers residing in the central city who work anywhere outside that city's boundaries.
Type 4: 'lateral commuting' takes place within the commuter range of the city but both workplace and residence locations are outside the central city.
Type 5: 'cross commuting' flows are those entering or leaving the central city's commuter zone, meaning that only the workplace or residence is located inside the urban field.

Application of this typology to data for 28 cities in New England revealed that 'within central city, inward and reverse flows together account for a surprisingly low percentage of the total commuting for any individual urban field. Considerably larger numbers of work trips are classified as Type 4 or Type 5 flows' (Plane 1981, p. 185). These findings are of significance despite the fact that the revealed patterns are influenced by national factors such as the large-scale decentralization of population and employment from American cities, and the choice of a densely settled study area in which the vast majority of the population live within the daily urban system of more than one major city.

As Connell (1974, p. 94) observes, 'the metropolitan village is essentially a product of the stringent planning regulations that have limited urban growth around the outer edge of the continuous built-up area of large cities. Since neither of these conditions occur to the same extent elsewhere, the phenomenon is primarily British; yet around many other cities of the Developed World there are incipient examples and parallel forms.' In North America planning regulations to curb urban sprawl are less well developed than in the UK and a combination of creeping suburbia and the coalescence of small-scale rural housing developments gradually engulfs the countryside around the cities. There is little organizational control over this and the high prices paid for land to be developed tend to weaken any informal opposition to this urbanization process. The fact that owner-occupation is the norm outside the American central city, together with the more general absence of old villages and hamlets, reduces the likelihood of social friction between established residents and newcomers. Finally the dominance of the automobile and highway permits a more sprawling form of suburbia than in the more densely settled metropolitan areas around British cities.

In Eastern Europe, where the housing market has been nationalized in an attempt to remove inequalities, there are no parallels with Western metropolitan villages. 'Rigorous centralized planning, the lack of capital for private-enterprise housing and inadequate public or private transportation beyond the city boundary are more than sufficient to prevent the emergence of this essentially capitalist phenomenon' (Connell 1974, p. 94).

In the Third World the main barrier to the development of metropolitan villages is not rigorous planning nor, in many cases, lack of capital, but the general conception that the 'good life' is to be found in the city (Rao 1970). In most rural villages there is complete absence of even the most rudimentary service provisions and in such a situation the 'metropolitan village' is far from being an ideal goal for the emerging middle class.

References

ALONSO, W. (1960) A theory of the urban land market, *Papers and Proceedings of the Regional Science Association* 6, 149–57.

BLACKWOOD, L. and CARPENTER, E. (1978) The importance of anti-urbanism in determining residential preferences and migration patterns, *Rural Sociology* 43(1), 31–47.

BRACEY, H. E. (1964) *Neighbours*. London: Routledge and Kegan Paul.

BRAY, C. (1981) *New Villages Case Studies: New Ash Green* Working Paper 51. Oxford: Polytechnic, Department of Town Planning.

BUNCE, M. (1982) *Rural Settlement in an Urban World*. London: Croom Helm.

CONNELL, J. (1974) The metropolitan village. *In* J. H. Johnston *Suburban Growth*. London: Wiley, 77–100.

COUNTRYSIDE REVIEW COMMITTEE (1977) *Rural Communities* Topic Paper No. 1. London: HMSO.

CRICHTON, R. (1965) *Commuters Village*. London: David and Charles.

CULLINGWORTH, J. B. (1966) *Housing and Local Government in England and Wales*. London: Allen and Unwin.

ELIAS, N. and SCOTSON, J. (1965) *The Established and the Outsider*. London: Cass.

GANS, H. J. (1969) *The Levittowners*. New York: Random House.

HOOVER, E. (1968) The evolving form and organisation of the metropolis. *In* H. S. Perloff and W. L. Wingo *Issues in Urban Economics*. Baltimore: Johns Hopkins Press, 237–84.

HORNBERRY, J. (1980) Harriston: a village reborn, *Architects Journal* 9th January, 78–88; 16th January, 130–9.

HOVINEN, G. (1977) Leapfrog developments in Lancaster County, *Professional Geographer* 29, 194–9.

KAIN, J. (1962) The journey to work as a determinant of residential location, *Papers and Proceedings of the Regional Science Association* 9, 137–60.

KENDALL, D. (1963) Portrait of a disappearing English village, *Sociologia Ruralis* 3, 157–65.

LANSING, J. and BARTH, N. (1964) *Residential Location and Urban Mobility*. Ann Arbor, Michigan: University of Michigan Institute for Social Research.

LEWIS, G. (1972) Population change in northern New England, *Annals of the Association of American Geographers* 62, 307–22.

MASSER, F. and STROUD, D. (1965) The metropolitan village, *Town Planning Review* 36, 111–24.

O'FARRELL, P. and MARKHAM, J. (1975) Commuting costs and residential location, *Tijdschrift voor Economische en Sociale Geografie* 66, 66–74.

PACIONE, M. (1980) Differential quality of life in a metropolitan village, *Transactions of the Institute of British Geographers*. N.S. 5(2), 185–206.

PACIONE, M. (1981) (Ed) *Urban Problems and Planning in the Developed World*. London: Croom Helm.

PAHL, R. (1965a) Class and community in English commuter villages, *Sociologia Ruralis* 5, 5–23.

PAHL, R. (1965b) *Urbs in Rure* Geographical Paper No. 2. London: London School of Economics.

PARKER, C. (1979) Martlesham Heath village, *Architects Journal* 5th September, 485–503.

PARSONS, D. (1980) *Rural Gentrification* Department of Geography Research Paper. University of Sussex.

PLANE, D. (1981) The geography of urban commuting fields, *Professional Geographer* 33, 182–8.

PLOCH, L. (1978) The reversal in migration patterns – some rural development consequences, *Rural Sociology*, 43(2), 293–303.

PRYOR, R. (1969) Urban fringe residence: motivation and satisfaction in Melbourne, *Australian Geographer* 11, 148–58.

RADFORD, E. (1970) *The New Villager*. London: Cass.

RAO, M. S. (1970) *Urbanization and Social Change: a study of a rural community on a metropolitan fringe*. New Delhi: Orient Longmans.

RICHARDSON, H. (1971) *Urban Economics*. Harmondsworth: Penguin.

STEGMAN, M. (1969) Accessibility models and residential location, *Journal of the American Institute of Planners* 35, 22–9.

STEVENS, J. (1980) The demand for public goods as a factor in the non metropolitan migration turnaround. *In* D. L. Brown and J. W. Wardwell *New Directions in Urban–Rural Migration*. New York: Academic Press, 115–35.

THORNS, D. (1968) The changing system of rural stratification, *Sociologia Ruralis* 8, 161–78.

US DEPARTMENT OF COMMERCE (1979) The journey to work in the United States 1975, *Current Population Reports, Special Studies, P-23, No. 99*. Washington: US Government Printing Office.

WALKER, G. (1977) Social networks and territory in a commuter village, *Canadian Geographer* 21, 339–50.

WINGER, A. (1970) The visibility of commuting costs and residential location, *Environment and Planning* 2, 89–94.

WINGO, L. (1961) *Transportation and Urban Land*. Baltimore: Johns Hopkins Press.

11 Seasonal suburbanization

The dispersal of the town into the country is aided and abetted by the phenomenon of seasonal suburbanization. This refers to the occupation of rural second homes by nonlocals whose primary residence is normally urban-based. Although such countryside retreats existed in ancient Egypt and classical Rome, and small numbers were found around North American and European cities in the eighteenth and nineteenth centuries, these were confined to the wealthier sections of society. As Clout (1974, p. 102) comments, 'the popularization and proliferation of second homes is essentially a post-1945 phenomenon'. This has resulted from a combination of factors including the ability to allocate part of one's income for nonessential items; sufficient time away from work; and increased personal mobility due to improvements in public and private transportation. Specific motives for acquiring a second home include: (a) the desire of many urban-dwellers to engage in rural recreation, (b) a wish to invest one's savings in property, (c) to provide a place for retirement, or (d) the status of owning a country cottage.

In 1966 Wolfe, with reference to Ontario, was able to state that 'going up to the cottage' is the accepted practice of many families. Ten years later the same conclusion could be applied to most of Western Europe as well as to many parts of Britain. Similar trends have been reported in Australia (Murphy 1977) and in parts of Eastern Europe (Gardavsky 1960, 1977). The temporal distinction between the occupation of primary and secondary residences is contracting and will continue to do so for some people as the working week becomes shorter and the era of telemobility (Berry 1970) lessens the need for daily travel to work. Second homes, therefore, must be regarded not as isolated phenomena but as part of the urban system. Mercer (1970), for example, has argued that second home settlements should be viewed as highly specialized ecological extensions of the city and as part of the city's living space, while Rogers (1977, p. 100) regards them as 'elements in the economy of the city-region'.

Second home development has occurred in three different ways. The first is through the conversion of existing rural buildings. This method is more widespread in Europe than in North America although Lewis (1972) refers to the purchase of abandoned houses in northern New England for second home use. A second form is the individual purpose-built structure set on its own private piece of land. This type of second home is more common in North America than in Europe largely due to the more stringent planning restrictions and land shortages in the latter area. Thirdly, second home estates have been constructed by property development companies, particularly in response to the growth in demand during the 1960s. These large-scale suburban-style developments are common in the US sunbelt areas of Florida and southern California, but are also found in recreational regions further north (Boschken 1975).

Clout (1972) suggests that the extension of the condominium formula from its source area on the American west coast will put the possession of a second home within reach of a growing number of families. This form of development means the common ownership of an area of land by a group of people who have individual possession of their own leisure home but enjoy a share in the grounds and facilities they pay to have provided.

The distribution of second homes

Second homes are widely found throughout Europe and areas of European settlement. In 1970 France was the most important European country in numerical terms with 1,232,000 second homes (Clout 1970), followed by Sweden with 490,000 (Bielckus 1977). Coppock (1977) offers a 'guestimate' of 3 million second homes in Western Europe in 1970, with an additional million in Eastern Europe. Ragatz (1970a) calculated a figure of 3 million for the United States in the same year, while in Canada Baker (1973) suggests a total of 500,000. In addition there are estimated to be approximately 250,000 second homes in Australia (Robertson 1977) with smaller numbers in white areas of South Africa and in New Zealand. According to Coppock (1977, p. 6) 'in all a world total of about ten million would not be an unreasonable estimate'. More significant, however, is the ratio of second homes to all households and here, as Table 11.1 shows, in 1970 Sweden occupied first rank with 22.0 percent of households owning a second home, followed by Norway (17.0 percent), Spain (17.0 percent) and France (16.0 percent). Figures for the English-speaking world are much lower but there is evidence that these have been increasing over the last decade. The second home phenomenon has been studied in most countries of the developed world including France (Clout 1970, 1971; Boyer 1980), Netherlands (Thissen 1978), Belgium (de Wilde 1968), Italy (Ruggieri 1972), Britain (Downing and Dower 1972; Aitken et al. 1977), Scandinavia (Bielckus 1977), Canada (Wolfe 1951), USA (Ragatz 1970a; Clout 1972), and Australia (Marsden 1969; Murphy 1977).

Several reasons may be suggested to explain the national differences in rates of second home ownership. These include:

(1)   Different levels of car ownership and in the quality and density of national highway networks which leads to different levels of personal mobility. Generally, people in North America and Australia travel further to their second homes than Europeans. Clearly, distance travelled also reflects the operation of other factors ranging from personal preferences to the availability of opportunities. Ragatz (1970b) for example, has suggested that long-distance travel in North America reflects the high prices of land closer to cities.
(2)   Differences in the lengths of paid holidays. In France, for example, annual paid holidays of at least one month are the norm.
(3)   Differences in general levels of affluence. Sweden with one of the highest standards of living in the world has the highest proportion of second home owners. This relationship is not perfect, however, and other factors must be employed to explain the low proportion of second homes in West Germany, one of the most prosperous countries of Europe.
(4)   Differences in the popularity of caravans (mobile homes), which provide alternatives to fixed second homes.

Table 11.1   *Second home owners as a percentage of all households in selected countries, 1970*

Sweden	22	Austria	8	Australia	5
Norway	17	Switzerland	8	USA	5
Spain	17	Belgium	7	West Germany	3
France	16	Finland	7	Netherlands	3
Portugal	10	Luxembourg	6	United Kingdom	3
Denmark	10	Italy	5	Ireland	2

Source: Aitken et al. (1977)

(5)   Differences in urban living conditions may also affect the growth of second homes in certain countries. For example, many city dwellers in continental Europe occupy high-density apartment buildings, a lifestyle which may promote a desire to obtain a second home in the country. This is less likely in Britain where urban population densities are generally lower and more houses have gardens attached which provide a small but accessible open space for weekends and leisure time.

Locational analysis

Early attempts to explain the location of second homes concentrated on identifying the physical and, to a lesser extent, human factors underlying observed patterns. Jacobs (1972) found that the distribution of second homes in Denbighshire (North Wales) was influenced by property prices, degree of urbanization, depopulation, the quality of agricultural land, and ease of access to the Merseyside conurbation. Scenic quality, local climate, and the view from a second home have also been shown to be of importance (Carr and Morrison 1972). Particular significance has been attached to the presence of water (Knetsch 1964; Marsden 1969; Bell 1977). Tombaugh (1970) found that of second homes purchased in Michigan, USA after 1952, 55.0 percent were on an inland lake, 24.0 percent on one of the Great Lakes and 10.0 percent on a river or stream. The existing settlement pattern, relative availability of land, and planning policies are also major determinants of second home location. Examples of locally important factors include the decline of the slate industry in parts of Wales (Tuck 1973), the availability of crofting cottages in the Scottish highlands (Ross and Cromarty County Planning Department 1972), and the presence of disused lead-miners' cottages in northeast England (Northumberland County Council 1971).

One of the most frequently cited factors determining second home location is the distance between the primary and secondary residences. This is the motive force of a descriptive model of second home development around the French city of Lyons, referred to by Clout (1974). In this the outermost boundary of second home developments at any date is determined by the distance weekend recreationists could travel in a maximum journey time of one hour. Thus in the horse-drawn carriage era of pre-1914 the ring of second homes reached only 15 km from the city; this distance increasing progressively over time with developments in transport technology so that by the mid 1950s the radius of 'weekend suburbs' extended to a distance of 65 km. A similar evolutionary model has been proposed for Queensland, Australia (Marsden 1969). A static 'period picture' model of this type, however, has a low explanatory power and ignores the processes of change constantly working on urban residential structure. Recast in a dynamic form the model would show how by the early 1950s the built-up suburbs of the city had expanded to absorb the pre-1914 zone of second homes; how the second ring of weekend homes would have been invaded by metro-politan villages as commuters moved out from the city; and how these centrifugal trends would in turn push the current area of second home development further into the rural countryside. Another major drawback of a concentric ring model of this type is that it is based on the unrealistic assumption of a homogeneous periurban environment uniformly endowed with sites for second home development.

The frictional effect of distance also underlies Ragatz's (1970a) schematic dis-tribution of vacation homes (Figure 11.1). 'This whole schematic distribution takes on a pulsating appearance during different seasons of the year as families leave their permanent residence to occupy their vacation home in the hinterland. During the summer, the major central city peak slumps and the minor peaks of vacation home concentrations rise. This appearance usually will be reversed during the winter except in areas suited to winter sports' (Ibid., p. 454). Others have employed a modi-fied version of the gravity model to explain the spatial distribution of second homes.

Figure 11.1 Schematic distribution of population by seasons.

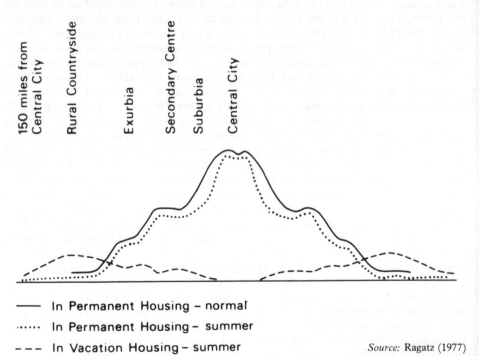

——— In Permanent Housing – normal

······ In Permanent Housing – summer

– – – In Vacation Housing – summer

Source: Ragatz (1977)

Ragatz (1970b) used regression analysis to investigate second home locations, but his major conclusion that the number of second homes in a State is in direct proportion to population and per capita income was hardly unexpected. At least of equal significance was his acknowledgement that 'numerous other variables are related to location. Many of these, especially ones related to recreation and aesthetics, cannot be easily quantified and therefore, are not included in the analysis' (Ibid., p. 123).

Models such as those reviewed are essentially deterministic and largely descriptive and their likelihood of providing a high level of explanation is low, for the basic reason that human behaviour rarely conforms to mechanistic 'natural laws'. Clearly what is required is a probabilistic-behavioural approach in which greater consideration is given to man's ability to make choices within a set of constraints.

One of the most thorough studies of the location of second homes was carried out by Aldskogius (1967, 1969) in central Sweden. He first employed a zonal multiple regression model to analyse the relationship between second homes in the Lake Siljan region and a range of place characteristics assumed to influence the locational decision-making of prospective second home owners. The place characteristics used as independent variables in the regression model were related to relief; presence of water bodies; Lake Siljan, the largest lake in the area and a landscape feature of particular importance; the open agricultural landscape, including seter settlements; accessibility in terms of local road transportation; and access to retail trade establishments. Levels of explanation of up to 70.0 percent were achieved. Using the results of this study Aldskogius (1969) went on to explore some of the problems associated with the building of a simulation model of second home settlement patterns. A basic assumption is that decision-making with respect to a second home for recreational use can be conceptualized as a spatial choice process in which different locations are evaluated by the individual in terms of their 'recreational place utility'. It is also assumed that the decision-maker evaluates recreational place utility in terms of both site attractiveness and the time-cost inconvenience associated with increasing distance between his place of permanent residence and his second home, and that he appreciates the possibilities of substitution between these two components of place utility. Finally he acknowledges that individuals will have imperfect knowledge of spatial variations in recreational place utility within an area and that they will receive or acquire adequate information (e.g. via friends who are already second home owners) only about a limited number of the whole set of alternative locations. Locational decision-making under this type of information constraint will produce a more clustered settlement pattern than would be expected under assumptions of perfect knowledge about existing spatial opportunities. Comparison of the observed distribution of second homes in the study area in 1965 and the mean pattern from five runs of the model revealed a reasonably close correspondence between the two patterns (r = 0.83); the model accounting for about 65.0 percent of the variation in the observed pattern of second home development. Nevertheless Aldskogius recognized that the degree of simplification required to represent the behavioural factors involved cast doubt on the ability of the model to explain the *process* of second home development.

Such a formulation relying heavily on spatial variations in landscape features and containing a built in distance-decay function has considerable value in revealing spatial aspects of second home acquisition, but a number of qualifying factors limit its general applicability.

(1)   In some countries, such as France, a large proportion of second homes are inherited by urbanites from parents or grandparents who lived in the countryside. In the uplands of Herault and the Chartreuse Iservise 45.0 percent and 40.0 percent respectively were inherited (Clout 1971). In such an instance the new owner is not faced with a locational choice per se, but rather with the decision of whether to use the property as a second home or to dispose of it in some other way.

(2)   The choice of location for a second home may be conditioned by social rather than landscape features. These include sentimental attachment to a birthplace and the presence of similar cultural groups, such as French Protestants in southeastern parts of the Massif Central (Clout 1970) or Jewish second home resorts around Toronto (Wolfe 1951).

(3)   Man's ability to modify the landscape (e.g. by flooding valleys to produce lakes) means that an analysis of landscape features at any point in time will not serve as a reliable basis for predicting the sites of second homes in the future.

(4)   Growing numbers of second homes are being constructed on special estates and variations in the desirability of different areas can depend to a large extent on the efforts of real estate developers and advertising companies (Henshall 1977).

(5)   Finally, in many countries the growing pressure for second homes has meant that land use planning controls are becoming more rigorous and will condition future patterns of second home development to a greater degree than in the past.

Burby et al. (1972) have attempted to apply models of urban residential development to simulate the process of vacation home location around two reservoirs in the Appalachians. Their model employs a randomizing procedure in which households are assigned to sites on the basis of supply of land available and its attractiveness for recreational residential use. Prior to programming the simulation model, interviews with reservoir owners, predevelopment landowners, developers and households were undertaken to identify 'pivotal attractiveness factors' (Ibid., p. 430). Practical limitations however meant that several variables had to be deleted from the actual analysis. The most significant of these were landowner characteristics (potentially a key indicator of whether land will be available for second home development) and land prices (a major determinant of the profitability of a site for a developer). In addition information on topography, water and sewerage availability, and zoning was not available for the whole area. A stepwise regression analysis of the 30 remaining measures identified several significant variables influencing 'seasonal shoreline' residential development (as opposed to permanent residential development in the surrounding area). These centred on accessibility to the lake and recreation facilities, and the quality of road access. Though only 20.0 percent of the variance was explained by the regression procedure, the authors judged the results to be acceptable for the purpose of isolating the key variables of site attractiveness to be used in the simulation model. As might be expected from the regression results, the ability of the simulation model to predict development patterns around the two reservoirs was disappointing. One interesting finding, however, was 'a tendency for development at one location to attract future development' (Ibid., p. 436). It was suggested that many of the 'under-allocations' in the model (i.e. where the predicted number of second homes was less than the observed number) could be corrected by recalculating attractiveness indices during the simulation process to take account of this clustering phenomenon. This was precisely the problem of information 'feedback' encountered by Aldskogius (1969).

A regression model was also employed by Thissen (1978) to analyse the distribution of second homes in the Netherlands. Independent variables measured the degree of urbanization; presence of water bodies; presence of forest; level of depopulation; and accessibility to Amsterdam. The final regression equation explained 56.0 percent of the variance and underlined the relative significance of variables related to the notion of recreational place utility (e.g. the presence of water bodies, and the 'rural' character of an area). Forces influencing the supply of second homes, and the distance from permanent residence to second home appeared to play a less important role in this instance. The minor significance of the distance factor may be explained by the small size of the country and the fact that the zone within which second homes occur has been extending rapidly and now covers most of the Netherlands. A strong spatial bias of Amsterdam-based second home owners in the north of the country was attributed to the operation of the 'multiplier effect' identified by Aldskogius (1969), whereby an area, once the process of vacation house settlement has been initiated, continues to attract new settlement more rapidly than other areas which may appear to be as well or better endowed in terms of 'recreational place utility'.

Gerking (1979) sidesteps the difficulties of identifying all the relevant physical and socio-economic factors underlying second home location decisions by developing a model based upon a univariate time series analysis of seasonal residential electricity utility connections in southwestern USA (this type of connection is provided to individuals who do not intend to use electrical services continuously and whose place of use is neither in an incorporated area nor on a farm). Time series analysis permits short-term forecasts of future observations on a particular series to be constructed exclusively from its own past history. Clearly this feature would be advantageous in research situations where the emphasis is on forecasting development rather than on explaining the process of second home development. The unavoidable risk is that numerous factors such as income, land availability, construction costs, and tastes could change, thereby causing second home development to shift away from its past trend, and so reduce the accuracy of forecasts. Nevertheless the evidence presented from Navajo and Apache counties in Arizona suggests that provided these underlying factors are relatively slow to change the time series approach is capable of providing short-term forecasts that are sufficiently accurate to be useful to planners.

Robertson (1977) supports the view that a better understanding of the decision-making process of second home buyers will increase the likelihood of developing successful models of patterns of second home development. He points out that 'second homes are not a homogeneous product' (Ibid., p. 136), being purchased and used for various reasons which themselves may change over time, so that in order to understand the decision process associated with their purchase they must be disaggregated into their various types. He suggests that this may be most effectively accomplished by categorizing second homes according to the utilities sought by prospective buyers, and proposes a framework of the second home decision process (Figure 11.2). Decision-making does not terminate once the second home has been purchased however; rather it is seen as an ongoing process of evaluating utility, the outcome of which results in the retention, alteration or disposal of the property (Figure 11.3). Support for this approach is found in a study of second home owners in the Caribbean (Henshall 1977) where retirement rather than recreation is generally the reason for investment in a second home. In such a case neither accessibility nor the concept of recreational place utility can explain the distribution of second homes; 'differences between territories are perceived in terms not so much of landscape or recreational facilities but rather of the political, fiscal and social advantages of investment in the area, the price of land, and the relative efficiency of local construction firms and rental agents' (Ibid., p. 76).

The complexity of the second home decision-making process is underlined by Ragatz (1977, p. 187) when he recognizes that 'different types of vacation home owners are probably concentrated in unique distributions throughout the schematic cone (Fig. 11.1). These various sectors may be concentrated according to age, income, neighbourhood of permanent home, family size and a series of other variables. Factors such as travel costs (in time and dollars), cost of land, property taxes, availability of certain types of recreational facilities and similarity in family types, all enter into the decision-making patterns of vacation home buyers and hence into the location of their vacation homes.' Ragatz (1977) suggests the components and structural framework of a complex model for predicting the location and occupancy patterns of vacation homes but this has yet to be operationalized.

Local variations in the presence and significance of the host of factors identified as important inputs to the second home location decision suggest that, while standardization of definitions and data collection techniques would aid international comparisons, the most penetrating insights into the locational pattern of second homes may be gained by studies at the regional and local level. Further, given the present state of expertise and the intricacy of the decision-making process it is possible that the utility of sophisticated quantitative modelling techniques may be limited by our inability to measure adequately such important but nebulous concepts as scenic attractiveness.

Social and economic impact of second homes

There are a number of conflicting views on the impact of second homes upon the landscape, upon existing communities, and upon the rural economy. Opponents characterize second homes as a drain on local resources, particularly in terms of housing for local residents; as a force for social and cultural disruption within the local area; and, as far as many purpose-built properties are concerned, as a blot on the landscape. Supporters argue that the owners of second homes bring significant financial benefit to the community by contributing more in rates than they consume in services and by making considerable local purchases. Some of the positive and negative aspects of second home development are summarized in Table 11.2.

In the North American context Ragatz (1970b, p. 126) concluded that 'the nega-

Figure 11.2   Schema of the second home decision process: preownership stage.

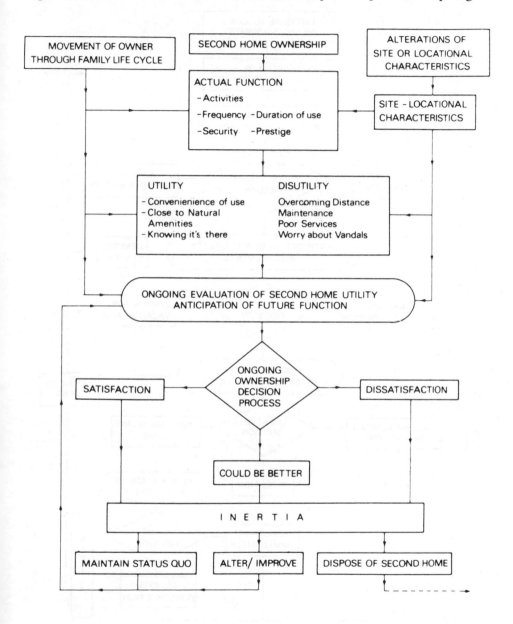

Source: Robertson (1977)

Figure 11.3 Schema of the second home decision process: ownership stage.

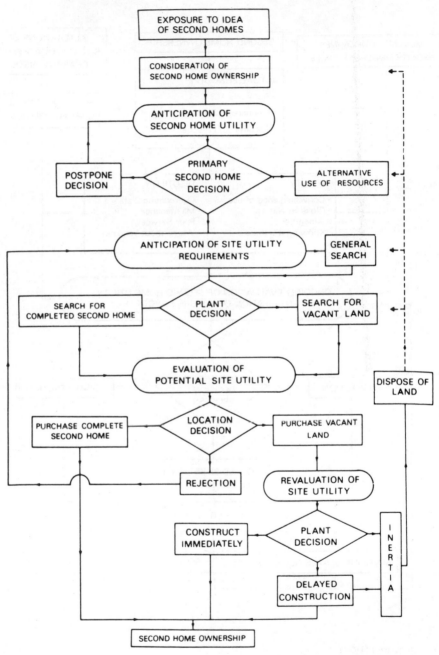

Source: Robertson (1977)

tive implications of a seasonal economy would appear to be secondary to its positive contributions'. This conclusion, however, may not be freely applied to the situation in other parts of the world. As Clout (1974) points out, any cost–benefit assessment would be influenced by the size of the second home colony in relation to the number of full-time residents, the degree of self-containment shown by the visitors, and the health of the local economy. Noneconomic factors are also of importance. In Britain, for example, members of the Welsh Language Society have expressed their opposition to the sale of cottages in Wales for use as second homes by interrupting auction proceedings, while more extreme forms of protest over the perceived loss of regional

Table 11.2 *Positive and negative aspects of second home development*

Advantages	Disadvantages
1. Brings new employment opportunities to areas previously dependent upon a contracting agricultural economy (e.g. building trade, gardening and domestic staff).	1. Concentrations of second homes may require installation of costly sewerage schemes, extension of water and electricity lines to meet peak season demand, and more frequent maintenance of rural roads, with the costs being partly borne by locals.
2. Local restaurants, shops and garages derive new business and additional profits (which may be essential to year-round economic survival).	2. Demand for second homes by urbanites pushes up house prices to the disadvantage of locals.
3. Specialized shops opened to cater for second home owners also benefit local residents.	3. Future schemes for farm enlargement or agricultural restructuring may be hindered by inflated land prices.
4. Property taxes imposed on second homes increase the finances of the local community.	4. Fragmentation of agricultural land.
5. Second home owners make fewer demands on local services since education and other community facilities are not required.	5. Destruction of the 'natural' environment (e.g. soil erosion and stream pollution).
6. Renovation of old buildings improves the appearance of the rural area.	6. Visual degradation may result from poorly constructed or inappropriately located second homes.
7. Rural residents have the opportunity to sell off surplus land and buildings at a high price.	7. Second home construction may distract the local workforce from ordinary house building and maintenance.
8. Contacts with urban-based second home owners can benefit local residents by exposing them to national values and information, broadening outlooks or stimulating self-advancement via migration.	8. The different values and attitudes of second home families disrupt local community life.

identity and Welsh language have included arson and subversive activity (Ashby et al. 1975; Bollom 1978).

The focus of concern over the effects of second home developments varies internationally. In a country like Britain where planning controls upon construction in the countryside have limited the possibilities for new purpose-built developments, the demand for second homes falls on the existing housing stock. Accordingly the main concerns are for the inequitable effects on housing access and the adverse consequences for poorer local people when faced with strong competition from outsiders. Some local authorities in Wales buy existing properties as they come onto the market using powers of compulsory purchase if necessary. These dwellings can then be rehabilitated and let to local people. In other countries, notably in North America and in Australasia where land resources are less of a constraint and where control upon development is far less rigorous, the concerns are more for the environmental excesses of second home growth (such as soil erosion and steam pollution) and in particular for the disadvantages of widespread recreational subdivision of land (Parsons 1972).

Reactions to second homes also tend to vary spatially within countries, between periurban and more remote stretches of countryside. Investigations in France by Clout (1970, 1971) have emphasized the disadvantages which arise when second home owners invade periurban areas such as the Paris Basin. These include: inflated prices which put land and houses beyond the reach of farm workers; the costs of providing additional facilities to cater for the summer peak demand; the fact that second home owners in periurban areas tend to buy their weekend provisions in city supermarkets and buy little in village shops; conflict in demand for limited local utilities, as for example between farmers who need water to irrigate crops and feed livestock and second home owners who wish to wash cars and fill swimming pools; and finally, the contraction of rural settlements as the permanent population declines and basic services disappear, which in turn promotes further depopulation and leads to a cycle of decline. On balance in periurban environments the disadvantages of second home development appear to outweigh the benefits for the resident population. In contrast, in more remote economically backward areas the advantages seem to be greater than the disadvantages. In parts of the Massif Central, for example, where second home owners often stay for long periods each summer, the major positive features identified by local mayors were first the increased trade for local shopkeepers and businesses, and secondly the increased activity and social life in the community.

Planning and prospect

'All the available evidence suggests that the demand for second homes will grow' (Coppock 1977, p. 12). Given that the supply of rural buildings suitable directly or by conversion for second home use is finite, it is likely that in future the demand for this form of leisure will turn into a pressure for new purpose-built accommodation. Clearly it is in the case of new accommodation that planning regulations are most easily enforced. These trends have been identified in North America by Clout (1972, 1974), as well as in Britain where according to Dower (1977, p. 159) 'we may be at a most significant turning point. Until now second homes were mostly converted from existing buildings, without the planning authority having much say. From now on, they may be mainly new built second homes, or newly-sited static caravans or chalets, and the planning authorities may have a significant influence on what is built where, and how many are built.'

Langdalen (1980) has provided a useful summary of the different interest groups involved in second home planning with reference to Norway but the framework can be applied equally well in other countries provided one recognizes that the import-ance of the different actors varies according to national ideologies (Table 11.3). In states where second homes are a long-established form of recreational land use deliberate protective planning has long been necessary to safeguard the countryside whilst meeting the demand for second homes. Sweden, the country with the highest level of second homes in Europe, has imposed a ban on new development within 300 m of the coast or above the tree line, and on schemes which do not include their own waste disposal system or which lack adequate roads and water supply. Similar legislation has been in force in Norway since the mid 1960s. Britain is another country with a strong planning tradition. Here, the development of second homes can be regulated by means of the appropriate sections of the Town and Country Planning Acts and statutory building regulations, together with any restrictions which local authorities wish to impose when granting permission for conversions of properties (other than dwellings) to second home use. While the national proportion of second home owners is still relatively low there are locally significant concentrations of second homes and several planning authorities have formulated planning policies specifically aimed at this form of development (Jacobs 1972; Tuck 1973; Pacione 1979). Landowners, property developers and potential second home owners have a freer rein in other countries but even in the relatively laissez-faire circumstances of the United States Clout (1972, p. 401) argues that 'a strong case could be made for the implementation of urban style systems of land use zoning in country areas to channel second home developments along the least disruptive lines'.

Table 11.3 *Interest groups involved in second home planning and development*

(a) Cabin owners who defend the status quo or attempt to improve it.	(g) Businessmen who supply or service second home builders or users.
(b) Potential purchasers who are looking for a plot or used cabin.	(h) Local population gaining no economic advantage from second home con-struction or use.
(c) Landowners who want to sell or rent plots, or build their own cabins for rental or sale.	(i) Nonprofessional, special interest groups who want plans to conform to their social or environmental ideals.
(d) Landowners who have no desire to rent or sell plots or cabins.	(j) Planners and consultants who advise landowners and communes.
(e) Professionals engaged in second home real estate development.	(k) Commune, county, and federal em-ployees responsible for related plan-ning, or who administer laws which control land use and development.
(f) Professionals engaged in second home construction.	

Source: Langdalen (1980)

In order to avoid the economic, environmental and social difficulties which can result from an influx of second homes into a rural area it may be desirable in future to concentrate all new development into exclusive second home settlements. In areas of high second home densities in Scandinavia and Britain where local planning authorities have directly tackled the question the general opinion has been in favour of a situation in which second homes do not exceed 20.0 percent of the local housing stock and where such dwellings are concentrated in purpose-built holiday villages. In Denmark, for example, future planning aims at more concentrated development of second homes in groups of up to 200 in an attempt to minimize their impact and to make provision of services more economic. The larger the development, however, the closer it comes to resembling the sort of urban environment second home owners seek to avoid.

References

AITKEN, R., DOWNING, P. and DOWER, M. (1977) *Second Homes in Scotland*. Totnes, Devon: Dartington Amenity Research Trust.

ALDSKOGIUS, M. (1967) Vacation home settlement in the Siljan region, *Geografiska Annaler* 49, 69–95.

ALDSKOGIUS, M. (1969) Modelling the evolution of settlement patterns: two studies of vacation house settlement, *Geografiska Regionstudier* 6. Uppsala University.

ASHBY, P., BIRCH, G. and HASLETT, M. (1975) Second homes in north Wales, *Town Planning Review* 46(3), 323–33.

BAKER, W. (1973) *The Nature and Extent of Vacation Home Data Sources and Research in Canada*. Ottawa: Statistics Canada.

BELL, M. (1977) The spatial distribution of second homes: a modified gravity model, *Journal of Leisure Research* 9, 225–33.

BERRY, B. J. L. (1970) The geography of the United States in the year 2000, *Transactions of the Institute of British Geographers* 51, 21–53.

BIELCKUS, C. L. (1977) Second homes in Scandinavia. *In* J. T. Coppock *Second Homes: Curse or Blessing?* Oxford: Pergamon, 35–46.

BOLLOM, C. (1978) *Attitudes and Second Homes in Rural Wales* Social Science Monograph No. 3. Cardiff: University of Wales Press.

BOSCHKEN, H. (1975) The second home subdivision: market suitability for recreational and pastoral use, *Journal of Leisure Research* 7, 63–72.

BOYER, J. (1980) Résidences secondaires et rurbanisation en région Parisienne, *Tijdschrift voor Economische en Sociale Geografie* 71(2), 78–87.

BURBY, R., DONNELLY, T. and WEISS, S. (1972) Vacation home location: a model for simulating the residential development of rural recreation areas, *Regional Studies* 6, 431–9.

CARR, J. and MORRISON, W. (1972) *A Survey of Second Homes in East Monmouthshire* Monmouthshire Studies Report No. 7, Planning Research Group, Enfield: College of Technology.

CLOUT, H. (1970) Social aspects of second home occupation in the Auvergne, *Planning Outlook* 9, 33–49.

CLOUT, H. (1971) Second homes in the Auvergne, *Geographical Review* 61, 530–53.

CLOUT, H. (1972) Second homes in the United States, *Tijdschrift voor Economische en Sociale Geografie* 63, 393–401.

CLOUT, H. (1974) The growth of second home ownership. *In* J. H. Johnson *Suburban Growth*. London: Wiley, 101–27.

COPPOCK, J. T. (1977) *Second Homes: Curse or Blessing*. Oxford: Pergamon.

de WILDE, J. (1968) Résidences secondaires et tourisme de weekend en milieu rural, *Revue Belge de Géographie* 92, 5–55.

DOWER, M. (1977) Planning aspects of second homes. *In* J. T. Coppock *Second Homes: Curse or Blessing?* Oxford: Pergamon 155–64.

DOWNING, P. and DOWER, M. (1972) *Second Homes in England and Wales*. Totnes, Devon: Dartington Amenity Research Trust.

GARDAVSKY, V. (1960) Recreational hinterland of a city, taking Prague as an example, *Acta Universitatis Carolinae: Geographica* 1, 3–29.

GARDAVSKY, V. (1977) Second homes in Czechoslovakia. *In* J. T. Coppock *Second Homes: Curse or Blessing?* Oxford: Pergamon, 63–74.

GERKING, S. (1979) A short term forecasting model for second home construction, *Regional Studies* 13, 259–67.

HENSHALL, J. (1977) Second homes in the Caribbean. *In* J. T. Coppock *Second Homes: Curse or Blessing?* Oxford: Pergamon, 75–84.

JACOBS, C. (1972) *Second Homes in Denbighshire*. Tourism and Recreation Research Report 3, Denbighshire: County Council.

KNETSCH, J. (1964) The influence of reservoir projects on land values, *Journal of Farm Economics* 46, 231–43.

LANGDALEN, E. (1980) Second homes in Norway, *Norsk Geografisk Tidsskrift* 34, 139–44.

LEWIS, G. (1972) Population change in northern New England, *Annals of the Association of American Geographers* 62, 307–22.

MARSDEN, B. (1969) Holiday homescapes of Queensland, *Australian Geographical Studies* 7, 57–73.

MERCER, D. (1970) Urban recreational hinterland, *Professional Geographer* 22, 74–8.

MURPHY, P. (1977) Second homes in New South Wales, *Australian Geographer* 13(5), 310–17.

NORTHUMBERLAND COUNTY COUNCIL (1971) *Second Homes in Northumberland, Summer 1970* Notes on Survey Report to the County Planning Committee. Newcastle: The Author.

PACIONE, M. (1979) Second homes on Arran, *Norsk Geografisk Tidsskrift* 33, 33–8.

PARSONS, J. (1972) Slicing up the open space: subdivisions without homes in northern California, *Erdkunde* 26, 1–8.

RAGATZ, R. L. (1970a) Vacation homes in the northeastern United States, *Annals of the Association of American Geographers* 60, 447–55.

RAGATZ, R. L. (1970b) Vacation housing: a missing component in urban and regional theory, *Land Economics* 46, 118–26.

RAGATZ, R. L. (1977) Vacation homes in rural areas. *In* J. T. Coppock *Second Homes: Curse or Blessing?* Oxford: Pergamon, 181–93.

ROBERTSON, R. (1977) Second home decisions: the Australian context. *In* J. T. Coppock *Second Homes: Curse or Blessing?* Oxford: Pergamon, 119–38.

ROGERS, A. (1977) Second homes in England and Wales. *In* J. T. Coppock *Second Homes: Curse or Blessing?* Oxford: Pergamon, 85–102.

ROSS AND CROMARTY COUNTY PLANNING DEPARTMENT (1972) *Holiday Homes: Progress Report.* Dingwall: The Author.

RUGGIERI, M. (1972) Modificazioni degli abitati Abruzzesi con particolare riferimento all' Abruzzo aquilano, *Bolletino della Societa Geografica Italiana* 10, 487–505.

THISSEN, F. (1978) Second homes in the Netherlands, *Tijdschrift voor Economische en Sociale Geografie* 69(6), 322–32.

TOMBAUGH, L. (1970) Factors influencing vacation home locations, *Journal of Leisure Research* 2, 54–63.

TUCK, C. (1973) *Second Homes* Merioneth Structure Plan Subject Report 17, Merioneth: County Council.

WOLFE, R. (1951) Summer cottages in Ontario, *Economic Geography* 27, 10–32.

WOLFE, R. (1966) Recreation travel: the new migration, *Canadian Geographer* 10, 1–14.

12 Quality of life

The meaning of the phrase 'quality of life' differs a good deal as it is variously used but, in general, it is intended to refer either to the conditions of the environment in which people live (air or water pollution, or poor housing) or to some attribute of people themselves (such as health or educational achievement). A feature of modern society is the paradox of affluence in which concern over quality of life has seemed to increase proportionately with technological progress and increases in income. People in developed countries have come to realize that quality of life is not necessarily a simple function of material wealth. Growing awareness of the social, political and environmental health of a nation has led to the search for indicators, other than those based on Gross National Product, which will more adequately reflect the overall health of a nation and the well-being of its population.

Several studies have attempted to identify the main components of life quality (Pacione 1982). Moser (1970) has suggested that most people, if asked to list the things in life which concern them, would include (1) having enough to eat, (2) being healthy, (3) being housed in a congenial environment, (4) achieving work satisfaction, (5) having sufficient leisure, and (6) personal security against crime. Other researchers have compiled similar lists (Smith 1973; OECD 1973; Knox 1974; Drewnowski 1974; Pacione 1980). These suggest that the basic elements of life quality are related to health, standard of living, housing, education, leisure, mobility, availability of services, and the social and physical environment. The sum total of these 'life concerns' adds up to the quality of life, although it must be remembered that the particular value or weight attached to each of the components varies from person to person and between social groups.

Situations characterized by low levels of life quality have been labelled 'deprived', and investigation of conditions at the disadvantaged end of the quality of life spectrum forms an area of particular concern in contemporary human geography. Central to the concept of deprivation is 'the idea of agreed standards for the provision of services and facilities against which the degree of disadvantage can be measured' (McLoughlin 1981, p. 31). In short, deprivation exists when needs which society feels should be satisfied are not met. Multiple deprivation occurs when two or more disadvantaged conditions coincide. In such circumstances it is not just the specific problems of unemployment, poor housing or lack of facilities that are of concern but the combination of these and other problems and the ways in which they act together to limit the range of opportunity open to individuals.

Since urban and rural deprivation are manifestations of the same forces emanating from the dynamic of late-industrial capitalism (Moseley 1980) they exhibit similar types of social problems. As Figure 12.1 illustrates, both involve high levels of unemployment, low wages and restricted job opportunities, stemming from local economic stagnation. These problems lead in turn to an erosion of community spirit and, eventually, to selective depopulation, leaving behind the aged and the socially

Figure 12.1 The overlap of urban and rural deprivation.

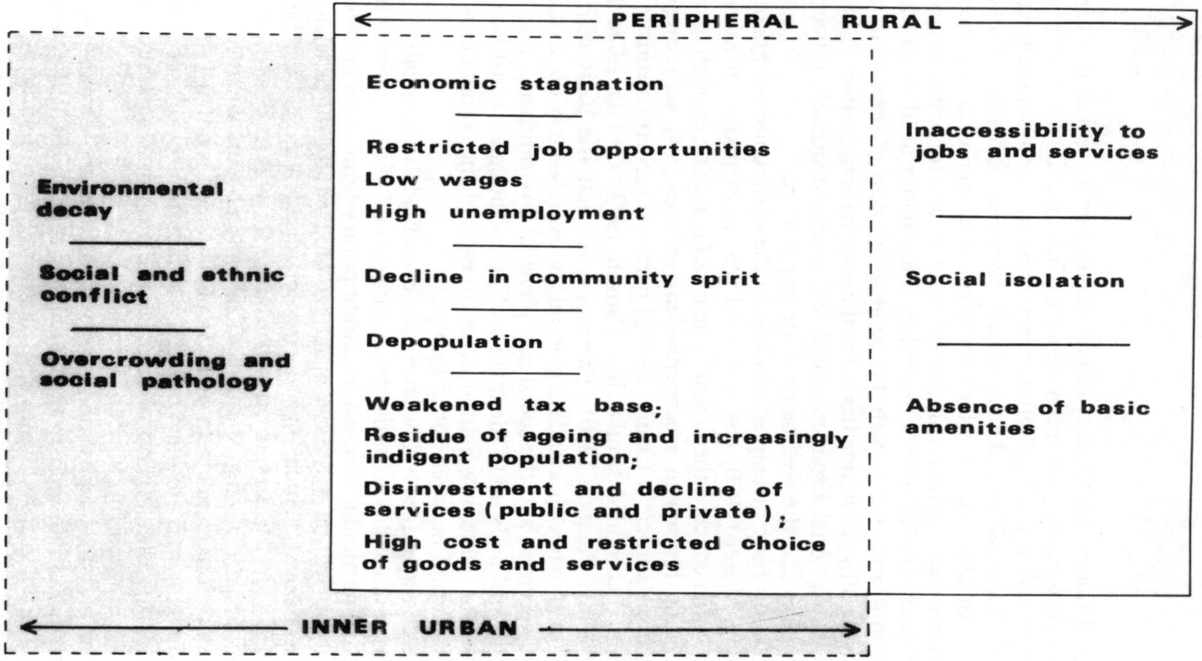

PERIPHERAL RURAL

Inaccessibility to jobs and services

Social isolation

Absence of basic amenities

Economic stagnation

Restricted job opportunities

Low wages

High unemployment

Decline in community spirit

Depopulation

Weakened tax base;

Residue of ageing and increasingly indigent population;

Disinvestment and decline of services (public and private);

High cost and restricted choice of goods and services

INNER URBAN

Environmental decay

Social and ethnic conflict

Overcrowding and social pathology

Source: Knox and Cottam (1981a)

and economically less competent who become trapped in the worst stock of both private and public housing submarkets. At the same time privately organized facilities and services decline or disappear, while public sector services struggle with the dilemma of an increasingly indigent population and a progressively smaller local tax base. There are also, however, important differences in the nature of urban and rural deprivation, stemming mainly from basic contrasts in the physical and social environments. Thus, whereas the fundamental dimensions of urban deprivation are associated with problems of environmental decay, class and ethnic conflict, over-crowding, delinquency, criminality and social disorganization, deprived rural areas suffer more from the problems of inaccessibility, social isolation, and the lack of a threshold population large enough to attract and maintain even the most basic village services and facilities. Clearly, while there are structural similarities between urban and rural deprivation, the latter is differentiated by its particular geographic milieu.

McLoughlin (1981) underlines the fundamental distinction between deprived places and deprived people. He observes that deprivation affects individuals and/or groups in society whose personal circumstances put them at a disadvantage wherever they live. However, the distribution of opportunities, services and facilities over space not only places such individuals or groups at a greater disadvantage but also other individuals or groups who might not otherwise be deprived. The effects of locational factors like settlement size and remoteness on levels of living in rural areas have been extensively studied (Rikkinen 1968; Hart and Salisbury 1965; Butler and Fuguitt 1970). It is clear that 'small settlement size and remoteness each bring their own associated problems but where they are combined the likelihood of an individual resident's social and economic opportunities being circumscribed is greatly increased' (Association of County Councils 1979, p. 4). Whether viewed within a centre–periphery or urban–rural dimension it is clear that, in general, residents of peripheral rural areas suffer a greater degree of deprivation than those in areas closer to urban population centres. As Dillman and Tremblay (1977, p. 121) conclude, 'rural areas are worse off than urban areas, and the more rural the area the greater the discrepancy'.

Shaw (1979) and the Association of County Councils (1979) have identified three broad components of rural deprivation:

(1)   Household deprivation stems primarily from the low incomes of rural workers. Clearly, income constitutes a major constraint on the ability of individuals or families to enjoy a reasonable level of living, and in many rural areas there is a par-ticularly high proportion of low-income groups including agricultural workers, the unemployed, the economically inactive and pensioners. These difficulties are re-inforced in many cases by rural housing problems as a result of rising prices in the private market, a limited supply of council housing in some settlements and the decline in the private rented sector. The combined effect of these income and housing factors has been to discriminate against the low-income families who wish to con-tinue living in rural settlements.

(2)   Opportunity deprivation relates to three broad categories of 'opportunity' in the spheres of employment, private sector facilities, and public sector services. Despite

the introduction of small manufacturing firms and the expansion of the service sector in recent years, which have replaced some of the jobs lost from agriculture since the Second World War, employment opportunities in rural areas remain severely limited, especially for school leavers and the older members of the work force. Moreover, in times of recession it is the rural areas with their low economic potential and narrow industrial base which are most vulnerable, with rural branch factories generally first to close. The result has been that many rural dwellers are faced with the choice of remaining unemployed, travelling long distances to work, or leaving their home area altogether.

The dispersed distribution of population in rural areas and the large catchment areas which are required to attain the threshold population to support certain fixed facilities, such as a school, doctor's surgery or shop, mean that many people live a considerable distance from these services. Some services are not available at all in rural areas, and many of those which are available provide only a limited range of service in comparison with their urban counterparts. In addition, the rural dweller pays a high price for food and has additional expenses to incur in order to obtain a similar standard of service to that generally available to urbanites.

(3)   Mobility deprivation is of paramount importance. The elderly, young children, teenagers, mothers at home, and the infirm, as well as the poor all tend to be disadvantaged if they lack access to a car, given the general decline in rural public transport services. Collectively these groups comprise the majority of the rural population. Although rising car ownership has increased the mobility of some sectors of the community, it has also undermined public transport provision and the viability of many village services. The distance from rural opportunities, whether measured in terms of time or cost, has a major effect on the ability or ease with which rural dwellers can benefit from the services provided. Rural residents often face the choice of bearing additional costs in order to avail themselves of opportunities or else of forgoing these opportunities.

The combined effect of these household, opportunity and mobility factors is to create a complex suite of problems for significant groups resident in rural areas. One reason for the current concern with rural deprivation is that present trends 'seem set to polarise the rural population broadly into two groups: the relatively affluent and the disadvantaged' (Association of County Councils 1979, p. 2).

Spatial variations in quality of life

The realization that 'inequalities may be exacerbated by geographical location' (Howes 1979, p. 82) has focused attention on spatial variations in quality of life and on the unequal distribution of deprivation in particular. Investigations have been carried out at several scales.

Interregional variations

In the United States there has long been an interest in spatial variations in quality of life, ranging from the early work of Hagood (1943) to more recent studies by Smith (1973), shown in Figure 12.2. More recently, Knox and Scarth (1977) have employed

Figure 12.2 Spatial variations in quality of life in the USA: top – Hagood's (1943) farm operator level of living index; bottom – Smith's (1973) index of social well-being.

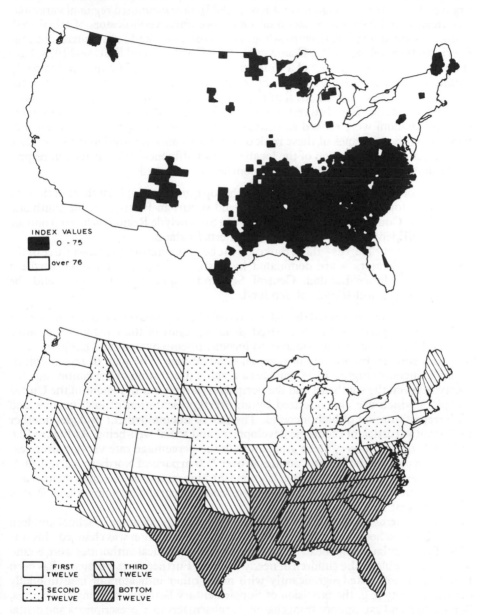

Source: B. E. Coates, R. J. Johnston and P. L. Knox (1977) *Geography and Inequality.* Oxford University Press.

cluster analysis of 41 social and economic variables to group French départements into nine types each with a distinctive quality of life profile. The characteristics of the nine groups are summarized in Table 12.1 and their spatial expression is portrayed in Figure 12.3. In Britain, Cottam and Knox (1982) have examined regional variations in affluence and deprivation based on four representative indicators of social well-being – infant mortality, overcrowding, unemployment, and substandard housing. Previous studies (Knox 1975; Coates et al. 1977; Goodyear and Eastwood 1978) have shown these to be diagnostic of a wider range of social and economic conditions. In addition they were found to be only weakly correlated with one another at the regional level, thus allowing the four measures to be combined in an aggregate index of social well-being. Based on census data for 1971, the 484 District Authorities in the United Kingdom were ranked according to their score on each of these measures. Examining the extremes of these rank distributions and the overlap between them provided a useful indication of the localization of affluence and deprivation respectively. In spatial terms, the following conclusions emerged:

(1)   The best-off areas – those ranked in the top quintile on at least three of the four indicators – are dominated by rural and suburban Districts in the south and Home Counties. Only one (Eastwood in Strathclyde Region) is located outside the affluent core of southern and eastern England.

(2)   The worst-off areas – those ranked in the bottom quintile on at least three of the four indicators – are dominated by Districts from four regions: Northern Ireland, Inner London, Central Scotland (especially Clydeside), and the Highlands and Islands of Scotland.

These findings confirmed the pattern revealed by an analysis of trends in levels of living over the period 1951–1971 based on an aggregate of the same four indicators (Figure 12.4). More recent evidence on income, unemployment and family poverty reveals a similar distribution of regional disadvantage. The map of regional deviations in income (Figure 12.5) provides a graphic illustration of the continuing disparity between the southeast and the peripheral (largely rural) regions of the United Kingdom which are characterized by an overrepresentation of low incomes and underrepresentation of high incomes. The rate of unemployment provides another important yardstick of economic development and social well-being. As Figure 12.6 indicates, there is a very steep gradient with the percentage rate varying from less than 5.0 in parts of the Home Counties to over 25.0 in parts of Northern Ireland. Outside Northern Ireland, the Western Isles had the highest rate of unemployment of any county, with similar high levels in western Scotland, rural Northumberland, Wales, and southwest England.

A valid surrogate measure of family poverty is the percentage of school children receiving free school meals. Prior to 1980, when the legislation was changed, this was a carefully regulated and means-tested benefit which all local authorities were bound to make available to the children of needy families. Furthermore, because it has been found to be correlated significantly with many other indicators of institutionally defined poverty (e.g. the provision of Supplementary Benefits, clothing allowances, home helps, and exemptions from charges for pharmaceutical prescriptions and dental care) it could be taken to be highly diagnostic of the incidence of poverty in general,

Figure 12.3 Quality of life in France, 1973.

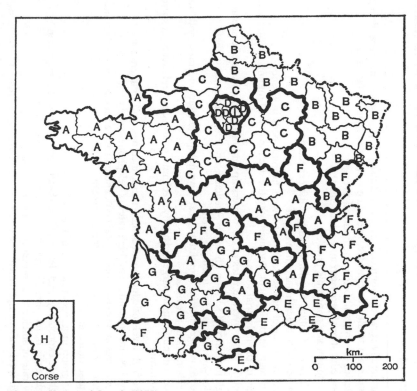

Source: Knox and Scarth (1977)

and not just the deprivation of households with dependent children. As Figure 12.7 shows, according to this indicator there is a marked concentration of family poverty in just a few areas. In the greater part of the United Kingdom the proportion of children receiving free school meals is less than 15.0 percent, while in parts of central and eastern Scotland and in a large tract of the English midlands and southeast the proportion falls to below 10.0 percent. The conurbations of Strathclyde, Tyneside, Merseyside and Greater Manchester exhibit relatively high levels of poverty with above-average levels also in North Wales, Northern Ireland, and the Western Isles.

Poverty has also been the subject of extensive investigation in the USA (Presidents National Advisory Commission on Rural Poverty 1967; National Academy of Sciences 1971; Brinkman 1974). As in the UK, a disproportionate share of America's poor live in nonmetropolitan areas – which contained 35.0 percent of the poor population in 1976 compared with only 27.0 percent of the total population (US Bureau of the Census 1978). Moreover, Davis (1979) has shown that all of the persistently low-

Table 12.1 *Socio-economic characteristics of the nine groups of French départements shown in Figure 12.3*

Type	Characteristics
A. Western France and the fringes of the Massif Central (25 *départe-ments*)	(i) a generally rural environment, with low density of population and rural depopulation (ii) houses are small, overcrowded, and often lacking in modern facilities (iii) salaries are low and below the national average (iv) poor educational provision and achievement (v) alcoholism is a noticeable problem
B. Northeastern France (15 *départements*)	(i) high rates of infant mortality and low life expectancy (ii) low levels of educational achievement (iii) high incidence of tuberculosis, but fewest hospital beds in France (iv) very high unemployment, due mainly to the decline in coal mining, textiles, and iron and steel in the industrial towns (v) slightly above-average rates of car ownership and of the provision of cinemas
C. The Paris Basin (12 *départements*)	(i) high incidence of social pathologies – suicide, divorce, delinquency, theft (ii) below-average rates of unemployment (iii) above-average housing conditions, car ownership, taxable incomes, and numbers of telephones and televisions (iv) good communications, large and highly mechanized farms, and relatively prosperous industrial towns
D. The metropolitan suburbs of Paris (6 *départements*)	(i) very high levels of educational achievement, incomes, and immigration (ii) good housing amenities and high rates of telephone ownership (iii) poor scores on provision of hospital beds, and on road accidents, divorce, crime, and over-crowding in the house and in the classroom (iv) a most varied area
E. Mediterranean France (7 *départements*)	(i) best group in terms of quality of life (ii) high life expectancy, high levels of health-care provision and immigration (iii) high levels of telephone ownership and well-appointed homes (iv) low rate of suicide and mortality from alcoholism (v) high levels of unemployment, especially in rural areas, and high divorce rates

F.	Southern France (I) (16 *départements*)	(i)	low levels of car ownership and job availability
		(ii)	good scores on education, housing conditions, and mortality from alcoholism
		(iii)	all départements experienced population increase between 1968 and 1975
		(iv)	close proximity to recognizable urban centres or growth poles
G.	Southern France (II) (12 *départements*)	(i)	below-average scores on educational attainment, salaries, and television ownership
		(ii)	above-average scores on social pathologies such as alcoholism, divorce, suicide, and delinquency
		(iii)	8 of the 12 départements are losing population
		(iv)	small market towns rather than large urban centres
H.	Corsica	(i)	extremely low salaries and low levels of car and television ownership
		(ii)	low levels of educational attainment and high rates of infant mortality
		(iii)	high rates of crime and delinquency, but low rates of suicide and alcoholism
		(iv)	small farm units and unfavourable terrain
I.	Paris	(i)	high provision of health-care facilities, research centres, hotels and restaurants, cinemas, libraries, roads, and newspapers
		(ii)	high educational attainment and life expectancy
		(iii)	high rates of divorce, crime, and car accidents
		(iv)	well above-average salaries
		(v)	congestion and overcrowding

Source: Ilbery (1981)

Figure 12.4   Trends in quality of life by UK local authority, 1951–1971.

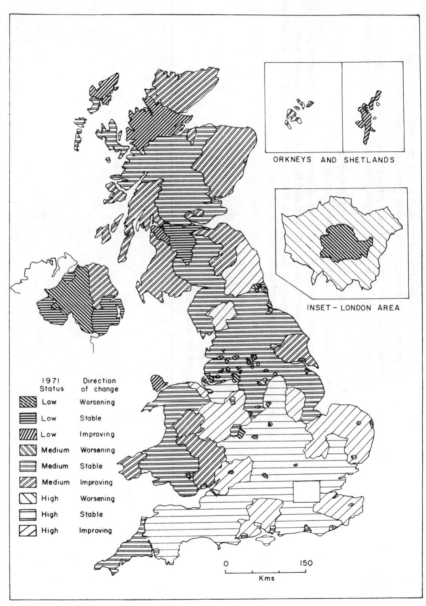

ORKNEYS AND SHETLANDS

INSET – LONDON AREA

1971 Status	Direction of change
Low	Worsening
Low	Stable
Low	Improving
Medium	Worsening
Medium	Stable
Medium	Improving
High	Worsening
High	Stable
High	Improving

0   150
Kms

Source: Cottam and Knox (1982)

Figure 12.5   Variation in incomes by region, 1977–1978.

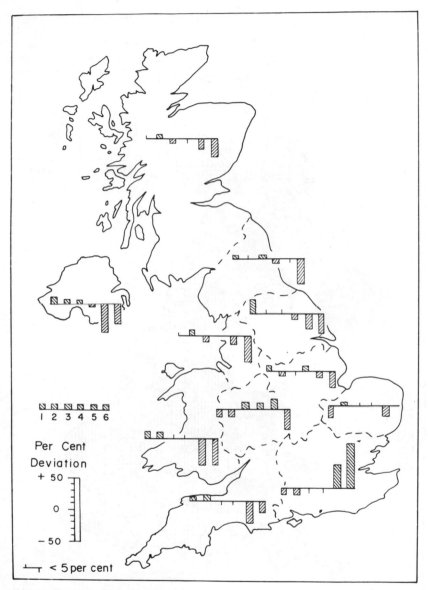

Source: Cottam and Knox (1982)

Figure 12.6 Total unemployment by local authority, 1980 (November).

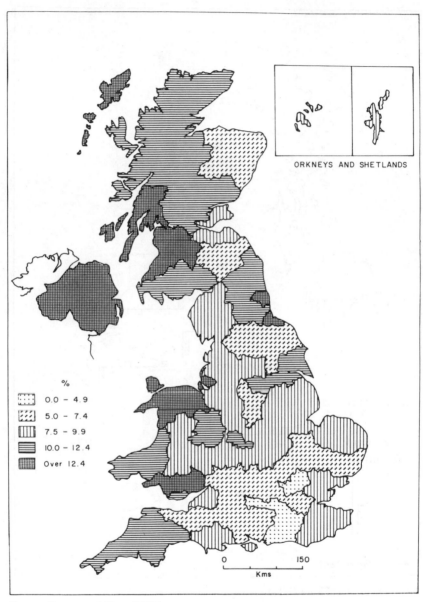

Source: Cottam and Knox (1982)

Figure 12.7 An index of family poverty: percentage of children present at school receiving free meals, 1980.

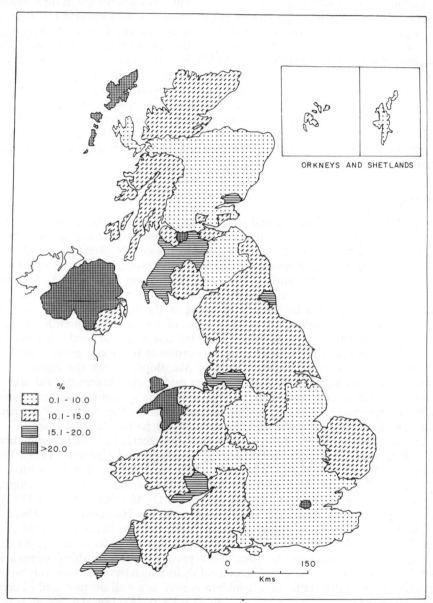

ORKNEYS AND SHETLANDS

%
0.1 - 10.0
10.1 - 15.0
15.1 - 20.0
>20.0

0   150
Kms

Source: Cottam and Knox (1982)

income counties in the USA (defined as those that have been in the lowest 20.0 percent by income rank in each decade since 1950) are located outwith Standard Metropolitan Statistical Areas. Poverty is not uniformly distributed in rural America – because of the residence pattern of rural minorities, and historic US economic development patterns, rural poverty is heavily concentrated in the South (Figure 12.8) where nearly two-thirds of the rural poor live (Deavers and Brown 1980). There is a close relationship between areas in which there is a concentration of poverty and a residential dominance of minority populations, principally blacks, Hispanics and American Indians (Durant and Knowlton 1978). Poverty is an aspect of deprivation which conditions other types of disadvantage. Poor people in rural America suffer from poor housing, low educational attainment, few marketable vocational skills, poor health services, and physical isolation. 'Paradoxically, the higher incidence of poverty in rural areas is accompanied by lower quality of public assistance available' (Chadwick and Bahr 1978, p. 185).

Intraregional patterns

The patterns described by regional studies provide a useful general indicator of differential quality of life in a country but one must beware the ecological fallacy of assuming that all people within a region experience the same level and kind of advantage or disadvantage. Studies of levels of living at an instrastate level were carried out in the American Mid-West as early as the 1930s (Lively and Almack 1938). Hagood et al. (1941) in a study of the socio-spatial structure of Ohio identified an urban–rural gradient extending from high levels of living in the northwest of the state, particularly adjacent to urban areas, to a zone of low living standards along the Appalachian foothills. Bertrand (1955) carried out a similar study in Louisiana. Lewis (1968) examining levels of living in counties of the northeastern USA found the best areas to be the urbanized core of Megolopolis, with the highest scores achieved by counties with rapidly expanding middle class commuter suburbs and booming service industries. At the poorer end of the spectrum was the relatively backward agricultural area extending eastwards from the Allegheny plateau of southern West Virginia to the Delmarva peninsula on the Atlantic coast.

In the UK the problem of rural deprivation has received detailed examination at the subregional level in Northern Ireland (Goodyear and Eastwood 1978), Wales (Bracken 1980; Thomas and Winyard 1979), southwest England (Gordon and Whittaker 1972), East Anglia (Moseley 1978) and Scotland (Scottish Development Department 1978; Knox and Cottam 1981a, 1981b; Cottam and Knox 1982). In terms of numbers of population and area affected, the Highlands of Scotland represent the most serious incidence of rural deprivation in Britain. Located on the periphery of Scotland, Britain and Europe, the Scottish Highlands have experienced a degree of disadvantage in their core–periphery relationships unparalleled elsewhere in the British Isles. The structural shifts which have cumulatively reduced the Highlands to the status of a 'problem region' are well documented (Turnock 1974; Geddes 1979). As Knox and Cottam (1981b, p. 435) observe, 'for most of the present century the Highlands have presented the classic syndrome of regional depression: a thin and depleted resource base, restricted job opportunities, low wages,

Figure 12.8 Nonmetropolitan low-income counties in USA.

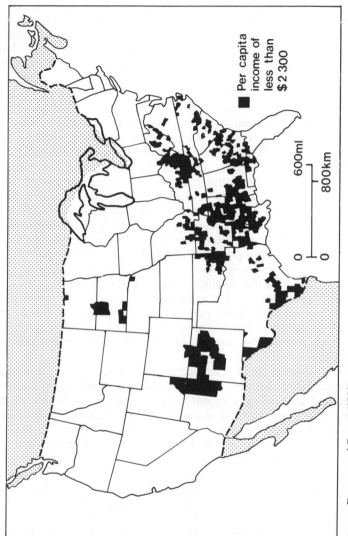

Per capita
income of
less than
$2 300

600ml

800km

0

0

Source: Deavers and Brown (1980)

low female activity rates, high levels of long-term unemployment, and above all depopulation'.

The region's isolation from the main centres of the British economy has been a major contributory factor. Peripherality influences social well-being in three ways. Its effect is seen, first, in the creation of separate local labour markets in which the long-standing excess of labour supply over demand has depressed wage rates to a level below those in other parts of Scotland, even for the same jobs. Secondly, it is apparent in the actual cost of basic goods and services to consumers. Housing, food and clothing are major items of household expenditure which are relatively expensive in the Highlands compared with the rest of the UK. This leaves these households with less disposable income for other items, notwithstanding their generally lower incomes. The third effect of peripherality can be seen in the quality, choice and availability of rural services. Small market size and the absence of competition make for a very restricted choice of goods in most food shops, whilst infrequent deliveries and low-volume sales severely limit the availability of fresh produce. Higher-order services do not exist within easy reach of many communities and the rising threshold population required for the economic viability of most services means that many existing establishments are vulnerable to closure. As Knox and Cottam (1981a) testify, rural communities with catchments of 500 or more are usually able to support a primary school, a sub-post office/shop and perhaps a public house; but where population falls much below this level it becomes difficult to sustain more than just the shop-cum-post office. The operation of many facilities is marginal and, in some cases, the future of a shop, a clinic or a primary school may rest on the migration decisions of a few families. Despite marked improvements in absolute levels of living throughout the UK in the postwar period, the overall pattern of inequality has changed little. While parts of the Highlands and Islands, particularly those affected by oil developments, have experienced a significant improvement in relation to the rest of the nation, the region as a whole remains severely disadvantaged.

A principal reason behind academic and professional interest in quality of life measures is the belief that they may be of value in identifying pockets of multiple deprivation, and in guiding decisions on the allocation of scarce resources. The geographer's major contribution to quality of life research, to date, has been the introduction of a spatial dimension in their work on territorial social indicators. Since most people, even in today's mobile societies, spend most of their time in their home areas and experience the benefits and disadvantages of their own localities, areally based measures of life quality are not merely a product of the geographer's peculiar perspective on the general social indicators movement but are a necessary and logical extension of any realistic system of social reporting. One of the major weaknesses of territorial quality of life indicators, however, is that they are normally based on aggregate data for administrative areas and do not lend themselves to the identification of socio-economic problems at the crucial level of individual households. This ecological trap remains a necessary evil of the spatial approach to quality of life; the larger the unit of enquiry, the greater the potential ignorance of internal variations from the mean position. Since assessments of social well-being can be effective only if one recognizes the complexity of social reality, this suggests a need for research at smaller geographic scales. This question is of particular concern for the study of rural deprivation since the phenomenon rarely involves the intense overlap and localization of disadvantages encountered among multiply deprived urban areas. While descriptive pattern identification and mapping may be of value at the larger scale as a pointer to detailed work, policy-relevant quality of life indicators are more likely to be derived at the local level. Such indicators are also likely to be concerned with specific life domains, such as housing conditions, employment, or access to public services; and to involve both objective and subjective measures (Pacione 1980, 1982).

References

ASSOCIATION OF COUNTY COUNCILS (1979) *Rural Deprivation.* London: HMSO.

BERTRAND, A. L. (1955) *The Many Louisianas, Rural Social Areas and Cultural Island 1950* Louisiana State University Agricultural Experiment Station Bulletin 496.

BRACKEN, J. (1980) Socio-economic profiles for rural areas: a study in Mid-Wales, *Cambria* 7(2), 29–44.

BRINKMAN, G. (1974) *The Development of Rural America.* Lawrence: The University Press of Kansas.

BUTLER, J. E. and FUGUITT, G. V. (1970) Small town population change and distance from larger towns: a replication of Hassinger's study, *Rural Sociology* 35, 396–409.

CHADWICK, B. A. and BAHR, H. M. (1978) Rural Poverty. *In* T. R. Ford *Rural USA: Persistence and Change.* Ames: Iowa State University Press, 182–95.

COATES, B. E., JOHNSTON, R. J. and KNOX, P. L. (1977) *Geography and Inequality.* Oxford: The University Press.

COTTAM, M. B. and KNOX, P. L. (1982) *The Highlands and Islands: A Social Profile* Occasional Paper No. 6, Department of Geography, University of Dundee.

DAVIS, T. F. (1979) *Persistent Low-Income Counties in Non-Metro America* Rural Development Research Report No. 12. Washington D.C.: US Department of Agriculture.

DEAVERS, K. L. and BROWN, D. L. (1980) The rural population turnaround: research and national public policy. *In* D. L. Brown and J. W. Wardwell *New Directions in Urban–Rural Migration: The Population Turnaround in Rural America.* New York: Academic Press, 51–66.

DILLMAN, D. A. and TREMBLAY, K. R. (1977) The quality of life in rural America, *Annals of the American Academy of Political and Social Science* 429, 115–29.

DREWNOWSKI, J. (1974) *On Meaning and Planning the Quality of Life.* The Hague: Mouton.

DURANT, T. J. and KNOWLTON, C. S. (1978) Rural Ethnic Minorities: adaptive response to inequality. *In* T. R. Ford *Rural USA: Persistence and Change.* Ames: Iowa State University Press, 145–67.

GEDDES, M. (1979) *Uneven Development and the Scottish Highlands* Working Paper 17, University of Sussex School of Urban and Regional Studies.

GOODYEAR, P. and EASTWOOD, M. (1978) Spatial variations in level of living in Northern Ireland, *Irish Geography* 11, 54–67.

GORDON, I. R. and WHITTAKER, R. M. (1972) Indicators of local prosperity in the South West region, *Regional Studies* 6, 299–313.

HAGOOD, M. J. (1943) Development of a 1940 rural farm level of living index for counties, *Rural Sociology* 8, 171–80.

HAGOOD, M. J., DANILEVSKY, N. and BEUM, C. O. (1941) An examination of the use of factor analysis in the problem of subregional delineation, *Rural Sociology* 6, 216–33.

HART, J. F. and SALISBURY, N. E. (1965) Population change in Middle Western villages: a statistical approach, *Annals of the Association of American Geographers* 55, 140–60.

HOWES, L. (1979) Review of A. Walker (1978) *Rural Poverty* (London: Child Poverty Action Group), *The Planner* 65, 82–3.

ILBERY, B. W. (1981) *Western Europe*. Oxford: The University Press.

KNOX, P. L. (1974) Spatial variations in level of living in England and Wales, *Transactions of the Institute of British Geographers* 62, 1–24.

KNOX, P. L. (1975) *Social Well Being: A Spatial Perspective*. Oxford: The University Press.

KNOX, P. L. and COTTAM, B. (1981a) Rural deprivation in Scotland: a preliminary assessment, *Tijdschrift voor Economische en Sociale Geografie* 72(3), 162–75.

KNOX, P. L. and COTTAM, M. B. (1981b) A welfare approach to rural geography: contrasting perspectives on the quality of Highland life, *Transactions of the Institute of British Geographers* New Series 6, 433–50.

KNOX, P. L. and SCARTH, A. (1977) The quality of life in France, *Geography* 62(1), 9–16.

LEWIS, G. M. (1968) Levels of living in the North-eastern United States c. 1960: a new approach to regional geography, *Transactions of the Institute of British Geographers* 45, 11–37.

LIVELY, C. E. and ALMACK, R. B. (1938) *A Method of Determining Rural Social Sub-Areas with Application to Ohio* Ohio State University Mimeograph Bulletin 106.

McLOUGHLIN, B. P. (1981) Rural deprivation, *The Planner* 67, 31–33.

MOSELEY, M. J. (1978) *Social Issues in Rural Norfolk*. Norwich: Centre of East Anglian Studies.

MOSELEY, M. J. (1980) Is rural deprivation really rural? *The Planner* 66, 97.

MOSER, C. A. (1970) Some general developments in social statistics, *Social Trends* 1, 7–11.

NATIONAL ACADEMY OF SCIENCES (1971) *The Quality of Rural Living*. Washington DC: National Academy of Sciences.

OECD (1973) *List of Social Concerns* The OECD Social Indicator Development Programme 1. Paris: The Author.

PACIONE, M. (1980) Differential quality of life in a metropolitan village, *Transactions of the Institute of British Geographers* New Series 5(2), 185–206.

PACIONE, M. (1982) The use of objective and subjective measures of life quality in human geography, *Progress in Human Geography* 6(4), 495–514.

PRESIDENTS NATIONAL ADVISORY COMMISSION ON RURAL POVERTY (1967) *The People Left Behind*. Washington DC: US Government Printing Office.

RIKKINEN, K. (1968) Change in village and rural population with distance from Duluth, *Economic Geography* 44, 312–25.

SCOTTISH DEVELOPMENT DEPARTMENT (1978) *Rural Indicators Study*. Edinburgh: Scottish Office Central Research Unit.

SHAW, J. M. (1979) *Rural Deprivation and Planning*. Norwich: Geo Books.

SMITH, D. M. (1973) *The Geography of Social Well Being in the United States*. New York: McGraw-Hill.

THOMAS, C. and WINYARD, S. (1979) Rural incomes. *In* J. M. Shaw *Rural Deprivation and Planning*. Norwich: Geo Books, 21–49.

TURNOCK, D. (1974) *Scotland's Highlands and Islands*. Oxford: The University Press.

US BUREAU OF THE CENSUS (1978) *Social and Economic Characteristics of the Metropolitan and Non Metropolitan Population: 1977 and 1970* Special Studies P-23 No. 75. Washington DC: Bureau of the Census.

13   Housing

Early geographical studies of rural housing concentrated on the links between regional economic and cultural characteristics and house type, and considered aspects such as vernacular style and building materials. This traditional approach was particularly strong in France during the early part of the twentieth century (Demangeon 1920), with more recent examples illustrated by the work of Houston (1964) in the Western Mediterranean, Kniffen (1936), Trewartha (1948) and Rickert (1967) in the USA, and Bonham-Carter (1952), Hoskins (1955) and Brunskill (1971) in Britain.

During the course of the twentieth century, however, rural housing in advanced capitalist societies has increasingly become divorced from the agricultural economy to which it was previously tied. Housing in the countryside now has to serve a variety of needs arising from a broadening rural employment structure and from the demands of recreation activities and retirement, in addition to its traditional function of providing shelter for the agricultural workforce. As a result the geography of rural housing has become as multifaceted as its urban counterpart. Consideration of the physical land use aspect of housing has been overtaken by questions of rural housing standards, tenure structure and 'issues of social justice and equity, state involvement and private interests' (Rogers 1983, p. 108).

Housing conditions

Until the 1960s problems of rural housing were generally equated with issues of housing quality. As Dunn et al. (1981) observe, the absence of amenities such as piped water or proper sewerage systems, the squalor of dampness and mould and gross overcrowding with children sharing parents' rooms were the focus of concern for rural reformers until at least the late 1940s.

Moves to improve the condition of rural housing began in the interwar period. Between 1918 and 1939 no fewer than 16 Acts of Parliament dealing with English and Welsh housing were passed, along with 10 Acts concerning rents and another 10 dealing exclusively with housing in Scotland (Clark 1982). The two major developments were the direct involvement of national and local government in the construction and control of rural housing, and the large-scale construction of new dwellings by private enterprise builders with or without government subsidy. As Table 13.1 shows, a total of over 870,000 new houses were built in England and Wales between 1919 and 1943 amounting to an increase of more than 50.0 percent in the rural housing stock. This total represented the efforts of rural district councils who had built nearly 160,000 new houses under the terms of the various Acts, and the contribution of private enterprise which had built over 135,000 houses with government subsidy. In addition county and district councils had built nearly 5,000 houses without subsidy. While the contribution of local authority house building accounted

Table 13.1 *Provision of housing in rural districts of England and Wales, 1919–1943*

	Rural District Councils	Private Enterprise	Total
1. *Housing Acts*			
Housing, Town Planning, etc. Act, 1919, (for general needs)	34,284	1,631	35,915
Housing (Additional) Powers Act, 1919, (for general needs)	—	15,979	15,979
Housing, etc. Act, 1923, (for general needs)	8,410	109,851	118,261
Housing (Financial Provisions) Act, 1924, (for general needs)	62,370	4,577	66,947
Housing Acts of 1910, 1936 and 1938, (for slum clearance)	31,746	1,246	32,992
Housing Acts of 1935, 1936 and 1938, (for abatement of overcrowding)	7,205	123	7,328
Housing Acts of 1925 and 1936, (for general needs), without subsidy	11,548	495	12,043
Housing (Financial Provisions) Act, 1938 (Section 2), (for agricultural population)	3,584	29	3,613
Housing (Financial Provisions) Act, 1938, (Section 3), (for agricultural population)	—	1,148	1,148
Total under the Housing Acts	159,147	135,079	294,226
2. *Houses built other than under the Housing Acts* (including those built by County Councils without subsidy)	4,936	571,448	576,384
Grand Totals	164,083	706,527	870,610

Source: Rogers (1976)

for only one-fifth of houses built in the period, it can be argued that this intervention had an influence out of all proportion to its numerical size in that the principle of public involvement in housing provision was established in practice. 'For the first time public housing was introduced into the countryside in significant numbers in many cases and often only the smallest villages failed to get their quota' (Dunn et al. 1981, p. 33). As Table 13.1 shows, however, the vast majority of new houses (more than 571,000) were built for the private market, largely in the newly emerging suburbs on the urban fringe where speculative developers were aided by cheap land and relatively unrestricted planning regulations. As these periurban developments were undertaken in response to housing demand rather than housing need they had little impact in improving the housing conditions of the average indigenous rural family who found access to the growing private market beyond their means.

As well as providing new housing the interwar legislation tried to tackle directly the major problems of overcrowding and substandard conditions in existing rural properties. The Housing (Rural Workers) Act of 1936 made funds available for cottage improvement, but its effect was mitigated by provisions in the same Act which required that any house which was refurbished with the aid of a grant should not be let at higher than agricultural rent. Although this was a genuine attempt to ensure that the benefit accrued to the working population rather than urban migrants it resulted in a much less than hoped for take up of the grants (22,000) by property owners, unattracted by the low return on investment. The problem of over-crowding was first tackled in the Housing Act of 1935 which provided special subsidies to rural districts to build cottages for farmworkers (Table 13.1).

The progress made between the wars in tackling the problems of rural housing was significant, with 30,000 unfit homes demolished and 22,000 renovated in addition to the new building. But in 1939 about one-third of all rural dwellings and over 90.0 percent of farmhouses were still not served by electricity. The Scott Report of 1942 found that over a million people in the countryside had no piped water supply and 46.0 percent of parishes had no system of sewerage. Thousands of cottages had only a single living room with no separate cooking accommodation and 'for the great majority of rural workers a bathroom is a rare luxury' (Ministry of Works and Planning 1942, p. 17). The Scott Report also identified new concerns which were developing and which, in time, were to assume principal importance in the debate over rural living conditions. These included a concern over the effect of isolation on the health and education of rural families; doubts over the cost of providing modern services to all rural dwellings; the question of the tied cottage; and disapproval of the purchase of country properties by 'week-enders'.

The period since the Second World War has seen the general improvement in rural housing conditions continued. Overcrowding is no longer a widespread problem in rural Britain; the physical condition of rural housing has improved steadily, and the stock is now much younger than before. The end result is that rural housing standards generally compare favourably with those in the nation as a whole. Some rural areas, however, have made less progress, and still have an above-average proportion of substandard housing. Concentrations of poorer housing have been found in northeast Scotland, Wales, East Anglia, Cornwall and the Peak District (Census Research Unit 1980). Significantly, those areas which have lagged behind the general improvement trend are to be found in the more rural and less accessible areas of the country where rural incomes are at their lowest. As Dunn et al. (1981, p. 41) conclude, 'it is clear that housing quality is still poor where the old rural economy remains, where newcomers from the town have been relatively few in number and where local authorities, for one reason or another (e.g. lack of finance, qualified manpower, or will to act), have been less able to enforce higher standards'.

Rural housing in Europe is generally older and in poorer condition than urban housing. In France, for example, more than 60.0 percent of all rural homes date from before the First World War and the majority of houses in the rural communes still lack basic amenities such as inside toilets and baths (Table 13.2). Thus 'despite substantial investment from the national government and from European Community sources French rural housing, particularly within the agricultural sector, remains in poor condition' (Rogers 1983, p. 111).

Similarly in the United States substantial improvements in rural housing conditions in the postwar era have not benefited all rural areas to the same extent. In the nation as a whole, between 1950 and 1975 the number of substandard rural houses fell from 9.08 million to 1.92 million (Bird and Kampe 1977); but rural areas, with only 28.0 percent of US households, still account for over half of the substandard housing. Some regions notably in the south and in Appalachia exhibit particularly bad conditions. As Table 13.3 shows, the Central Appalachian Region typifies this residual problem – as late as 1960, nearly 44.0 percent of all housing was officially considered as deteriorating or dilapidated (Deaton and Hanrahan 1973).

In addition to geographical concentrations of poorer housing there remain groups of households (e.g. the elderly or, notably in USA, ethnic minorities) which suffer an

Table 13.3 *Housing amenities in the central Appalachian region, USA, 1970*

Region	Number of housing units	Housing units lacking full plumbing facilities	
		No.	%
Kentucky (26 counties)	163,444	74,608	45.5
Tennessee (18 counties)	103,217	33,083	32.2
Virginia (17 counties)	61,402	24,780	40.2
West Virginia (9 counties)	119,856	32,164	26.7
Central Appalachian region (60 counties)	447,919	164,635	36.7
Four state total	4,433,892	721,184	16.3
United States total	68,418,062	5,168,646	7.6

Source: Rogers (1983)

Table 13.2 *Rural housing conditions and amenities, France, 1975*

	No inside flush toilet		No bath/shower		No central heating		Inadequate water supply	
	Principle residence with 1 dwelling %	Farms %	Principle residence with 1 dwelling %	Farms %	Principle residence with 1 dwelling %	Farms %	Principle residence with 1 dwelling %	Farms %
Rural communes	41	63	43	58	65	82	6	10
Urban areas (excluding Paris)	28	55	27	49	48	76	2	9
Greater Paris	14	25	18	20	23	32	2	2
Total	32	62	32	57	52	81	3	9

Note: Principle residences exclude second homes.
Source: Rogers (1983)

unacceptably low standard of housing. Particular concern in recent years has therefore been afforded to questions of social equity in the distribution of housing resources. As Dunn et al. (1981, p. v) observe, 'housing has always featured as a matter of concern for those with an interest in rural social policy. Historically, that concern centred on housing quality and rural living conditions. Today, while poor living conditions can still be found in rural areas (particularly in parts of upland Britain), the focus is rather on inequality of opportunity and the unfair effects of competition for a limited supply of houses in the countryside.'

Under normal market conditions prevalent in the Western capitalist world, access to different classes of housing is essentially determined by household income. In parts of rural United States, however, this direct relationship is complicated by the effect of race on housing market structure. The three largest ethnic minorities in rural America, blacks, Mexican-Americans and Indian-Americans, share a common position of relative deprivation and inequality. The adaptive response of each of these groups to inequality has been outlined by Durant and Knowlton (1978). While all three ethnic minorities have made economic gains in rural areas in the postwar era, their statuses continue to rank well below that of white occupants. Simple census tabulations indicate that housing occupied by rural minority groups is inferior to that of white households. While low income levels provide the major explanation of the poor housing conditions of rural blacks there is also clear evidence of discrimination on ethnic grounds. Marantz et al. (1976) working in Arkansas, Georgia, North Carolina and Tennessee, discovered that ethnic discrimination was built into the operations of the housing market. They found no black lenders or real estate agencies and only one black builder and concluded that 'a single set of white-dominated institutions serves both white and black consumers, but serves them separately and unequally' (Ibid., p. 144).

More generally, to assess the relative strength of different population groups with regard to housing access it is necessary to identify the nature of the housing supply mechanism, and the major types of households in competition for housing.

Housing supply

The rural housing stock comprises a mix of owner-occupied or mortgaged properties, local authority housing and private-rented accommodation, with smaller proportions of semipermanent dwellings such as mobile homes. The latter are particularly important in the USA where, in 1976, 10.0 percent of rural houses were of this type. Numerically owner-occupied housing dominates the tenure structure both in Western Europe and North America. While the proportion is over 50.0 percent in English rural districts it is generally higher in other countries and reaches about 80.0 percent in the USA (Limmer and McGough 1979).

The main problems of rural housing need are felt by those in the lower-income groups who either have to live in a rural area because of their employment or wish to do so as a result of family ties or for other social reasons, but who cannot afford to compete in the private housing market. Traditionally the main housing opportunities for all low-income groups in rural areas have been in the private-rented sector which in the case of agricultural workers and some others is often tied to their employment. In Britain the declining profitability to the landlord (as a result of progressive rent controls and increased security of tenure for the tenant) and rising property prices have led to a situation where 'a decreasing pool of rented housing in rural areas is available to a part of the rural population which is least able to take advantage of the private market' (Rogers 1976, p. 100).

The level of provision of council housing in rural areas is also below the national average, with 22.0 percent in rural England and 27.0 percent in rural Wales compared with 29.0 percent in England and Wales as a whole. In Scotland the figure of over 50.0 percent is again lower than the regional average of 55.0 percent. Several reasons have been advanced to explain the decline in the rate of publicly financed house building which has occurred in rural Britain since the mid 1960s. Building costs are usually higher in rural areas, and central government has been occupied by the more visible social crisis in urban areas. In addition to financial constraints, historically there has been a degree of unwillingness by some Conservative-controlled councils to undertake council house building. In general, council house building rates in rural areas have not been sufficient to offset the decline in the private-rented sector nor to prevent a gradual decline in council housing as a proportion of rural housing.

Housing and household types

Both Pahl (1966) and Ambrose (1974) have attempted to provide a typology of social groups relevant to the study of rural housing. Pahl's 8 main social groupings have received much attention (Table 13.4), but this simple classification can be criticized

Table 13.4   *Major social groupings according to Pahl (1966)*

1. *Large property owners:* owner-occupiers who are also property landlords.

2. *Salaried immigrants with some capital:* owner-occupiers whose main influences are in the improvement and gentrification of rural housing.

3. *Spiralists:* transient owner-occupiers characteristically occupying a recent housing development in an accessible village.

4. *Those with limited incomes and little capital:* reluctant commuters who have been forced out of towns by the need for cheaper but larger housing in response to a growing family.

5. *The retired:* either as owner-occupiers or tenants in small towns and large villages where accessibility is high and service provision comparatively good.

6. *Council house tenants:* marks the definite transition from groups who can buy to those who must rent housing; characterized by relative inflexibility of tenure and location compared with owner-occupiers.

7. *Tied cottagers and other tenants:* the rural poor with low wages, poor housing and isolation.

8. *Local tradesmen and owners of small businesses:* rather indeterminate in its housing characteristics and may include both owner-occupiers and tenants.

Source: Pahl (1966)

on several counts. It fails to explicitly consider important rural social groups such as second home owners, mobile home dwellers, people living in winter lets (i.e. holiday accommodation which becomes available during the winter months and which can be used by the local authority to relieve overcrowding or homelessness albeit temporarily), and members of the armed forces living in rented accommodation. Further, only very general spatial variations throughout the country can be suggested and then only imprecisely.

Dunn et al. (1981) employed a more rigorous multivariate procedure to derive 7 'rural housing profiles' based on a cluster analysis of 30 socio-economic variables extracted from the 1971 census. Table 13.5 describes these profiles and their spatial

Table 13.5   *The character of rural housing profiles, England 1971, shown in Figure 13.1*

1. *Agricultural – farmworkers (42 cases)*
   A high proportion of agricultural workers and low proportions of professional and non-manual workers. Above-average proportion of private-rented unfurnished tenancies and also a greater than average number of households lacking exclusive use of one or more basic amenities. High unemployment rates. Low level of car ownership.

2. *Agricultural – farmers (91 cases)*
   A predominantly agricultural group with low population totals and high proportions of farmers and agricultural workers. Many households living in rented unfurnished accommodation. Low occupancy rates. Above-average proportion of pensioners.

3. *Owner-occupiers – retired (42 cases)*
   Large retired population. Low economic activity rates; high unemployment rates. High levels of owner-occupation and underoccupancy of dwellings.

4. *Transitional rural (90 cases)*
   A large profile incorporating a variety of characteristics. High female economic activity rate. Above-average proportion of nonmanual workers; slightly more than average percentage of children. Fewer pensioners and agricultural workers than the average for rural districts. Renting privately unfurnished is a smaller than average tenure category and there is less underoccupancy.

5. *Owner-occupiers – high status (88 cases)*
   High proportion of heads of household employed in professional and nonmanual occupations and correspondingly above-average levels of education. Two car ownership and owner-occupation are both above average.

6. *Armed forces (36 cases)*
   A small profile dominated by armed forces personnel and households living in rented furnished accommodation. Above-average proportion of children leading to more overcrowding. High male economic activity rate. Few pensioners.

7. *Local Authority housing (26 cases)*
   A small group of rural districts with high proportions of households living in local authority rented accommodation. Skilled manual workers dominate the occupational structure. Relatively few households own cars. Some overcrowding of dwellings.

Source: Dunn et al. (1981)

distribution is depicted in Figure 13.1. This analysis recognizes the importance of tenure as an explanatory variable but it also acknowledges the equally important distinction between areas which have remained essentially rural in nature and those which have been progressively affected by urban influences. As Table 13.5 and Figure 13.1 indicate, the more truly rural areas of the north of England, the eastern counties, the Welsh borders and the southwest are particularly associated with profiles 1, 2, and 3; that is where agricultural employment is strong or where retirement, either of the indigenous population or because of inmigration, is an important func-

Figure 13.1 Rural housing profiles, England 1971.

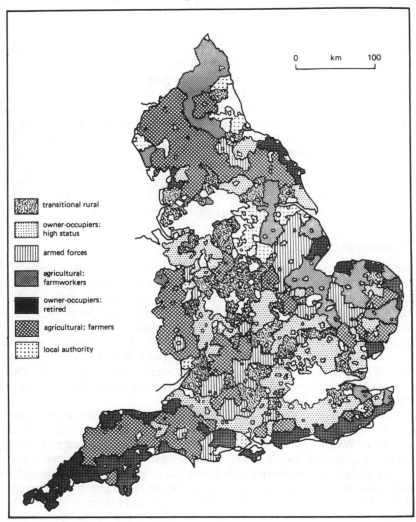

Source: Dunn et al. (1981)

tion of the rural housing stock. In contrast, in the more urban districts, stretching in a broad band from London and the southeast northwest towards Merseyside, profiles 4, 5, 6 and 7 are dominant; that is where incomes are generally higher, employment opportunities are more varied, housing quality is better, the demographic structure is more vibrant or where State involvement in housing provision has been particularly effective (Rogers 1983). A similar multivariate study by Ogden (1978) in the eastern Massif Central of France also stressed the important links between rural housing and regional socio-economic structure.

The work of Dunn et al. (1981) culminates in the identification of the major social groups in competition for housing in rural areas. Clearly, however, while such national or regional studies provide a useful indication at an aggregate level of the social and spatial differences in rural housing, policy-relevant indicators are more likely to be derived at a local scale. Figures 13.2 and 13.3 and Tables 13.6 and 13.7 describe the local rural housing profiles for the Cotswold and South Oxfordshire Districts. At the national level most of the former district was described by the 'agricultural: farmers' profile with the southern part classed as 'transitional rural'; while much of the latter district was classed as 'traditional rural' with an area of high-status owner-occupiers in the south, reflecting the urban influences of London, Oxford and Reading. Local scale analysis uncovers 'less widespread, though not necessarily less important, types and tenures' (Dunn et al. 1981, p. 120) and leads away from broadbrush spatial statements and closer to consideration of the housing needs of minority groups. For socially disadvantaged minority groups in rural society access to housing is restricted to the declining opportunities in the council and private-rented sectors. Two types of private-rented housing of importance in rural areas are tied accommodation and housing association property.

Tied accommodation

Tied accommodation is housing owned by employers and provided as part of their workers' terms of employment. Such accommodation is occupied by many different groups including miners, policemen, nurses, soldiers and clergymen but, despite the fact that it accounts for only one-seventh of the British total (Jones 1975), it is the agricultural tied cottage that has received greatest attention. Gasson (1975) estimated that there were between 100,000 and 110,000 tied cottages on farms in Britain, 75,000–85,000 in England and Wales and 20,000–25,000 in Scotland (Smythe 1976). Nearly 60.0 percent of full-time hired workers lived in tied accommodation with the higher-paid specialist workers being most likely to receive free accommodation of this type.

The distribution of tied cottages is shown in Figure 13.4 which reveals considerable regional variations, ranging from a figure of 98.0 percent in Dumfriesshire to 30.0 percent in Wales. Gasson (1975) suggests that the incidence of tied cottages is greatest for specialist livestock workers and lowest for general workers, those in horticulture and those in new types of farming like large-scale poultry production. A regression analysis based on eight farm-employment (e.g. farm type, acreage, total cost of hired labour) and population-related (population density in the administrative area, distance to nearest town) variables failed to explain more than 20.0 per-

Figure 13.2 Rural housing profiles, Cotswold District.

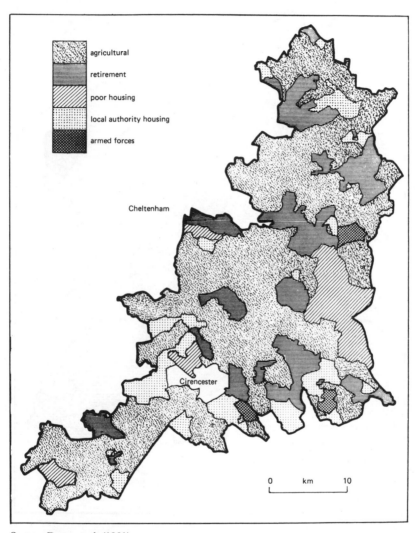

Source: Dunn et al. (1981)

Figure 13.3 Rural housing profiles, South Oxfordshire District.

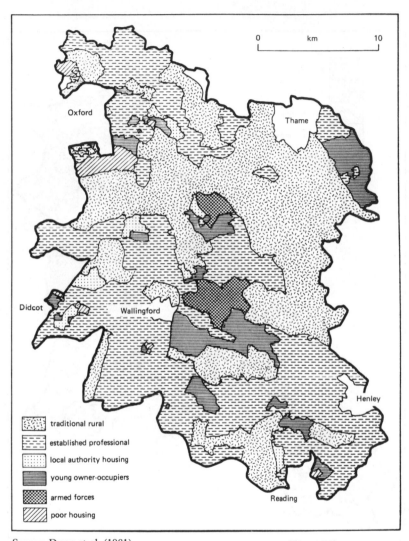

Source: Dunn et al. (1981)

Table 13.6   *The character of rural housing profiles, Cotswold District, shown in Figure 13.2*

Profile 1:   *Agricultural (88 cases)*
Much the largest cluster and therefore average in many respects, but predominantly agricultural in character, with high proportions of both farmers and farmworkers, many living in relatively high-standard privately rented accommodation. Higher than average level of car ownership.

Profile 2:   *Retirement (42 cases)*
A group dominated by retired people, with greater than average numbers of small households, pensioners and owner-occupier households, but few households with children and a smaller proportion of the population economically active.

Profile 3:   *Poor Housing (10 cases)*
A small cluster exhibiting very poor housing conditions. Very small enumeration districts, predominantly with small houses lacking exclusive use of basic amenities and with a very immobile population consisting largely of older households. A very high proportion of households renting privately unfurnished accommodation (36.4 percent of the Cotswold District mean; 58.4 percent of the profile mean).

Profile 4:   *Local Authority Housing (34 cases)*
A group of enumeration districts with high proportions of dwellings rented from a local authority. High average household size, with a certain degree of over-crowding; low level of car ownership; a high proportion of heads of household are skilled manual workers.

Profile 5:   *Armed Forces (4 cases)*
A very small group dominated by armed forces personnel living in furnished, privately rented accommodation. Most households have young families, thus reducing the proportion of females able to work. Very few retired people and, con-versely, a large number of children.

Source: Dunn et al. (1981)

cent of the observed variation in tied cottage provision. This led Gasson to postulate the importance of historical factors to explain the present distribution (Figure 13.4). Differences in hiring practices in the past may be of significance. In Wales, for example, a large proportion of the farm labour force was traditionally accommodated in farm buildings whereas in the Scottish Borders almost all workers lived in cottages.

Though the absolute number of agricultural tied cottages is decreasing as the farm labour force shrinks the relative provision has increased since the last war. Whereas there were 35.3 tied cottages for every 100 full-time hired men in England and Wales in 1947 the corresponding provision in 1972 was 54.2. The increased significance of the tied cottage is open to several interpretations. It could indicate that those in tied accommodation are trapped in agriculture by low wages and the availability of a free or subsidized house. Alternatively it could be that as urban demand for rural housing has increased more potential employees are insisting on a house with the job, particularly the more skilled livestock workers who are in shortest supply.

Table 13.7 *The character of rural housing profiles, South Oxfordshire, shown in Figure 13.3*

Profile 1: *Traditional Rural (52 cases)*
A group of relatively small enumeration districts with a high proportion of households renting unfurnished accommodation. The standard of housing is generally much lower than average, especially where households are owner-occupiers. A higher than average proportion of farmers; average age higher than the South Oxfordshire District mean, with fewer children than average.

Profile 2: *Established Professional (99 cases)*
Naturally, as the largest group, fairly average in many respects, but weighted towards older age groups and higher social classes, living in slightly larger houses in good condition. Fewer households with children and fewer young married couples.

Profile 3: *Local Authority (24 cases)*
A cluster dominated by large households in local authority accommodation, with generally low car ownership and a relatively low terminal educational age. High level of use of the housing stock (low vacancy rate), with a moderate degree of overcrowding.

Profile 4: *Younger Owner-Occupiers (42 cases)*
A group consisting largely of younger owner-occupiers, often with children, and with a high proportion of young married households. Conversely, few pensioners – hence a high proportion economically active – and few households without a car.

Profile 5: *Armed Forces (6 cases)*
A small and very distinctive group of enumeration districts, dominated by armed forces personnel living in rented furnished accommodation. Many have young families, hence the reduced number of married women able to work.

Profile 6: *Poor Housing (10 cases)*
A small cluster dominated by poor housing conditions: a remarkable proportion of households in nonpermanent dwellings, many lacking some or all basic amenities, and with a considerable degree of overcrowding. Generally small households, often consisting of young marrieds, but in very small accommodation.

Source: Dunn et al. (1981)

The debate on the merits of the tied cottage system has gone on for most of the century. The main arguments proposed by farmers in favour of the arrangement are: (a) it is essential for certain key workers to live close to the farm, (b) it facilitates mobility within agriculture, and (c) the offer of accommodation is essential to attract and retain skilled workers on farms. The main objections to the system are: (a) the provision of a cottage depresses wages, (b) it gives the employer undue influence over the lives of employees and their families, and (c) the lack of security puts workers in an uncertain position when they retire from a low-pay industry with few savings with which to obtain alternative accommodation. Until the 1976 Rent (Agriculture) Act, if for any reason, including accident, redundancy or retirement, the worker's employment ceased, so did his security of tenure. The 1976 legislation extended the pro-

Figure 13.4 Tied cottages in Great Britain, 1972–1973.

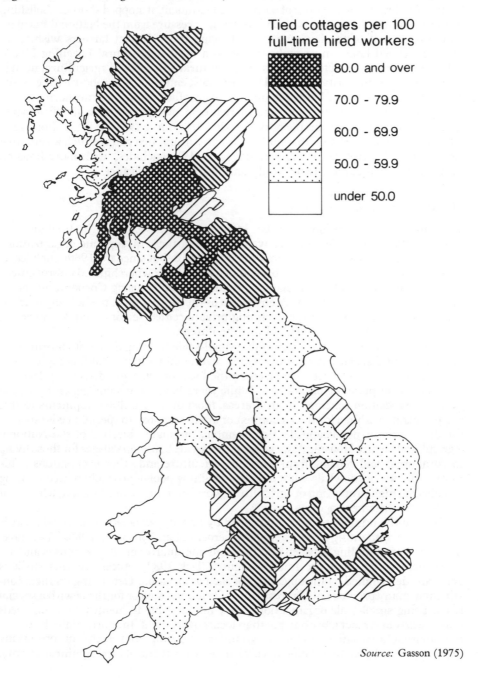

Tied cottages per 100
full-time hired workers

80.0 and over

70.0 - 79.9

60.0 - 69.9

50.0 - 59.9

under 50.0

Source: Gasson (1975)

visions of the 1965 Rent Act to the occupants of farm tied cottages in England and Wales, but, despite the presence of a Labour government, it stopped short of abolishing the system outright, largely as a result of strong pressure from the National Farmers Union on behalf of the landowners. Following the 1976 Act farmers wishing to repossess a tied house must make a case to a local Agricultural Dwelling House Advisory Committee on the grounds of agricultural efficiency. If agricultural need is proven the local authority is charged to use its best endeavours to rehouse the current occupants. Faced with a limited council housing stock, some local authorities have been reluctant to accept this duty and there is evidence that others will only allocate their poorest housing for this purpose (Larkin 1978; Burke 1981). It is the shortage of alternative accommodation that makes the agricultural tied cottage such an emotive issue in the countryside. As Gasson (1975, p. 119) concludes, 'with more housing available the tied cottage issue would shrink into insignificance'.

Housing associations

The Housing Corporation recorded 3,020 housing associations in England and Wales in 1981. As originally conceived the role of these quasipublic organizations was to provide houses to rent for low-income groups, but since the 1960s such 'cost-rent' and 'fair-rent' schemes have been joined by shared ownership and improvement for sale projects. Housing associations, funded by the Housing Corporation set up under the Housing Act 1964, were envisaged as the 'third arm' of the housing market, providing an alternative to the declining private-rented sector. To date, however, most action has been concentrated in urban areas.

In order to provide financially viable small-scale housing developments in rural areas housing associations must overcome several difficulties including higher construction costs and restrictions placed on the location, size and density of developments by local planning authorities. While there have been some general purpose housing association schemes in rural areas, most of the rural developments in this sector operate within a local area context or are in response to special needs (such as for the elderly or handicapped). For example, the main objective of the National Agricultural Centre Housing Association is to provide houses in villages for those living in rural areas and retiring from work in agriculture and other occupations. This motive directly acknowledges not only the declining pool of privately rented housing but also the high proportion of agricultural workers living in tied housing who are at or close to retirement age.

In total the number of houses provided by housing associations in rural areas is still limited, amounting to only about 2.0 percent of all housing in 1980. They have, however, been building between one-fifth and one-quarter of all new houses and are even more active in house improvement (Clark 1982). Access to this stock is generally determined by the objectives of each association. Depending on their constitution, many provide only for residents of a defined area or for those with a special need. Being small-scale organizations, they may be able to identify housing needs more clearly and react more quickly than local government. In short, while the role of the housing association sector or voluntary housing movement in preserving privately rented accommodation in rural areas is as yet one of local significance only, there is potential for greater housing association involvement in supplementing council housing and attracting extra money into the provision of privately rented property.

Council housing

Public housing represents the obvious solution to the housing needs of lower-income sections of the community yet, while the incidence of housing stress is often as great as in urban areas, there is proportionately less council housing in rural Britain than in the country as a whole. Apart from the small proportion of publicly owned dwellings there is also a high degree of spatial concentration in the towns and larger villages as a result of the centralizing effects of key settlement policies (Cloke 1979); the provision of government subsidies for higher-density developments, which favours building large estates as opposed to scattered dwellings (Shucksmith 1981); the higher costs associated with using local building materials for housing in some villages (Larkin 1979); the domination of the construction industry by large companies; and the derivation of economies of scale in construction and infrastructure provision (Rogers 1976).

The expressed housing needs of those on the waiting and transfer lists exhibit considerable variety ranging from elderly owner-occupiers unable to maintain their homes to young married couples with children who are perhaps sharing a house with relatives or living in a short-lease let. The major responsibility of housing authorities is to match this myriad complex of housing needs with the available housing stock. Access to council housing is primarily determined by local authority housing managers within the constraints imposed on them by national policy (e.g. on council house sales). Housing authorities have certain statutory duties to fulfil, including rehousing from slum clearance schemes, emergency provision for the homeless and, in rural areas under the Rent (Agricultural) Act 1976, rehousing families from tied accommodation. Outside these statutory obligations the two main sources of expressed need are the housing 'waiting list' (for those who want to enter the system) and the 'transfer list' (for those who wish to move house within the system). Waiting lists may not reveal the full extent of felt housing need since many families in poor conditions may not approach the local authority. Others may be excluded from the waiting list by residential qualification and rules which prevent certain categories (e.g. owner-occupiers) from applying. Nevertheless in many instances this source is often the only measure of housing need available.

The priority of those on the waiting list for council housing is determined by an assessment of an applicant's need as measured against a set of locally defined criteria. This is usually achieved by one of three methods. Some authorities operate simple queues on a 'first come, first served' basis. Unless there are very short waiting lists this method will be insensitive to actual housing need (Cullingworth 1979). A few authorities operate 'merit schemes' under which each applicant is evaluated by a committee. This is an informal version of the third method, the 'points scheme', which is used in most areas. Points schemes allocate scores to applicants on the basis of criteria such as length of time on the waiting list, present housing situation, family size, and medical needs. After their need has been assessed applicants are placed in queues for different types of accommodation. These are usually differentiated by the size of the house needed but other criteria such as the type of dwelling and preferred area may be used (Phillips and Williams 1982). Some authorities, as in the South Oxfordshire and Cotswolds districts, award additional points to those with established connections in a village and who wish to remain there. This strategy attempts to counter the arguments that the scarcity of council accommodation in many villages results in a drift to the towns, and causes applicants to specify locations where they feel their chances of gaining a tenancy are higher rather than specifying where they would like to live (Dunn et al. 1981).

The major problem for local housing authorities is that the available stock of dwellings is rarely sufficient to meet demand. In many rural local authorities concern over this shortfall has been heightened by the passing of the 1980 Housing Act and in particular the provisions for the sale of council houses.

Council house sales   According to Schifferes (1980, p. 10) the 1980 Housing Act introduced the 'most far reaching changes in the council housing system since its effective origins at the end of the First World War'. The most controversial of these was the section giving tenants the 'right to buy' council houses. While local authorities had been permitted to sell houses since the 1925 Housing Act (with 260,000 council and New Town houses sold between 1951 and 1980), the 1980 Act gave all tenants of more than three years the statutory *right* to buy at a discount of 33.0 per-cent of market price for the first four years of occupancy and 1.0 percent for each complete year thereafter, up to a maximum of 50.0 percent. A possible outcome of council house sales in attractive rural areas was the loss of housing stock to incomers seeking a second home should extenants later decide to resell their houses. Pressure from rural councils and other interest groups resulted in safeguards in the form of resale conditions for houses purchased under the 1980 Housing Act. In Areas of Outstanding Natural Beauty, National Parks, and 'Designated Rural Areas' (Figure 13.5) the council must either be allowed first refusal on resale during the first ten years or the houses can only be resold to someone who has lived or worked in the area for at least three years. In fact, out of 130 English authorities who applied for desig-nation, only 18 were accorded powers over resale. While these included Cornwall and much of rural Northumberland, substantial areas of the London green belt and regions such as the Cotswolds and East Anglia, where the incomer and second-homer are active in the market, failed to obtain powers. Furthermore, in practice the escalating price of desirable rural properties (e.g. in the smallest and most rural villages) which are most likely to be sold off, makes it unlikely that a council could exercise its rights to repurchase.

For individuals purchase offers clear advantages but for the remainder of the community the end result may be that the poorest tenants are left with the least desir-able properties. Also, in the more attractive areas with small stocks, the reduction in public housing available will result in longer queues for a dwindling resource. Phillips and Williams (1982) suggest that these trends could force people either to move out of their local area in order to improve their housing conditions or else to occupy inferior accommodation locally. For the local community the implications of such outmigration for the continued viability of smaller rural centres can be crucial.

Figure 13.5 Designated rural areas under the 1980 Housing Act.

National Parks

Areas of Outstanding Natural Beauty

Designated Rural Areas

0 _____ 100 Kilometres

Source: Phillips and Williams (1983)

As Dunn et al. (1981, p. 216) observe, the 1980 Housing Act 'provides a clear instance of the dangers of the unthinking application of a national policy to rural areas without a true appreciation of the probable consequences'.

Local needs policies

The cutbacks in public housing expenditure, the sale of council houses, and the reducing stock of private-rented accommodation have led some local authorities to consider means of protecting local needs; particularly in pressured rural areas where the outcome of the inmigration of affluent commuters, second home owners or retirees is 'intense competition for rural housing with all the odds stacked against the local person' (Thurgood 1978, p. 143). The position of disadvantaged locals may be exacerbated by the structure planning process which limits development in smaller settlements to that catering for local need only, since in practice the operation of the free market inevitably means that at least some of these will be occupied by affluent outsiders. Penfold (1974) in the Peak District and Bennett (1976), Shucksmith (1981) and Rogers (1981) in the Lake District have all demonstrated how the combination of attractive surroundings and strict building controls with relatively low local incomes has resulted in incursions of outsiders to the detriment of local people. As Rawson and Rogers (1976, p. 28) comment, 'only rarely do plans consider more than the simple spatial attributes of the housing stock'.

Some local authorities, such as Suffolk, Cornwall and Northumberland, have operated build-for-sale schemes whereby council tenants and those on the waiting list can buy new houses at a reasonable price while the council retains a right to repurchase within five years. A related strategy is for the local authority to buy private houses for relet or resale. This could be appropriate where a mismatch between size of house and owner's need has arisen with life-cycle change. Other possible schemes to assist local residents to enter the housing market include (a) assisting individuals and self-help groups by acquiring and servicing suitable land, (b) entering into more short-term letting agreements to ensure that houses do not stand empty unnecessarily, (c) rehabilitation of existing property, (d) promoting starter-home, equity-sharing and self-build schemes, and (e) encouraging housing association action. In Canada home ownership for the marginal buyer is subsidized by an interest-free government loan to supplement the amount they can borrow from private financial institutions. In West Germany local government will pay a subsidy to the owner of rented property to allow him to rent it at a lower cost to a low-income family. In the USA the Farmers Home Administration (FmHA) has been responsible since 1949 for providing aid, mainly in the form of mortgage loans, for rural housing projects; and the aid is now available to most farming and nonfarming rural people. All of these schemes, however, are dependent upon the availability of public funds.

Planning powers may be used in an attempt to ensure local people gain access to local housing. Measures include: (a) the local planning authority could require builders to provide a range of dwelling types; (b) compulsory purchase can minimize the land cost element in house prices; (c) restrictions on density, on the basis that higher densities will result in smaller house sizes and prices which may be affordable by local people and first-time buyers; (d) release of larger development sites in small units aimed at local builders, on the assumption that they will tend to sell a greater proportion of houses to local people than their national counterparts; (e) planning for a controlled supply of land at current-use value for residential development; and (f) refusal of planning permission where the development does not accord with planning priorities.

A more radical approach would be to legislate for the exclusion of nonlocals from certain rural areas. Such legislation exists in Jersey and Guernsey where heavy external demand for housing has conflicted with the need to safeguard a limited supply of land. The Guernsey authorities operate a system of 'controlled accommodation', access to which is confined to those who either hold a residential qualification or are employed in an occupation essential to the community, such as schoolteachers, doctors or dentists. The only other means of entry via the open market excludes all but a wealthy minority. It is unlikely that such close bureaucratic control over housing would be acceptable elsewhere.

Some pressured rural areas in Britain, however, have adopted variants of this type of exclusionary policy in an attempt to protect local housing needs. The best example is provided by the debate over private housing development and planning policy in the Lake District. The Lake District has a relatively small stock of 17,000 houses, 87.0 percent of which are privately owned or rented. These have been subject to purchase by outsiders for decades, and the large number of second homes has tended to make it more expensive for native Lakelanders to obtain a house, thus exacerbating the central problem of rural depopulation. Prior to 1974, the policy was to give planning permission for relatively large numbers of new houses in order to accommodate the rural–urban drift of population within the region, to replace substandard stock to be demolished, to accommodate new household formation, and to stem depopulation. By the early 1970s, however, this expansionist policy was subject to attack on several grounds: (1) the increased supply of houses had no discernible effect on reducing the high cost of housing in the Lake District; (2) concern was expressed over the extent to which houses of all types, including new houses, were being converted for use as holiday homes; (3) there was concern over the visual impact of the new house building; (4) finally, the 45.0 percent increase in the number of houses had not halted rural depopulation.

Accordingly, the late 1970s witnessed a reversal of housing policy (Clark 1982). The new policy increased public intervention in the private housing market and the main thrust was two-pronged. First, the rate of new house building was severely restricted to only 70 houses per year. Secondly, the small number of houses which were built would be reserved exclusively for local people, using powers vested in all planning authorities under Section 52 of the 1971 Town and Country Planning Act. Permission to build a new house would only be given if it was to be sold to a local person who had been or who would be employed locally and who would live in the house for more than six months of each year. This restricted covenant would be binding on all subsequent owners of the house. Since the demand from potential second home owners would be excluded, these new houses ought to be cheaper than comparable property open to all bidders. Thus, the intention was that positive discrimination in favour of local workers would counter the inflationary effect of the restricted number of new houses.

The effects of the Section 52 policy are difficult to assess given its short duration. It is not clear whether, in practice, it is the marginal house-buyer who will benefit. There has been some evidence, for example, that building societies will advance only 70.0–80.0 percent of the purchase price of Section 52 houses compared with 85.0–95.0 percent which is normal for most other properties. This would partly negate any benefit from a lower selling price particularly for first-time buyers with limited savings (Clark 1982). Although the use of Section 52 agreements has been opposed by central government the strategy represented a particular local response to a widespread problem created by external demand for housing in rural areas. The pressures which have created the general problem of meeting local housing needs are as insistent as ever.

The structure planning framework is not equipped to deal with such issues. A structure plan is a policy document primarily concerned with physical planning and not with social policy issues, such as housing need. The statutory planning system controls neither the occupancy of houses nor the price at which a dwelling is sold. Furthermore, planning policy can only influence the scale and location of new dwellings and cannot assist the entry of local people into the existing, noncouncil, housing stock. As Dunn et al. (1981, p. 206) remark, 'planners are on more certain ground when they are viewing rural housing in the context of settlement policies and development control ... but when issues of tenure choice or of identifying households as "locals" or second home owners are involved, the planner has moved away from his area of experience and, more particularly, from the area where he has powers to control'. Clark (1982, p. 110) echoes this view when he summarizes the views of the Secretary of State on the draft structure plans for the Lake District and Peak District in the words, 'clearly planning is about land use and not land users'. Nevertheless 'so many of the problems of rural housing and indeed of rural planning generally come back to the inhabitants of the houses rather than the houses themselves' (Rawson and Rogers 1976, p. 27). In this situation it is inevitable that strictly land use planning procedures will be found wanting when faced with human problems.

References

AMBROSE, P. (1974) *The Quiet Revolution*. London: Chatto and Windus.

BENNETT, S. (1976) *Rural housing in the Lake District*, Lancaster University.

BIRD, R. and KAMPE, R. (1977) *Twenty Five Years of Housing Progress in Rural America* Agricultural Economic Report No. 373. Washington DC: US Department of Agriculture.

BONHAM-CARTER, V. (1952) *The English Village*. Harmondsworth: Penguin.

BRUNSKILL, R. W. (1971) *Illlustrated Handbook of Vernacular Architecture*. London: Faber and Faber.

BURKE, G. (1981) *Housing and Social Justice*. London: Longman.

CENSUS RESEARCH UNIT (1980) *People in Britain – a Census Atlas*. London: HMSO.

CLARK, G. (1982) *Housing and Planning in the Countryside*. Chichester: Wiley.

CLOKE, P. J. (1979) *Key Settlements in Rural Areas*. London: Methuen.

CULLINGWORTH, J. B. (1979) *Essays on Housing Policy: The British Scene*. London: Allen and Unwin.

DEATON, B. J. and HANRAHAN, C. E. (1973) Rural housing needs and barriers: the case of Central Appalachia, *Southern Journal of Agricultural Economics* 5(1), 59–67.

DEMANGEON, A. (1920) L'habitation rurale en France: essai de classification, *Annales de Géographie* 29, 325–52.

DUNN, M., RAWSON, M. and ROGERS, A. (1981) *Rural Housing: Competition and Choice*. London: Allen and Unwin.

DURANT, T. J. and KNOWLTON, C. S. (1978) Rural ethnic minorities: adaptive response to inequality. *In* T. R. Ford *Rural USA: Persistence and Change*. Ames: Iowa State University Press, 145–67.

GASSON, R. (1975) *Provision of Tied Cottages* Occasional Paper No. 4. Cambridge: University Department of Land Economy.

HOSKINS, W. G. (1955) *The Making of the English Landscape*. London: Hodder and Stoughton.

HOUSTON, J. M. (1964) *The Western Mediterranean World*. London: Longman.

JONES, A. (1975) *The Agricultural Tied Cottage*. London: Bell.

KNIFFEN, F. B. (1936) Louisiana house types, *Annals of the Association of American Geographers* 26, 180–81.

LARKIN, A. (1978) Rural housing: too dear, too far, too few, *Roof* 3, 15–17.

LARKIN, A. (1979) Rural housing and housing needs. *In* J. M. Shaw *Rural Deprivation and Planning*. Norwich: Geo Books, 71–80.

LIMMER, R. and McGOUGH, D. (1979) *How Well Are We Housed?: 5 Rural* HUD-PDR-500. Washington DC: Department of Housing and Urban Development.

MARANTZ, J. K., CASE, K. E. and LEONARD, H. B. (1976) *Discrimination in Rural Housing*. Lexington: D. C. Heath.

MINISTRY OF WORKS AND PLANNING (1942) *Report of the Committee on Land Utilisation in Rural Areas* (The Scott Report) Cmd 6378. London: HMSO.

OGDEN, P. E. (1978) Analyse multivariée et structure régionale: transformations socio-économiques récentes dans le Massif Central de l'est, *Méditerranée* 3, 45–58.

PAHL, R. E. (1966) The social objectives of village planning. *Official Architecture and Planning* 29(8), 146–50.

PENFOLD, S. F. (1974) *Housing Problems of Local People in Rural Pressure Areas: the Peak District Experience and Discussion of Policy Options*. Department of Town and Regional Planning, University of Sheffield.

PHILLIPS, D. and WILLIAMS, A. M. (1982) *Rural Housing and the Public Sector*. Aldershot: Gower.

PHILLIPS, D. and WILLIAMS, A. (1983) The social implications of rural housing policy. *In* A. W. Gilg *Countryside Planning Yearbook* 4, 77–102.

RAWSON, M. and ROGERS, A. (1976) *Rural Housing and Structure Plans* Working Paper No. 1. Countryside Planning Unit, Wye College, University of London.

RICKERT, J. E. (1967) House facades of the Northeastern United States, *Annals of the Association of American Geographers* 57, 211–38.

ROGERS, A. (1976) Rural housing. *In* G. E. Cherry *Rural Planning Problems*. London: Leonard Hill, 85–122.

ROGERS, A. (1981) Housing in the national parks, *Town and Country Planning* 50(7), 193–95.

ROGERS, A. (1983) Housing. *In* M. Pacione *Progress in Rural Geography*. London: Croom Helm, 106–29.

SCHIFFERES, S. (1980) Housing Bill 1980: the beginning of the end for council housing, *Roof* 5, 10–15.

SHUCKSMITH, D. M. (1981) *No Homes for Locals?* Farnborough: Gower.

SMYTHE, J. (1976) *Tied Housing in Scotland.* Edinburgh: Shelter.

THURGOOD, G. (1978) Rural housing initiatives – are we doing enough? *The Planner* 64(5), 143–45.

TREWARTHA, G. T. (1948) Some regional characteristics of American farmsteads, *Annals of the Association of American Geographers* 38, 169–225.

14   Employment and rural development

The principal energizing force behind rural emigration is the lack of local employment opportunities (Figure 14.1). This deficiency is reflected in high levels of unemployment, low activity rates, particularly among women, and low incomes, in addition to outmigration of young people. As the example of England and Wales indicates (Figure 14.2), there is a clear positive relationship between the severity of these problems and degree of rurality as measured by distance from the urban heart of the country. Similarly, in the USA Chadwick and Bahr (1978, p. 188) also found that 'generally, as rurality increased, labor force participation decreased'. In terms of particular population groups the impact of these problems falls most heavily on school-leavers, women, the elderly and the unskilled (Packman 1979; Dower 1980).

Prospects for primary sector employment

Though seldom the only source of work in the countryside, farming has long been a central component of the rural economy. The decline in agricultural employment as a result of increased mechanization and modernization is a widely observed trend in most developed countries (Table 14.1). This labour-shedding process has gone furthest in the UK where only about 2.0 percent of the workforce are now engaged in agriculture. Even at this low level, however, it is estimated that the labour force is still

Figure 14.1 The principle of circular and cumulative causation.

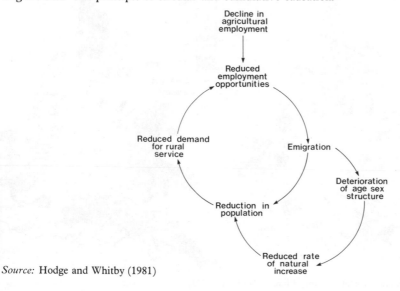

Source: Hodge and Whitby (1981)

243

Figure 14.2 Selected socio-economic characteristics for rural England and Wales: (a) percentage change in 1961 5–14 age group on becoming 1971 15–24 age group by county rural areas; (b) population over retirement age as a percentage of total population by county rural areas, 1971; (c) male employees in the five lowest paid industrial orders (SIC Orders: I – agriculture, forestry and fishing; XV – clothing and footwear; XVII – timber and furniture; XXIII – distribution; and XXVI – miscellaneous) as a percentage of total male employees, by county rural employment areas, 1976; (d) percentage economic activity among females aged 15–59, by county rural area, 1971.

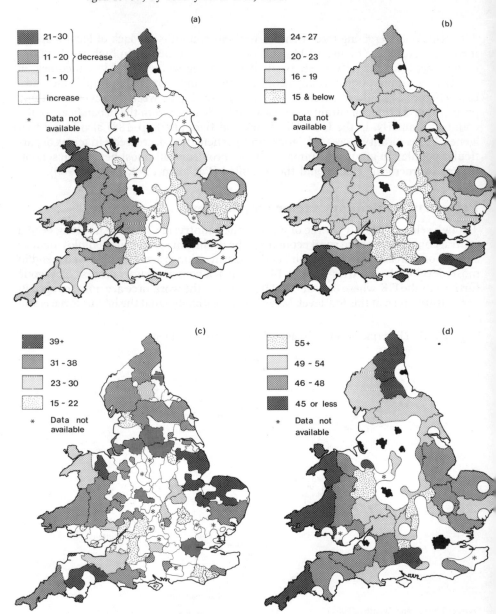

Source: J. M. Shaw, Norfolk County Planning Officer (1979)

declining at a rate of approximately 3.0 percent per annum, and British experience may well presage events elsewhere (Gilg 1983). Despite some movement 'back to the land' by 'urban dropouts', agriculture is unlikely to support a large part of the rural population in the future.

The modernization of agriculture has been accompanied by an increase in the economic interdependence between it and other industries. Farm inputs are now purchased from the chemical and engineering industries and a range of transport, communication and professional services are also required. On the output side the share of sales requiring further processing beyond the farm gate has increased with the spread of manufactured food products and convenience foods. As Hodge and Whitby (1981, p. 61) point out, however, 'the new industries on which agriculture now depends are not necessarily tied to rural areas, indeed in many cases their dependence on economies of scale (agricultural machinery) or imported inputs (fertilisers) often makes it unlikely that they will locate in rural areas'. Only for certain industries, such as food processing, will the balance favour rural locations when transport costs, availability of raw materials and of labour are taken into account. Thus, the loss of jobs in agriculture has not been offset by growth of alternative employment opportunities in other sectors (Commins 1978; Doeksen and Schriener 1971).

Table 14.1   *Proportion of the labour force employed in agriculture, 1965, 1977*

	Percent of economically active population in agriculture	
	1965	**1977**
World	54.2	46.2
Developed countries	23.4	13.6
Developing countries	69.4	60.7
North America	5.6	2.7
W. Europe	24.6	11.4
Oceania	10.3	6.8
Canada	10.7	5.6
USA	5.1	2.4
Belgium-Luxembourg	6.6	3.4
Denmark	14.4	7.7
France	17.9	9.5
GDR	15.3	10.2
Ireland	31.4	22.0
Italy	24.8	12.5
Netherlands	9.4	5.8
Norway	15.7	8.5
Spain	34.0	18.9
Sweden	11.0	5.6
Switzerland	9.4	5.6
UK	3.4	2.2
Australia	9.6	6.2
New Zealand	13.2	9.7

Source: Hodge and Whitby (1981)

Forestry is another extensive primary land use. In the United Kingdom the Forestry Commission is the country's biggest single landowner and owns or manages almost half of the country's 2 million hectares of forest. Forecasts of labour requirements in British forestry under three different planting strategies have been produced by the Commission (Table 14.2). Such forecasting is notoriously difficult, however, since assumptions must be made on a host of variables including future timber prices and the demand for timber products, the age structure of plantations, and the effect of scale economies and the impact of technology on the industry. The distribution of age classes within a forest is of great importance in determining the demand for labour, since there is a peak labour requirement at planting and at felling but very little demand in between. According to Inglis (1977) over a 50-year production cycle more than two-thirds of all the employment generated by initiation of new planting will not appear until the final year. About one-seventh of the total employment arises in the first 3 years. In Britain the maturation period of conifers and the age distribution of forests (Table 14.3) suggest that the demand for labour will mainly reflect the rate of new planting over the next decade or two but thereafter felling will become important as the post World War II plantings mature. Clearly

Table 14.2   *Forecasts of labour requirements in UK forestry*

	Assumed rate of productivity change	Labour requirements in thousand man-years		
		1985	2000	2025
Forestry Labour				
Alternative 1 –				
No more planting	0	19.0	25.4	33.2
	+2.5%	14.8	13.7	9.7
	+4.0%	12.9	9.6	4.7
Alternative 2 –				
Planting another 1 million	0	22.3	30.2	47.7
hectares	+2.5%	17.4	16.3	13.9
	+4.0%	15.1	11.3	6.7
Alternative 3 –				
Planting another	0	23.6	33.0	55.7
1.8 million hectares	+2.5%	18.5	17.8	16.3
	+4.0%	16.0	12.4	7.8
Net job loss in agriculture				
Alternative 1		0	0	0
Alternative 2		0.6	1.0	0.7
Alternative 3		0.8	1.4	1.2

Source: Forestry Commission (1977)

Table 14.3   *The age class distribution of forests in Great Britain*

	Planting years						
	post-1970	1961–1970	1951–1960	1941–1950	1931–1940	1901–1930	pre-1900
			(thousand hectares)				
Conifers	383	362	325	113	100	53	12
Broad-leaves	13	14	25	16	15	55	183

Source: Centre for Agricultural Strategy (1980)

though, improvements in harvesting techniques will also influence forest labour requirements. Employment opportunities in downstream wood processing industries also depend on which planting strategy is adopted (Table 14.4). While these labour requirements in processing are of modest proportions they do relate entirely to rural areas, where absolute increases of this order may guarantee sufficient income to sustain many vulnerable communities.

Table 14.4   *Forecasts of employment in wood processing in rural areas assuming traditional cutting regime (thousand man-years)*

	1975	2000	2025
Alternatives			
1. No more new planting	4.0	4.6	3.5
2. Plant another 1 million hectares	4.0	4.6	4.6
3. Plant another 1.8 million hectares	4.0	4.6	5.0

Source: Forestry Commission (1977)

The location of employment opportunities in other primary activities like mining and quarrying is entirely dominated by the distribution of natural resources, exploitation of which is determined primarily on the basis of quality of the raw material and its ease of extraction. Such operations tend to be highly capital intensive, require few locally produced inputs, and operate with a limited time horizon. Consequently they are unlikely to have a significant effect on rural employment beyond their immediate location.

Rural industrialization

The transfer of employment opportunities from the primary to secondary and tertiary activities is a concomitant part of the development process. Agriculture, forestry and the extractive industries are no longer major rural employers and, to an increasing extent, the employment prospects for rural dwellers will be found in manufacturing and service industries. Processing of rural products would appear to be an activity well suited to employment creation in rural areas. This would include the canning and freezing of vegetables or meat, and the processing of dairy products, sugar, cloth, wool or timber. There are, however, several limitations. The first is that the capital investment involved in processing often requires that equipment be operated for most of the year to obtain an acceptable return, whereas a region may be able only to supply agricultural produce over a limited period. Secondly, the close relationship between processing plants and the agricultural enterprises from which they obtain their raw materials means that instability either in supply or market demand will have serious consequences for regions whose incomes are heavily dependent upon these two sources alone.

In theory the majority of manufacturing activities could be undertaken in rural areas. For example, Summers et al. (1976) found a wide variety of products in a survey of 198 manufacturing plants in nonmetropolitan areas of the USA. These included chemicals, textiles, shoes and apparel, paper, glass, electronics, furniture and engineering, in addition to the traditional food-related operations. In the UK Howard (1968) and Spooner (1972) found a similar range of activities among migrant firms, with significant representation in engineering and electrical goods, and clothing and footwear manufacture. Among the reasons for this is that many light engineering factories are characterized by standardized production, dependence on semiskilled labour, unspecialized requirements for buildings, use of a ubiquitous power source in electricity, and high value to weight products. In addition many electrical and electronics factories have become oriented towards large-scale component assembly by women, while the importance of clothing and footwear plants reflects the unspecialized requirements of these industries.

The facilities which are required in an area, whether urban or rural, to allow the establishment of manufacturing will clearly depend on the type and scale of activity being considered, but in general the following factors will be of importance to most enterprises: (a) the availability, quality and cost of labour; (b) costs of transporting inputs and products; (c) availability and cost of energy supplies; (d) attractiveness of area to key workers and management; (e) presence of local or regional markets; (f) linkages with other firms or parent plant; (g) availability of suitable site and premises; (h) local authority cooperation, for example in the provision of housing for key workers; and (i) availability of government grants and incentives. Rural areas can face particular problems stemming from the difficulty of acquiring and maintaining a sufficient pool of local labour, the inability to exploit external economies available to firms in urban locations, and the impact of distance from markets and raw materials on a firm's competitive position. Rural locations, however, do possess compensating advantages that may offset these difficulties for some producers. Land prices are generally lower than in cities; space is normally available for manufacturing and storage of bulky products or for subsequent expansion; the absence of congestion can reduce the frictional effect of distance in terms of travel time; and a degree of 'psychic income' may be derived from an attractive environment.

Particular importance has been attached to the role of small firms in generating employment in rural areas. While there is evidence to suggest that small businesses are important in generating new employment in manufacturing both in the USA and

Britain (Storey 1980), small firms are also likely to be more liable to closure, a fact which has significant implications for small communities with limited alternative employment opportunities. A constant source of new employment through plant openings and company growth is therefore necessary in order to maintain employment levels. Barkley and Paulsen (1979), for example, found that in nonmetropolitan Iowa an average of more than 4,000 jobs were eliminated during each of the previous 11 years due to plant failures and outmigrations. The continuing challenge for rural areas, therefore, is to attract manufacturers in sufficient numbers to make industrial employment in the area self-generating. As well as the question of the longevity of new enterprises, the type of labour required (male or female; full-time or part-time; skilled or unskilled) will determine the value of a new factory to the local economy (Bertrand 1978; Hodge and Whitby 1981).

The service sector

It can be argued that with the advent of a postindustrial society manufacturing industry will experience the same fate as agriculture, leaving the tertiary sector as the only substantial employment growth area. Employment in the service sector includes wholesale and retail trading, banking and finance, transport and communications, and government services and administration. Much of this, however, tends to be concentrated in the larger places within the rural area, and, with the exception of popular retirement areas and the metropolitan commuter zones, the withdrawal of many services has exacerbated the shift of employment away from the countryside. Furthermore, many service industries are susceptible to the displacement of labour by modern technology. Some decentralization of office-based employment from urban areas is technically possible for services which do not require face-to-face contact with the populations they serve (e.g. insurance and finance companies), but, as with other types of enterprise, service activities will not locate in rural areas unless the advantages of the new location outweigh those of a central city site. The remoter rural areas would seem to be unlikely locations for most service activities (Hodge and Whitby 1981).

The quality of the environment represents rural areas' greatest asset in the competition for jobs, either directly by encouraging recreation and tourism, or indirectly by providing an attractive living environment for those working in secondary or tertiary activities. Tourism is one service activity with particular potential to bring more jobs and income to rural areas. Measuring the total employment impact of recreation and tourist activities is extremely difficult, however, given the part-time nature of providing services such as bed and breakfast for tourists, the seasonality of many recreational and tourist activities, and the likelihood that many facilities will also be used for nontourist purposes. Nevertheless Dower (1980) has estimated that in terms of direct and indirect employment tourism supports at least 9.0 percent of the total civilian workforce in southwest England, 11.0 percent in Cornwall and 10.0 percent in Pembrokeshire. On the island of Anglesey Archer (1974) calculated that each £10,000-worth of tourist expenditure generated 4.3 direct and 0.49 indirect jobs; a figure which compared well with the effects of general expenditure which generated 1.9 direct and 0.49 indirect jobs per £10,000. Smith and Wilde (1977) have provided a similar impact study for tourism in western Tasmania. In many peripheral rural areas, such as the crofting communities of north and west Scotland, part-time involvement with tourism can offer an important additional source of income (Dartington Amenity Research Trust 1974; Denham 1978). Significantly, in this respect, Archer (1974) found that the single highest income multiplier impact of tourism expenditure among hotels, caravans, tents and 'farmhouse and bed and breakfast' provision was in the last category. Thus, the small-scale, labour-intensive facilities seem to offer the best return per unit of tourist expenditure. As Hodge and Whitby (1981) emphasize, however, farmhouse developments are likely to be very small and their absolute economic impact will not be regionally significant unless a high proportion of small farmers provide facilities.

The discussion so far has assumed the largely unfettered operation of market forces in the generation of rural employment opportunities. Alternative patterns of development will result where governments intervene to stimulate new jobs. Among the reasons for government action are the following: (a) unequal standards of living and other general inequalities create rifts and divisions in society; (b) agriculture and other primary activities cannot by themselves support economically efficient communities; (c) most rural areas have substantial reserves of labour which if brought into employment would not only boost the Gross National Product but would also save government expenditure on unemployment and other State benefits; (d) a continued exodus of people and jobs from the remote to the already overcrowded urban areas would lead to intensification of congestion in the latter areas; (e) rural areas contain social capital which in a period of low economic growth is expensive to replace and reconstruct in another location; (f) most people living in rural areas do not wish to leave, and many who have left would return given the opportunity. Such arguments do not advocate that all rural settlements should be retained, but that efforts should aim to maintain regional totals. It follows, therefore, that employment policies for rural areas must first of all be regional policies, within which local policies can be evolved (Gilg 1976).

Rural development agencies

The need for a comprehensive integrated approach to the development of rural areas is widely recognized (Green 1971; Wibberley 1976; Northfield 1977; Gilg 1980). Comprehensive development is an approach which emphasizes the combined effects of individual policies and tries to ensure that activities are planned with interaction in mind, so that they work together to further overall objectives. This goes beyond post-facto coordination of sectoral plans to which agencies are already largely committed and which have been prepared separately within a strictly limited outlook. Robinson (1972) has detailed the characteristics which a rural comprehensive development agency should possess. It would (1) operate on a regional scale, (2) treat economic, social and physical planning as a combined operation, (3) be innovative in outlook, (4) have powers of intervention and its own budget, (5) have a continuing role and be allowed to take a long-term view of problem solving, and (6) be an indigenous agency, thus avoiding problems of alienation, misinformation and misinterpretation which can accompany planning from a distance.

Rural development agencies have been established in several countries in attempts to alleviate the inequitable distribution of social and economic opportunities.

Great Britain

Several agencies currently operate in rural Britain.

1.   The Development Commission   The Commission has no executive function but recommends projects to the Department of the Environment for financing from the Development Fund, the general aim being to assist any scheme calculated to benefit the rural economy. Since 1976 the Commission's responsibilities have been limited to England with separate Development Agencies established for Scotland and Wales. The scope of the Commission's activities has altered considerably since its creation in 1909. Its current interests are (a) building advance factories in problem rural areas, (b) assisting, advising and offering training to rural industries, and (c) giving financial support to voluntary and self-governing organizations providing rural services, to assist their work of sustaining the social fabric. The main agents of the Development Commission are the Council for Small Industries in Rural Areas (COSIRA) and the English Industrial Estate Corporation (EIEC).

The construction of small advance factory premises (140 m^2–1400 m^2) in selected growth points is undertaken within the government's Assisted Areas by the EIEC on the Commission's behalf, and elsewhere by COSIRA. In the mid 1960s the Commission designated several 'trigger areas' as experiments in concentration of resources on small-growth zones for greater impact. By 1973 50 factories and nursery clusters of workshops had been established in three trigger areas, mainly in Scotland and Wales. Since 1975 attention has been focused on two types of area: (1) Special Investment Areas which are those suffering from a variety of symptoms of rural deprivation including depopulation, high unemployment and an ageing population; and (2) Pockets of Need seen as smaller areas with more localized and less severe problems (Hillier 1982). An important distinction between the Commission's activities and the more general government regional aid policies is that 'the Department of Trade and Industry seek a reduction of unemployment by the attraction of footloose industry whereas the Commission's activities have been aimed more clearly at the development of indigenous industry in order to stem depopulation' (Clarkson 1980, p. 5).

On the whole the Development Commission has been successful in finding tenants for its advance factories. The position in mid 1976 was that the total factory space constructed since 1959 represented just over 50.0 percent of the floor space approved and less than 10.0 percent of it remained unallocated. Since then the rate of factory building in England has increased and by March 1979 689 factories had been approved covering nearly 2 million square feet; 160 of the factories had been completed and a further 202 were under construction. Of the units completed only 20.0 percent were unoccupied. The Commission estimated that 1,600 jobs had been created in the factories and that completion of all approvals would bring another 6,200 jobs (Development Commission 1980). Although such employment figures are minute in a national context, they can have a considerable impact on the small local communities in which the developments are located. While it is difficult to identify the numbers of jobs actually created through COSIRA's assistance, 'the organisation would appear to be making a valuable contribution to the growth of small firms in rural areas' (Hodge and Whitby 1981, p. 114). In cost terms Hodge and Whitby (1979) found that discounting the cost per direct employee over time, and taking into account savings in unemployment benefit and the extra tax revenue, COSIRA investment in the eastern Borders showed a positive rate of return over 25 years. A recurrent problem, however, is that in both the eastern Borders (Hodge and Whitby 1979) and eastern England (Hillier 1982) most employment opportunities created were for full-time males, with few jobs for part-time workers, females, or out-workers. The latter study also found that COSIRA developments have provided very few new opportunities for school-leavers.

Overall the scale of Development Commission/COSIRA intervention is limited by the size of its budget allocation so 'it is unlikely that its development projects alone will greatly increase the chances of rural recovery' (Hillier 1982, p. 194). However, COSIRA units do provide opportunities for entrepreneurs, if not to start up new establishments, at least to relocate to accommodation more conducive to growth. COSIRA appears to plug a market gap with the type of accommodation it provides, offering premises for about five years during which time the firm is able to consolidate its operations to a point at which it may seek a move to larger premises elsewhere. This is a valuable service for small firms as the private speculative industrial developer is unlikely to be attracted by the uncertain returns from such schemes in areas suffering from the lack of a traditional industrial base, high unemployment rates, a general shortage of facilities, and an isolated location remote from the main national transport routes and markets. COSIRA advice and training schemes are also important.

It has been suggested that in order to maximize its impact the remit of the Development Commission should be expanded to enable it, for example, to provide venture capital throughout rural areas either by directly lending money or by standing security on loans. Northfield (1977) suggests that a logical development would be towards an independent executive rural development agency for England, on the lines of the Scottish and Welsh bodies, operating within its own priorities and budget.

2. Rural Development Boards These agencies stemmed from the proposals in the 1967 Agriculture Act to establish in areas of hill land Rural Development Boards designed to (1) overcome difficulties in formation of commercial units of agricultural land, (2) guide decisions on the complementary use of land for agriculture and forestry, (3) improve public services, and (4) preserve and exploit the amenities and scenery. The origins, rationale and operation of these agencies have been discussed elsewhere (House 1976; Childs and Minay 1977).

In pursuit of these objectives and with the slow natural rate of change in the structure of agriculture in mind, the Boards were given powers to acquire land by compulsory purchase if necessary; to manage, improve, farm, sell or let the land; and to use it to promote the amalgamation of small uneconomic holdings. There are clear similarities here with the principles behind the SAFERs (Sociétés d'Aménagement

Foncier et d'Établissement Rural) which were introduced in France in the early 1960s with the twin objectives of improving the structure of agricultural holdings and reducing speculation in the land market. Most importantly, all sales of agricultural land in a SAFER region must be approved by the SAFER. Not surprisingly, the most controversial of the Rural Development Board powers were those which gave authority to intervene in land transfers and to object to changes in land use considered detrimental to the community good.

In practice, only one Rural Development Board was established in Britain: for an area of 800,000 ha of the northern Pennines containing 6,246 farms, one-third of which were nonviable according to the Ministry of Agriculture's economic criterion of units requiring 275 SMDs (Standard Man Days) of labour input. Three-fifths of the farms did not provide enough work for a full-time worker, and providing only a bare subsistence for the farmer they did not allow any capital to be accumulated for improvements that might raise productivity. The efforts of the North Pennines Rural Development Board, however, were short-lived as the agency was disbanded after only 17 months by a Conservative government to which the principle of public power over land transfer was an anathema. The proposal for a second Rural Development Board for Mid Wales was also abandoned in 1970; this region has evolved an alternative development structure, however, culminating in the formation of the Development Board for Rural Wales in 1977 (Jones 1972; Minay 1976; Carney and Hudson 1979; Broady 1980).

3.   The Highlands and Islands Development Board   Established in 1965 by Act of Parliament, this agency has the two-fold purpose of assisting the people of the Highlands and Islands to improve their economic and social conditions, and enabling the region to play a more effective part in the economic and social development of the nation. The Board has wide powers and finance to make grants and loans to private enterprises, to carry out projects itself, to enter into and acquire private land and buildings, to concert and assist other activities, and to keep the economy and welfare of the area under review (Grieve 1972).

These powers of interaction allow the Board to influence almost all aspects of Highland life and resource use, but its work has become increasingly selective and concentrated upon particular subregions such as the 'growth areas' of Fort William, Inverness and Caithness, and on particular activities such as fishing, bulb growing in the Hebrides, a range of large and small craft industries, new hotels and other tourist accommodation, as well as major industrial developments. Such a concentration of effort is tacit acknowledgement of the fact that 'the task of taking jobs to every one of the pockets of unemployment is an impossible one' (Highlands and Islands Development Board 1967, p. 14).

It is also significant that the Board has involved itself more in the nonagricultural field by developing forestry, fishing, tourism and manufacturing activities. Although in 1968 the Board acquired the same powers as the North Pennines Rural Development Board to intervene in the land market it has not used them (Clark 1979). This decision is based on the belief that the benefits to be gained, in terms of agricultural productivity, from compulsory land purchase and farm enlargement are outweighed in this region by the social costs in terms of resentment by local farmers. The

Highlands and Islands Development Board, therefore, has made only cautious moves to improve the structure of Highland agriculture and has concentrated instead on fostering alternative sources of employment.

At first sight the Highlands and Islands Development Board seems to be very similar to the short-lived North Pennines Rural Development Board and the aborted Rural Development Board for Mid Wales – with the important difference that it appears to work successfully. The long-standing problem of depopulation has been halted, and even reversed in parts of the region, unemployment levels have been reduced, and regional incomes have been brought closer to the national average. It is, of course, difficult to disentangle the effects of North Sea oil and those of the Board's policies in improving the regional economy. The most dramatic reversal of population trends, in the eastern Highlands, is clearly attributable to oil-related factors, but the more modest net reversal of depopulation in the western Highlands is strong evidence of the Board's impact. A number of reasons may be suggested for the Board's success: (1) the failure of earlier isolated improvement projects and recognition that the region was living on or beyond the physical, economic and social margins instilled a general willingness in the Highlands and Islands to try out a more comprehensive approach to the problems; (2) the Highlands and Islands Development Board has recognized that different areas within the depressed region have special difficulties that require sympathetic individual treatment – while the growth area concept has been applied, particularly in relation to major industrial development, assistance has also been given to other activities, ranging from small businesses to the large tourism and recreation complex at Aviemore; (3) in contrast to the North Pennines Rural Development Board the HIDB has moved with great caution into agricultural improvement through intervention in the land market; and (4) the Board deals with a well-defined geographic region and is an indigenous agency with its headquarters in Inverness. The Highlands and Islands Development Board is now an established part of British rural planning, and is the rural development agency which most closely resembles Robinson's (1972) ideal type.

Europe

Integrated management schemes have been implemented by rural development corporations operating in parts of France, such as Languedoc and the Massif Central, as well as other regions of Western Europe (Moore 1979; Grafton 1980). Most of these attract investment funds both from national governments and from EEC organizations such as the European Investment Bank (EIB), European Social Fund (ESF), and European Agricultural Guidance and Guarantee Fund (FEOGA).

The Italian Mezzogiorno is the largest problem region on the Continent. The area, which covers 40.0 percent of the national territory and contains 36.0 percent of the population, exhibits all of the characteristics of economic infirmity. In the early 1950s per capita income was just over half of the national average, only 40.0 percent of that in the north of Italy, and 22.0 percent of that in the USA. Even more seriously, the disparity in income levels between north and south was progressively widening. The creation of a regional development corporation (Cassa per il Mezzogiorno) in 1950 marked the first comprehensive attempt to tackle the region's problems. The work of the Cassa can be divided into three main phases: (1) a preindustrialization period (1950–1957) in which the emphasis was on schemes related to agrarian reform; (2) the period between 1957 and 1965 when explicit recognition was given to the need to invest more of the Cassa's funds in industrial projects than in agriculture – this new policy direction has underlain all subsequent planning for the region; (3) from 1965 to the present time, in which reaffirmation of the importance of industry has been combined with increasing attention to and growing expenditure on developing the tourist potential of the region.

The two most important elements of economic policy since 1957 have been the use of State-controlled firms in the pursuit of southern industrialization and the development of a growth centre strategy (Pacione 1976, 1982). Doubts have been cast on the effectiveness of growth poles to spread benefits to surrounding small towns and rural areas. Moseley's (1973) studies of small-growth centres in Brittany and East Anglia, for example, indicated that the 'trickle down' effect cannot be relied on. He did admit, however, that 'large centres may be much more effective as sources of trickle down' (Ibid., p. 93). Richardson (1976, p. 8) maintains that effective regional planning requires a 15–25 year time horizon and concludes that 'a well-located growth pole, promoted with vigor in appropriate economic conditions and resistant to political trimming, should pay off as a regional planning policy instrument if the planning horizon is long enough'.

The Cassa per il Mezzogiorno has been concerned with industrial development of the south for the last quarter of a century. Many of its past efforts were of a long-term nature and are only now beginning to pay dividends. Although the long-standing crisis has not been solved, significant strides have been made to reduce the life quality disparities between the region and the rest of the country. Much of the credit for this must go to the Cassa's efforts to reorient the economic structure of the region which is now better prepared for growth with a lower weighting of agriculture and a higher proportion of modern industry, utilizing a better-trained labour force. Infrastructural improvements are widespread and include one of the finest motorway networks in Europe. While the region is still poor relative to the north, private consumption and per capita incomes have increased while other deprivation indicators, such as infant mortality, illiteracy and overcrowding, have all been reduced. Given the established tendency for people and prosperity to concentrate in the main industrial-growth areas of a country to the detriment of outlying regions, these improvements in social and economic conditions must be considered a real achievement.

USA

Postwar persistence of pronounced regional disparities in economic opportunity and living standards led the US government to endorse the idea of revitalizing rural areas through other than strictly agricultural policies. Legislation designed to encourage capital investment in rural areas includes the Economic Opportunity Act 1964, the Public Works and Economic Development Act 1965, the Appalachian Regional Development Act 1965, and the Rural Development Act 1972. An important feature was the formula for establishing cooperative federal and multistate regional planning commissions for problem areas straddling state lines. Under the 1965 legislation five 'Title V' Commissions were initially established and a separate Regional Planning Commission was provided for Appalachia (Figure 14.3). The former agencies have not fulfilled expectations, largely due to a low level of funding, the indifference of successive Federal administrations, and an unproductive relationship with the Economic Development Administration, the main Federal agency established in 1965 to pursue nationwide area development objectives (Gibson 1981). Thus, 'a realistic assessment of the Title V Commissions would be that they have largely failed in their task of promoting the economic development of lagging regions in a cooperative multi-state planning context' (Estall 1982, p. 37).

The regional commission set up for Appalachia has been more successful and has been cited as a possible model for rural development planning elsewhere. Like the Title V Commissions the Appalachian Regional Commission (ARC) is a comprehensive planning agency with Federal authority to produce a multistate development plan, but it has particular characteristics which distinguish it from the other agencies. It is controlled by representatives of both state and Federal government which ensures regular consultation on the disposition of Federal resources within the region. As well as involving both major tiers of government the Appalachian formula also embraces county and city authorities in a requirement that multicounty development districts be formed; these districts have been given an important mandatory role in programme development. The ARC was also unique among the early regional planning commissions in size terms, covering an area of 195,000 square miles, embracing parts of 13 states and enclosing almost 18 million (10.0 percent) of the USA population. Finally the ARC was not simply a *planning* agency and from the outset was given sizeable funds to encourage the *implementation* of its plan. As Estall (1982, p. 38) concludes, 'in sum, the Appalachian Regional Commission has no parallels. The Title V Commissions, nominally similar, lack funds; other multistate organisations (such as the river basin commissions) are limited in the scope of their operations; the T.V.A. (Tennessee Valley Authority), with which the A.R.C. is sometimes compared, is simply another federal agency.'

The poverty and related disabilities of life in rural Appalachia prior to the ARC were documented by the report of President Kennedy's Appalachian Regional Commission (PARC 1964), the recommendations of which were accepted as a basis for action. Two policy features are worthy of note. First, particular emphasis was given to highway building in an effort to lessen the region's isolation, with 60.0 percent of ARC funds over the period 1965–1979 devoted to this end. A similar motive underlay the extensive autostrada building programme in southern Italy. At the same time significant amounts have been spent on 'human resource' programmes with health, education and child development schemes accounting for more than two-thirds of total ARC spending on nonhighway programmes (Table 14.5). A second feature of the Appalachian Regional Development Act 1965 was its requirement that public investments should be concentrated in areas where there is a significant potential for future growth and where the expected return on public dollars invested will be the greatest. While the official designation of growth centres has included most communities of any size and, as Hansen (1972) suggests, may well have more value in political and morale terms than in any economic sense, in practice actual spending

Figure 14.3 Economic development regions in the USA, 1980.

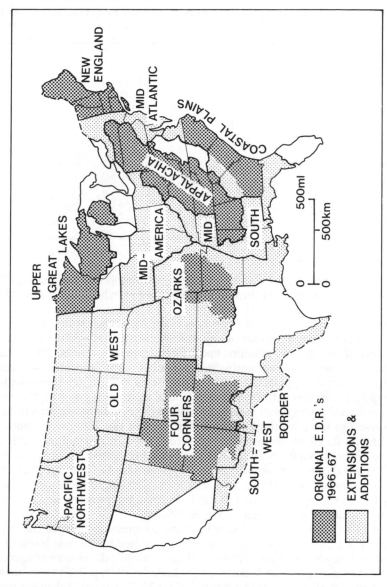

Source: Estall (1982)

Table 14.5   *Appalachian Regional Commission patterns of spending for nonhighway programmes, 1965–1978*

Programme	ARC funds $ million	%	Total projects costs $ million	%	Apparent multiplier*
Vocational and other educational	433	30.5	1315	25.9	3.0
Health projects	388	27.3	1449	28.6	3.7
Child development	137	9.6	305	6.0	2.2
Community development	270	19.0	1632	32.2	6.0
Local development district support, research etc.	91	6.4	132	2.6	1.5
Environmental and natural resource projects	74	5.2	96	1.9	1.3
Other (chiefly nonhighway transport)	32	2.3	143	2.8	4.5
Total	1420	100	5073	100	3.6

*Total project costs – ARC Funds
Source: Estall (1982)

has been more concentrated. By 1971, for example, almost one-third of the total ARC funds had been spent in 20 of the region's 397 counties, while over one-half had gone to only 60 counties.

Assessment of the impact of a rural development agency is far from simple. It is difficult to determine the extent of any improvements that might have occurred in the absence of the regional planning body. Further, many of the social consequences of planning are not readily quantifiable, and only become apparent over the longer term. In the case of Appalachia many of the forces recently operating nationally – including reaffirmation of the importance of coal as an energy source, the population turnaround, and the regional shift in balance of development from north to south – have worked to the advantage of the region. Within this framework, however, the ARC through its efforts to improve and extend basic infrastructure (such as water supplies, sewerage systems, industrial sites, and highways) has created conditions favourable for the development of new enterprises. The ARC has solid achievements to its credit, and as Estall (1982, p. 52) observes, 'a balanced judgement of its role to date is that, in the overall context, it has been small but positive, while in particular local circumstances it has been highly significant'.

Nominally, similar regional development commissions carpet the rest of the USA, but their effectiveness has been severely limited by the low levels of Federal funding; and, as elsewhere, the future of these economic development agencies rests to a great extent on political decisions. In Schaller's (1978, p. 207) view, 'meagre and uneven funding' of the Rural Development Act 1972 and only token support for its provisions by the United States Department of Agriculture raise doubts as to whether a bona fide national rural development policy exists in the USA.

References

ARCHER, B. H. (1974) The impact of recreation on local economies, *Planning Outlook* 14, 16–27.

BARKLEY, D. L. and PAULSEN, A. (1979) *Patterns in the Openings and Closings of Manufacturing Plants in Rural Areas of Iowa.* North Central Regional Center for Rural Development, Iowa State University.

BERTRAND, A. L. (1978) Rural social organization implications of technology and industry. *In* T. R. Ford *Rural U.S.A.: Persistence and Change.* Ames: Iowa State University Press, 75–88.

BRADSHAW, T. K. and BLAKELEY, E. J. (1979) *Rural Communities in Advanced Industrial Society.* New York: Praeger.

BROADY, M. (1980) Mid-Wales: a classic case of rural self-help, *The Planner* 66(4), 94–6.

CARNEY, J. G. and HUDSON, R. (1979) The Welsh development agency, *Town and Country Planning* 48(1), 15–16.

CENTRE FOR AGRICULTURAL STRATEGY (1980) *Strategy for the U.K. Forest Industry* Report 6. Reading: The Author.

CHADWICK, B. A. and BAHR, H. M. (1978) Rural Poverty. *In* T. R. Ford *Rural USA: Persistence and Change.* Ames: Iowa State University Press, 182–95.

CHILDS, B. and MINAY, C. L. W. (1977) *The Northern Pennines Rural Development Board* Working Paper No. 30. Department of Town Planning, Oxford Polytechnic.

CLARK, G. (1979) Farm amalgamations in Scotland, *Scottish Geographical Magazine* 95(2), 93–107.

CLARKSON, S. (1980) *Jobs in the Countryside* Occasional Paper No. 2. Department of Environmental Studies and Countryside Planning, Wye College, University of London.

COMMINS, P. (1978) Socio-economic adjustments to rural depopulation, *Regional Studies* 12, 79–94.

DARTINGTON AMENITY RESEARCH TRUST (1974) *Farm Recreation and Tourism in England and Wales* CCP83. Cheltenham: Countryside Commission.

DAVIDSON, J. and WIBBERLEY, G. P. (1972) *Planning and the Rural Environment.* London: Pergamon.

DENHAM, R. (1978) *Recreation and Tourism on Farms, Crofts and Estates.* Edinburgh: Scottish Tourist Board.

DEVELOPMENT COMMISSION (1980) *Encouraging Enterprise in the Countryside* 37th Report of the Development Commissioners 1978–9. London: HMSO.

DOEKSEN, G. A. and SCHRIENER, D. F. (1971) Contributions of agricultural processing industries to rural development objectives, *American Journal of Agricultural Economics* 53, 847.

DOWER, M. (1980) *Jobs in the Countryside.* London: National Council for Voluntary Organisations.

ESTALL, R. (1982) Planning in Appalachia: an examination of the Appalachian regional development programme and its implications for the future of the American Regional Planning Commissions, *Transactions of the Institute of British Geographers* 7(1), 35–58.

FORESTRY COMMISSION (1977) *The Wood Production Outlook in Britain – A Review*. Edinburgh: Forestry Commission.

GARBETT-EDWARDS, D. P., POWELL, B., HOWELL, E. W. G. C., BROADY, M. and RYAN, A. (1979) *New Agencies in Wales* Discussion Paper No. 12. London: Regional Studies Association.

GIBSON, L. J. (1981) Contemporary strategies and policy issues for U.S. sparsely populated areas. *In* R. E. Lonsdale and J. H. Holmes *Settlement Systems in Sparsely Populated Regions*. New York: Pergamon, 361–76.

GILG, A. (1976) Rural employment. *In* G. E. Cherry *Rural Planning Problems*. London: Leonard Hill, 135–70.

GILG, A. (1980) Planning for rural employment in a changed economy, *The Planner* 66(4), 91–3.

GILG, A. (1983) Population and employment. *In* M. Pacione *Progress in Rural Geography*. London: Croom Helm, 74–105.

GRAFTON, D. (1980) *Planning for Remote Rural Areas: The Swiss Experience* Discussion Paper No. 5. Department of Geography, University of Southampton.

GREEN, R. J. (1971) *Country Planning*. Manchester: The University Press.

GRIEVE, R. (1972) Problems and objectives in the Highlands and Islands. *In* J. Ashton and W. H. Long *The Remoter Rural Areas of Britain*. Edinburgh: Oliver and Boyd, 130–45.

HANSEN, N. M. (1972) *Growth Centres in Regional Economic Development*. New York: Free Press.

HIGHLANDS AND ISLANDS DEVELOPMENT BOARD (1967) *First Annual Report*. Inverness: The Author.

HILLIER, J. (1982) The role of COSIRA factories in the provision of employment in rural Eastern England. *In* M. J. Moseley *Power, Planning and People in East Anglia*. Norwich: University of East Anglia, 177–98.

HM TREASURY (1972) *Forestry in Great Britain: An Interdepartmental Cost Benefit Study*. London: HMSO.

HODGE, I. and WHITBY, M. (1979) *Jobs in the Eastern Borders*. Agricultural Adjustment Unit, Department of Agricultural Economies, University of Newcastle.

HODGE, I. and WHITBY, M. (1981) *Rural Employment*. London: Methuen.

HOUSE, J. W. (1976) The geographer and policy-making in marginal rural areas: the northern Pennines rural development board. *In* J. T. Coppock and W. R. D. Sewell *Spatial Dimensions of Public Policy*. London: Pergamon. 86–103.

HOWARD, R. S. (1968) *The Movement of Manufacturing Industry in the U.K., 1945–1965*. London: HMSO.

INGLIS, C. J. (1977) A forest employment model for the Highland region, *Scottish Forestry* 32(2), 101–10.

JONES, J. M. (1972) Problems and objectives in rural development board areas. *In* J. Ashton and W. H. Long *The Remoter Rural Areas of Britain*. Edinburgh: Oliver and Boyd, 109–29.

MINAY, C. L. W. (1976) A new rural development agency, *Town and Country Planning* 45(10), 439–43.

MOORE, D. (1979) *Disadvantaged Rural Europe*. Langholm: The Arkleton Trust.

MOSELEY, M. J. (1973) The impact of growth centres in rural regions, *Regional Studies* 7, 77–94.

NORTHFIELD, LORD (1977) The role of the Development Commission, *Town and Country Planning* 45(6), 304–7.

PACIONE, M. (1976) Development policy in Southern Italy: panacea or polemic, *Tijdschrift voor Economische en Sociale Geografie* 67, 38–47.

PACIONE, M. (1982) Economic development in the Mezzogiorno, *Geography* 67(4), 340–3.

PACKMAN, J. (1979) Rural employment: problems and planning. *In* J. M. Shaw *Rural Deprivation and Planning*. Norwich: Geo Books, 51–69.

PARC (1964) *Appalachia: A Report by the President's Appalachian Regional Commission*. Washington DC.

RICHARDSON, H. W. (1976) Growth pole spillovers: the dynamics of backwash and spread, *Regional Studies* 10, 1–9.

ROBINSON, D. G. (1972) Comprehensive development. *In* J. Ashton and W. H. Long *The Remoter Rural Areas of Britain*. Edinburgh: Oliver and Boyd, 215–24.

SCHALLER, W. N. (1978) Public policy and rural social change. *In* T. R. Ford *Rural USA: Persistence and Change*. Ames: Iowa State University, 199–210.

SHAW, J. M., Norfolk County Planning Officer (1979) *Rural Areas in England and Wales*. Norwich: County Planning Department.

SMITH, V. and WILDE, P. (1977) The multiplier impact of tourism in Western Tasmania. *In* D. Mercer *Leisure and Recreation in Australia*. Malvern: Sorrett.

SPOONER, D. J. (1972) Industrial movement and the rural periphery: the case of Devon and Cornwall, *Regional Studies* 6, 197–215.

STOREY, D. (1980) *Job Generation and Small Firms Policy in Britain* Policy Series No. 11. London: Centre for Environmental Studies.

SUMMERS, G., EVANS, S., CLEMENT, F., BECK, E. and MINKOFF, J. (1976) *Industrial Invasion of Non-Metropolitan America*. New York: Praeger.

WIBBERLEY, G. P. (1976) Rural resource development and environmental concern, *Journal of Agricultural Economics* 27(1), 1–16.

15   Service provision

The number and range of services and facilities available to rural dwellers has exhibited a marked and steady decline in the postwar era. In 'deep rural' areas depopulation has undermined the economic threshold for many services while in less remote areas the spreading competitive influence of towns combined with increased personal mobility has had a similar effect on service viability. These difficulties have been compounded by a general trend towards centralization by public and private service providers in an effort to achieve economies of scale.

The scale of the problem

The poor level of service provision in rural areas has been well documented (Standing Conference of Rural Community Councils 1978; Association of County Councils 1979; Norfolk County Council 1979). In England and Wales in 1979 almost 4 million people lived in parishes without a doctor's surgery, while for dispensing chemists the figure was over 6 million. For many of these accessibility to health care was further reduced by long and expensive journeys and inadequate public transport. About 750,000 people had no sub-post office in their parish, and a similar number lacked a food shop. Despite rapid extension of public utility systems in the postwar years nearly 1 million people still live in parishes without mains sewers and many more in unconnected dwellings in partially served parishes. Around 5 million people are unable to benefit from the relatively cheap heating provided in all urban areas by mains gas. Important information facilities, such as the Citizens Advice Bureau, Area Social Services offices and offices of the Department of Health and Social Security, are usually only available in urban areas. Many local areas fall below even this generally low level of provision. Over 13.0 percent of the villages in Gloucestershire and Wiltshire which had a village shop in 1972 had lost that service five years later. Over the same period 8.0 percent of villages in the same counties lost their sub-post office. In Cornwall, 19.0 percent of villages with a doctor's surgery in 1967 had lost that service by 1976; a situation which is exacerbated by the absence from most villages of a dispensing chemist who can often also act as a source of informal medical advice. Finally in Wiltshire 9.0 percent of the village schools closed between 1972 and 1977; part of 800 primary school closures recorded in rural England between 1967 and 1977. Numerous studies have indicated that the smallest villages are being hardest hit (Stockford 1978; Standing Conference of Rural Community Councils 1978). In West Dorset, for example, almost half the population live in villages of less than 500 inhabitants – 75.0 percent of these villages have no school, 68.0 percent no garage, 61.0 percent no pub, 50.0 percent no sub-post office, and 30.0 percent no shop. In general 'the more rural and isolated the area is the poorer the service appears to be' (Stockford 1978, p. 68). This situation is repeated throughout the rural parts of Europe (House of Lords 1979), North America (Bradshaw and Blakeley 1979; Ford 1978) and Australia (Lonsdale and Holmes 1981).

Health services

Health care services are concerned with the provision of facilities for diagnosis, treatment and care of those who become ill and with promoting the health of and preventing disease in the population. A distinction may be drawn between primary health care facilities and secondary health care. Primary health care covers general practitioner services including the work of doctors, dentists, opticians and pharmacists supported by community health services such as clinics for expectant and nursing mothers and the health visitor service. The public have direct access to these services. Secondary health care comprises hospital inpatient and outpatient services and access is normally by referral from the primary sector.

The majority of people require health care at some time during their lives and access to health facilities is an essential component of life quality. In both Britain and North America, however, there is a disproportionate provision of medical services in urban as opposed to rural areas. As Roemer (1976, p. 74) notes, 'in the rural areas of America, as elsewhere in the world, the supply of physicians and other health workers is much lower than in the city'. General practitioners have tended to centralize into group practices, with adverse effects on rural levels of provision. In Britain GPs are independent contractors with the National Health Service. A Medical Practices Committee tries to ensure an even distribution of services based on a 'carrot and stick' policy under which areas of the country with low patient–GP ratios are 'restricted', meaning that new practices will not be authorized, while in areas with a high patient–GP ratio establishment of new practices is encouraged by an additional cash allowance. However the motives underlying the locational behaviour of GPs are more complex (Knox and Pacione 1980) and, as a result, after more than 30 years of this mixture of mild coercion and financial incentive there remain disturbing disparities in the provision of primary medical care. Such problems are not unique to Britain. Many Western countries, whatever their methods of employing and controlling medical personnel, have experienced similar imbalances between the distribution of population and of medical services (Shannon and Dever 1974; Barnett and Sheerin 1978).

Arguments in favour of centralization of GP services include the advantages of mutual support, shared costs, a range of technological equipment beyond the reach of a single practice, and close proximity to other members of the primary health team engaged in complementary services to the community. In the USA in particular, group practices can also enable each doctor to develop a specialized practice. Inevitably, however, such locational trends lead to problems of access for some rural patients, especially those in sparsely populated areas affected by deteriorating transport services. With the exception of births, the greatest financial demands on the health services are made by the elderly and, as recent migration trends in Britain, Europe and North America have demonstrated, the age structure of the rural population is biased towards this section of society. In addition, for housewives with strong time-space constraints on their activities and for people who do not own a car, primary health care facilities in rural areas are becoming increasingly inaccessible.

In those countries where a national health service is more limited than in the United Kingdom these problems are even more acute (Walmsley 1978). The low availability of health services in rural USA, for example, is reflected in the lower usage of such services by rural people compared with their urban counterparts. As Dillman and Trembley (1977, p. 123) observe, 'this difference can hardly be due to a lower need for medical attention on the part of rural Americans'. In fact, rural areas exhibit a higher incidence of chronic disease, more days lost from work due to illness, and a greater rate of work-related injuries. The most rural areas also experience morbidity and infant mortality rates far in excess of the general population. In addition many poor rural people, who do not have medical insurance to pay for treatment, are excluded from the Medicaid programme which provides benefits largely to one-parent families (Fiedler 1981). The pattern suggested by these data is of a chain that is difficult to break – fewer medical personnel, contributing to the practice of less preventive medicine, and as a result a greater need for medical services.

A comparable policy of centralization has operated in the provision of secondary health care facilities. In the UK the National Health Service inherited a diverse collection of hospitals including many small ones serving their immediately local population. The first national hospital plan (Ministry of Health 1962) and a subsequent Central Health Services Council (1964) report both recommended the replacement of this historically determined pattern by a network of large district general hospitals, each providing a wide range of diagnostic and treatment facilities that cannot economically be offered in smaller units. District general hospitals are situated in large urban areas and service a population of approximately 250,000 with catchment areas of 20–30 miles in radius. A consequence of this programme was the closure of older and smaller hospitals, many of which are in rural areas. As Haynes and Bentham (1979a, p. 180) point out, 'there is clearly a potential conflict between the desire to minimise internal costs by concentrating services in large units and the need to make the service accessible to its public'. A survey of hospital facilities in Norfolk found that accessibility affected the use made of hospitals by both patients and visitors. 'This means that decisions about the location of hospitals are also (in part at least) decisions about who will benefit from their services' (Ibid., p. 190). The potential impact of distance or accessibility on consulting behaviour is appreciable but difficult to quantify. Girt (1973) in Newfoundland has studied how consultation rates depended on a complex relationship between distance and the nature of the ailment. As in the case of primary medical care, the adverse effects of centralization of facilities will be felt more by the less mobile members of the community, housewives, the elderly and the poor, groups which often have the greatest need for health care. More recently the district general hospital programme has been supplemented by a Department of Health and Social Security (1974) policy for community hospitals serving populations of between 30,000 and 100,000 and normally located in market towns. These community hospitals provide locally based services for patients not in need of acute treatment, and a facility where GPs may treat their own patients. In the USA current Federal programmes which provide incentives to physicians to serve in rural areas have had only a limited impact on the enduring problem of under-provision of medical care. It has been realized that 'improving rural health care will require deliberate planning, control by state or federal government (especially in facility location and construction) and the development of integrated health care systems' (Rainey and Rainey 1978, p. 144).

Improving patient access

Realistic attempts to tackle the problem of rural health care must acknowledge two barriers: first, the low population density which is often below the minimum required to support medical personnel and equipment; and secondly, the locational preferences of general practitioners. The problem is particularly acute in rural parts of the USA. Hence, access to medical care services usually means access to primary care, as the low resource base of the rural areas, generally low incomes and low population density make it uneconomical to provide tertiary or usually even secondary care. The most common primary care provider is the GP but the trends of increasing centralization and specialization in medicine are making the GP a rare species, and are concomitantly reducing the ability of ruralites to secure access. Fiedler (1981) identifies five main difficulties for primary health care provision in rural USA:

(1)   primary care, especially in rural areas, provides little opportunity to practice the sophisticated type of medical care the physician has been trained in;
(2)   rapid advances being made in modern medicine also make urban areas, where most research and development is occurring, much more attractive;
(3)   physicians who enter primary care, particularly in solo-rural practices, often abandon their practices within a few years to go to urban areas to join group practices and/or to concentrate on a speciality;
(4)   work loads are higher in rural than urban areas, and general practitioners see far more patients and have more irregular hours than other types of doctors;
(5)   physicians have been poorly trained to provide primary care, a greater emphasis being placed on specialist medicine in medical school curricula.

Apart from the community hospitals initiative of the Department of Health and Social Security (1974) and suggestions to improve access to clinic-based services by making more use of mobile facilities (Martin 1976) little progress has been made in the United Kingdom to reverse the decline in level of medical care available to rural dwellers. In the USA among the ad hoc Federal government policies which have encountered only limited success are (a) increasing the number of medical schools and the number of graduates from each; (b) the practice commitment-loan forgiveness programme designed as an incentive for doctors to locate in rural preceptorships; (c) the development and promotion of family (general) practice programmes in medical schools; and (d) establishment of the National Health Service Corps to help train family physicians and place them in rural areas. Most of these efforts have been preoccupied with getting the physician into the rural area and have not addressed the question of keeping him there. As a result, although the programmes are improving rural access they tend to do so only on a short-term basis, as most of their participants spend only two or three years in rural areas. Despite recent moves to enhance the image of general practice in the curriculum of medical schools and to develop a more flexible approach to training it is evident that a shortage of general practitioner services in areas of greatest need will continue for some time to come.

Given this mismatch between supply and demand, a more radical approach to improving access has been gaining momentum over the last decade. This is the use of mid-level health personnel (Reid 1975) or new health practitioners (NHPs). These are ancillary medical staff trained to function at a particular level within the health care delivery system. They can perform tasks such as interviewing patients, performing physical examinations, keeping case records, taking X-rays, and treating minor ailments. More serious complaints are referred to a qualified physician. Numerous studies have shown that increased use of NHPs can raise physician productivity substantially and increase access to and utilization of health care services (Rafferty 1974), particularly in rural areas (Miles and Rushing 1976; Blake and Guild 1978). A basic difficulty, given the shortage of rural-based GPs, concerned the adequate monitoring of these medical auxiliaries. In short, how could an NHP working under the direct supervision of a GP improve the situation? One answer to this dilemma was to endorse the idea of independently functioning NHPs. Evidence from several studies which indicate that NHPs deal competently with all of the minor medical problems brought to them has helped to temper initial opposition to this alternative form of health care delivery.

Dhillon et al. (1978) see expanded utilization of NHPs as a possible solution to the scarcity of doctors in rural America, particularly if it is related to the development of telemedicine. Supervision of the NHP would be achieved by a set of protocols which guide an NHP towards a diagnosis of the problem and a plan for treatment. The protocols also specify those observed patient conditions that warrant physician intervention; the patient would either be sent for a physician visit or alternatively, in some cases, the personal visit could be replaced by a telecommunication consultation. Protocols have also been devised for a form of self-help medical care for use by people in isolated areas or small communities.

Figure 15.1 shows a portion of a protocol for diagnosing upper respiratory infection (URI). This shows the sequential format, the detail and the delineation of specific decision or branch points at which the NHP should either consult with or send the patient to a physician. Two decision points are shown in the diagram; one, stemming from an undescribed anomaly, requires an MD referral and the other, associated with the presence of ear discharge or other abnormalities of the tympanic membrane, requires an MD consultation. Dhillon et al. (1978, p. 47) conclude that 'the application of telecommunications-based technology in support of remotely located non-physician providers offers considerable potential for: (1) expanding the role of these personnel, and (2) lowering costs and enhancing access to primary health care for isolated rural populations due to the reduced requirement for physician referrals'. Application of such a system to sparsely peopled rural areas elsewhere may represent the only means of providing local access to primary health care.

Education

The education system extends from preschool provision through the statutory school-age years to a variety of further education opportunities in schools and colleges. In addition the service provides facilities for community education in the form of adult education classes, youth service programmes and opportunities for leisure and recreation. The school is often the focal point of local social life and provides villages with the opportunity for natural growth with a balanced age and sex

Figure 15.1 A protocol for diagnosing upper respiratory infection (URI).

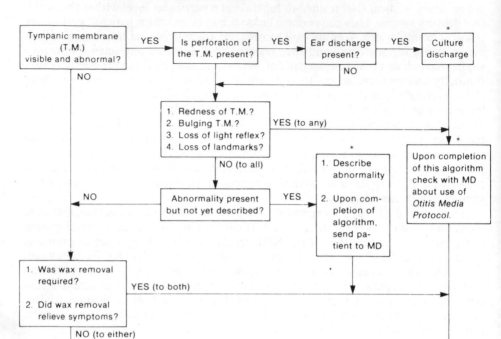

Source: Dhillon et al. (1978)

structure. As Neate (1981, p. 17) observes, for all sections and age groups in a community 'the village school has a significance beyond its ostensible educational one'.

Despite this key role the closure of rural schools in Britain has been proceeding apace since the beginning of the present century, initially reflecting the growth of cities and the reduction of the rural population, and more recently in response to the combined impact of a falling birthrate and economic stringency. An early stimulus to primary school closures was the Hadow Report (1926) which recommended the establishment of separate 'secondary' schools for children over the age of 11. In theory these recommendations would have left many rural primary schools with too few pupils under the age of 11 to merit continuation. However, the national economic climate of the 1920s and 1930s dictated that few secondary schools were built and thus school reorganization was a slow process. The 1944 Education Act and an increase in central government finance for local authorities quickened the pace of reorganization and primary school closure. By the late 1940s the current situation had emerged in which most rural schools are primary schools and most rural children over the age of 11 are transported to secondary schools in the nearest town or city.

A fresh impetus for closure came after 1967 with the Plowden and Gittins Reports, which examined the advantages and disadvantages of small rural schools. A case was made against the small primary school on both educational and economic grounds and it was concluded that, while in certain circumstances small rural schools should remain open, the majority of such schools should be closed down. The Gittins Report (1967) proposed a minimum size for primary schools, of 50 pupils; and called upon rural education authorities to draw up long-term plans for the amalgamation of all one- and two-teacher schools in order to create a centrally located primary school which would ideally be located in a 'key village', well served by existing transport networks. The Plowden Report's (1967) recommendation that schools with an age range of 5–11 should usually have at least three classes, each covering two age groups, threatened the existence of many village schools, since to meet this criterion schools would have to guarantee a minimum number of 90 children. As Rogers (1979, p. 4) observes, 'that immediately put six and a half thousand primary schools at risk throughout England and Wales'. In practice few rural local authorities adhered rigidly to the size recommendations of the Plowden and Gittins Reports. According to the Standing Conference of Rural Community Councils (1978) only four counties are known to have set a minimum of 50 pupils for their schools and only Gloucestershire has set the minimum number of teachers at three. Two counties, Lincolnshire and Leicestershire, are willing to retain one-teacher schools, whilst Durham is willing to retain schools of 12 pupils. Closures have been accelerated by the trends towards a three-tier schooling system with the introduction of middle schools for those aged 9–13 in between the primaries (renamed first schools) and secondaries. Reducing the age range in the village school to four years (i.e. 5–9) compared to six years has increased the difficulty for a small community of 'filling' the school, since the school age group has been reduced by one-third.

Arguments for closure   The case against small schools can be argued on both education and economic grounds. Small schools usually cost more to run than large schools. Powys County Council's (1978) analysis of annual revenue costs suggested that in a school of 10 pupils the cost per place would be £1,071, while in schools of 20, 35 and 55 pupils the corresponding figures would be £766, £566 and £472 respectively. If all four schools were to be closed and the 120 pupils were to attend a single area school then, although transport costs would rise by over 50.0 percent, economies would be achieved elsewhere – particularly in teachers' salaries which can cover 60.0 percent of running costs – and unit costs would fall to £398. While some local authorities are prepared to carry the extra expenditure to keep some of their small schools open, others are not. The cost of building and maintaining schools also favours the larger school.

The educational arguments against small rural schools are that:

(1)   the range of subjects in a modern curriculum is too wide for one or two teachers to cope with, with the result that pupils in small schools could be disadvantaged by the limited range offered to them compared with their peers in larger schools;

(2)   all-age classes are difficult to teach, and special needs cannot be adequately catered for;
(3)   it is difficult to overcome any personality clash between teacher and child when they are together for four to six years;
(4)   while a school could thrive under the influence of a good teacher, pupils may suffer under a mediocre one;
(5)   larger schools are more flexible and can cope with changes in the birthrate by using portable classrooms;
(6)   children do not receive the stimulation from varied contact with adults and others of their own age;
(7)   there is a difficulty in recruiting teachers to isolated schools;
(8)   teachers are isolated and lack professional contacts;
(9)   the buildings are often old and in need of repair, many having outside lavatories and limited space for games.

Arguments against closure   The proponents of small schools can also marshal arguments in their defence. They point out that:

(1)   small classes mean more individual attention, a closer relationship between child and teacher, and the generation of a 'family' atmosphere;
(2)   the advantages of a generous pupil–teacher ratio are linked with a high level of parental involvement and commitment to the local school;
(3)   discipline is rarely a problem;
(4)   smallness enables a high degree of flexibility in the organization of teaching and the conduct of the school day;
(5)   academic achievement is as good as in larger schools;
(6)   vertical grouping in primary schools enables younger and older children to learn together;
(7)   contrary to the findings of the Plowden Report (1967) teachers are now more eager to work in small rural schools;
(8)   the demand for a wide range of subjects can be met by peripatetic teachers serving a group of schools;
(9)   long journeys (in excess of 30 minutes) to and from centralized schools can affect attainment, and preclude children from after-school activities.

Even the economic rationale for closure has been challenged. Although the basic fact that it costs more to keep a small school running than a larger one is rarely disputed, the plea is for a wider economic criterion to be employed in the interests of equity of opportunity. Thus Nash et al. (1976) admit that in crude terms rural children are expensive to educate. Even if all small primary schools were closed the cost would still be large, for the costs of transport are significant. However, they go on to argue that in many ways rural children make few demands on local authority services; for example, few are in care, on probation, or take up the time of child guidance services. Considered in this light the small rural school may be a bargain. This social dimension to the value of the small rural school is also pursued by the Standing Conference of Rural Community Councils (1978) who point out that since rural communities take less in total out of the public purse than urban areas they are entitled to their 'expensive' village school. Clearly evaluation of the economic, educational and social arguments for and against closure of the small primary school in rural villages involves complex analysis of costs and benefits. Whatever the financial savings might be, whether or not they are worth making is a political decision that has to be made separately.

The continued existence of many rural primary schools is endangered because, as currently organized, the Education Committee of a local authority is not empowered to adopt a comprehensive view. In Scandinavia the local coordination of schooling with housing, employment, transport, health and other services is achieved much more readily. Although these fall under different Ministries and have different sources of support from central government, the municipal councils have overall responsibilities and know the local situation intimately. Thus the buildings can be planned with multiple usage in mind and the running costs of all the activities can be brought together within the council's overall budget. The administrative system in Britain makes joint planning of capital and recurrent expenditure for the shared use of buildings more difficult. In the early discussions of the small rural school problem in Denmark, Sweden and Norway the minimum size of class was set at 25 children in all three countries. In the last two decades, however, the recognized strain on children, parents and local community of enforced travel to an area school has led to a reversal of this policy and retention of small schools whenever possible (D'Aeth 1981).

Means of saving the village school

There are various projects under way in Britain which attempt to improve the future for the small rural school and offer an alternative to closure. These include:

(1)   *Use of mobile resources*: vehicles can be fitted out as mobile resource units or classrooms for specialized teaching. Mobile resource centres can keep teachers in touch with new developments. Peripatetic teachers can also travel around supplementing the basic teaching force of a school.

(2)   *Resource sharing*: groups of small schools may organize themselves to share the cost of expensive or sophisticated equipment and staff. In the USA the educational service district comprises the school districts of several rural counties banded together under a voluntary and cooperative arrangement to undertake projects beyond the resources of individual districts, e.g. hiring a remedial teacher or offering in-service training courses for teachers.

(3)   *Topping up funds*: some communities argue that a local education authority should continue to fund a local school to the level it would have to expend on providing education elsewhere, including transport costs. Any additional finance required to keep the school running would be the responsibility of the community itself.

(4)   *Parent-teacher cooperative*: a more radical alternative is for some communities to take over the financing and running of their school aided by a local authority grant based on their average annual expenditure per pupil. The teacher's salary may be negotiable, with assistance provided by parents. An example of such a scheme is provided by Madingley School near Cambridge, which was closed by the local education authority as educationally and economically unviable. Other countries, including

Denmark, the Netherlands and the USA, have successful state-funded alternative schemes.

(5) *Amalgamation*: an amalgamation between two schools can be an acceptable alternative to closure if both schools are within a well defined and popularly acknowledged community. Travel distances will be only slightly larger and one of the schools can be 'mothballed' in case of a future upturn in demand.

(6) *Market-determined salaries*: the main reason for closure is the high cost of salaries per pupil. A controversial strategy would be to allow teachers' salaries to find their level in the market place. Rural schools offer many attractions and with an over-supply of teachers nationally it might be possible to retain a school if a lower salary could be paid to those willing to trade off some financial remuneration for a country lifestyle.

(7) *Cluster schools*: this is a more radical and formal extension of school resource sharing. The scheme unites a group of small schools administratively and philosophically under one headmaster. There is one central school with three or four smaller ones as annexes. The first such scheme was the Cheveley Federation school in Cambridgeshire, which was formed in 1978 as an alternative to closing three small primary schools and concentrating all of the pupils at Cheveley School. For core subjects children will be taught by their 'own' teachers in their 'own' school, while for more specialized subjects teachers will travel among schools in the cluster; and for activities such as sports the children themselves will be bussed to the central nucleus. Equipment and resources will also be transported between the schools. Such a scheme has advantages for children and teachers. It keeps open schools which could not survive on their own, allows greater educational resources to be put into small schools, provides larger peer groups for the children, reduces staff isolation, and offers a new career structure for the small-school teacher. Clustering is not necessarily a cost-cutting solution in the short term but because of the social and educational advantages similar experiments are under way elsewhere (e.g. in Norfolk and Gwynedd).

Retail services

The most significant changes in the organization and operation of the retail system in the postwar period have been the expansion of the multiple retailers' share of turnover, which has occurred largely at the expense of independent shopkeepers, and the development of larger shop units in response to the need for economies of scale, culminating in the growth of supermarkets, superstores and hypermarkets. In rural areas depopulation combined with significant increases in personal mobility for many residents have undermined the ability of many villages to satisfy the minimum thresholds needed to maintain services.

The number of shops has declined dramatically in rural areas throughout Britain and Europe (House of Lords 1979). As noted earlier, the Standing Conference of Rural Community Councils (1978) found that 13.0 percent of villages in Gloucestershire and Wiltshire which had a shop in 1972 had lost that service by 1977; 8.0 percent of the villages in the same counties had lost their sub-post office over the same five-year period; and 10.0 percent of villages served by a mobile shop in Devon lost that service in the eight years up to 1975. As the study points out, however, percentage figures are only part of the story – for the villages affected the impact is absolute. Similar findings have been reported from Norfolk (Moseley and Spencer 1978; Harman 1978) and in rural Scotland (Cottam and Knox 1982; Mackay and Laing 1982). As Table 15.1 shows in the latter region, over the twenty-year period 1960–1980 the number of parishes with a shop and sub-post office was almost halved.

As is the case with other basic services, the loss of a village shop has greatest impact on the elderly, the poor, and those without private transport. Public transport to the nearest facilities may be unavailable or expensive. Bulk-buying trips to urban superstores are not possible for every household, and the village shop will often sell small quantities to suit the needs of pensioners or those without home storage facilities. The village shop is also one of the traditional focal points of community life and nonmobile villagers suffer not just the loss of the economic role played by the shop but a significant social role which cannot be replaced by a trip to the nearest town. Moreover, many shops house a sub-post office with the important agency services it provides. In Britain about 80.0 percent of all sub-post offices are run in conjunction with private businesses like grocery shops and newsagents, and the shop-cum-post office represents a key element in many villages. Such establishments are run by sub-postmasters who are not themselves Post Office employees but are agents who provide their own premises, employ their own assistants, and are paid in relation to the actual volume of business transacted, including an arranged sum to cover overheads according to a 'scale payment scheme'. Significantly, only about 27.0 percent of post office business is concerned with postal matters, with the bulk of transactions relating to agency work for other bodies, the most important of which is the Department of Health and Social Security. Thus to the pensioner or mother with young children the post office provides the weekly pension or child allowance payment. It can also act as a village bank where National Girobank is available, it dispenses dog and television licences, and in some areas accepts payments for rates or local authority rents (Taylor and Emerson 1981). The close physical and functional

Table 15.1 *Availability of services in remote Scotland*

Service	1960	No. of parishes containing service			
	1960	1970	% change	1980	% change
Shop	334	283	−15.3	180	−36.4
Sub-P.O.	202	172	−14.8	117	−32.0
Primary school	166	130	−11.7	102	−21.5
Doctor	114	100	−12.2	80	−20.0
Bank	99	95	−4.0	88	−7.4
Pub/hotel	93	96	+3.2	89	−7.3
	(maximum 354)				

Source: Mackay and Laing (1982)

relationship between the village shop and the sub-post office often means that a threat to the continued viability of a village store can represent a severe danger to the local community which may suffer more than loss of a retail facility.

Methods of aiding rural shops

1.   Government assistance   Central government 'directive' measures such as simplification of Value Added Tax (VAT) or reduction of rates for commercial premises, as suggested by a survey of retailers in Norfolk (Harman 1978), would have to be applied as a form of positive discrimination in favour of rural shops if they were to produce a significant advantage. Disquiet could be anticipated from other retailers, particularly those in declining inner city areas; and such a strategy would imply higher domestic rates to enable the local authority to maintain its income. Neither could such a broad brush approach guarantee that the shops saved from closure would necessarily be those in 'needy' villages. This suggests that policies to aid village shops should be 'enabling' and locally determined within broad government guidelines.

The system of government aid to private rural retailers in Scandinavia may be capable of wider application. From the early 1970s the governments of Finland, Norway and Sweden have shown concern for the plight of rural consumers following the closure of small stores in sparsely populated areas. In each country legislation has been introduced to improve the economic situation for small stores and so prevent their closure. It is important to note that the support has not been introduced out of consideration for the trade itself, or for the employment situation, or because of the importance of the small store within the local or national economy, to which its contribution is comparatively modest. In contrast to most general policies of public support to private business the Scandinavian measures in favour of small stores have been introduced out of concern for the consumers' plight, which is particularly serious in a 'last-shop' situation (Ekhaugen et al. 1980).

The first measures in support of small stores in peripheral areas were introduced in Sweden in 1973, in Finland in 1975 and in Norway in 1976 (Table 15.2). Four different types of measures are involved:

(1)   *Investment aid*: this is the most common type of measure and forms an important part of the support policy in all three countries. Investments supported include the acquisition of new buildings and equipment as well as the modernization of old facilities. Most of the financial support for investment is provided as direct subsidies although in Sweden some of the support is also given in the form of loans or loan guarantees.

(2)   *Management aid*: financial support for running the store is granted as a direct subsidy to stores that are not profitable but are important for the supply of groceries, and for maintaining the level of population in the local community.

(3)   *Home deliveries*: this may be considered as a special form of management aid which is granted only in Swedish peripheral areas, to facilitate continuation of the traditional practice whereby grocery stores have offered home deliveries to customers at no extra charge.

Table 15.2   *Summary of public policy measures for retailing in Finland, Norway and Sweden*

Aspect of the public policy	Finland	Norway	Sweden
Year of appointing public committees	1971	1973	1970
Year of introducing support measures	1975	1976	1973
Types of measures	Investment aid	Investment aid Management aid Consultant aid	Investment aid Management aid Home deliveries
Conditions for getting support	Importance of the store Expectations of the store Minimum distance to nearest competing store Maximum amount of sales	Importance of the store Expectations of the store Minimum distance to nearest competing store Maximum amount of sales	Importance of the store Expectations of the store Consistency with municipal distribution plans
Administration of the support system	Decisions by Ministry of Commerce Advice by county authorities	Decisions by Ministry of Commerce Advice by county and municipal authorities	Decisions by county authorities Advice by municipal authorities and a consultative group

Source: Ekhaugen et al. (1980)

(4)   *Consultant aid*: this is available in Norway. The aim is to improve the professional and business ability of small shop keepers, through training and offering advice on management techniques, market analysis and stock-keeping.

To be eligible for financial support the shops (a) must provide a significant proportion of the community's supply of groceries, offer a satisfactory variety of goods, and be open all year; and (b) should be expected to remain in business for some time. In addition to these two general conditions, specific conditions apply in individual countries. In Sweden the store will not obtain public financial support unless its location and sales activities fit into the local authority's overall plan for the distribution system within the municipality. In Finland and Norway no support will be granted unless there is a minimum distance of 3 km and 4 km respectively between the supported store and its nearest competitor; and a store will only obtain support if its annual sales do not exceed a certain level.

The effect of public policies is notoriously difficult to isolate. In Norway, however, it has been observed that since the introduction of the legislation in 1976 nearly 50.0 percent of the grocery shops situated more than 4 km from the nearest outlet have received some kind of investment subsidy, and the number of shop closures has been reduced from approximately 650 per annum in the early 1970s to about 300 by the end of the decade (Roven 1979). Similarly Mackay and Moir (1980, p. 23) have shown that within an overall decline of 324 in the number of rural shops throughout Norway between 1976 and 1980, the number of assisted shops had increased by 55 whereas the nonassisted had fallen by 379. They conclude that of the four different types of financial support 'the investment subsidy seems to have been the most effective and there has been a very marked improvement in the physical quality of and range of goods stocked by many shops, with the result that more people are using the local shop for their requirements'. It would seem on the basis of the limited evidence available that the aid systems are achieving their objective of main-taining essential shopping facilities for the rural consumer. Similar legislation also exists in France and the Netherlands, while Mackay and Laing (1982) list 10 recom-mendations to aid rural shops and consumers in Britain. Given that service decline is a common problem throughout rural areas, social arguments for some form of government intervention may be difficult to refute.

2. Self-help Some countries are less inclined to intervene in the market process than others. In addition, fierce competition among statutory public service agencies for scarce resources can often relegate the notion of government support for private sector shops to a low priority level. Under such circumstances self-help is often the only way to counter many deficiencies. Self-help can operate on two planes: it can either be initiated by the shopkeeper or, following loss of a facility, by the community in general.

Shopkeepers may band together in order to achieve the price advantages of a large buying organization, and several companies operating in Britain (such as Mace, Spar and VG) perform the same functions as a cooperative. To join this type of organiz-ation the shopkeeper normally pays a fee and undertakes to purchase a minimum amount of goods each week. In return the company supplies goods at relatively cheap rates, delivers them to the village shop and undertakes advertising, promotional and other retailer services.

Most villages in rural Britain are well below the population threshold at which the majority of services can be supported and should a shop closure occur the only alternative is often self-help by the community. This may take the form of com-munity shops, bulk-buy schemes, cooperative markets, parish council-run pubs, or adapting rooms in houses to serve as sub-post offices (Dungate 1980; Woollett 1981). In England rural service provision has been improved through wider use of village halls for a variety of purposes such as weekly markets, doctors' consultations, playgroups and sub-post offices; benefiting from the fact that the village hall is nor-mally owned and controlled by the village rather than the local authority. An ex-tension of this use of village halls is the 'multipurpose village centre'. This involves the alteration or extension of existing village premises to provide centres which are capable of accommodating a wide range of services and facilities which would not otherwise be present in the village. In certain circumstances such as at Mundford in Norfolk (Packman and Wallace 1982) the centre might be purpose-built, but in view of the expense this would not be common. The aim of the multipurpose village centre is primarily to group activities so that costs are shared and the maximum use is made of existing premises (Development Commission 1981). Space in the centre could be rented out for retailing, post office, banking, health services, library, advice and information services, social clubs or a parish council office, manned permanently or by visiting specialists according to the required frequency of the particular use. Much of the success, or otherwise, of a village centre inevitably depends on the people who form its management committee and who participate in its activities.

Implicit in this notion is the concept of corporate management of village service provision. This would involve a more comprehensive form of decision-making, and some form of corporate resource allocation in rural areas. Clearly, this would require significant political direction from central government in the first instance. The Working Party on Rural Settlement Policies (1979, p. 23) support this principle on the grounds that 'costs would then be examined in terms of benefits and trade offs between the various services to provide an overall financial assessment for a given policy package and, as necessary, a comprehensive analysis of its likely effects on individual groups or areas'. Corporate rather than disparate resource management in rural areas could become a powerful method for the fulfilment of needs in rural communities.

References

ASSOCIATION OF COUNTY COUNCILS (1979) *Rural Deprivation*. London: The Author.

BARNETT, J. R. and SHEERIN, I. G. (1978) *Public policy and urban health: a review of selected policies designed to influence the spatial distribution of physicians in New Zealand* Proceedings, Fifth New Zealand Geography Conference. Dunedin: New Zealand Geographical Society, 10–16.

BLAKE, R. L. and GUILD, P. Q. (1978) Mid-level practitioners in rural health care: a three year experience in Appalachia, *Journal of Community Health* 4, 15.

BRADSHAW, T. K. and BLAKELEY, E. J. (1979) *Rural Communities in Advanced Industrial Society*. New York: Praeger.

CENTRAL HEALTH SERVICES COUNCIL (1964) *The Functions of the District General Hospital*. London: CHSC.

COTTAM, M. B. and KNOX, P. L. (1982) *The Highlands and Islands: A Social Profile* Occasional Paper No. 6. Dundee: University Department of Geography.

D'AETH, R. (1981) *A Positive Approach to Rural Primary Schools*. Cambridge: University Institute of Education.

DEPARTMENT OF HEALTH AND SOCIAL SECURITY (1974) *Community Hospitals: their role and development in the National Health Service* HSC(IS)75. London: HMSO.

DEVELOPMENT COMMISSION (1981) *Multi-Purpose Village Centres: a study of their feasibility design and operation.* London: The Author.

DHILLON, H. S., DOERMANN, A. C. and WALCOFF, P. (1978) Telemedicine and rural primary health care: an analysis of the impact of telecommunications technology, *Socio-Economic Planning Sciences* 12, 37–48.

DILLMAN, D. A. and TREMBLEY, K. R. (1977) The quality of life in rural America, *Annals of the American Academy of Political and Social Science* 429, 15–129.

DUNGATE, M. (1980) Rural self-help. *Voluntary Action* 2, 17–21.

EKHAUGEN, K., GRONMO, S. and KIRBY, D. (1980) State support to small stores: a Nordic form of consumer policy, *Journal of Consumer Policy* 4(3), 195–211.

FIEDLER, J. L. (1981) A review of the literature on access and utilization of medical care with special emphasis on rural primary care, *Social Science and Medicine* 15c, 129–42.

FORD, T. R. (1978) *Rural USA: persistence and change.* Ames: Iowa State University Press.

GIRT, J. L. (1973) Distance to general medical practice and its effect on increased ill-health in a rural environment, *Canadian Geographer* 17(2), 154–66.

GITTINS REPORT (1967) *Primary Education in Wales* Central Advisory Council for Education. London: HMSO.

HADOW, W. H. (1926) *The Education of the Adolescent.* London: HMSO.

HARMAN, R. G. (1978) Retailing in rural areas: a case study of Norfolk, *Geoforum* 9, 107–26.

HAYNES, R. M. and BENTHAM, C. G. (1979a) Accessibility and the use of hospitals in rural areas, *Area* 11(3), 186–91.

HAYNES, R. M. and BENTHAM, C. G. (1979b) *Community Hospitals and Rural Accessibility.* Farnborough.

HAYNES, R. M., BENTHAM, C. G., SPENCER, M. B., and SPROTLEY, J. M. (1978) Community attitudes towards the accessibility of hospitals in West Norfolk. *In* M. J. Moseley *Social Issues in Rural Norfolk.* Norwich: University of East Anglia, 45–58.

HOUSE OF LORDS (1979) *Policies for Rural Areas in the European Community* 27th Report of the Select Committee on the European Communities 5720/79. London: HMSO.

KNOX, P. L. and PACIONE, M. (1980) Locational behaviour, place preferences and the inverse care law in the distribution of primary medical care, *Geoforum* 11, 43–55.

LONSDALE, R. E. and HOLMES, J. H. (1981) *Settlement Systems in Sparsely Populated Regions: the United States and Australia.* New York: Pergamon.

MACKAY, G. A. and LAING, G. (1982) *Consumer Problems in Rural Areas.* Edinburgh: Scottish Consumer Council.

MACKAY, G. A. and MOIR, A. C. (1980) Norwegian policies for assisting rural shops. *In* G. A. Mackay and A. C. Moir *Rural Scotland Price Survey Autumn 1980.* Aberdeen: University Institute for the Study of Sparsely Populated Areas, 21–6.

MARTIN, I. (1976) Rural communities. *In* G. E. Cherry *Rural Planning Problems.* London, Leonard Hill: 49–83.

MILES, D. L. and RUSHING, W. A. (1976) A study of physicians assistants in a rural setting, *Medical Care* 14, 987.

MINISTRY OF HEALTH, (1962) *A Hospital Plan for England and Wales*, Cmnd 1604. London: HMSO.

MOSELEY, M. J. and SPENCER, M. B. (1978) Access to shops: the situation in rural Norfolk. *In* M. J. Moseley *Social Issues in Rural Norfolk*. Norwich: University of East Anglia, 33–44.

NASH, R., WILLIAMS, H. and EVANS, M. (1976) The one-teacher school, *British Journal of Educational Studies* 24(1), 12–32.

NEATE, S. (1981) *Rural Deprivation: an annotated bibliography of social and economic problems in rural Britain*. Norwich: Geo Books Ltd.

NORFOLK COUNTY COUNCIL (1979) *Rural Areas in England*. Norwich: County Planning Department.

PACKMAN, J. and WALLACE, D. (1982) Rural services in Norfolk and Suffolk. *In* M. J. Moseley *Power Planning and People in Rural East Anglia*. Norwich: University of East Anglia, 155–75.

PLOWDEN REPORT (1967) *Children and their Primary Schools* Central Advisory Council for Education. London: HMSO.

POWYS COUNTY COUNCIL (1978) *Structure Plan* Topic Study 7 – Health, Education and Welfare Appendix 1.

RAFFERTY, J. (1974) *Health, Manpower and Productivity*. Lexington: Heath.

RAINEY, K. D. and RAINEY, K. G. (1978) Rural government and local public services. *In* T. R. Ford *Rural USA: persistence and change*. Ames: Iowa State University Press, 126–44.

REID, R. A. (1975) Simulation and evaluation of an experimental rural medical care delivery system, *Socio-Economic Planning Sciences* 9, 111–19.

ROEMER, J. M. (1976) *Rural Health Care*. St Louis: Mosby.

ROGERS, R. (1979) *Schools under threat: a handbook on closures*. London: Advisory Centre for Education.

ROVEN, E. (1979) The Norwegian assistance programme for small shops in sparsely populated areas. *In* PTRC *Retailing*. London: Planning Transportation and Computation (International) Ltd, 98–102.

SHANNON, G. W. and DEVER, G. E. (1974) *Health Care Delivery: Spatial Perspectives*. McGraw Hill: New York.

STANDING CONFERENCE OF RURAL COMMUNITY COUNCILS (1978) *The Decline of Rural Services*. London: The Author.

STOCKFORD, D. (1978) Social services provision in rural Norfolk. *In* M. J. Moseley *Social Issues in Rural Norfolk*. Norwich: University of East Anglia, 59–75.

TAYLOR, C. and EMERSON, D. (1981) *Rural Post Offices: retaining a vital service*. London: National Council for Voluntary Organisations.

WALMSLEY, D. J. (1978) The influence of distance on hospital usage in rural New South

Wales, *Australian Journal of Social Issues* 13, 72–81.

WOOLLETT, S. (1981) *Alternative Rural Services*. London: National Council for Voluntary Organisations.

WORKING PARTY ON RURAL SETTLEMENT POLICIES (1979) *A Future for the Village*. Bristol: HMSO.

16   Transport and accessibility

The well-being of individuals, families and rural communities depends on access to employment and to basic services and amenities. Transport is the main agent enabling people to satisfy these needs. In rural areas the proportion of car-owning households is typically above the national average. In Great Britain in 1976, for example, the national level of car ownership was 56.0 percent but in rural areas the figure was 10.0–20.0 percent higher (Department of the Environment 1976, 1978). Car ownership levels have continued to rise since then despite increases in the prices of fuel and of new vehicles. Rural America is almost totally dependent on the private vehicle, with public transport practically nonexistent in many areas. High levels of car ownership in rural areas, however, do not reflect greater prosperity but a degree of 'enforced ownership' in response to the declining level of public transport provision. In addition, as Rainey and Rainey (1978, p. 140) observe in North America, 'although the incidence of car ownership is higher among the poor in rural areas than in urban areas, the poor drive older, less reliable cars. Their problem is compounded by the effects of inflation and the energy crisis.' Moreover, high levels of car ownership cannot disguise the fact that significant numbers of rural dwellers are without private means of transport. The 'mobility-deprived' include the elderly, young children, teenagers, the poor and the infirm as well as housewives without use of the family car. Collectively these groups comprise a large proportion of the rural population, and 'the view that the rural accessibility problem affects only a residual minority is a myth' (Moseley 1979, p. 40). For the groups without ready access to cars the ability to reach certain facilities has been greatly restricted in the postwar era, both by the reduction in conventional public transport services and by the decline of village-based activities, notably the closure of village shops and schools and the replacement of local GPs by Area Health Centres. Similar transport and accessibility problems to those encountered in Britain and North America are experienced throughout the Developed World (Chujo 1979; Andersen 1979; Pedersen 1976).

The decline of public transport

The chief factor determining the demand for public transport is the level of car ownership in rural areas. Thus, as private car ownership has increased in the postwar era there has been a corresponding decrease in demand for the alternative modes of rail and bus travel. Oldfield (1979) estimated that for every additional car, 300 bus trips were lost each year since 1952, and that the increase in car ownership directly accounted for about 45.0 percent of observed public transport patronage decline. Fullerton (1982) refers to Swedish studies which have suggested that when car ownership passes the level of one car per seven people public transport begins to have economic difficulties. This figure was reached in some areas of rural Britain by the early 1960s. The low usage of public transport was also illustrated by studies in

Devon and West Suffolk (Department of the Environment 1971a, 1971b) where (a) only 3.0 percent of journeys made by car owners were on public transport; (b) as many journeys were made in the form of 'lifts' as on stage bus services; (c) only 6.0 percent of all trips took place on public transport, including 7.0 percent of journeys to work and 13.0 percent of shopping trips; and (d) half the population never used public transport.

In general, public transport patronage has declined by about 50.0 percent from its peak levels in 1952. At that time, nationally, nearly 40.0 percent of all vehicular passenger kilometres were by bus, but by 1974 it had fallen to 12.0 percent, with the current level around 8.0 percent in rural areas. The smaller decline in the annual vehicle kilometres covered (19.0 percent between 1969 and 1980) indicates that buses are now running emptier, meaning that vehicle productivity has fallen despite increases in staff productivity. The decline of the rural rail network has been even more dramatic.

Passenger rail services

Many rural railway lines have been closed and the tracks taken up because they carried too few passengers to be viable, and intercity trains linking the major centres of population no longer stop at small country stations. Patmore (1966) has described how many railway closures took place during the 1930s due to the general economic depression; in 1930 and 1931 alone passenger services were withdrawn from 800 km of line in England and Wales, a figure which exceeded all previous closures taken together. Since the nationalization of Britain's railway companies in 1948 many more sections of line have been lost; between 1952 and 1962, for example, 6,750 km were closed throughout Britain.

The low economic justification for much of the rail network was underlined in the Beeching Report (1963) on the reshaping of British railways. This revealed that in 1962, 40.0 percent of the rail network had carried only 3.0 percent of the total traffic. In order to rationalize the system the British Railways Board announced its intention to close almost 2,500 stations and halts (55.0 percent of the total) and to withdraw services from 8,000 km of line (29.0 percent of the 1962 total). Naturally it was the low-volume rural lines which suffered most severely. Many rural routes had been constructed in the railway boom era of the late nineteenth century to feed traffic onto the main lines, but even in their Victorian heyday many of these branch lines did not yield an economic return (Nock 1957). The traffic from them helped to swell that on trunk routes but their role as traffic feeders was vulnerable to the development of effective road transport. Other parts of the railway system were unnecessary because of duplication arising from the fierce competition between railway companies in the nineteenth century (Whitby et al. 1974).

The economic problem of providing passenger rail transport in rural areas was stated succinctly in the Beeching Report (1963). Railways are distinguished by the provision and maintenance of a specialized route system for their own exclusive use, giving rise to high fixed costs. This route system permits dense flows of traffic and, *provided the flows are dense*, the fixed costs per unit are low. Unfortunately rural areas do not produce dense traffic flows and 'the fact remains that for the majority of rural branch lines and duplicated main lines, traffic generated is not sufficient to justify even single-track operations' (Whitby et al. 1974, p. 191). Rather than pondering on the severity of the Beeching cuts we should perhaps marvel that so many rural lines survived for so long. As a result of the implementation of the 1963 proposals most of highland Britain and many rural areas in lowland Britain are now without rail services.

Since 1964 it has been argued strongly that proposals to withdraw railway services should not be decided purely on financial grounds but on broader economic and social criteria (Hillman and Whalley 1980). This view was expressed in the 1966 White Paper on Transport Policy which stated that there were some railway services 'which have little or no prospect of becoming directly remunerative, in a commercial sense, on the basis of revenue from users . . . yet their value to the community outweighs their accounting cost to the railways' (Ministry of Transport 1966, p. 4). Consequently, cost–benefit analyses have attempted to evaluate the effects of withdrawing a railway service. Studies of individual loss-making rural routes include an analysis by Clayton and Rees (1967) of the Shrewsbury–Llanelli line in central Wales and an examination by Williams et al. (1976) of the Exeter–Barnstaple line. Under the provisions of Section 39 of the Transport Act 1968, central government may undertake to pay a grant towards loss-making railway services where this is deemed desirable for social or economic reasons, and in practice 'the Government has supported all but the hopeless cases' (Whitby et al. 1974, p. 192). Since 1968 the rate of closure of the rural railway network has slowed but by 1979 local train services were virtually extinct in much of rural Britain, with only 1.0 percent of people in rural areas using the train as the main mode of transport to and from work. A similar process of railroad abandonment has operated in the USA (Cherington 1948; Black 1977; Due 1979; Briggs 1981).

The financial predicament of rural lines as a result of operating deficits is intensified by the fact that many of the surviving rural services are operated with obsolete equipment whose replacement would be difficult to justify economically. In the early 1980s British Rail stated that there would need to be an expensive programme of capital renewal on the rural lines if they were to continue to function into the 1990s and that there was little prospect of finding the money for this investment from fare revenues or cross-subsidy. Further, any 'cascading' of rolling stock would require the introduction of new vehicles somewhere on the system (Policy Studies Institute 1981).

One means of retaining a level of public passenger transport in rural areas which has been advocated is the replacement of uneconomic rail lines by bus services. Coach services replaced many rail services lost in the Beeching round of closures. However, without any grant system and oriented mainly to local needs rather than connection with the trunk rail network, many of these substitute services have disappeared. Furthermore, between 1968 and 1978 about one-third of the replacement bus services introduced as conditions of rail closure consents had closed down and another one-third had been substantially modified (Keen 1978). A major criticism of bus substitution for rail is the uncertain life of the replacement service compared with rail under a Public Service Obligation grant (introduced under Section 3 of the 1974 Railways Act). A related but radical solution proposed by Hall and Smith (1976,

p. 122) suggested the conversion of uneconomic railway lines to passenger coach services running along the same route. They provided cost–benefit evidence for six types of railway line, including a 'rural service threatened with closure', a 'rural shuttle service', and a 'busy rural single track', and concluded that in all cases 'the community would benefit from replacing trains with buses and lorries, and save where the existing road is adequate, converting the railway formation to a public road'. An important consideration for any bus-rail system is the need to coordinate replacement bus services and surviving train timetables. In the Netherlands, for example, the national railways issue a comprehensive bus guide giving for all towns and most villages details of the nearest railhead with connecting bus service details.

By the late 1970s rural passenger services accounted for 5.0 percent of the British Rail total passenger mileage and provided all the traffic at 500 stations out of a total of 2400. In revenue terms rural lines contributed 5.0 percent of British Rail income but absorbed 32.0 percent of the passenger network grant. Thus despite experiments with 'low-cost' rural trains (Hodge 1981) rail services seem destined to play an increasingly small role in rural transport provision. During the course of the 1970s the focus of attention turned to the problem of maintaining even a rural bus service in many parts of the country.

Road transport

During the 1930s rural bus services and the bus industry in general expanded as traffic was attracted from the railways to a new, cheaper and more flexible service. In the immediate postwar period the growth of the network was fostered by petrol rationing and the limited production of private cars. Besides the regional bus companies formed under the Road Traffic Act 1930, there were a large number of small operators who provided stage carriage, coach and charter services between villages and market towns until the late 1950s. By 1955, however, the number of passenger journeys on bus routes began to decline, and between 1955 and 1959 passenger journeys fell by over 10.0 percent. As demand declined many rural routes became no longer viable and, although some operators cross-subsidized these routes with profits from urban services, the total number of rural services was reduced and the steady process of service contraction commenced (Figure 16.1).

The growth of private transportation both contributed to and resulted from such a downward spiral of public service provision. Several other factors also acted to reduce demand for bus travel: (a) changes in entertainment habits and in particular the spread of television drastically reduced the need for evening coach trips to urban cinemas as well as travel at other off-peak periods; (b) the growing practice of lift-giving in rural areas, which was partly a response to inadequate transport, also aggravated the situation; (c) the changing distribution of the rural population was another factor – as people moved into larger towns and cities demand for bus services between smaller settlements fell; and (d) the spread of mobile shops may also have been a contributory factor, although for many rural dwellers a shopping trip to town is also partly a social outing. In addition to the reduced demand for their services bus operators were faced with steady increases in labour costs which represent the largest proportion (over 60.0 percent) of overall costs. The viability of smaller firms was further weakened by rising costs of petrol, replacement vehicles and more stringent

Figure 16.1 The effect of increasing levels of car ownership on public transport services.

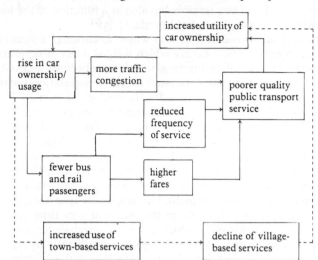

Source: M. J. Moseley (1979) *Accessibility: the rural challenge.* Methuen and Co.

safety standards. During the 1960s as their urban routes became less economic the regional bus companies found cross-subsidization of their loss-making rural routes less possible. They ceased to take over the routes of small operators when the latter suspended services and increasingly sought permission from the Ministry of Transport to abandon routes or to reduce services.

The difficulties facing rural bus transport by the late 1950s were investigated by the Jack Committee (1961). The most positive conclusion reached was that adequate rural transport could only be provided given a measure of financial assistance from outside the industry. The committee argued against indirect assistance in the form of a reduction or partial remission of fuel tax and recommended that direct financial aid should be provided partly by the central government and partly by local authorities. This proposal was embodied in the 1968 Transport Act which empowered local authorities to provide financial aid at their own discretion to improve or maintain passenger transportation in the countryside. Exchequer grants would cover half of the approved subsidies. The Act did not however place an obligation on local authorities to support rural transport and, despite the legislation, many services disappeared during the 1970s. The number of passenger journeys on services run by the National Bus Company declined by 38.0 percent over the period 1969 to 1980.

The concept of accessibility

The decline of rural public transport services and the uneven distribution of private transport in rural society form only part of the wider problem of rural accessibility which also involves consideration of the availability of rural services. The concept of accessibility basically refers to the ease with which people can obtain necessary goods and services. In the postwar period the ability of most carless rural residents to reach required services and facilities has deteriorated not only as a result of the disappearance of many rail and bus services but also as a function of the loss of village-based opportunities to satisfy household needs.

Accessibility can be considered in two ways. *Locational* accessibility can be viewed either as a comparative measure which weighs units of separation (such as distance) against the number of destinations which have become accessible (Mitchell and Town 1977), or as a composite measure (such as population potential) which combines the two factors into a single index (Baxter and Lenzi 1975). Such techniques have traditionally been employed in transport planning (Pirie 1979; Morris et al. 1979). Secondly, for *personal* accessibility the unit of study is the individual rather than the location. This perspective has been developed by Hagerstrand (1970) who has outlined a framework for the study of time-geography based on the environment of resources and opportunities which surrounds each individual. The basic premise is that evaluation of accessibility levels should concentrate not on what people do or are likely to do but on what they are able to do. This approach, therefore, concentrates on the opportunities which are available to the individual in time and space. Each individual has his own 'action-space' which limits the activities he can engage in. The time-space budget of any individual can be depicted graphically by representing distance along a horizontal axis and time along a vertical axis; the effective action-space of a person during the day is then described by a prism. As Figure 16.2 shows, the shape of the prism depends on the available mode of transport. The time-space budgets of some population subgroups will permit more effective access to opportunities than will those of others. One group which is particularly vulnerable to time-related constraints is women. Moseley (1979) describes the hypothetical case of a rural housewife (Figure 16.3). For certain periods of the day she is confined to her home – until 09.15 by sleep and family commitments, from 12.00 to 13.00 by family lunch time, from 16.00 to 18.00 when she welcomes the children from school and prepares tea, and after 22.00 when she again prepares for bed. The challenge for rural accessibility planning is first to determine the dimensions of the action-space of significant population subgroups; and secondly to expand it or to place more opportunities within it (Carlstein et al. 1978).

A time-space approach to personal accessibility was employed by Moseley et al. (1977) in rural Norfolk. This study focused upon certain group-activity combinations such as 'housewives–food shops' or 'teenagers–extra mural education'. Several alternative land use and transport strategies were evaluated in terms of the benefits of accessibility that they offered. The key question asked of each strategy was how far it permitted groups of carless people to reach specified activities without an unreasonable amount of inconvenience. As Moseley (1979, p. 71) explains, 'the various alternative strategies comprised statements of the spatial distribution of people and of activities and of the public transport network, with precise bus and rail time-tables and the times of availability of the various activities being carefully specified. Whether these strategies were deemed to be successful in ensuring access to the various activities for the groups in question, was in practice determined with reference to a number of "reasonable standards" relating to acceptable waiting time, journey time, walking distance, frequency per week etc. These "standards" were based on crude empirical evidence and varied between groups and between

Figure 16.2 Time budgets and daily prisms.

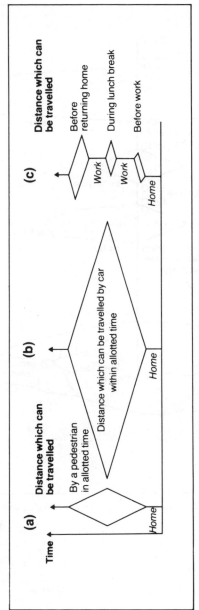

Source: Pred and Palm (1978) *In* D. A. Lanegran and R. Palm (1978) *An Introduction to Geography.* McGraw-Hill. Reproduced with the permission of the publisher.

Figure 16.3 The time-space realm of a rural housewife.

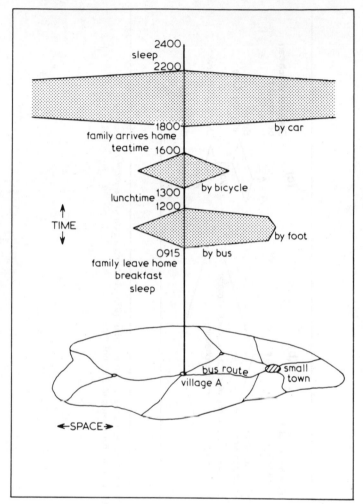

Source: M. J. Moseley (1979) *Accessibility: the rural challenge.* Methuen and Co.

activities.' Figure 16.4 illustrates the effect of six different strategies on general accessibility levels for five different population subgroups; and Figure 16.5 the effect of each strategy on general access to four health services. Accessibility studies have also been carried out in northwest Scotland (Nutley 1979), Skye (Stanley and Farrington 1981) and Wales (Nutley 1980). It has generally been agreed that much depends on the geographical scale of analysis, with potential problems emerging more clearly at greater levels of resolution. Nutley (1980, p. 351), for example, working at the parish scale in Wales concluded that although large-scale mapping may reveal likely problem areas, in most cases 'the determination of remedial policy inputs for the areas affected requires the identification of specific access deficiencies at a village level'.

A constraints-based approach to the evaluation of rural accessibility for villages within a region was employed in Strathclyde, where the local authority has recognized the essential difference between a demand-based and a need-based methodology. Although the definition of need can present complex problems this approach does avoid the mistaken assumption that people's aspirations can be ascertained simply by recording and projecting facts about their present behaviour. To identify what people would like to do with what they actually do is to assume that the situation in which their behaviour is observed offers them a satisfactory range of choice (Plowden 1972). As Stanley and Farrington (1981, p. 65) point out, 'a by-product of behaviour-based transport planning is that these individuals who do not show a "demand" for movement are assumed not to "need" to move. Hence future plans based upon demand projection will offer little to help those probably experiencing the worst problems at the present time.'

A village's mobility requirement depends on the interaction of its population structure and the type of facilities present in the settlement. In order to evaluate the effectiveness of existing transport services in promoting accessibility for residents it is necessary to consider the balance between transport 'demand' and 'supply' characteristics of each settlement. To achieve this in Strathclyde the Greater Glasgow Passenger Transport Executive (GGPTE) constructed two indices. The first estimates relative levels of service based on current timetables, taking into account departure times and dwell times in the main towns. The second estimates the need for public transport by considering local population structure, car ownership and local facilities. The composite supply/demand score for any village reflects how well its public transport meets its need for access to essential services and facilities. A ranking of the rural settlements of mainland Strathclyde in terms of adequacy of service revealed that the main problem areas were in Argyll and Lanark districts. Such areas may be singled out for priority treatment and/or experimentation with nonconventional transport services.

An ideal solution to the inaccessibility problem would be to redistribute financial support for public transport on the basis of a measure of 'need for access', thus ensuring that any subsidy provided is used to support socially necessary services. Clearly, in practice, much depends on what is considered a 'fair' amount of subsidy and what is deemed a 'reasonable' service. These are essentially political decisions. The Strathclyde approach was to divide the region into rural catchment areas with each

Figure 16.4 North Walsham area: six strategies (numbered 1–5b) compared in terms of the access they afford to different social groups. The horizontal axis relates to the proportion of resident population. The key to the shadings is white – access only by car; horizontal lines – by car and public transport; cross hatching – by public transport or by foot; stippled – access impossible.

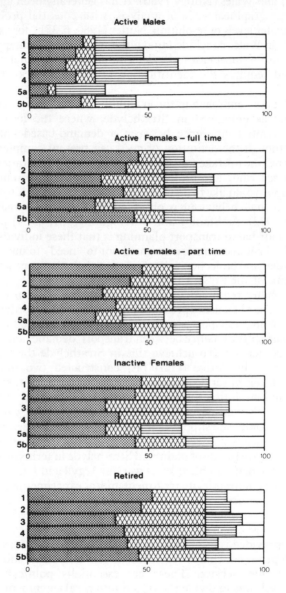

Source: M. J. Moseley (1979) *Accessibility: the rural challenge.* Methuen and Co.

Figure 16.5 North Walsham area: six strategies compared in terms of the access they afford to health activities (see Figure 16.4 for key).

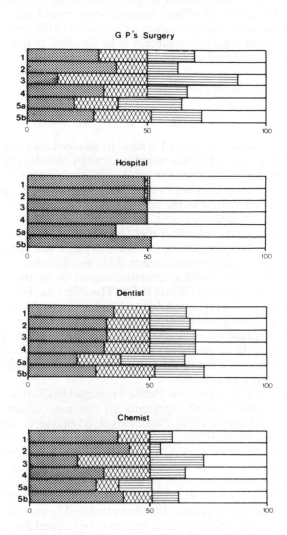

Source: M. J. Moseley (1979) *Accessibility: the rural challenge.* Methuen and Co.

under the supervision of a transport coordinator (Figure 16.6). Within each area the role of public transport is to achieve the most cost-effective means of concentrating the market into serviceable units, which can then be fed into the local centre where activities are offered and from whence longer journeys can be undertaken. For each catchment area the combined village demand score would indicate the need for movement out of the area, and this score as a proportion of the regional total demand score suggests the percentage of the subsidy to be allocated to that area. In this way revenue support is distributed on the basis of need for access while the coordinator must develop, within his support ceiling, local transport networks, the nature of which will depend to a great extent on local demand and operating conditions.

Policy responses

The major policy developments related to rural transportation in postwar Britain are summarized in Table 16.1 and are discussed in detail by Moseley (1979) and Banister (1983). Briggs (1981) also describes the increasing involvement of Federal government in rural transportation planning in the USA. In the United Kingdom, in addition to government initiated activity in the late 1970s the National Bus Company, in response to the need to rationalize services, introduced its own Market Analysis Project (MAP) as a selective service planning tool. The MAP seeks to avoid a piecemeal approach to service cuts by examining the entire network in a defined area with the aim of reducing the peak vehicle requirement. This may be achieved, for example, by substituting one route for two with a minimum impact on the majority of travellers, or through rescheduling services (White 1978). The effect has been to match service provision more closely with expressed demand, but an inevitable outcome is the loss of services from the least profitable rural areas, in the absence of local authority financial support. A similar rationalization exercise, based on local user surveys and data on ticket sales, has been carried out in Belgium by SNCV (Société Nationale des Chemins de fer Vicinaux), a bus operator providing a network similar to that of the National Bus Company in Britain.

The three-part OPTIC (Operation Public Transport in Carrick) strategy effected by Strathclyde Regional Council represents an extension of the MAP approach (Strathclyde Regional Council 1978). Phase I involved an on-bus survey to build up a full picture of bus use. Phase II comprised a household survey to ascertain the travel behaviour primarily of non-bus users, and Phase III an attitude survey designed to elicit information on the perceptions of local bus and rail services. An advantage of the OPTIC procedure is that it brings operator and local authority together to design and cost rural networks which incorporate an injection of financial support and which seek to satisfy a market greater than that identified by current public transport usage. Perhaps one of the most important lessons to be learned from government and operator experience in tackling the rural transport/accessibility problem on both sides of the Atlantic is the need for 'careful pragmatism' and to 'closely monitor the situation on an area-by-area and year-by-year basis' (Briggs 1981, p. 355). Ideally strategies such as MAP and OPTIC should be undertaken at regular intervals in order to more effectively relate the available level of services to revealed need.

No single agency is alone responsible for, or capable of, maintaining adequate

Figure 16.6 Village accessibility ratings and transport catchment areas in Strathclyde.

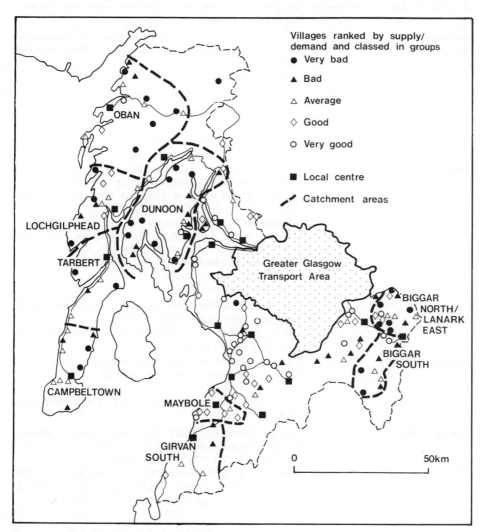

Source: Strathclyde Regional Council (1978)

Table 16.1 *Principal transport policy changes and their impact on rural areas*

	Date	Recommendations and actions
Jack Committee's Report on Rural Bus Services	1961	Selective direct financial assistance to unremunerative services. Fuel-tax rebate.
Beeching Report on the Reshaping of British Railways	1963	Closure of 5,000 km of rural railways.
Series of surveys in six areas	1963	To examine the problems of and the demand for rural transport services.
Transport Act	1968	System of direct grants with central government paying half where the services covered half their operating costs. Revenue grants to cover losses on unremunerative rail services. National Bus Company set up. School service contracts could now take fare-paying passengers if there was excess capacity. Fuel-tax rebates increased. New bus grants introduced. Concessionary fares.
Local Government Act	1972	Coordinating function for the county councils through the Transport Policies and Programmes. County councils to administer the distribution of the Transport Supplementary Grant.
Passenger Vehicle (Experimental Areas) Act	1977	Relaxation of the licensing laws in certain areas so that innovative services could be introduced.
	1977	Rural Transport Experiments set up in four 'deep' rural areas.
Transport Act	1978	County Public Transport Plans to coordinate passenger transport to meet the 'needs' of the public. Guidelines set for concessionary fares. Minibuses (8–16 seats) exempt from Public Service Vehicle Licences and Road Service Licences, provided that the drivers were from approved voluntary organisations. Traffic commissioners permitted to introduce short-term Road Service Licences. Car-sharing allowed for payment. Overall, explicit recognition of the social importance of rural transport services.
Transport Act	1980	Major changes in bus licensing – deregulation. Small vehicles (fewer than 8 seats) no longer classified as Public Service Vehicles. Express services (minimum journey length over 30 miles) no longer required Road Service Licences, thus facilitating competition between bus operators.

Recommendations and actions
Road Service Licences 'create a presumption in favour of the applicant'. Trial Areas could be designated where there were no Road Service Licences in existence. Overall, reemphasis of the economic criteria for rural transport provision.

Source: Banister (1983)

levels of accessibility in rural areas. Future improvement requires a high level of cooperation and coordination between the various authorities and private concerns which provide services to the rural areas. Options include both transport-based and non-transport-based strategies.

Transport-based options

1. Stage carriage bus services These operate to a specified timetable and comprise the great majority of bus services. The decline in these services in the face of rising car ownership is well documented. To assist the carless or 'captive' rural population greater use could be made of drivers and buses in off-peak periods when the marginal costs of operation are effectively low since the driver's wages and other fixed costs are already covered. An example is the Cromer Market bus in Norfolk which provides off-peak shopping trips for rural housewives at the expense of Cromer traders. Another possibility is for a community 'bus club' in which members pay an annual subscription that entitles them to use an off-peak service without further charge. The Horncastle bus club was established in 1975 as a twice-weekly shopping service between Louth and Horncastle in east Lincolnshire, using a driver and vehicle hired from a local independent bus company between school peaks. Costs are met from cash fares from casual passengers, members' subscriptions, and some assistance from Lincolnshire County Council.

2. Demand-actuated transport On these the route and/or timing responds, at least in part, to ad hoc passenger requests. The most obvious example is the taxi but the high per capita charges for this form of transport generally place it beyond the means of the 'mobility-disadvantaged'. Dial-a-ride schemes in which a would-be passenger telephones for a flexibly routed minibus to divert to his home is superficially attractive but expensive to operate (Oxley 1976). A more realistic alternative is the selective diversion of scheduled bus services. The decision whether to divert from the main intertown route or not can be made in two ways. The simplest is for the passenger to ask the driver directly to divert to the required village. More complicated to arrange would be a system to pick up passengers from villages off the main road but the difficulties could be overcome by some form of advance-booking. Clearly under such a scheme passengers would have to forgo the benefits of a precise timetable.

3. Multi-purpose services This involves the use of a single vehicle and driver to perform several distinct tasks. In Scandinavia a 50:50 division of passenger and goods space is common on public transport. In Huntingdonshire the driver of the St Ives midibus is entrusted with shopping orders and medical prescriptions; and in Scotland, Borders regional council has established a 'Border Courier' bus service which moves stores, goods and fare-paying passengers between the locations of their various establishments.

The most common form of multipurpose service is the postbus. Such services are well developed in Norway, Sweden, Austria, Germany and Switzerland. In the UK the first postbus was introduced in the late 1960s and by 1976 over 100 were in operation, mainly in Scotland (Turnock 1977). The guidelines laid down by the Post Office Corporation for the introduction of a new postbus service are that (a) there should be a demand for the service; (b) it should not make a loss, that is receipts should cover the marginal cost incurred by transforming the mail service into a mail passenger service (in practice the marginal costs of conversion are not great and passenger loadings do not have to be high for a service to break even); (c) it should not compete with an existing transport operator; and (d) it must be compatible with the prime task of collecting and delivering the mail. As Moseley (1979, p. 127) explains, 'typically, postbuses link a rural area with an urban centre. Four trips are normal: a slow trip out from the town in early morning, a fast trip back in mid-morning, a fast trip out in early afternoon, and a late afternoon slow return trip with mail being collected. Clearly it is the second and third of these trips which are most attractive to the rural resident, providing the possibility of a reasonably speedy return shopping trip to town.' Postbuses would seem to be ideal for areas where no other public transport services exist or in replacing existing marginal services, as they can be provided at little additional cost. There are, however, two disadvantages. First, the circuitous and time-consuming routes make them unattractive except to the most captive passenger, and secondly, as currently timed they are not suitable for school or work trips which tend to focus on the town when the mail van is travelling in the opposite direction.

Provision of transport for school children is a major obligation of rural authorities, and schoolbuses account for a significant portion of total subsidies to transport services. It has been suggested that adults should be permitted to travel on schoolbuses, particularly if there is no reasonable alternative service available. Unfortunately, (a) most services are run close to full capacity, with many buses carrying 50.0 percent more children than seats according to the three for two seating rule, (b) schoolbuses do not operate during school holidays, and (c) passengers must follow the route and timings dictated by the school day. A more radical approach to the closer integration of schools transport with regular rural services has been suggested by Oxfordshire County Council (1976). Its 'extended school contract scheme' links school contracts with a requirement that the bus operator also runs certain off-peak services which are specified by groups of local people in conjunction with the County Council.

Other alternatives to the declining stage carriage bus service place an emphasis on self-help and voluntary action by communities. These options include making greater use of the private car through car-sharing and social car schemes, and the use of village-based midi- and minibuses, which may be well suited to cater for irregular excursions such as hospital visiting or trips to health centres. Discussion of a wide range of these less conventional services and experiments is provided by Moseley (1979); Peddle (1977); National Council for Social Services (1977). The future for rural public transport would appear to depend on a multicontributor system with a basic stage carriage service on main interurban routes and less conventional forms of transport serving much of the remaining countryside.

Non-transport-based options

These aim to reduce the disadvantaged groups' *need* for transport. This may be achieved in several ways; for example (1) by taking the activity to the people via mobile services and communications; (2) by locating the activity closer to the people; (3) by locating the people nearer to the activity; and (4) by reducing the time constraints on individual activity (Moseley 1979).

Mobile services include delivery vans and grocery shops, playbus facilities for preschool children, the meals-on-wheels service for the housebound elderly, mobile libraries and banking services, and the provision of community and social welfare information by travelling van. There may also be a greater role for telecommunications technology linking rural homes with a national information network. Impersonal links via television and telephone, however, will not remove the need for a basic transport system in rural areas.

Efforts to locate activities such as shops, employment, schools and medical services closer to the people are constrained by the natural economic trends towards concentration of such activities in larger centres of population. Advance factories can be built to generate local employment and a case can be made for State aid to support rural shops but in the private sector the planners' powers are largely indicative, permissive and negative rather than directive, compulsory and positive. Even within the public sector the multitude of organizations involved in service provision makes implementation of a 'desirable pattern' of activities and facilities problematic, at least in the short term.

In cost terms the clustering of the rural population around the main points of service provision is an attractive strategy for improving individual accessibility. In the absence of compulsory migration, however, this must be seen as a long-term objective. The natural process could be accelerated to some extent if local authorities increased council house building in selected settlements. They could also give greater weight to the location of a potential tenant's existing residence in allocating houses, as well as to the traditional criteria of family size and quality of current dwelling. Provision of more 'sheltered housing' in key settlements might attract elderly people from outlying villages and hamlets. Such policies, however, would not have any direct bearing on the private housing sector which accounts for the greatest part of new rural housing; and there would continue to be pressure for development to be permitted in the smaller villages where land prices tend to be lower and the environment particularly attractive to exurbanites.

Time constraints can be reduced either by enabling people to better arrange the blocks of time they have available for extradomiciliary activities or by altering the opening hours at which activities are available to the public. A simple example of the first type of strategy would be a weekly village-based child-minding service to enable mothers to make a trip into town. Opening-hour policies may include (a) making certain services (e.g. banking, hospital visiting, or local government offices) available outside 'normal' working hours; (b) coordination of public transport timings and of relevant opening hours so as to avoid wasted time; and (c) having part-time outlets in several locations rather than a full-time outlet in a single place. Such a system of peripatetic service provision has clear parallels with the periodic markets of the Third World.

Transport accessibility has been defined as the ability of people to get to or be reached by the opportunities which are perceived to be relevant to them (Jones 1981). As Banister (1983) concludes, to further this objective there is an urgent need for a comprehensive rural accessibility policy that seeks to make the best use of all forms of communication.

References

ANDERSEN, B. (1979) Rural transport in Norway: past, present and in the future, *Eighth Annual Seminar on Rural Public Transport*. Polytechnic of Central London, 1–49.

BANISTER, D. (1983) Transport and accessibility. *In* M. Pacione *Progress in Rural Geography*. London: Croom Helm, 130–48.

BAXTER, R. S. and LENZI, G. (1975) The measurement of relative accessibility, *Regional Studies* 9(1), 15–26.

BEECHING REPORT (1963) *The Reshaping of British Railways*. London: HMSO.

BLACK, W. R. (1977) Negotiating for local rail service continuation: the major issues, *Traffic Quarterly* 31, 455–69.

BRIGGS, R. (1981) Federal policy in the United States and the transportation problems of low-density areas. *In* R. E. Lonsdale and J. H. Holmes *Settlement Systems in Sparsely Populated Regions: the United States and Australia*. New York: Pergamon, 238–61.

CARLSTEIN, T., PARKES, D. and THRIFT, N. (1978) *Human Activity and Time Geography*. London: Arnold.

CHERINGTON, C. R. (1948) *The Regulation of Railroad Abandonment*. Cambridge, Mass: Harvard University Press.

CHUJO, U. (1979) A review of rural public transport in Japan, *Eighth Annual Seminar on Rural Public Transport*, Polytechnic of Central London, 117–137.

CLAYTON, G. and REES, J. H. (1967) *The Economic Problems of Rural Transport in Wales*. Cardiff: University of Wales Press.

DEPARTMENT OF THE ENVIRONMENT (1971a) *Study of Rural Transport in Devon*. London: HMSO.

DEPARTMENT OF THE ENVIRONMENT (1971b) *Study of Rural Transport in West Suffolk*. London: HMSO.

DEPARTMENT OF THE ENVIRONMENT (1976) *Transport Policy: a consultative document.* London: HMSO.

DEPARTMENT OF THE ENVIRONMENT (1978) *Transport Statistics, Great Britain 1966–1976.* London: HMSO.

DUE, J. F. (1979) State rail plans and programs, *Quarterly Review of Economics and Business* 19, 109–30.

FULLERTON, B. (1982) Transport. *In* J. W. House *The U.K. Space.* London: Weidenfeld and Nicolson, 356–425.

HAGERSTRAND, T. (1970) What about people in regional science? *Papers of the Regional Science Association* 24, 7–21.

HALL, P. and SMITH, E. (1976) *Better Use of Rail Ways* Geographical Paper No. 43. Reading: University Department of Geography.

HIBBS, J. (1972) Maintaining transport in rural areas, *Journal of Transport and Economic Policy* 6, 10–22.

HILLMAN, M. and WHALLEY, A. (1980) *The Social Consequences of Rail Closures.* London: Policy Studies Institute.

HODGE, P. R. (1981) Low-cost rural railways and the B.R.-Leyland railbus, *Tenth Annual Seminar on Rural Public Transport.* Polytechnic of Central London.

JACK COMMITTEE REPORT (1961) *Rural Bus Services.* London: HMSO.

JONES, S. R. (1981) *Accessibility Measures: a Literature Review* LR967. Crowthorne: Transport and Road Research Laboratory.

KEEN, P. A. (1978) Rural rail services. *In* R. Cresswell *Rural Transport and Country Planning.* London: Leonard Hill, 139–46.

MINISTRY OF TRANSPORT (1966) *White Paper on Transport Policy* Cmnd 3057. London: HMSO.

MITCHELL, C. G. B. and TOWN, S. W. (1977) *Accessibility of Various Social Groups to Different Activities* SR258. Crowthorne: Transport and Road Research Laboratory.

MORRIS, J. M., DUMBLE, P. L. and WIGAN, M. R. (1979) Accessibility indicators for transport planning, *Transportation Research* 13A, 91–109.

MOSELEY, M. J. (1979) *Accessibility: the rural challenge.* Methuen: London.

MOSELEY, M. J., HARMAN, R. G., COLES, O. B. and SPENCER, M. B. (1977) *Rural Transport and Accessibility* 2 vols. Norwich: University of East Anglia, Centre for East Anglian Studies.

NATIONAL COUNCIL FOR SOCIAL SERVICES (1977) *Rural Transport: New Developments in Rural Transport Provision.* London: The Author.

NOCK, O. S. (1957) *Branch Lines.* London: Batsford.

NUTLEY, S. D. (1979) Patterns of regional accessibility in the N.W. Highlands and Islands, *Scottish Geographical Magazine* 95(3), 142–54.

NUTLEY, S. D. (1980) Accessibility, mobility and transport-related welfare: the case of rural Wales, *Geoforum* 11, 335–52.

OLDFIELD, R. (1979) *Effect of Car Ownership on Bus Patronage* LR872. Crowthorne: Transport and Road Research Laboratory.

OXFORDSHIRE COUNTY COUNCIL (1976) *Local Transport in Oxfordshire*. Oxford: The Author.

OXLEY, P. R. (1976) *Dial-a-Ride in the U.K.: A General Study Symposium on Unconventional Bus Services*. Crowthorne: Transport and Road Research Laboratory.

PATMORE, J. A. (1966) The contraction of the network of railway passenger services in England and Wales 1836–1962, *Transactions of the Institute of British Geographers* 38, 104–18.

PEDDLE, J. (1977) An independent view of rural transport innovation, *Sixth Annual Seminar on Rural Public Transport*. Polytechnic of Central London, 26–58.

PEDERSEN, P. O. (1976) Rural public transport in Denmark: its past and its future development. *In* P. R. White *Rural Public Transport*. London: Polytechnic of Central London, 169–84.

PIRIE, G. H. (1979) Measuring accessibility: a review and proposal, *Environment and Planning A* 11, 299–312.

PLOWDEN, S. (1972) *Towns Against Traffic*. London: Deutsch.

POLICY STUDIES INSTITUTE (1981) *The Future of Rural Railways*. London: The Author.

PRED, A. and PALM, R. (1978) The status of American women: a time-geographic view. *In* D. A. Lanegran and R. Palm *An Introduction to Geography*. New York: McGraw-Hill, 99–109.

RAINEY, K. D. and RAINEY, K. G. (1978) Rural government and local public services. *In* T. R. Ford *Rural USA: Persistence and Change*. Ames: Iowa State University Press, 126–44.

STANLEY, P. A. and FARRINGTON, J. H. (1981) The need for rural public transport: a constraints-based case study, *Tijdschrift voor Economische en Sociale Geografie* 72(2), 62–80.

STRATHCLYDE REGIONAL COUNCIL (1978) *Rural Movement: Transport Policy Studies*. Glasgow: The Author.

TURNOCK, D. (1977) The postbus: a new element in Britain's rural transport pattern, *Geography* 62(2), 112–18.

WHITBY, M. C., ROBINS, D. L. J., TANSEY, A. W. and WILLIS, K. G. (1974) *Rural Resource Development*. London: Methuen.

WHITE, P. R. (1978) Midland Red's Market Analysis Project, *Omnibus Magazine*, May/June, 61–68.

WILLIAMS, S. R., WHITE, P. R. and HEELS, P. (1976) The Exeter-Barnstaple line: a case for improvement or closure? *Modern Railways* 300–303.

17 Resource exploitation and management

Attributes of the environment only become resources when they are considered as having utility for mankind (Zimmerman 1933). Thus attributes of nature are no more than 'neutral stuff' until man is able to perceive their presence, to recognize their capacity to satisfy human wants, and to devise means to utilize them. Four environmental resources of particular significance in rural areas are minerals, water, woodlands, and landscape.

Minerals

It is difficult to exaggerate the importance of minerals in an industrial society. Fertilizers for agriculture; bricks, mortar, plaster and glass for housing; concrete and steel for major structures; raw materials for the chemical industry; metals for engineering; and aggregate for roads are all mineral products (Stevens 1976). To these we could add coal, china clay, special earths and sands, as well as precious metals and stones (Nutley et al. 1978).

Mineral exploitation has a long history in rural Britain. Precious metals have never been found in great quantities and in the case of base metals such as lead, tin, zinc and copper, peak production occurred in the nineteenth century. But there are significant deposits of limestone, sandstone, igneous and metamorphic rocks, sands and gravels, whilst china clay and slate have been mined since the eighteenth century. Coal remains a major national resource while fluorspar and barytes are examples of nonmetallic minerals once not valued as commodities but which have become of significance in the twentieth century. Other less extensive recent developments have involved the working of talc in Shetland, diatomite in Cumbria, silica sand at Loch Aline in Scotland, and potash under the North Yorkshire Moors (Blunden 1978; Roberts and Shaw 1982).

1. Aggregates The products of the aggregate industry are key raw materials in the process of urban development. Demand for aggregates, therefore, is strongly urban-oriented. The natural raw material, however, may be widely distributed in the form of unconsolidated material (e.g. glacial drift, alluvial or beach deposits) or rock. The high-bulk-low-value nature of these commodities leads to high transport costs, which ensures that proximity to markets is a major factor in the development of resources. In postwar Britain, a shortage of sand and gravel in many areas combined with a growing demand from the construction industry led to the increased utilization of limestone, sandstone and igneous rocks in crushed form. In the case of limestone extraction additional demands came from the chemical industry.

Limestone now represents the largest single source of crushed aggregate, the bulk of which is supplied to the construction industry. The three main quarrying areas are in the Peak District (including the largest limestone quarry in Europe at Tunstead), the Craven district of the North Pennines, and South Wales; with two smaller production zones in the Lake District and North Wales. All of these areas coincide with areas of scenic value and in the majority of cases lie within National Parks. As Blunden (1978, p. 225) points out, while mineral extraction was viewed as an acceptable activity by the Act establishing National Parks, 'no-one in 1947 could foresee the scale or the level of output of the modern quarry, let alone the extent of its working life'. The aftermath of limestone quarrying may scar a landscape for decades before natural weathering processes can mellow the worked face. Of more immediate significance is the question of mitigating the impact of active quarries, most of which have a minimum working life of 30 years. A major problem is the visual impact of plant and machinery. A large quarry supplying aggregates is likely to have an on-site complex of crushing, asphalt, concrete batching and mixing plants; while a modern lime burning kiln will be over 30 m in height. Other problems associated with the daily working of limestone quarries are common to all types of hard rock extraction and are primarily noise, vibration, dust and traffic generation.

Other sources of aggregate are sandstone, igneous and metamorphic rocks, and sand and gravel. Important sandstone production areas are located adjacent to the large urban areas of Lancashire, with the chief concentration of workings in the Rossendale area. The thick deposits, heavy demand and cost advantages of local sandstone over alternatives from elsewhere have given rise to a complex of large workings.

In Britain igneous and metamorphic rocks are less widespread than either limestone or sandstone and are heavily concentrated in the upland zones of the north and west. The higher costs of extraction and processing than for competing hard rock materials, and their relative remoteness from areas where they are needed in quantity, has so far largely precluded the development of these resources to meet more than localized markets. Environmental problems are less for sandstone and igneous exploitation since the scale of workings is much smaller than for limestone quarrying, and activities take place largely outside the National Parks.

Sand and gravel working is an extensive activity around many urban areas. In London's green belt, for example, the Standing Conference on London and South East Regional Planning (1976) found that 3,320 ha of land were in active mineral workings with another 3,040 ha approved for future workings. While this represented less than 2.0 percent of the metropolitan green belt area the local impact of such operations is considerable. Similarly, in the smaller Waterloo area of southern Ontario, McLellan et al. (1979) identified 2,400 ha of land occupied by 60 active sand and gravel operations and an additional 127 abandoned pit sites occupying 307 ha of land, making the industry the second largest land use after agriculture in the rural area of the county. Some attempts have been made to rehabilitate land following aggregate extraction. Within Toronto's city boundaries, for example, sand and gravel sites now accommodate recreation or conservation areas, housing, schools, industrial uses, sanitary landfill sites and shopping centres. In Britain, flooded gravel workings in the Colne valley have been zoned to support different activities linked by a footpath network. In general, however, only in a minority of schemes will the shape and extent of current and future excavations be strongly influenced by the needs of subsequent land activity whereby the creation of functional but attractive new landscapes could be phased with the destruction of the old (Davidson and Wibberley 1977).

2. Slate   The economic importance of slate is due to its resistance to weathering and its fissility. However, the high cost of skilled labour and of transporting the split slates to markets from remote deposits in North Wales, the Lake District, and the Grampian Mountains of Scotland, plus the competition from clay and concrete tiles, has reduced sales to the housing market. Slates required for the maintenance of existing buildings now constitute a larger percentage of the roofing market than those for new houses. There remains a speciality market for architectural slate for cladding, facing, paving and flooring, and the high value of the green Cumbria slate, for example, means that the product can bear the transport costs to reach an international market. The major environmental problems created by slate workings stem from the high ratio of waste to cut slate (Moss 1981). The Blaenau Ffestiniog area of North Wales was deliberately omitted from the Snowdonia National Park for this reason. Although slate powders and granules prepared from waste can be used for surfacing asphaltic roofing felts, and for inert fillers in a variety of products (e.g. insecticides, paints, and pipeline coatings), this can only dispose of a fraction of accumulated waste. Attempts to vegetate slate tips are also slow and difficult (Countryside Commission 1978).

3.   China Clay   China clay is a kaolinized granite. It is produced in two areas of Britain, in Cornwall near St Austell and at Lee Moor on the edge of Dartmoor, and with worldwide deposits limited it is an important export. High-quality china clay is used in paper making and coating as well as in the pottery industry. Unfortunately, the working of the clay demands the removal of large quantities of quartz sand with which it is intermixed, meaning that the problem of waste disposal is considerable. Ironically the waste quartz sand would be a valuable commodity in southeastern England where it is needed as concreting sand, building sand and in brick making. One strategy might be for the government to subsidize the transport of waste sand from the southwest, with the subsidy being considered as a positive contribution to environmental conservation.

Other important minerals currently being worked in Britain include fluorspar, barytes and potash (Blunden 1975, 1978) while changes in world market conditions could lead to pressure for the exploitation of presently noneconomic but proven reserves such as copper in Snowdonia (Searle 1975). Government approval has been granted to explore for oil and gas in the Peak District and North Yorkshire Moors National Parks, and to exploit large coal reserves in the previously unspoiled Selby area in Yorkshire and Vale of Belvoir in Nottinghamshire (North and Spooner 1978). These decisions indicate the considerable conflicts which exist between the needs of the national economy, local job creation and conservation.

Water

Water is essential to life. In England and Wales public water supplies (which serve 99.0 percent of dwellings) are derived in approximately equal proportions from rivers

(32.0 percent), upland reservoirs (35.0 percent) and groundwater sources (33.0 percent), with private abstractions being mainly from surface and groundwater sources (National Water Council 1978). Scottish public supplies are drawn almost exclusively (96.0 percent) from natural lochs, reservoirs and rivers. The fact that an average of 190 million cubic metres of water per day is made available by rainfall in Britain compared to a demand of 14 million cubic metres per day suggests an abundance of supply. National averages, however, disguise the fact that there exists an inverse relationship between areas of water surplus and the main centres of demand (Porter 1978; Kirby 1979). The basic problem, therefore, is one of storage for times of deficit, and to transfer water from areas of plenty (such as Scotland, Wales, Northumbria and the Southwest) to areas where it is scarce (e.g. the Southeast).

Prior to the Water Resources Act 1963 there was little attempt at integrated management of water resources, with a multiplicity of over 1,000 authorities in England and Wales providing a fragmented competitive water use pattern in which many demand centres were not served from the most economic sources (Rees 1976; Gilg 1978). Between 1963 and 1973 the number of water undertakings was reduced to 160 but the Water Resources Act 1963 did not overcome the problem of divided responsibilities, there being an additional 29 river authorities with general responsibility for water conservation and river basin management, and over 1,200 sewerage and sewage disposal authorities. In 1974 these were abolished (with the exception of 28 private/statutory water companies) and their functions taken over by 10 integrated Regional Water Authorities designed to take a comprehensive and long-term view of all aspects of Water Management. In addition the post-1974 Regional Water Authorities have a duty to develop the recreation and amenity potential of their water spaces and to have due regard for the needs of conservation. Overall national policy is in the hands of the National Water Council. In Scotland the 13 regional water boards set up under the Water (Scotland) Act 1967 were dissolved at the time of local government reorganization in 1975 and their functions transferred to the new Regional Councils (Figure 17.1). The major benefits of the new water authorities, over and above a regular supply of potable water, have been the provision of extra recreational facilities, new habitats for wildlife and, in particular, application of the concept of overall management of the drainage system successfully pioneered by the Tennessee Valley Authority in the USA in the 1930s (Smallwood 1981).

In the United Kingdom 'future demand is the basic planning requirement around which other water management plans have to revolve' (Gilg 1978, p. 140). As Table 17.1 shows, the National Water Council forecasts a 42.0 percent increase in public water supply demands between 1975 and the end of the century. There are two chief ways of meeting these demands. The first approach, used extensively up until the Second World War, is to construct direct supply storage reservoirs in the water-rich uplands and pipe water to areas of demand. Public supply in Wales and in the English Midlands still relies on direct supply from upland reservoirs for 80.0 percent of its water. Aquaducts carry water from the Elan reservoir on the river Wye to Birmingham; from the Vyrnwy, a tributary of the Severn, to Liverpool; and direct supplies from the Derwent, a tributary of the Trent, serve Sheffield, Derby, Nottingham and Leicester. Manchester receives water directly from Lake Thirlmere in the Lake District. Such long-distance transfers of water have been the focus of

Figure 17.1 Water authorities in Great Britain.

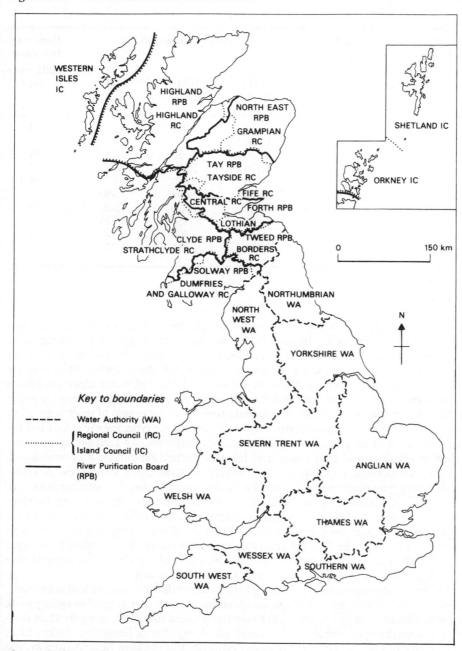

Source: Parker and Penning-Rowsell (1980)

Table 17.1 *Water authority forecasts for public water supply demands, 1981–2001*

Water authority	Actual supply	Forecast demand			Forecast increase 2001 over 1975
	1975 (Ml/d)	1981 (Ml/d)	1991 (Ml/d)	2001 (Ml/d)	(%)
North West	2,450	2,630	3,040	3,280	34
Northumbrian	960	1,200	—	—	—
Severn–Trent	2,180	2,230	2,660	3,020	38
Yorkshire	1,280	1,430	1,700	1,940	52
Anglian	1,450	1,730	2,250	2,670	84
Thames	3,360	3,400	3,640	3,880	15
Southern	1,090	1,220	1,500	1,800	65
Wessex	710	750	850	970	37
South West	380	420	500	590	55
Welsh	1,130	1,300	1,510	1,720	52

Source: Hanna (1982)

nationalistic protest in Wales. Other problems of these schemes are that reservoirs occupying the better valley bottom land undermine the fragile hill-farming operation, and that large areas of upland are effectively sterilized from public use because of the need to keep reservoir water, treated only by filtration, untainted by organic matter. The second approach relies on the use and reuse of water abstracted from rivers nearer to the centres of demand. This process places the emphasis on water quality and on the maintenance of adequate river flows by means of river-regulation reservoirs. Most new reservoirs and extensions are of this type; meaning that few restrictions need to be placed upon the use of the surrounding land for agriculture, including grazing; and that water and lakeside recreation can be accommodated. Modern landscaping techniques also provide less intrusive structures. A river-regulation system permits flood control as well as maintaining dry-weather flow and, as Hanna (1982) points out, the building of a downstream sewage works to raise river water to the required quality to permit abstraction may offset the need for a new upland reservoir and has the additional advantage of improving amenity values in general. Since 1980 the Kielder reservoir in Northumbria has regulated the river Tyne for abstraction by Newcastle and Gateshead with pipelines and tunnels also providing a link to the rivers Wear and Tees further south.

Other possible methods for meeting future demands for water are less important, at least in the short term. Although desalination of sea water is used to satisfy peak summer demands in Jersey and Guernsey the process is still more costly than conventional methods available on the mainland. A number of feasibility studies have been carried out on the damming of major estuaries like the Dee, Severn, Solway, the Wash and Morecambe Bay. In addition to the financial cost of such a project the environmental impacts would be far-reaching and this strategy is again unlikely in the short term. An alternative is to use underground aquifers for storage. The main aquifers in England are the chalk and Jurassic limestone areas (e.g. the Thames Basin) and the Bunter sandstones, mainly in the Midlands and on the flanks of the Pennines. In areas of Triassic rocks, however, much of the ground water is mineralized.

Both the direct-supply and river-regulation strategies are examples of the 'supply-fix' approach to water management, according to which facilities are automatically extended to meet increasing demand. As Rees (1976) observes, in all developed countries when estimating future requirements it is assumed that no attempts to control demand will be made and that all peak needs should be met. Additionally, authorities normally attempt to guard against very low probability drought occurrences, and calculate potential supply on the basis of extremely dry conditions. An alternative to supply extension is to attempt to manage demand (e.g. by metering) and to increase efficiency in use of existing resources. There is a range of techniques which could make it possible to defer expenditure on new storage facilities:

(a) Supply transfer – Interregional transfer of water formed a key element in the Water Resources Board's assessment of water management strategies until the end of the present century (Jones 1975), and stimulated suggestions for a national water grid. This type of strategy has formed the basis of water resource planning in California since 1935. The aim is to transfer 'surplus' water from the Sacramento basin in the northern part of the state and from the Colorado river in the southeast to satisfy the demands from irrigation and urban-industrial interests in the semiarid southwest (Wilcock et al. 1976).

(b) Reduce distribution losses – The most important of these losses occurs through pipeline leakage although in dry summers evaporation from water surfaces is also significant. Rees (1976) estimates that a 20–30 percent leakage loss is common with the figure rising to over 50 percent in some British residential areas. Similar levels of leakage have been reported in the USA. Opportunities for reduction are related to programmes to replace ageing water mains and to advances in leak detection technology.

(c) Dual quality supply systems – In most industrial societies only about 10–25 percent of water is used for functions which require high purity and yet the overall quality of supplies is dictated by this usage. Dual water supplies use one system for potable water and another for nonpotable water. In Hong Kong, for example, sea water is provided on a separate system for toilet flushing in many government-built high rise blocks; while in Australia towns in New South Wales give a nonpotable supply for all uses of water outside the home, such as garden watering or car washing.

(d) Water reuse – This can be achieved either by reclaiming sewage effluent to provide supplies of low quality, perhaps for dual-supply systems; or by recycling water in homes and factories. The Water Resources Act 1963 made it obligatory for industry to obtain a licence and pay a charge for private water supply, and industrial recycling of water has grown as the price of metered water has risen. Domestic bath or washbasin water could be stored and used for toilet flushing, as in parts of Sweden.

(e) Domestic water metering – This attempts to use the price mechanism to reduce current consumption and to control the rate of increase in demand. A central issue is the price elasticity of demand for water (Russell 1974; Lingard 1975; Dugdale 1975; Okun 1977). Research in the USA and Netherlands found that water demand is price sensitive so that the effect of metering depends on the size of charge levied (Rees 1976; Parker and Penning-Rowsell 1980). In Britain experience of domestic metering is mainly limited to Malvern where meters have been in operation since 1872 following a local water shortage. Given the variation in resource availability, domestic metering, though legalized by the Water Act 1973, is more likely to be introduced in locally pressured areas rather than as a national measure. Before any such policy could be implemented, however, authorities would have to overcome the common belief that an abundant water supply is a basic human right, too vital to be restricted through charges.

Woodlands

Woodland is the natural climatic-climax vegetation cover over much of the British Isles. A thousand years of exploitation by man had reduced the forest cover to 5.0 percent of Britain's land surface in 1900, and while this proportion has risen to 9.0 percent it is still well below the average of 21.0 percent for Europe, 23.0 percent in USA, and 54.0 percent in both Canada and Sweden. As a consequence, Britain must import 90.0 percent of its timber needs mainly from Canada, Finland, Norway, Sweden and USSR, a group of producers which dominates the world wood market (Centre for Agricultural Strategy 1980).

In Britain the main agency responsible for woodland management is the Forestry Commission, which was established by the Forestry Act 1919 with the principal duty of building up a strategic reserve of timber following the demands of the First World War. Between 1945 and 1951 a series of Forestry Acts increased the Commission's powers for the purchase and management of land and provided for the dedication of land to forestry purposes by allowing private owners or tenants to make covenants with the Commission. The Commission has a dual role. As the Forest Authority it seeks to ensure the best use of the country's timber resources, undertakes research and education, and supervises private forestry schemes. As the Forestry Enterprise its main aim is to produce timber from its own estates. In 1958 the emphasis changed from building up a strategic reserve to social-economic aims such as providing employment in depressed rural areas and producing raw materials for home-based industries (Gilg 1978). Since the Forestry Act 1962 and the Countryside Act 1968 the Forestry Commission is also required to develop the recreational potential of its properties, to conserve the natural beauty and amenity of the countryside, and to integrate with other land uses as far as is possible.

In addition to the activities of the Forestry Commission afforestation is also undertaken by private interests (including financial institutions, pension funds, commercial companies and private landowners) aided by favourable tax provisions, government grants and Forestry Commission advisory services. Private forestry accounts for 60.0 percent of the total forest area in Britain and contains most of the mature and semimature timber and most of the hardwoods. Much of this woodland is in small plots, 40.0 percent of which have an area of less than 80 ha; and is of particular importance in the southern half of the country. Under the Forestry Acts, the Commission has two main controls over private forestry: first, the power to control the felling of trees by means of a licensing system; and secondly, the power to enter into forestry dedication covenants (with owners receiving a grant and tax concessions in return for managing dedicated woodland in accordance with Commission advice).

The vast majority (over 90.0 percent) of trees planted by the Forestry Commission are conifers. As Green (1981, p. 120) explains, 'a crop of native hardwoods like oak or beech may be worth as much or more as one of conifers such as Corsican pine or Sitka spruce, but they grow at only half the rate (4–6 c.f. 10–20 m³/annum/ ha.) so that the hardwood crop is harvested in about 140 years and the conifer at 60 years. Discounted revenues can thus make the conifers as much as ten times more valuable.' Although monocultures of conifers are more productive than mixed stands, more easily established, managed, harvested and marketed, they have been criticized by conservationists on aesthetic grounds. Particular concern has been expressed over the impact of this form of afforestation on the landscape in the National Parks (Price 1980; MacEwan and MacEwan 1982).

Most private and public tree planting has taken place in the uplands where the main competitive land uses have been hill sheep and cattle farming (Mather 1971, 1978). Private interests have found it easier to purchase land than has the Forestry Commission which is constrained to acquire land of low agricultural value. State forestry is therefore pushed onto the higher ground where hill farming is either static or on the retreat, whereas private forest interests are free to bid in the open market for land (Davidson and Wibberley 1977). Between 1919 and 1976 the Forestry Commission acquired and planted 0.80 million hectares of productive forest. Since the 1960s, however, it has found it increasingly difficult to obtain land and the acquisition rate has fallen to below that required to meet an annual planting target of 22,000 ha. If the supply of hill land on the open market continues to fall short of needs the Commission may have to resort to its hitherto unused power of compulsory purchase.

Arguments against large-scale afforestation cite its adverse effects on water catchments (pollution of streams and loss of supply through evapotranspiration); sedimentation and erosion after clear felling; and loss of scenic quality. The case for upland afforestation has been argued at various times on economic, strategic, employment and amenity grounds. The economic case rests on a comparison of the long-term returns from poor land under trees with those from poor land under sheep or other livestock. A cost–benefit analysis by HM Treasury (1972) calculated a rate of return from upland forestry of 4.0 percent, possibly rising to 7.0 percent if allowance was made for the recreational benefits. On the basis of these figures it was concluded that afforestation could not be justified purely on economic grounds. The strategic argument, which was the original basis for establishing the Forestry Commission, retains a degree of validity and could assume increased importance if forecasts of a world wood shortage by the end of the century prove to be accurate (Centre for Agricultural Strategy 1980; Food and Agriculture Organisation 1980). The 1947 government White Paper on Post-War Forest Policy strongly argued for afforestation as a means of providing more permanent employment than hill farming in certain upland areas. The number of jobs created has been less than envisaged but the HM Treasury (1972) analysis concurred that afforestation did provide more employment than hill farming, with the actual ratio varying regionally from 2:1 in southern England to 10:1 in northern England. Although the cost of providing these forestry jobs was at least twice as much as for hill farming, in any policy seeking to maximize rural employment forestry would be preferable to farming. Moreover, the HM Treasury (1972) analysis was limited in that it failed to consider the benefits of combined enterprises involving forestry, agriculture, tourism and other rural industries. Finally, although forest parks have been provided since the 1930s the importance of amenity aspects of afforestation were only recognized officially in the late 1960s. Landscape and recreation factors now have a significant influence on the planting programmes of the Forestry Commission, and the new Dedication Scheme in operation since 1974 indicates that, while the planting and management of private woodland will continue to be grant-aided by the State and helped through preferential tax arrangements, environmental improvement will play a major role in deciding on the schemes to be agreed.

In the United Kingdom, forestry and agriculture have been viewed as competing land uses in the uplands, in contrast to many hill areas of Europe where there is a tradition of combined forest and farming holdings. Hill farming represents a major source of income in the uplands which supply the bulk of Britain's mutton, lamb and wool; but without government subsidies, which may account for one-third of an individual farmer's income, the local economy of many hill areas would collapse. One solution has been for farmers to sell land to the Forestry Commission. An alternative goal may be to combine agriculture and forestry within a multiple-use management policy. On the Fassfern estate in Inverness-shire, for example, forests occupy the middle ground on hills which rise in places to 650 m, the lower parts have been converted into a more intensive type of sheep and cattle rearing operation, and the hill tops have been left for deer (Grainger 1981). Matthews et al. (1972) and Newton (1978) cite several examples of integrated farming and forestry schemes.

The creation of 'farm-forest units' can provide increased financial returns as a result of improvements such as (a) the construction of new access roads for forestry operations which also facilitate stock movement and the cultivation of hill land, (b) the division of land into more manageable units, (c) the provision of shelter belts for crops and stock. These are particularly important at lambing time, and also promote improved grass growth through a longer period of the year. In addition to the immediate production benefits, forestry normally provides more employment than hill farming and the two run together can maintain a higher year-round rural population. Labour requirements in farming and forestry can also be smoothed out and dovetailed to take account of slack and busy seasons, and equipment may be shared. Finally the appearance of the countryside will be more varied – less bleak than extensive hill farming and more interesting than large tracts of forest. It will also support a greater variety of fauna and flora. Although a Scottish study concluded that small tenanted upland farms integrated with forestry offer the possibility of holding large numbers of people in the countryside (Mutch and Hutchinson 1980), progress towards farm-forestry production units has largely been confined to larger farms and estates.

Regarding the overall role of forestry in the rural land use pattern, Gilg (1978) suggests that a minimum of forest land essential to national security should be planted on the best land but that, on the poorest land where most afforestation takes place, the expense of planting and managing trees for a minimum of 60 years can only be justified by using forestry as a core land use, around which a coordinated rural land management strategy can be evolved, including recreation, water management and wildlife conservation.

Landscape

'For many people the outward appearance of the countryside is the single most obvious and most valued component of its fabric' (Davidson and Wibberley 1977, p. 87). Landscape is a cultural as well as physical resource and its appreciation will change over time and among human groups. Nevertheless, a great many attempts have been made to develop methods for the assessment of landscape quality (Penning-Rowsell 1973; Dunn 1974; Zube et al. 1975; Dearden 1977). The underlying aims include: (1) to assist land use planning and management decisions by evaluating the potential impact of a proposed development, such as an industrial enterprise (Weddle 1969), power line (Haggerty 1974) or road; (2) to define areas best suited to conservation or recreation needs (Anderson 1981) or to design scenic routes and trails (Priddle 1973); and (3) to monitor landscape change.

One of the earliest ways of deriving landscape evaluations is the concensus approach based upon the judgement of 'experts'. This has been the basis of management decisions in several countries despite its apparent lack of objective method. It has been employed extensively in Britain and as Turner (1975, p. 157) comments, 'few of us can argue that concensus methods which produced the designations of the National Parks and Areas of Outstanding Natural Beauty were in error'. The same approach was used in the USA to designate outstanding streams as part of a National Wild and Scenic Rivers programme (Knudson 1976). The concensus approach has both strengths and weaknesses. It is flexible and normally minimizes time and expense but it does not provide systematic evidence to support decisions and there is no evidence to suggest that the views of a group of experts resemble those of people in general (Bukyoff et al. 1978).

In North America interest in landscape evaluation has been more broadly based than in the United Kingdom with significant contributions being made by landscape architects (Litton 1972), social psychologists (Craik 1972) and geologists (Leopold 1969) as well as by geographers. Leopold (1969) adopted a pragmatic view arguing that it was necessary for environmentalists to describe landscapes objectively in a quantitative manner in order to counter the numerical advocacy employed by economists and others in debates over alternative uses for the environment. Stimulated by a proposal to build a hydro-electric dam in the Hell's Canyon area of the Snake river in Idaho, he employed a total of 46 criteria to calculate a uniqueness index for 16 river valleys (with Hell's Canyon ranked second overall). It is important to note, however, that Leopold's uniqueness score was not an indication of the attractiveness or unattractiveness of a site – river pollution at one site, for example, gave it the highest uniqueness value. Despite its deficiencies (Hamill 1975), several studies have been developed on the basis of this technique (Chubb and Bauman 1977).

Among the first significant British contributions to landscape evaluation were Linton's (1968) analysis of Scottish landscapes, Fines's (1968) view analysis in Sussex, Clark's (1968) attempt to devise a national system of landscape analysis, and Tandy's (1971) method of landscape character and quality assessment. Fines (1968, p. 43) set out to provide 'a method of evaluating the basic three-dimensional landscape under average conditions and in relation to the average intelligent observer'. He first established a scale of landscape values by asking 10 observers with 'training and experience in a design discipline' to grade the scenic quality of 20 landscape colour photographs. The scores of 0–32 were divided into six descriptive categories (Figure 17.2). The scenic value of each landscape tract was then judged in the field by a single observer using the photographs as reference points. Despite criticisms of the method and in particular the dependence on the views of only 10 'experts' (Brancher 1969) Fines's work was a seminal contribution to landscape evaluation research in Britain.

Linton's (1968) landscape appraisal technique was offered as an alternative to Fines' approach which was considered to be overly complicated, costly, time-consuming, and based on an unverified measurement scale. Linton believed that scenic quality was the product of two landscape features: landform and landuse. He identified six landform landscapes and seven landuse landscapes and assigned numerical values to each (Table 17.2). Both characteristics were mapped for Scotland and the results amalgamated to produce a map of scenic quality (Figure 17.3) which, in essence, reinforced Murray's (1962) intuitive classification of the Highlands' landscape. Crofts and Cooke (1974, p. 16) tested Linton's approach against that suggested by Fines and concluded that the former provided a 'simpler, quicker, cheaper and more comprehensible way of producing a general statement of landscape quality'. Gilg (1975, 1976) also argued in favour of the Linton method based on the replicability of results, and considered that deficiencies could be overcome by modifying the technique rather than the approach.

Reaction to the criticisms of excessive subjectivity in these intuitive methods of landscape appraisal led, in the early 1970s, to the development of more complex statistical techniques – the intention being to maximize both reliability (i.e. the capacity of being replicable) and validity (i.e. the fit between what is being measured and the substantive interpretation to be placed upon the measurement). The Coventry-Solihull-Warwickshire (CSW) team was one of the first to propose such an approach (Coventry-Solihull-Warwickshire Sub-Regional Planning Study Group 1971). The procedure had six stages (Figure 17.4). First, data were collected from air photographs and map sources on three groups of landscape components: (1) landform – number of intersections of 25' contour lines with the periphery of the grid; (2) land use – area of farmland, woodland, developed land, industry, parkland, heathland, unused land; (3) land features – incidence of hedgerows, watercourses, roads, power lines, railways, buildings and mining. In addition an index of inter-visibility was calculated based on the product of the number of survey units visible from any one unit and an index of slope. In stage B, the visual quality of each of the 2,316 km^2 landscape tracts in the study area was evaluated in the field by two members of the research team. A step-wise multiple regression of the 24 landscape variables against the dependent variable of visual quality found that 15 variables

Figure 17.2 Fines' scale of landscape values.

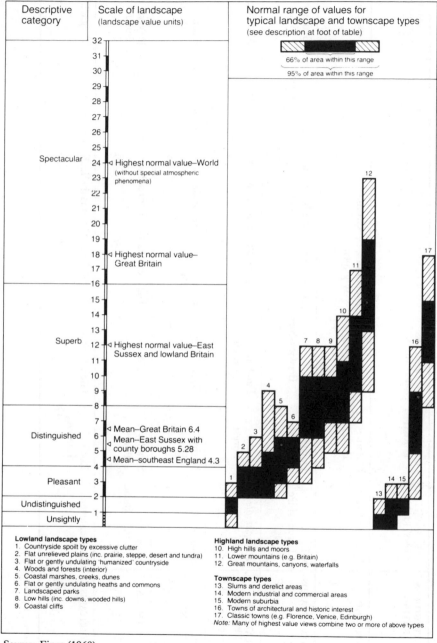

Descriptive category	Scale of landscape (landscape value units)	Normal range of values for typical landscape and townscape types (see description at foot of table)

Spectacular
24 ◁ Highest normal value—World (without special atmospheric phenomena)

18 ◁ Highest normal value— Great Britain

Superb
12 ◁ Highest normal value—East Sussex and lowland Britain

Distinguished
7 ◁ Mean—Great Britain 6.4
6 ◁ Mean—East Sussex with county boroughs 5.28
◁ Mean—southeast England 4.3

Pleasant

Undistinguished

Unsightly

Lowland landscape types
1. Countryside spoilt by excessive clutter
2. Flat unrelieved plains (inc. prairie, steppe, desert and tundra)
3. Flat or gently undulating 'humanized' countryside
4. Woods and forests (interior)
5. Coastal marshes, creeks, dunes
6. Flat or gently undulating heaths and commons
7. Landscaped parks
8. Low hills (inc. downs, wooded hills)
9. Coastal cliffs

Highland landscape types
10. High hills and moors
11. Lower mountains (e.g. Britain)
12. Great mountains, canyons, waterfalls

Townscape types
13. Slums and derelict areas
14. Modern industrial and commercial areas
15. Modern suburbia
16. Towns of architectural and historic interest
17. Classic towns (e.g. Florence, Venice, Edinburgh)
Note: Many of highest value views combine two or more of above types

Source: Fines (1968)

Table 17.2   *Linton's landscape evaluation categories*

CATEGORY & RATING	URBANIZED & INDUSTRIALIZED −5	CONTINUOUS FOREST −2	TREELESS FARMLAND +1	MOORLAND +3	VARIED FOREST AND MOORLAND +4	RICHLY VARIED FARMLAND +5	WILD LANDSCAPES +6
LOWLAND 0	Ayrshire Coast −5	Culbin Forest −2	Machars of Wigtown +1	Moors of Wigtown +3	Cromar +4	Strathearn +5	Colonsay +6
LOW UPLANDS +2	N.E. Lanarkshire −3	Darnaway Forest 0	N.E. Berwickshire +3	Loch Shin +5	Methven and Glenalmond +6	Gifford (East Lothian) +7	Gruinard Bay +8
PLATEAU UPLANDS +3	(No example) −2	Kielder Forest +1	Falahill (Midlothian) +4	Monadhliath +6	Potrail Water +7	(No example) +8	Mid Argyll +9
HILL COUNTRY +5	Bathgate Hills 0	Nethy Forest +3	Gala Valley +6	Crawick Water +8	Speyside +9	Middle Tweed +10	Loch Moidart +11
BOLD HILLS +6	Leadhills – Wanlockhead +1	Strathyre Forest +4	Loch Chon +7	Dalveen Pass +9	Bennachie +10	(No example) +11	Morvern and Sunart +12
MOUNTAINS +8	Kinlochleven +3	Loch Lubnaig +6	Glen Elchaig +9	Glen Clova +11	Achnashellach +12	(No example) +13	Coigach +14

Source: Linton (1968)

Figure 17.3 Linton's composite scenic assessment for Scotland.

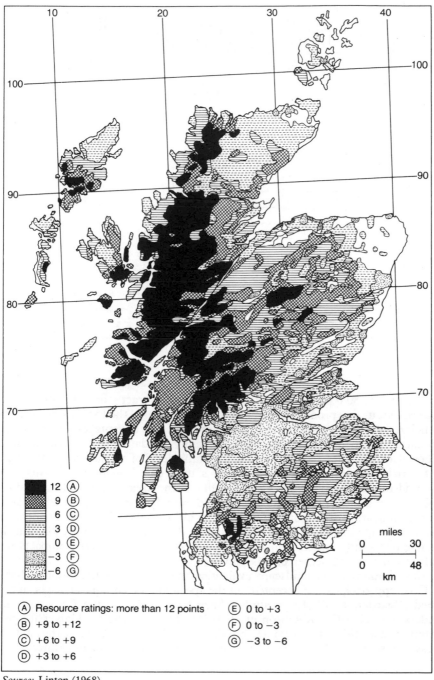

A Resource ratings: more than 12 points   E 0 to +3
B +9 to +12   F 0 to −3
C +6 to +9   G −3 to −6
D +3 to +6

Source: Linton (1968)

Figure 17.4 The Coventry-Solihull-Warwickshire method of landscape evaluation.

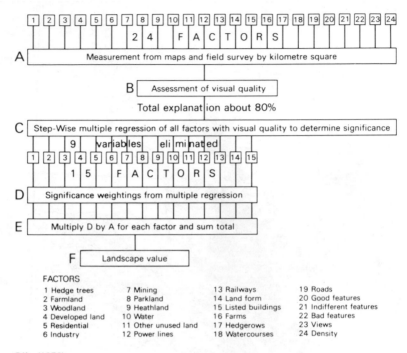

FACTORS

1 Hedge trees	7 Mining	13 Railways	19 Roads
2 Farmland	8 Parkland	14 Land form	20 Good features
3 Woodland	9 Heathland	15 Listed buildings	21 Indifferent features
4 Developed land	10 Water	16 Farms	22 Bad features
5 Residential	11 Other unused land	17 Hedgerows	23 Views
6 Industry	12 Power lines	18 Watercourses	24 Density

Source: Gilg (1978)

explained up to 80.0 percent of the variation between tract scores. Finally a map of landscape value was produced by multiplying the values of the 15 measured variables by their respective regression weights (Figure 17.5). The advantages of this statistical approach are: (a) the R^2 statistic can be readily validated; (b) if variation in the independent variables accounts for an acceptable level of explanation of the dependent variable a clear link exists between a map based on measurements of the independent variables and the visual quality of the area (and therefore landscape quality for areas not visited could be predicted from data on the measured variables); (c) some indication of the correlation between individual landscape components and visual landscape quality is given by the simple R values of the regression, thus it is possible to identify which components have positive and negative impacts upon quality, and also the degree of this impact.

As with many other landscape evaluation methodologies, the rationale behind the CSW approach can be accepted but the operational techniques have been questioned (Dearden 1980). Later studies have tried to refine the CSW technique (Anderson et al. 1976; Robinson et al. 1976). The Manchester University group (Robinson et al. 1976), for example, introduced a device to standardize the landscape assessment scores of the observers in order to meet the requirement of interval scale

Figure 17.5 The landscape evaluation map produced by the CSW method shown in Figure 17.4.

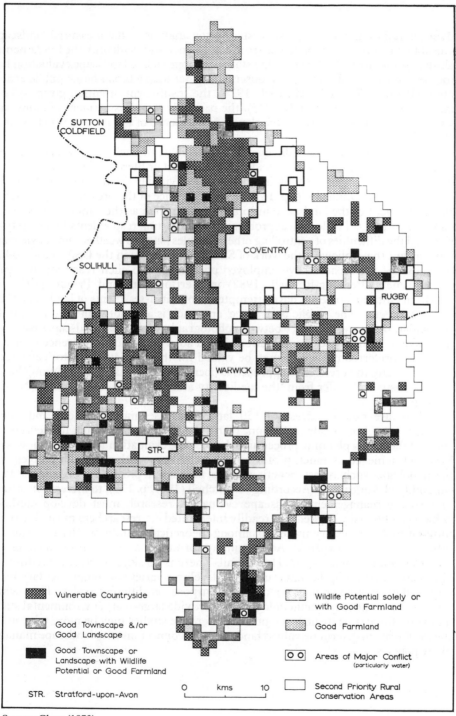

Vulnerable Countryside

Good Townscape &/or Good Landscape

Good Townscape or Landscape with Wildlife Potential or Good Farmland

STR. Stratford-upon-Avon

Wildlife Potential solely or with Good Farmland

Good Farmland

Areas of Major Conflict (particularly water)

Second Priority Rural Conservation Areas

0   kms   10

Source: Clout (1972)

data for valid regression, and suggested factor analysis of the measured landscape variables prior to regression to ensure independence and to identify the fundamental landscape elements. Criticism of the statistical approach to landscape evaluation has focused on the use of professional observers rather than a broad-based public evaluation (Penning-Rowsell and Searle 1977), the insufficient attention given to how landscape is perceived (Tandy 1977), the narrowly visual assessment of landscape value (Turner 1977), and the complexity and expense of the procedures (Penning-Rowsell 1981).

A third approach seeks to discover landscape value through expressed preferences, identified either indirectly from evidence such as art or literature (Rees 1977; Salter and Lloyd 1977) or directly by interviewing individuals (Shafer and Tooby 1973; Dunn 1976). As Dunn (1976, p. 16) notes, the essence of the preference approach is the 'judgement of the landscape in totality' rather than as the sum of a number of component parts. The logistical problem of transporting respondents to a variety of sites and the difficulties of controlling other variables (such as weather, time of viewing) have meant that, following the work of Shafer et al. (1969) in the USA, most studies of landscape preferences have employed photographs to elicit reactions to scenic attractiveness. Penning-Rowsell (1982) in Hertfordshire and Priddle (1973) in southern Ontario, however, have attempted to obtain assessments of landscape preferences directly. The 'public preference' approach is also not without criticism. In particular, the correspondence between photographs and actual landscapes has been questioned. Also landscape evaluations based solely on visual preference overlook areas not preferred but which may be valued for their variety or historical associations. Finally the preference approach is open to the criticism that planning based on concensus will suffer from 'the mediocrity associated with the average' (Newby 1978, p. 349).

There are now in excess of 150 landscape assessment methods and many attempts have been made in Britain, North America and Australia to incorporate some of these into planning procedures. Landscape evaluation techniques, however, have not achieved as much professional acceptance as other equally problematic methodologies such as cost-benefit analysis, population projection models, and land capability classifications. According to Mitchell (1979, p. 171), to increase its utility in resource management, landscape evaluation research must develop methods 'which can be easily applied and readily interpreted . . . researchers must give more thought to the necessary trade-offs among theoretical soundness, elegance, ease of interpretation, and expense'. Attempting to formulate a universal methodology is akin to pursuing an academic Holy Grail. There is no single correct procedure for landscape evaluation; the aim must be to develop a variety of complementary techniques that may be applied for different purposes at different scales. Thus while intuitive and statistical methodologies may provide large-scale environmental statements useful at a strategic level, public preference studies may be more relevant at the local scale to determine valued landscapes in connection with landscape management policies.

References

ANDERSON, M. A. (1981) The proposed High Weald Area of Outstanding Natural Beauty, *Landscape Research* 6(2), 6–10.

ANDERSON, T. W., ZUBE, E. H. and MacCONNELL, W. P. (1976) Predicting scenic resource values. *In* E. H. Zube *Studies in Landscape Perception* Institute for Man and Environment Publication No. R-76-1. Amherst: University of Massachusetts, 6–69.

BLUNDEN, J. R. (1975) *The Mineral Resources of Britain*. London: Hutchinson.

BLUNDEN, J. R. (1978) The future of the extractive industries in upland Britain. *In* R. B. Tranter *The Future of Upland Britain* Vol. 1. Reading: Centre for Agricultural Strategy, 220–60.

BRANCHER, D. M. (1969) Critique of K. D. Fines: landscape evaluation, *Regional Studies* 3, 91–2.

BUKYOFF, G. J., WELLMAN, J. D., HARVEY, H., and FRASER, R. A. (1978) Landscape architects' interpretations of peoples' landscape preferences, *Journal of Environmental Management* 6, 255–62.

CENTRE FOR AGRICULTURAL STRATEGY (1980) *Strategy for the U.K. Forest Industry*. Reading: The Author.

CHUBB, M. and BAUMAN, E. H. (1977) Assessing the recreation potential of rivers, *Journal of Soil and Water Conservation* 32, 97–102.

CLARK, S. B. K. (1968) Landscape survey and analysis on a national basis, *Planning Outlook* 4, 15–29.

CLOUT, H. (1972) *Rural Geography: an introductory survey*. Oxford: Pergamon.

COUNTRYSIDE COMMISSION (1978) *Upland Land Use in England and Wales* CCP111. Cheltenham: HMSO.

COVENTRY-SOLIHULL-WARWICKSHIRE SUB-REGIONAL PLANNING STUDY GROUP (1971) *A Strategy For the Sub-Region Supplementary Report No. 5*. Coventry: The Author.

CRAIK, K. H. (1972) Psychological factors in landscape appraisal, *Environment and Behaviour* 4, 255–6.

CROFTS, R. S. and COOKE, R. U. (1974) *Landscape Evaluation: A comparison of techniques* Occasional Paper No. 25 Department of Geography. London: University College.

DAVIDSON, J. and WIBBERLEY, G. (1977) *Planning and the Rural Environment*. Oxford: Pergamon.

DEARDEN, P. (1977) *Landscape Aesthetics: An annotated bibliography* Exchange Bibliography 1220. Monticello, Illinois: Council of Planning Librarians.

DEARDEN, P. (1980) Landscape assessment: the last decade, *Canadian Geographer* 24(3), 316–25.

DUGDALE, W. (1975) Universal metering, the case against, *Water* 4, 9–10.

DUNN, M. C. (1974) *Landscape Evaluation Techniques* Working Paper No. 4. University of Birmingham: Centre for Urban and Regional Studies.

DUNN, M. C. (1976) Landscape with photographs: testing the preference approach to landscape evaluation, *Journal of Environmental Management* 4, 15–26.

FINES, K. D. (1968) Landscape evaluation: a research project in East Sussex, *Regional Studies*, 2, 41–55.

FOOD AND AGRICULTURE ORGANISATION (1980) *The State of Food and Agriculture 1978*. Rome: The Author.

GILG, A. W. (1975) The objectivity of Linton type methods of assessing scenery as a natural resource, *Regional Studies* 9, 181–9.

GILG, A. W. (1976) Assessing scenery as a natural resource, *Scottish Geographical Magazine* 92, 41–9.

GILG, A. W. (1978) *Countryside Planning*. London: Methuen.

GRAINGER, A. (1981) Reforesting Britain, *The Ecologist* 11(2), 56–81.

GREEN, B. (1981) *Countryside Conservation*. London: Allen and Unwin.

HAGGERTY, J. (1974) A regional level landscape evaluation for the analysis of visual impact of high voltage transmission lines, *Geographical Inter-University Resource Management Seminar Vol. 4*. Waterloo, Ontario: Wilfrid Laurier University, 67–81.

HAMILL, L. (1975) Analysis of Leopold's quantitative comparisons of landscape esthetics, *Journal of Leisure Research* 7, 16–28.

HANNA, L. W. (1982) Environment and land use. *In* J. W. House *The U.K. Space* 3rd edition. London: Weidenfeld and Nicolson, 204–81.

HM TREASURY (1972) *Forestry in Great Britain*. London: HMSO.

JONES, P. (1975) Future water resources for England and Wales, *Geography* 60(4), 298–300.

KIRBY, C. (1979) *Water in Great Britain*. Harmondsworth: Penguin.

KNUDSON, D. M. (1976) A system for evaluating scenic rivers, *Water Resources Bulletin* 12, 281–90.

LEOPOLD, L. B. (1969) Landscape esthetics, *Natural History* 78, 37–44.

LINGARD, J. (1975) Universal metering, the case for, *Water* 4, 6–9.

LINTON, D. L. (1968) The assessment of scenery as a natural resource, *Scottish Geographical Magazine* 84, 219–38.

LITTON, R. B. (1972) Aesthetic dimensions of the landscape. *In* J. V. Krutilla *Natural Environments: Studies in Theoretical and Applied Analysis*. Baltimore: Johns Hopkins, 262–91.

MacEWAN, A. and MacEWAN, M. (1982) *National Parks: Conservation or Cosmetics?* London: Allen and Unwin.

MATHER, A. S. (1971) Problems of afforestation in north Scotland, *Transactions of the Institute of British Geographers* 54, 19–32.

MATHER, A. S. (1978) Patterns of afforestation in Britain since 1945, *Geography* 63(3), 157–66.

MATTHEWS, J. D., PHILIP, M. S., and CUMMING, D. G. (1972) Forestry and the forest industries. *In* J. Ashton and W. H. Long *The Remoter Rural Areas of Britain*. Edinburgh: Oliver and Boyd, 25–49.

McLELLAN, A. G., YUNDT, S. E., and DORFMAN, M. L. (1979) *Abandoned Pits and Quarries in Ontario* Ontario Geological Survey Miscellaneous Paper 79. Toronto: Ontario Ministry of Natural Resource.

MITCHELL, B. (1979) *Geography and Resource Analysis*. London: Longman.

MOSS, G. (1981) *Britain's Wasting Acres*. London: Architectural Press.

MURRAY, W. H. (1962) *Highland Landscape – a Survey*. Edinburgh: National Trust for Scotland.

MUTCH, W. E. S. and HUTCHINSON, A. R. (1980) *The Interaction of Forestry and Farming* Economics and Management Series No. 2. Edinburgh: University Department of Forestry and Natural Resources.

NATIONAL WATER COUNCIL (1978) *Water Industry Review 1978*. London: The Author.

NEWBY, P. T. (1978) Towards an understanding of landscape quality, *British Journal of Aesthetics* 18, 345–55.

NEWTON, J. P. (1978) Farming and forestry in the hills and uplands: competition or partnership. *In* R. B. Tranter *The Future of Upland Britain* Vol. 1. Reading: Centre for Agricultural Strategy, 114–35.

NORTH, J. and SPOONER, D. (1978) On the coal mining frontier, *Town and Country Planning* 46, 155–63.

NUTLEY, W. G. et al. (1978) *Planning and Mineral Working* Journal of Planning and Environmental Law Occasional Paper No. 4. London: Sweet and Maxwell.

OKUN, D. A. (1977) *Regionalization of Water Management*. London: Applied Science Publishers.

PARKER, D. J. and PENNING-ROWSELL, E. C. (1980) *Water Planning in Britain*. London: Allen and Unwin.

PENNING-ROWSELL, E. C. (1973) *Alternative Approaches to Landscape Appraisal and Evaluation* Planning Research Group Report No. 11. Middlesex: The Polytechnic.

PENNING-ROWSELL, E. C. (1981) Fluctuating fortunes in gauging landscape value, *Progress in Human Geography* 5(1), 25–41.

PENNING-ROWSELL, E. C. (1982) A public preference evaluation of landscape quality, *Regional Studies* 16(2), 97–112.

PENNING-ROWSELL, E. C. and SEARLE, G. H. (1977) The Manchester landscape evaluation method: a critical appraisal, *Landscape Research* 2(3), 6–11.

PORTER, E. (1978) *Water Management in England and Wales*. Cambridge: The University Press.

PRICE, C. (1980) Afforestation and the fate of the National Parks, *Town and Country Planning* 48, 184–7.

PRIDDLE, G. B. (1973) Measuring the view from the road, *Geographical Inter-University*

Resource Management Seminar Vol. 4. Waterloo, Ontario: Wilfrid Laurier University, 67–81.

REES, J. (1976) Rethinking our approach to water supply provision, *Geography* 61(4), 232–45.

REES, R. (1973) Geography and landscape painting, *Scottish Geographical Magazine* 89, 147–57.

ROBERTS, P. W. and SHAW, T. (1982) *Mineral Resources in Regional and Strategic Planning*. Aldershot: Gower.

ROBINSON, D. G., LAURIE, I. C., WAGER, J. F. and TRAILL, A. C. (1976) *Landscape Evaluation*. University of Manchester: Centre for Urban and Regional Research.

RUSSELL, C. S. (1974) Restraining demand. *In* B. M. Funnell and R. D. Hey *The Management of Water Resources in England and Wales*. Farnborough: Saxon House.

SALTER, C. L. and LLOYD, W. J. (1977) *Landscape in Literature* Resource Paper for College Geography No. 76–3. Washington D.C.: Association of American Geographers.

SEARLE, G. H. (1975) Copper in Snowdonia National Park. *In* P. J. Smith *The Politics of Physical Resources*. Harmondsworth: Penguin.

SHAFER, E. L. and TOOBY, M. (1973) Landscape preferences: an international replication, *Journal of Leisure Research* 5, 60–5.

SHAFER, E. L., HAMILTON, J. E. and SCHMIDT, E. A. (1969) Natural landscape preferences: a predictive model, *Journal of Leisure Research* 1, 1–19.

SMALLWOOD, J. B. (1981) An American way to conservation: comments on Federal river basin development. *In* R. Kain *Planning For Conservation*. London: Maxwell, 159–76.

STANDING CONFERENCE ON LONDON AND SOUTH EAST REGIONAL PLANNING (1976) *The Improvement of London's Green Belt*. London: The Author.

STEVENS, R. (1976) *Planning Control Over Mineral Working*. London: HMSO.

TANDY, C. R. V. (1971) *Landscape Evaluation Techniques*. Croydon: Land Use Consultants.

TANDY, C. R. V. (1977) Review of D. Robinson et al. (1976) *Landscape Evaluation* (University of Manchester), *Landscape Planning* 4, 100–2.

TURNER, J. R. (1975) Applications of landscape evaluation: a planner's view, *Transactions of the Institute of British Geographers* 66, 156–61.

TURNER, T. H. D. (1977) Landscape evaluation, *Town and Country Planning* 45, 282–93.

WEDDLE, A. E. (1969) Techniques in landscape planning, *Journal of the Royal Town Planning Institute* 55, 387–9.

WILCOCK, D. N., BURCH, B. P. and CANTOR, L. M. (1976) Changing attitudes to water resource development, *Geography* 61(3), 127–36.

ZIMMERMAN, E. W. (1933) *World Resources and Industries*. New York: Harper and Brothers.

ZUBE, E. H., BRUSH, R. O., and FABOS, J. G. (1975) *Landscape Assessment: value perceptions and resources*. Stroudsburg P.A.: Dowden, Hutchinson and Ross.

18   Conservation

The term conservation is open to several interpretations. It is clearly related to the notion of resource management, but can encompass (a) the materialistic cost-minimization motives of those concerned with the efficient use of scarce resources; (b) the cultural or architectural values attached to a particular built environment (Woodruffe 1976; Gray 1979); and (c) the aesthetic, scientific or recreational attributes of the countryside. Westmacott and Worthington (1974, p. 91) define conservation as 'the optimum use of a resource to meet the various demands made upon it but, at the same time safeguarding and maintaining the quality of the resources in the long term'. More specifically Green (1981, p. 1) defines countryside conservation as 'the protection and management of the environment for the essentially amenity objectives of maintaining wildlife, landscape and access to them for their non-consumptive use and appreciation for ethical, cultural, aesthetic and recreational purposes'. Both definitions explicitly acknowledge the conflicts which exist in the contemporary countryside. Sharply defined conflicts have arisen between conservationists and developers intent on copper mining in Snowdonia, oil platform construction (e.g. at Drumbuie), reservoir creation (e.g. Cow Green in upper Teesdale, or Swincombe on Dartmoor), and road improvement (e.g. the A66 through the Lake District), in addition to those generated by the centrifugal pressures exerted by urban areas. Equally important, however, are the conflicts which occur between traditional rural land uses, such as farming, and forestry, hunting, water gathering, mineral extraction, military training, and, more recently, recreation and amenity use.

Green (1977, p. 68) has summarized these conflicts in a land use compatibility matrix (Figure 18.1). Although reciprocal impacts are disguised (the effects of agriculture on wildlife, for example, are different from those of wildlife on agriculture) the structure does offer an indication of the levels of compatibility of different rural activities. Out of 625 possible conflicts between the 26 activities only 53 major conflicts (8.5 percent) and 55 minor ones (8.8 percent) are identified, suggesting that 'over 80.0 percent of the different land uses seem to be compatible with one another'. Significantly, however, arable cultivation and ley grazing (sown grass) – the most productive agricultural activities and therefore those most likely to continue as dominant rural land uses – are by far the least compatible with other land uses. As Figure 18.1 indicates, arable land conflicts in some way with 84.0 percent of other land uses. A more detailed statement of the kinds of conflict that can occur between different land uses is provided in Figure 18.2.

The growth of a conservationist movement

The development of the conservation ethic has been well documented (O'Riordan 1971; Warren and Goldsmith 1974; Kain 1981; Green 1981). As a concept in land use management, conservation dates from the end of the nineteenth century, with the

Figure 18.1 A compatibility matrix of competing rural activities.

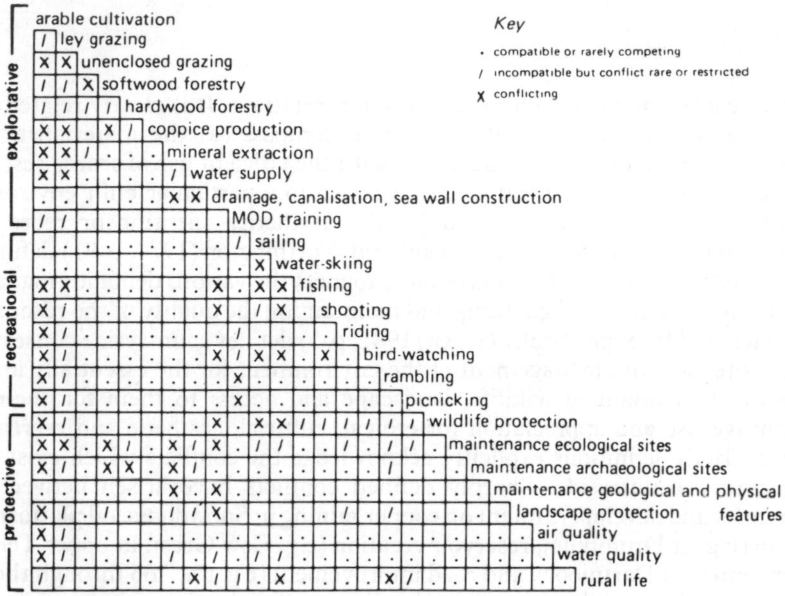

```
                arable cultivation                        Key
              / ley grazing                               · compatible or rarely competing
            x x unenclosed grazing                        / incompatible but conflict rare or restricted
          / / x softwood forestry                         x conflicting
        / / / / hardwood forestry
        x x . x / coppice production
        x x / . . . mineral extraction
        x x . . . . / water supply
        . . . . . . x x drainage, canalisation, sea wall construction
        / / . . . . . . . MOD training
        . . . . . . . . / sailing
        . . . . . . . . . x water-skiing
        x x . . . . . x . x x fishing
        x / . . . . . x . / x . shooting
        x / . . . . . / . . . . riding
        x / . . . . . x / x x . x . bird-watching
        x / . . . . . . x . . . . . rambling
        x / . . . . . . x . . . . . . picnicking
        x / . . . . . x . x x / / / / / / wildlife protection
        x x . x / . x / x . / / . / / / . maintenance ecological sites
        x / . x x . x / . . . . . / . . . maintenance archaeological sites
        . . . . . x . x . . . . . / . . . . maintenance geological and physical
        x / . / . / / x . . . . / . / . . . . landscape protection   features
        x / . . . . . . . . . . . . . . . . . air quality
        x / . . . / . / . / / . . . . . . . . . . water quality
        / / . . . . x / / . x . . . x / . . . . / . . rural life
```

Source: Green (1977)

National Parks movement in the USA and the establishment of voluntary groups (such as the Sierra Club) concerned with the protection of rare species and their habitats.

In Britain the period up to the First World War also witnessed the rise and growth of voluntary conservation organizations concerned with protecting wildlife and landscape (e.g. Royal Society for the Protection of Birds 1889; The National Trust 1895) and with gaining access to the countryside (e.g. The Commons, Open Spaces and Footpaths Preservation Society 1865). Between the wars, in the face of significant urban expansion, these organizations and the Councils for the Preservation of Rural England, Scotland and Wales (1926, 1927, 1928) were active in lobbying the government to develop a State organization to protect the countryside and establish national parks (Sandbach 1978; Sheail 1981). These efforts led to the setting up of two government committees to explore the case for a national park system. The reports of the Hobhouse and Huxley committees and their Scottish equivalents strongly influenced the nature of the National Parks and Access to the Countryside Act 1949. This established a National Parks Commission which was given powers to prepare a national park programme with the twin objectives of preservation and enhancement of natural beauty, and promotion of enjoyment by the public. In Scotland the idea of national parks foundered largely on the resistance of the landed

Figure 18.2 Diagramatic representation of levels of incompatibility between land use and resources.

Legend:
- ☐ No apparent conflict
- ▦ Conflicts which could be substantially overcome
- ▨ Apparently insuperable conflicts

	AGRICULTURE	FORESTRY	RECREATION/ TOURISM	NATURE CONSERVATION	MILITARY TRAINING	TOWNS	COALMINING/ INDUSTRY	ROADS	WATER SUPPLY
LANDSCAPE	Prairie farming. Loss of trees/hedges. Unsympathetic buildings. Loss of forest identity.	Alien conifers. Rigid plantation boundaries. Felling problems.	Litter. Impact of cars.			Air pollution. Unattractive modern development—urban fringe problems.	Pollution subsidence. Absolute visual conflict.	Unsympathetic design and scale of engineering improvements.	
AGRICULTURE		Forests harbour agricultural pests.	Trespass. Fire damage to crops and animals. Removal of rights of way. Unattractive modern farming.	Loss of natural habitat i.e., hedges, tree clumps, Pesticides, Stubble burning.	Major conflict i.e. damage to crops and animals.	Fire. Trespass. Air pollution. Damage to crops and animals.	Pollution subsidence.	Access problems on minor roads.	Lowering of water table.
FORESTRY			Fire damage to young trees. Conifer plantations lesser attraction.	Coniferous plantations less attractive for Flora & Fauna. Conservation versus cropping.	Fire damage to trees. Plantations too dense for fieldcraft.	Air pollution.	Pollution Poor environment.	Access problems on minor roads.	Pollution.
RECREATION/ TOURISM				Erosion by feet & cars. Damage to plants. Reduction of natural habitats.	Major conflict between vision and guns and tanks.	Air Pollution Unattractive modern development.	Pollution subsidence.	Large lorries & heavy traffic versus people. Tourist traffic on minor roads.	Lowering of water table.
NATURE CONSERVATION					Erosion. Some damage to flora by tanks, etc. Noise frightens wildlife. Preserves land from other incursions.	Pollution. Urban extensions reducing natural habitat.	Pollution subsidence.	Noise danger to wildlife. Reduction of habitat.	Lowering of water table.
MILITARY TRAINING							Terrain and cover interfered with.	Large Military vehicles and dangerous crossing.	
TOWNS							Pollution. Subsidence poor Environment.	Environmental problems—people versus traffic.	Pollution of rivers and aquifer.
COALMINING/ INDUSTRY								Subsidence.	Possible pollution.

Source: Davidson and Wibberley (1977)

interests to the radical proposals of the Ramsey report, the counterpart of Hobhouse, which recommended that land required for national park purposes, including the open moorlands, should be designated for free public access as a right and should be acquired outright, if possible by agreement but if necessary compulsorily (MacEwan and MacEwan 1982). The actual management of the park areas in England and Wales was the responsibility of local government. Apart from designating National Parks and Areas of Outstanding Natural Beauty (subject to ministerial confirmation) the National Parks Commission's role was entirely advisory and supervisory. Thus the original concept of an executive land-holding authority similar to the US National Park Service was seriously diluted – largely due to opposition to the new body from private landowners, as well as from existing government agencies like the Forestry Commission and Ministry of Agriculture, Fisheries and Food (MAFF), and the local planning authorities newly created under the terms of the Town and Country Planning Act 1947. The national park system that emerged 'was national in name only. It was not nationally administered, it had no nationally enforceable policy, and it was not nationally owned' (Ratcliffe 1981, p. 311). Between 1951 and 1957 ten national parks were created; since 1957, although three further parks have been put forward for designation – the South Downs, the Norfolk Broads, and the Cambrian Mountains – all have been rejected by the government.

In contrast to the limited powers given to the National Parks Commission, the Nature Conservancy, established separately in 1949 with responsibility for wildlife protection, was an autonomous research, advisory and land-holding council. Thus, a far more powerful State organization was created for the promotion of national nature reserves from which the public are largely excluded than had been provided for the promotion of national parks. As Green (1981, p. 46) observes, this government action 'consolidated a split in the conservation movement in Britain, which now had two distinct objectives. One was the protection and provision of access to natural landscapes for their scenic beauty and use for informal recreation, and the other was the protection of wildlife for research and education.'

Despite these early developments, only since the 1960s can concern for the environment be described as a 'popular movement'. But the period since then has witnessed 'an exponential growth in environmental awareness' (Newby 1980, p. 21) and the conservation movement has developed into a considerable lobby in land management. A central element in the upsurge of 'environmentalism' has been a disillusionment with agriculture as a force for rural conservation. As Strutt (1978) acknowledged, concern about the adverse effects of many current farming practices upon both landscape and nature conservation is coupled with a widespread feeling that agriculture can no longer be accounted the prime architect of conservation nor farmers accepted as the natural custodians of the countryside. Some conservationists have argued that the situation requires a move away from a negative protective approach towards a positive attacking position which advocates a fundamental rethinking of national priorities in land use planning and management (Mabey 1980; Shoard 1980; Green 1981). Table 18.1 summarizes some rural activities which public authorities may wish to influence in the national interest. Clearly though, however desirable in principle, the success of any intervention is dependent upon the organizations and powers available.

Table 18.1 *Prospective activities which public authorities may wish to influence*

AGRICULTURE

A. Activities related to changes in agricultural infrastructure

(i.e. the reclamation of land for increased farm production, the restructuring and redesigning of the farm holding, and the carrying out of capital works)

1. Ploughing of grass and heather moor, rough pasture, heath and downland for cropping or pasture.
2. Surface renovation: 'topping', burning, scrub clearance and other means of converting and agriculturally improving grass and heather moorland/rough pasture/heath and downland other than by ploughing, e.g. by direct drilling. (See also B.1 below.)
3. Reclamation of wetlands, mires, bogs and ponds by new or improved drainage schemes.
4. Grubbing out of hedge banks, hedges and hedgerow trees.
5. Demolition or conversion of obsolete farm buildings.
6. Demolition or removal of other obsolete structures, e.g. walls, gates.
7. Erection of new farm buildings.
8. Erection of new fencing and other structures, e.g. yards, pens, silage clamps.
9. Creation or improvement of access roads and tracks for agricultural purposes.
10. Tipping, excavation; earth moving and mineral workings related to agricultural purposes.

B. Activities related to changes in agricultural management practices.

(i.e. adoption of new or different agricultural systems and practices, and the modification or abandonment of certain maintenance work)

1. Intensified grazing management and an increase in stocking rates.
2. Changes in nature of farm enterprise, e.g. sheep to arable, beef to milking.
3. Changes in fodder systems and practices, e.g. switch from hay to silage, and adoption of a zero graze system.
4. Neglect or modification of traditional maintenance practices affecting:
   i.   stone walls, e.g. stop-gap fencing
   ii. earth banks, e.g. failure to bank up
   iii. hedges, e.g. mechanical trimming
   iv. ditches, ponds, drains and other water-courses, e.g. tree felling to facilitate mechanical clearance, silting or infilling of ponds
   v.   woodland, copses, spinneys and shelter-belts, e.g. failure to protect, manage or replenish
   vi. parkland and individual trees.

FORESTRY

C. Forestry and land use change

(i.e. likely to have major impact on landscape character)

1. Afforestation of bare land.
2. Clear felling and nonreplacement of existing woodland.

D. Other situations involving forestry

1. Clear felling or selective felling of mature woodland and replanting with:
   i.   hardwood/indigenous species
   ii. soft wood/commercial species
2. Neglect of, or inadequate management of small woodland, tree belts, and individual trees with resulting failure to ensure a healthy continuation of tree cover and/or supply of timber. (See B.4.v. and vi. in farmland situations), e.g. lack of protective fencing, weeding or thinning.
3. Erection of buildings, construction of access roads and other operations on land in accordance with forestry practices.

RECREATION

E. Recreational development

(i.e. provision of facilities by landowners or others in the interests of recreation)

1. Provision of recreational accommodation facilities of specified types under specified conditions, e.g. tied to farm business.
2. Provision of other facilities for visitors, e.g.
   i.   car parks and lay-bys
   ii. picnic sites
   iii. permissive paths across agricultural land
   iv. farm trails
   v.   interpretation facilities
   vi. fishing piers

F. Other recreational activities and situations

1. Continuation, by sufferance of landowner, of *de facto* or specifically authorised activities on all types of agricultural or forestry land on a regular, seasonal or occasional basis, e.g. rallying, picnicking, walking, canoeing, car parking, camping etc.
2. Discontinuation of informal *de facto* activities and certain forms of permitted development, e.g. temporary caravan/camping and car parking (see also G.2 below).
3. Creation of permissive paths and access on all types of agricultural and forestry land.
4. Provision of wardening and other services and application of byelaws where appropriate in the interests of visitor management.

CONSERVATION AND ENHANCEMENT OF THE COUNTRYSIDE

G. Landscape enhancement

1. Removal, repair or camouflage of derelict or unsightly buildings, structures and other development or dereliction, e.g. old prefabs, farm machinery, rubbish tips.
2. Discontinuation of activity considered injurious to the visual or other amenities of the countryside, e.g. caravan sites, scrap yards.
3. Provision of litter collection service.
4. Creation of new, or extension and conservation of existing natural or other attractive features including changes in management where appropriate: e.g.
   i.   replanting or reinforcement planting of trees and woodlands of all sizes and species
   ii. hedges and sympathetic fencing
   iii. ponds

H. Historical conservation

1. Conservation of historic landscapes and their essential components, e.g. boundary hedges and dykes, lynchetts.
2. Protection and conservation of historical monuments and structures, e.g. mounds and earthworks.
3. Conservation of other structures and vernacular buildings of historic or aesthetic merit, e.g. buildings and developments associated with rural industries – mills, mine-buildings, leats.
4. Conservation of certain designed landscapes, e.g. historic gardens, parkland.

I. Nature conservation

1. Retention and management of noteworthy wildlife habitats.
2. Retention of geological and geomorphological sites of scientific importance.

Source: Feist (1978)

Organizations and powers

Local authority development controls   The 1947 Town and Country Planning Act, although amended and extended particularly in 1968 and consolidated in 1971, remains the basis of the British planning system. In marked contrast to the USA where absolute ownership of land exists this system reflects the long tradition in English land law that possession of freehold does not confer absolute ownership. Ever since the 1947 Act was passed the right to develop land has been vested in the State, and anyone who wishes to make the changes in land use defined as development, even on land over which they possess the freehold, must first apply to their local planning authority for permission to proceed. The definition of development is wide ranging embracing 'the carrying out of building, engineering or mining operations in, on, over, or under land or the making of any material change in the use of any building or other land'. Some land uses, however, are automatically excluded from the need to obtain planning permission by a device known as the General Development Order. These include minor developments within the curtilage of a dwelling house, as well as those carried out by local authorities and statutory undertakings. Most significantly, it also excludes the whole area of forestry and farming because these were not regarded as development by those responsible for framing the 1947 Act. At that time agriculture was seen as in need of protection rather than as a force for radical change in the countryside. Those classes of rural land use exempted from development control by the GDO may be brought under planning control by the use of Article IV Direction Orders. These, however, require the approval of the Secretary of State and are normally only used in special circumstances. In effect, despite minor constraints (e.g. Tree Preservation Orders) agriculture and forestry lie outside the statutory planning system.

Nature Conservancy Council   The Nature Conservancy (since 1973 the NCC) has powers to enter into agreements with landowners for establishing nature reserves, to compulsorily purchase land, to establish or manage reserves, and to make byelaws for the protection of nature reserves (Blackmore 1974; Williams 1982). It also has the duty of informing local authorities of Sites of Special Scientific Interest (SSSI). The aim of these areas is to preserve a cross-section of the most interesting ecological communities or geological sections and to protect areas with particularly rich habitats or rare species of plants and animals. Although the local authority are required to consult the NCC if any planning permission for development affecting these sites is sought, agriculture and forestry operations, which lie outside development control, are not covered. A survey in 1977 of the outcome of threats to SSSI on the Isle of Wight, for example, showed that 90.0 percent of proposed agricultural improvements actually took place (Tubbs 1977). More generally Moore (1981) found that in 1980 between 8.0 and 15.0 percent of the SSSI received significant known damage or loss. The most important causes of damage related to agricultural activities, but a substantial number of sites were damaged by forestry, recreation and by other industrial activities over which the planning authorities should have had some control.

The NCC must rely on persuasion to conserve any site threatened by agricultural change. Section 15 of the Countryside Act 1968 enables it to make agreements with landowners under which the owners refrain from carrying out certain operations on the SSSI, usually in return for compensation. The agreements are not binding on the land, only on the owner with whom they are made. Thus, to protect a site absolutely the NCC has to purchase the land but, as the 1979 acquisition of 6,000 acres of coastal marshland in the Ribble estuary demonstrated (Jones 1979), this option can be very costly and with a limited budget can be resorted to only in exceptional cases.

Countryside Commission   The inadequacies of the existing machinery to safeguard the natural beauty of the national parks and the growth in and changing character of outdoor recreation (Dower 1965) were major stimuli for legislation to modify the 1949 National Parks and Access to the Countryside Act. The Countryside Act 1968, which replaced the National Parks Commission with the Countryside Commission (Cripps 1980), extended informal recreation policies to the countryside as a whole instead of concentrating them on national parks and Areas of Outstanding Natural Beauty. The Commission was able to offer 50.0 percent grants to both the private and public sector for Country Parks and other recreational facilities which hitherto had been grant-aided only in national parks. It was also given new powers to undertake or grant-aid experimental projects such as the Upland Management Experiment (UMEX) which aimed to reduce conflict between agriculturalists and recreationists by offering farmers financial encouragement to become involved in landscape maintenance (tree planting; repair of stiles, walls, gates, paths, fences) and provision of simple facilities for visitors (car parks, picnic sites). The project has been extended from the first trial areas in Snowdonia and the Lake District to all national parks as well as to lowland areas such as the Bollin valley in Manchester's urban fringe, Havering in London's green belt, and around St Helens on Merseyside (Bucknall 1977).

An important provision of the 1968 Countryside Act was the requirement that public bodies consider the effects of their intended actions on the natural beauty and amenity of the countryside. This 'amenity clause' marked a change in official attitudes towards conservation by shifting the onus of proof from the conservationist to the developer. This line of thought has been extended significantly in the USA by the National Environmental Policy Act 1969 with its requirement that all government-sponsored developments be first assessed for their environmental impact (Clark et al. 1978; Garner 1979; Clark et al. 1980).

The passing of the 1968 Countryside Act did not mean an end to the criticisms and difficulties voiced by conservationists. In the late 1960s and early 1970s national park authorities were finding it difficult to resist extensive afforestation and the reclamation of moorland. Against this background, in 1971, the government appointed a National Park Policies Review Committee (Sandford Committee, NPPRC). One conclusion of the review was that where the two purposes were seen to be irreconcilable the preservation and enhancement of natural beauty should have priority over the promotion of public enjoyment. An important recommendation was that powers should be provided to enable park authorities to make management agreements with owners or occupiers in order to secure park objectives. The NPPRC (1974, p. 55) was also critical of the existing management arrangements for national parks, concluding that 'the planning and management of the parks has in general followed rather than anticipated or even kept abreast of changing circumstances'. As a result fundamental changes in the administrative structure of national parks were embodied in the 1972 Local Government Act which was implemented in 1974. Under the new arrangements the Peak District and Lake District parks were to be the responsibility of special or joint planning boards, and it became the duty of local authorities in whose areas the parks lay to establish a single committee for each of the remaining parks. In an attempt to ensure adequate representation of people who live and work within the park, two-thirds of the members of these boards and committees were to be appointed by the county councils and one-third, after consultation with the Countryside Commission, by the Secretary of State. Each national park authority must produce a management plan to be reviewed every five years in consultation with the Countryside Commission and with district planning authorities within the park boundary (Dennier 1980). These management plans are intended to complement the land use planning undertaken by structure (development) plans. The potential conflicts to be considered in framing a cohesive management plan include (a) the mineral potential of national parks, (b) the extent of military land within the parks, (c) the demands of water collection, (d) attempts by hill farmers to improve pasture or undertake private afforestation, (e) traffic problems, and (f) visitor pressure on the landscape resource.

Nationally, however, one of the most striking weaknesses of the UK national park system is that it concentrates on the uplands and affords no protection to farmed lowland countryside. As Shoard (1980, p. 141) observes, 'our national parks enshrine only three types of countryside: moors, mountains and, to a lesser extent, dramatic coastal scenery. There is certainly no chalk downland, fen country or lowland heath in any of our national parks nor are there any sizeable stretches of coastal marshland.' The reasons for this spatially biased selection centre on (a) the preferences for 'wild country' of Dower and others instrumental in framing the early legislation, (b) the influence of North American examples, and (c) the postwar pressure for food production on the lowlands. While Areas of Outstanding Natural Beauty have embraced a much larger proportion of lowland countryside, these areas do not have the special planning and administrative arrangements provided for national parks. To correct this imbalance Shoard (1980) has advocated the creation of six new national parks in lowland England (Figure 18.3).

Conservation trusts   The National Trust, founded in 1895, was formally established by the National Trust Act 1907 with the purpose of permanently preserving for the benefit of the nation land and buildings of beauty and historic interest (Fedden 1974). The Trust is the oldest and largest conservation trust in existence and, apart from the Forestry Commission, is Britain's largest private landowner. It acquires land and properties in three ways: (1) by purchase, (2) by donation, and (3) by a system of leasehold whereby the landholder remains in residence but the land is run by the Trust. Virtually all of the National Trust land is inalienable, meaning that it cannot be compulsorily acquired by government departments, local authorities or any other agency without Parliamentary approval. The National Trust is a major landowner in all of the national parks and in Tunbridge's (1981, p. 112) view 'it is

Figure 18.3 Main protected areas in England and Wales and proposed national parks.

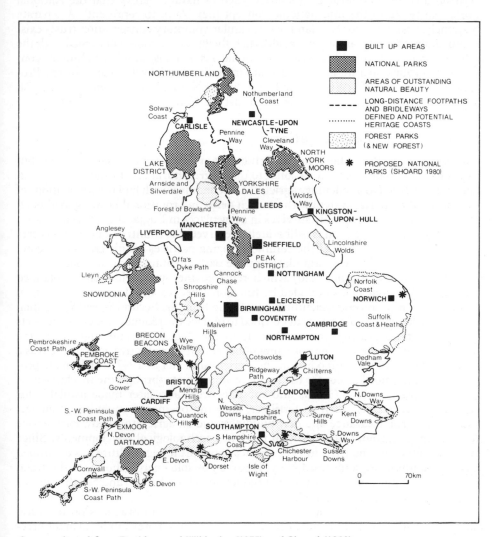

Source: adapted from Davidson and Wibberley (1977) and Shoard (1980)

primarily through the existence of Trust lands, providing guaranteed conservation, controlled access and strategic facilities (such as nature walks), that the National Parks can relate to the international concept they claim to represent'. A separate National Trust exists for Scotland, while similar voluntary conservation trusts exist in Australia, the USA and Canada, although the latter are more concerned with the built environment. In addition to the National Trust a host of other voluntary conservation groups operate in rural Britain, including the Royal Society for the Protection of Birds, the Society for the Promotion of Nature Conservation, the British Trust for Ornithology, and the British Trust for Conservation Volunteers.

Agriculture and conservation

The present agricultural landscape of Britain has evolved over thousands of years but can conveniently be seen as a response to three agricultural revolutions. The first in neolithic times led to a sedentary agricultural economy which laid the foundations of the medieval manorial system with its open fields and rotational farming. Although the strip cropping system only survives in a few places in England, such as at Laxton in Nottinghamshire where it is deliberately preserved, the country's one million acres of common land are relics of the common grazing pastures of this era. The second agricultural revolution was stimulated by the parliamentary enclosure acts (passed mainly between 1750 and 1820) which replaced the open fields with a planned landscape of regular fields bounded by functional hedges and ditches. The roots of the third and most recent agricultural revolution lie in the Second World War which stimulated demand for home produced food to replace the reduction of cheap imports (e.g. wheat from North America, beef from the Argentine, and sugar from the Caribbean). After the war the government belief that a productive agriculture was a strategic necessity was embodied in the Agricultural Act of 1947 which made provision for guaranteed prices for the major farm products through the mechanism of an annual price review. Grants and subsidies were also later made available for agricultural materials, such as fertilizer, and improvements, including drainage, ploughing, scrub clearance and new buildings; and an agricultural advisory service was set up to acquaint farmers with the latest technological developments. Since Britain's entry into the EEC in 1972 financial support for agriculture has continued via the Common Agricultural Policy. Despite possible energy shortages the trend towards intensification of agricultural production in both Britain and North America is likely to continue for the foreseeable future.

The impact of these changes in farm management and practices on the rural landscape of lowland Britain has been seen in many ways; for example (1) in the erection of large-scale industrialized farm buildings to store machinery, fertilizers and grain, and to house livestock, with a corresponding diminution in use of local building materials and styles; (2) in the enlargement of fields and the consequent removal of hedges which obstruct machines, require maintenance, impede drainage schemes, and harbour pests and weeds – on average 4,500 miles of hedgerow disappeared every year between 1945 and 1970 and in total around one-quarter of all hedges in the countryside have been destroyed since the Second World War (Pollard et al. 1974); (3) in the disappearance of trees without replacement, a loss which has been compounded by Dutch Elm disease; (4) in the use of inorganic fertilizers to improve crop yields, and fungicides, herbicides and pesticides to reduce weeds, which has had significant ecological consequences. Carson (1962) has documented the effects of an accumulation of organo-chloride insecticides (such as DDT, aldrin, isodrin, entrin and dieldrin) on the natural food chain. The ecological problems deriving from the application of artificial fertilizers are often equally complex and extensive. Run-off of nitrate fertilizers via drainage ditches leads to eutrophication of streams and rivers; nitrate can also seep into aquifers which are used as sources of domestic water supply (as occurred in parts of East Anglia during the 1976 drought). Controversy has also surrounded the long-term effects of artificial fertilizer on the soil structure, particularly in arable areas where the decline of outdoor grazing and mixed farming has led to a decline in the organic content of the soil. Heavy machinery and continuous cereal cultivation have produced signs of soil breakdown on clay lands (Agricultural Advisory Council 1970). In the USA an agricultural policy equally biased towards maximization of production has also had 'unintended, but dramatic, environmental consequences including: (1) increased cultivation of marginal lands; (2) increased grain production and reduced pasture and hay acreage; (3) further drainage of wetlands and field ditching and tiling; and (4) removal of fence rows, windbreaks, terraces, grass waterways, and strip-cropping to facilitate use of advanced technology for planting, fertilizing, irrigating, harvesting, and other more intensive farming techniques' (Wilkening and Klessig 1978, p. 22). Green (1981), with reference to the United Kingdom, introduces an explicitly spatial dimension to these impacts when he identifies three main kinds of environmental change effected by modern agriculture: (1) more intensive use has been made of the farmed land on the better soils, as in East Anglia; (2) some, mainly upland, pastoral land has been abandoned, e.g. in the North Pennines; (3) pastoral land has been brought into arable cultivation with the resultant loss of heath, down, and wetland as on Exmoor, the Dorset Downs or in the Somerset Levels.

'The conflict between farming and conservation is now arguably the major problem in conservation planning and management' (Green 1981, p. 52). Along with the creation of the prairie landscapes in the arable areas of eastern England, the grant-aided reclamation of wetlands, downs and moorlands has been one of the most visually striking impacts of agriculture on the landscape. Green (1981) reports that nearly 50.0 percent of the Wiltshire downland (26,000 ha) was lost to the plough between 1937 and 1971; nearly 25.0 percent of the Dorset downland (20,000 ha) between 1957 and 1972; almost 20.0 percent of North Yorkshire Moors National Park moorland (15,000 ha) between 1952 and 1975; as well as a similar proportion (5,000 ha) of moorland in the Exmoor National Park. The example of Exmoor serves to illustrate the nature of the argument.

Since the mid 1960s Exmoor has been a scene of conflict between those to whom the national park objectives were of primary importance and those to whom the moorland was an agricultural resource (MacEwan and MacEwan 1982). In 1968 the National Park Authority, concerned at the loss of moorland to agricultural use, designated 41,000 acres as a Critical Amenity Area and reached a 'gentleman's agreement' with the National Farmers Union and Country Landowners Association whereby farmers in the area would voluntarily give six months' notice to the park authorities of intention to plough. In return the park authorities agreed to refrain from invoking a Section 14 order under the 1968 Countryside Act which would make such notification compulsory. The park authorities hoped in this way to persuade farmers to enter into management agreements which would conserve the moorland. Between 1968 and 1977, however, a further 1,000–1,500 acres of moorland were ploughed, including 650 acres within the Critical Amenity Area (Newby 1980).

The Porchester Committee, which had been set up in 1977 to examine the problem, expressed serious reservations about informal management agreements, considering it unrealistic to expect a mutually acceptable agreement to be concluded as long as MAFF was offering reclamation grants, there were no back-up powers to deal with the farmer who was determined to proceed, and there were no statutory rules for determining compensation for compliant farmers. Porchester (1977) recommended that statutory force be given to the notification system and that national park authorities should have the power to make Moorland Conservation Orders binding in perpetuity, for which a lump sum would be paid in compensation. However, the Conservative government which came into office in 1979 declined to support these recommendations, favouring instead a voluntary system. In addition, farmers and landowners have consistently argued that for any voluntary system to work compensation must take the form of annual payments related to loss of profit, rather than a once and for all lump sum. Clearly such a scheme would be costly and could only be financed with government assistance which would itself be based on different governments' views of the role of conservation.

The recent history of Exmoor is typical of plateau uplands in Britain (Parry et al. 1981). Over the past 30 years 15,060 ha of moorland have been reclaimed for afforestation or agriculture in the Brecon Beacons, Dartmoor, North Yorkshire Moors and the northern part of Snowdonia National Parks. The fact that moorland reclamation is largely promoted by MAFF improvement grants and that a farmer can be compensated by one arm of government for not taking advantage of a grant or subsidy from another underlines the fragmented nature of rural planning in Britain. There would appear to be scope for rationalizing the subsidy to farmers in areas where agriculture cannot survive without support by directing it to be derived from and used for amenity rather than food production. In other European countries, for example, 'hill farming is more important in places for keeping ski slopes open than producing food and is subsidised by the tourist industry to do so' (Green 1981, p. 94).

While the specific circumstances of the Exmoor dispute are local, the implications are of national significance for conservation. The conflict between agriculture and conservation is not confined to the uplands. Pressure to bring lowland areas into cultivation has also been exerted on natural wetland ecosystems in the Fens, Broads, Somerset Levels, Romney Marsh, Pevensey and Ribble estuary (George 1976; Shoard 1980; Green 1981; O'Riordan 1982).

Conservation strategies

There are three main types of strategy open to conservation interests: (1) voluntary arrangements with landowners and operators, (2) statutory land use development controls, and (3) direct acquisition and management of land.

Management agreements   A management agreement has been defined as 'an agreement between two or more parties to voluntarily adhere to an agreed course of action or inaction usually in return for some form of compensation, consideration or practical assistance' (Feist 1978, p. 27). Management agreements can be used for a variety of purposes (e.g. landscape and wildlife conservation, archaeology, recreation); can be adapted to national and local criteria and budgetary circumstances; may be initiated by either party; can be used as a stop-gap measure pending legislation or the introduction of more radical options; and, it is argued, foster by the absence of compulsion a climate of cooperation between public agencies and landowners. Management agreements, however, have several limitations. The first is that they cannot remedy the causes of conflict (e.g. divergent policies of government departments) or the underlying structural problems of agriculture in marginal areas. Secondly, without adequate back-up powers management agreements cannot offer long-term security for the public interest or public investment. Thirdly, there are practical problems: (a) management agreements are difficult to enforce; (b) landowners have proved unwilling to sign away for all time their right to improve or develop land; (c) negotiation of agreements requires a great deal of professional time and manpower; (d) there is uncertainty over whether many existing agreements remain with the land if the title passes to another owner. The most formidable difficulty is the cost of compensation payments, which limits the ability of the conservation agencies to employ this option more generally. There is also the risk that landowners might demand and receive payments either towards the cost of operations which they would have carried out in any event or for refraining from operations which they had no real intention of carrying out. Under the provisions of the Wildlife and Countryside Act 1981 the Nature Conservancy Council, Countryside Commission, National Park Authorities and Local Authorities have an obligation to pay compensation whenever a farmer is refused grant aid by MAFF on the grounds of conservation in a national park or SSSI if objections to agricultural development are raised by the statutory conservation bodies. In such cases the National Park Authority or NCC will have to enter into a management agreement with the landowner to whom compensation is payable. The Act provided no extra funds for compensation payments. In the final analysis the successful implementation of management agreements rests upon the goodwill of landowners. A positive response is more likely in marginal areas than in prosperous lowland agricultural areas where the loss of income from forgoing land improvement will greatly outweigh any compensation available.

Dawson (1983) has suggested the use of the American concept of transferable development rights (TDRs) to remove the burden of compensation costs from conservation agencies. Under such a system it would be possible to grant farmers a form of agricultural TDR by way of compensation for not developing land if areas of similar land use were designated as being improvable only by farmers who have purchased an 'improvement right' from those in the protected area. This could be applied, for example, if a distinction was made between core and fringe moorland. Agricultural improvement in the core area might be forbidden, and in fringe areas permitted only after the purchase of improvement rights. Thus the valued environment would be protected without loss to the farmers on it or cost to public funds.

Extension of statutory controls   The extension of planning control to cover the major rural land uses of agriculture and forestry has been strongly advocated (Shoard 1980). A necessary complementary measure would be an increase in penalties for breaking the law or failing to comply with specific conditions, so that no economic or other benefits can be obtained by disregarding the law. As well as the benefit of direct control it is argued that the legislative threat would make landowners more amenable to 'reasonable-cost' management agreements. The disadvantages of controls are, first, that they are negative by nature and offer no inducement to positive actions. Secondly, their use might be counterproductive through their tendency to foster a climate of antagonism. Thirdly, the current planning system is concerned with land use rather than land management. Given the wide range of agricultural activities that are potentially harmful to amenity values, the definition and enforcement of controls would be difficult. Finally, requirements of minimum standards of landscaping, tree cover or building design would fall unevenly on different operators in the agricultural industry, and under normal planning practice, while grant aid would be available, compensation would not be paid.

Public land acquisition   Landownership is a powerful planning tool. The main arguments advanced in favour of greater public ownership are that, first, in a property-owning democracy public ownership of land is the only absolute guarantee that public interest will prevail and that valued landscapes will be protected. Secondly, public ownership gives full security for public investment in perpetuity; there being no question of subsequent owners negating previous public efforts to conserve land. Thirdly, it enables the authority to implement management policies towards landscape and visitor usage, and to experiment with various aspects of multiple land use. The major disadvantages of this strategy are that (a) the scope of acquisition for conservation purposes is so large that short of land nationalization this strategy could be prohibitively expensive meaning that the policy must be selective in practice, (b) a desired area of land may not come on the market when required, (c) public land acquisition on a significant scale would be a politically contentious issue, and (d) extension of ownership among single-minded public agencies pursuing a narrow range of policies (e.g. Forestry Commission or NCC) could worsen the situation and encourage a more rigid and exclusive system of rural land zoning. While widespread public acquisition of land for conservation purposes is unlikely in Britain, Davidson and Wibberley (1977) suggest that there are parts of the country, such as the uplands and the urban fringe, where the fragmentation of administration and the lack of interest of private land-holders in environmental trusteeship make a strong case for some extension of public ownership.

The scant use made of land acquisition powers and the limited effectiveness of development controls in the countryside mean that the management agreement is currently the main weapon in the conservationists' armoury. Two other methods of promoting rural conservation have been proposed.

Modification of the agricultural support system   The availability of grants for certain agricultural operations has been a major stimulus for change in the farmed landscape. In considering applications for grant aid the MAFF has been primarily concerned with the technical and economic feasibility of farm improvement schemes rather than the aesthetic and ecological effects likely to stem from their implementation. Despite the fact that it is MAFF's duty to have due regard for the latter, it is rare for agricultural grants to be refused on the grounds of conservation. Feist (1978) suggests that the system of agricultural support via capital grants and subsidies could usefully be modified in two ways. First, landscape or other conditions could be attached to agricultural grants. Secondly, there could be a change in emphasis in agricultural support policies so that grants and subsidies are related to the landowner's contribution to amenity as well as agricultural production. Such a shift in emphasis would be in keeping with EEC practice, and with the 1975 Directive on Mountain and Hill Farming in Less Favoured Areas. The major advantage of such modifications is that they would help 'to remove problems at their source and resolve the current conflict, whereby MAFF actively encourages undesirable changes in the landscape while the Department of the Environment tries to prevent such changes, or at least mitigate their effects' (Feist 1978, p. 25). The main drawbacks of the system are, first, that farmers may be discouraged from applying for grants and hence increasing national food production, and secondly, if a farmer considers the landscape conditions too onerous and if his scheme is economically viable even without a grant, he may not notify his intentions and implement his scheme unaided.

Fiscal measures   The principle behind fiscal measures is that farmers and landowners would be offered tax concessions to improve and manage their properties in ways that would benefit the landscape and the conservation of wildlife habitats. The principal arguments in favour of tax incentives are, first, that they are more likely to appeal to those institutions, absentee landlords and agribusinesses whose motivation is primarily financial; secondly, they need not be tied to development or to applications for agricultural improvement grants and hence are capable of more flexible usage; and thirdly, they could be used as a positive inducement to raise amenity standards throughout the countryside. The major arguments in opposition are that there would be no compulsion to accept tax concessions, and a landowner could opt out of an arrangement if he thought any tax advantages were outweighed by financial or operational disadvantages. Secondly, unless the more radical concept of negative income tax were to be introduced, annual tax allowances would be of little attraction to marginal farmers who are making little taxable profit. Equally, if tax concessions were related to land value they would be of limited appeal to farmers in marginal situations, or where farmers were required to *refrain* from action. The farmers would be caught in a vicious circle whereby the tax allowance would be assessed on relatively cheap, unimproved land the value of which could only be enhanced by undertaking actions that would disqualify it for tax exemption (Feist 1978).

As Britain is a country with a limited land resource on which increasing demands are being made it is not surprising that 'a precept central to its countryside planning is that multi purpose use must be made of the land' (Green 1977, p. 67). Multiple land use can mean either (a) the common integrated use of the same tract of land for two or more purposes, or (b) parallel use where individual activities are segregated spatially within a tract administered as a single unit. The preparation of National Park Plans is a move towards the latter strategy, but outside these areas individual government agencies pursue their own objectives many of which place a low priority on conservation.

Careful planning is a prerequisite for successful multiple use of land. A fundamental question is how to assess the most effective combination of activities. Statham (1972) provides a detailed example of the application of capability analysis in the North Yorkshire Moors while Selman (1978) reviews four main approaches to reconciling interests and achieving a degree of multiple use. A realistic appreciation of rural land use conflict must acknowledge that the better quality land will almost inevitably be used for the production of food and fibre, and that amenity interests can only compete with a reasonable likelihood of success on agriculturally marginal land. Green (1981, p. 69), for example, argues that the best strategy for conservationists is to accept the changes in modern agriculture and work with them rather than against them. In his view 'the best agricultural land must be exploited as intensively as possible without any amenity constraints so that low-grade agricultural land can be set aside for amenity (i.e. recreation and conservation)'. More radical solutions suggested include a national land use plan (Tranter 1978) and a British land reform (MacEwan and MacEwan 1982). Others see a need for some form of national rural planning agency (Wibberley 1976) or at least greater coordination among the agencies of central government so that conflicts of policy are resolved at the centre and not passed down to local government where they are insoluble. More generally, the basic need is for a broader conceptualization of conservation as an integral part of rural resource development.

References

AGRICULTURAL ADVISORY COUNCIL (1970) *Modern Farming and the Soil.* London: HMSO.

BLACKMORE, M. (1974) The Nature Conservancy. *In* A. Warren and F. B. Goldsmith *Conservation in Practice.* London: Wiley, 423–36.

BUCKNALL, S. (1977) Experiments in landscape management, *The Planner* 63, 70–2.

CARSON, R. (1962) *Silent Spring.* London: Hamilton.

CLARK, B. D., BISSETT, R. and WALTHERN, P. (1980) *Environmental Impact Assessment: A bibliography with abstracts.* London: Mansell.

CLARK, B. D., CHAPMAN, K., BISSETT, R. and WALTHERN, P. (1978) *Environmental Impact Assessment in U.S.A.: A Critical Review* Research Report No. 26. London: HMSO.

CRIPPS, J. (1980) The Countryside Commission: its first decade. *In* A. Gilg *Countryside Planning Yearbook* Vol. 1. Norwich: Geo Books, 38–48.

DAVIDSON, J. and WIBBERLEY, G. (1977) *Planning and the Rural Environment.* Oxford: Pergamon.

DAWSON, A. (1983) *Selling the idea of T.D.R.s* Paper presented to the Planning Study Group of the Institute of British Geographers, Edinburgh.

DENNIER, A. (1980) National park plans. *In* A. Gilg *Countryside Planning Yearbook* Vol. 1. Norwich: Geo Books, 49–66.

DOWER, M. (1965) The fourth wave: the challenge of leisure, *Architects Journal* 141, 123–90.

FEDDEN, R. (1974) *The National Trust: Past and Present*. London: Fontana.

FEIST, M. J. (1978) *A Study of Management Agreements* ccp 114. Cheltenham: Countryside Commission.

GARNER, J. F. (1979) *Environmental Impact Statements in United States and in Britain*. Cambridge: University Department of Land Economy

GEORGE, M. (1976) Land use and nature conservation in Broadland, *Geography* 61(3), 137–42.

GRAY, J. (1979) Rural conservation problems, *Planning Outlook* 22, 65–70.

GREEN, B. (1977) Countryside planning: compromise or conflict, *The Planner* 63, 67–9.

GREEN, B. (1981) *Countryside Conservation*. London: Allen and Unwin.

JONES, P. (1979) Wetlands, *Town and Country Planning* 48(9), 296–8.

KAIN, R. (1981) *Planning for Conservation*. London: Mansell.

MABEY, R. (1980) *The Common Ground*. London: Hutchinson.

MacEWAN, A. and MacEWAN, M. (1982) *National Parks: Conservation or Cosmetics?* London: Allen and Unwin.

MOORE, N. W. (1981) *Loss and Damage to SSSI in 1980*. London: Nature Conservancy Council.

NATIONAL PARK POLICIES REVIEW COMMITTEE (1974) *Report (Sandford)*. London: HMSO.

NEWBY, H. (1980) *Green and Pleasant Land*. London: Pelican.

O'RIORDAN, T. (1971) *Perspectives On Resource Management*. London: Pion.

O'RIORDAN, T. (1982) Environmental issues, *Progress in Human Geography* 6(3), 409–24.

PARRY, M., BRUCE, A. and HARKNESS, C. (1981) The plight of British moorland, *New Scientist* 90(1255), 550–1.

POLLARD, E. P., HOOPER, M. D. and MOORE, N. W. (1974) *Hedges*. Glasgow: Collins.

PORCHESTER, LORD (1977) *A Study of Exmoor*. London: HMSO.

RATCLIFFE, J. (1981) *An Introduction to Town and Country Planning*. London: Hutchinson.

SANDBACH, F. R. (1978) The early campaign for a national park in the Lake District, *Transactions of the Institute of British Geographers* N.S. 3(4), 498–514.

SELMAN, P. (1978) Alternative approaches to the multiple use of the uplands, *Town Planning Review* 49, 163–74.

SHEAIL, J. (1981) *Rural Conservation in Inter-War Britain.* Oxford: The University Press.

SHOARD, M. (1980) *The Theft of the Countryside.* London: Temple Smith.

STATHAM, D. (1972) Natural resources in the uplands, *Journal of the Royal Town Planning Institute* 58, 468–77.

STRUTT, N. (1978) *Agriculture and the Countryside.* London: Advisory Council for Agriculture and Horticulture in England and Wales.

TRANTER, R. B. (1978) *The Future of Upland Britain.* Reading: Centre for Agricultural Strategy.

TUBBS, J. (1977) *The Concept of Sites of Special Scientific Interest: a review.* Southampton: The University.

TUNBRIDGE, J. E. (1981) Conservation trusts as geographic agents, *Transactions of the Institute of British Geographers* N.S.6, 103–25.

WARREN, A. and GOLDSMITH, F. B. (1974) *Conservation in Practice.* London: Wiley.

WESTMACOTT, R. and WORTHINGTON, T. (1974) *New Agricultural Landscapes* C.C.P. 76A. Cheltenham: Countryside Commission.

WIBBERLEY, G. (1976) Rural resource development in Britain and environmental concern, *Journal of Agricultural Economics* 27, 1–16.

WILKENING, E. A. and KLESSIG, L. (1978) The rural environment: quality and conflicts in land use. *In* T. R. Ford *Rural U.S.A.: Persistence and Change.* Ames: Iowa State University Press, 19–29.

WILLIAMS, H. (1982) *The role of the Nature Conservancy Council* Paper presented to the Rural Geography Study Group of the Institute of British Geographers, Southampton.

WOODRUFFE, B. J. (1976) *Rural Settlement Policies and Plans.* Oxford: The University Press.

19 Leisure and recreation

Leisure is time free from work and other obligatory activities. The related, though narrower, concept of recreation may be viewed as pleasurable activity engaged in during leisure time. Outdoor recreation is an aspect of leisure time usage which is of growing significance in the Developed World, as a consequence of rising standards of living, increased discretionary spending, shorter working hours, longer holidays and greater car ownership (Figure 19.1). Clearly, comparison of the changing amount of leisure time available to Man over time is conditioned by the base point selected. Compared with the situation in Rome around AD 350, for example, when the average citizen worked only about half a year due to public holidays, the present burden of work has increased substantially (Wilensky 1961). During the course of the last 150 years, however, the working week has been reduced from an estimated 70-hour 6-day week in the mid nineteenth century to around 40 hours or less spread over 4 or 5 days. The right to several weeks of paid annual leave has been established and, in some countries like Italy and Australia, is accompanied by a holiday pay supplement to enable workers to take better advantage of their vacations. The age of retirement too has fallen to the point where 60 is the accepted norm and even earlier retirement is commonplace. Dower (1965) has characterized the growth of the leisure phenomenon as a 'fourth wave' comparable with the advent of industrialization, the railway age, and urban sprawl. While energy shortages and inflation can have an effect on recreation activity patterns, the underlying long-term trend is one of containment of work time and increasing prosperity. Despite the difficulty of extrapolation based on past and

Figure 19.1 Estimated change in factors affecting recreation 1965–2000.

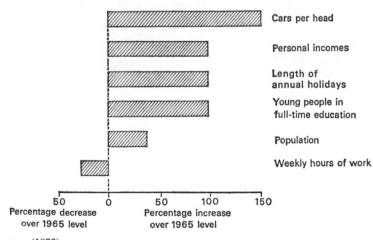

Cars per head

Personal incomes

Length of
annual holidays

Young people in
full-time education

Population

Weekly hours of work

| 50 | 0 | 50 | 100 | 150 |

Percentage decrease
over 1965 level

Percentage increase
over 1965 level

Source: Patmore (1972)

Table 19.1 *Percentages of respondents participating in recreational activities as reported by four national outdoor recreation surveys*

Activity	1960	1965	1972[a]	1977
Picnicking	53	57	47	72
Driving for pleasure	52	55	34	69
Sightseeing	42	49	37	62
Swimming (Pool)			(18)	(63)
(Other)	45	48	(34)	(46)
Walking for pleasure and jogging	33	48	34	68
Playing outdoor games or sports	30	38	22	56
(Golf)		(9)	(5)	(16)
(Tennis)		(16)	(5)	(33)
Fishing	29	30	24	53
Attending outdoor sports events	24	30	12	61
Other boating	22	24	15	34
Bicycling	9	16	10	47
Nature walks	14[b]	14	17	50
(Bird watching)		(5)	(4)	
(Wildlife and bird photography)		(2)	(2)	
Attending outdoor concerts, plays	9	11	7	41
Camping	8	10		
Developed			11	30
Backcountry			5	21
Horseback riding	6	8	5	15
Hiking or backpacking[c]	6	7	5	28
Water skiing	6	6	5	16
Canoeing	2	3	3	16
Sailing	2	3	3	11
Mountain climbing	1	1		
Visiting zoos, fairs, amusement parks			24	73
Off-road driving (motorcycles/other vehicles)			5/2	26
Other activities category	5		24	

Note: 1960, 1965 and 1972 participation rates are for the summer only.
a. 1972 Survey data are not directly comparable to previous surveys due to sampling differences.
b. Includes bird watching and photography.
c. Includes mountain climbing from 1972 and 1977 surveys.
Source: Finsterbusch (1980)

present trends it is highly improbable that the upward curve in available leisure time and outdoor recreation participation will be reversed in the foreseeable future (Roberts 1978).

In Britain the Cobham Committee (1974, p. xxi) predicted an increase of at least 25.0 percent in outdoor recreation by the end of the century. Growth estimates for particular recreational activities included camping (+64.0 percent), golf (+74.0 percent) and motor sports (+42.0 percent) with overall 'a 10–15 per cent compound increase in the rate of recreational activity in the countryside'. Equally striking increases have been noted in Europe, for swimming, angling, and other water sports; and in casual family activities such as picnicking and pleasure motoring. In the USA participation in outdoor recreation is expected to triple by the year 2000 (Gold 1980). The trends in individual activities over the period 1960–1977 are shown in Table 19.1. Picnicking is a perennial favourite as are driving for pleasure and sightseeing but more active outdoor pursuits such as swimming, pleasure walking, jogging and sports also have high participation levels. Table 19.2 presents the 10 most popular outdoor recreational activities, the 10 fastest growing activities, and the 10 with the

Table 19.2 *The 10 top outdoor recreational activities, ranked by three indicators of popularity and growth**

10 Most Popular[1]	10 Fastest Growth[2]	10 Highest Potential Growth[3]
(73) Visit zoos, aquariums, fairs, carnivals, amusement parks	(25) Cross-country ski	(6) Downhill ski
(72) Picnic	(17) Downhill ski	(6) Tennis
(69) Drive for pleasure	(13) Tennis	(5) Water ski
(68) Other walk or jog	(11) Sail	(4) Horseback ride
(63) Pool swim or sunbathe	(11) Snowmobile	
(62) Sightsee at historical site or natural wonders	(10) Water ski	(3) Camp in primitive area
(61) Attend sports events	(9) Canoe, kayak or river run	(3) Sail
(56) Other sports or games	(9) Golf	(3) Golf
(53) Fish	(5) Drive vehicles or motorcycles off-road	(3) Snowmobile
(50) Walk to observe nature, bird watch, or wildlife photography	(4) Horseback ride	(2) Canoe, kayak or river-run

* Percentages of respondents to 1977 General Population Survey
[1] Percentage of total population participating in an activity at least once during a 12-month period.
[2] Percentage of participants just starting activity for the first time during previous 12 months.
[3] Percentage nonparticipants that would like to begin participating during 'next year or two'.
Source: Finsterbusch (1980)

highest potential growth. Recreation in Australia reflects similar trends. Pigram (1983) suggests an annual rate of expansion in recent years of 12.0 percent in activities such as water-based and wilderness recreation, camping and picnicking.

Recreation demand assessment

Recreation demand is made up of several components. Effective demand comprises the people who actually participate in outdoor recreation activities. Deferred demand refers to those who could participate but do not, through lack of knowledge and/or lack of facilities. Potential demand consists of those who are unable to participate at present and who require a change in their social and economic circumstances to do so (Lavery 1975). The basic distinction between recreation demand and participation (i.e. effective demand) must be underlined. Clearly, it would be fallacious to equate the two since effective demand is a function of the opportunities available. As Knetsch (1972) points out, adoption of attendance figures as a measure of demand confuses revealed behaviour with people's recreation propensities and preferences. For a full appreciation of recreation demand consideration must be given to latent demand, that is, to the reasons for nonparticipation or underparticipation in particular activities and locations. A number of researchers have examined this issue (Stein and Sessoms 1977) as well as the related equity question of minority group access to recreation opportunities (Fitton 1976). Most attention, however, has been devoted to actual participation or effective demand and its relationship with the factors underlying the supply of recreation opportunities.

The growth of recreation demand has resulted in (a) competition among different land uses for available space, as well as (b) pressure on the existing recreation space, particularly in the most favoured locations. The relative value of recreation as a land use has been examined by means of techniques such as potential surface analysis and demand curve analysis; while the effects of recreation pressure on sites have been studied using the concept of land capability or carrying capacity.

Potential surface analysis

Various systems of classifying recreational resources have been employed ranging from the early work of Clawson et al. (1960) to that proposed by the Outdoor Recreation Resources Review Commission (1962) and the comprehensive classification scheme carried out as part of the Canada Land Inventory (1969). More recently, attempts to identify suitable environments for selected categories of outdoor recreation have been based on the technique of potential surface analysis, which may be seen as a refinement of the seive map technique (Countryside Commission 1974). This provides a comparative evaluation of the spatial distribution of recreation potential according to the capability of the resource base to meet certain predetermined objectives. The degree to which each subunit of the study area (e.g. a 1 km square) satisfies the specified objectives is quantified and weighted and the scores aggregated to produce a 'potential surface' of high and low capacity.

The procedure involves three stages:

(1)   Classification of the study area into grades reflecting the potential of the land for each activity. In the North Yorks Moors, for example, Statham (1972) employed five grades to assess land potential for agricultural use, forestry, conservation, and recreation. The example of the agricultural ratings is shown in Figure 19.2b.
(2)   Compilation of composite maps to examine the possible patterns of optimum uses under a range of weightings and to identify conflict and opportunity areas. The weighting attached to each land use indicates the assumed importance of each for different scenarios. Thus in the 'amenity' situation recreation and nature conservation are assigned equal weight and given one grade priority over agriculture and forestry (Figure 19.2c). In the 'economic' situation the position is reversed. In the 'competitive' situation all four land uses are given equal weight.
(3)   Detailed analysis of the main conflict areas. By comparing the derived potential surfaces with existing land uses areas of conflict and opportunity emerge (Figure 19.2d). Zetter (1974) provides another example of potential surface analysis, with reference to Sherwood Forest.

A refinement of the potential surface analysis technique has been designed to delineate areas of tourism and recreation potential in Scotland according to the presence and capacity of relevant resources and constraints on their use and development (Owen et al. 1974). The computer-based Tourism and Recreation Information Package (TRIP) system is flexible and has almost unlimited scope for experimentation so that weighting factors may be applied to individual resource attributes and new data on demand or supply factors incorporated as they become available.

Demand curve analysis

The economic evaluation of outdoor sites or regions was pioneered in the USA by Clawson (1959). The method seeks to derive a demand curve for a recreation site indicating how many visitors would be expected at various admission charges, that is it attempts to elicit consumer values for normally free (nonpriced) recreation resources. From such demand curves, overall measures of benefit to the recreation consumer may be derived, usually using the concept of consumer surplus (Norton 1970), that is the extent to which utility gained exceeds cost. Such values expressed in standardized monetary terms can then be used for comparison with those arising from competing rural land uses and so assist in the determination of priorities.

The Clawson method involves four steps:

(1)   The initial requirement is basic data on the geographical origin of visitors so that each visit can be allocated to a 'distance zone', usually defined by concentric circles drawn around the recreation site. A visit rate (number of visits were 100,000 population is calculated for each zone (Figure 19.3).
(2)   The relationship between visit rates and distance is converted into one between visit rates and cost, by assuming a certain cost per mile for travelling to the recreation site. Clearly, the choice of cost per mile has a crucial influence on the final result. Among the variety of measures employed are fuel cost, full motoring cost including depreciation, and perceived costs. The relationship, shown in Figure 19.3, is termed

Figure 19.2 Potential surface analysis of North Yorks Moors: (a) Existing uses; (b) Agricultural capability; (c) Optimum uses – amenity situation; (d) Potential conflict and opportunity areas.

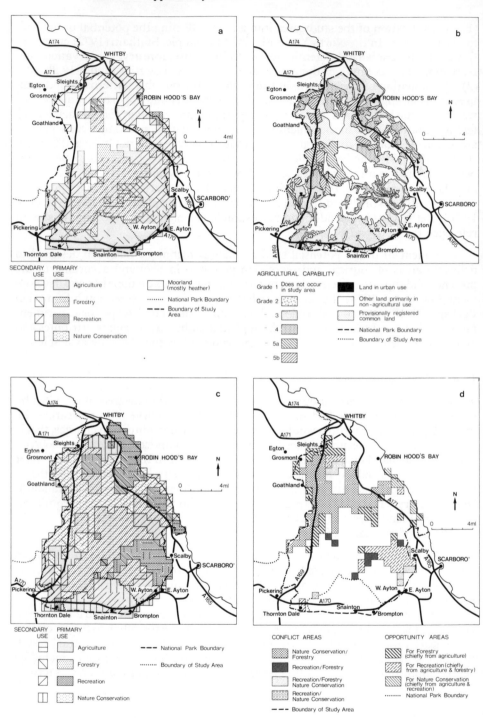

Source: adapted from Statham (1972)

'the demand curve for the whole recreation experience', or the initial demand curve.

(3)   From the initial demand curve, the demand curve for the recreation site per se (final demand curve) is derived. This requires consideration of the absolute level of population in each zone. The final demand curve exhibits a relationship between the number of visits to the recreation site and an assumed set of admission charges. For example, considering the raw data tabulated in Figure 19.3, one point (point A) on the final demand curve can be fixed immediately, because the number of visits made at the current admission price of zero is already known (i.e. the sum of visits from each zone = 135). Similarly for different admission charges the number of visits to the site can be calculated. Thus, if the admission charge is raised to 25 pence and, as Clawson assumed, the consumer responds to this increase in the same way as he reacts to transport costs (i.e. a reduced propensity to visit) then the total cost (travel + admission) of a visit from the closest zone A is 50 pence, from zone B 75 pence, from zone C £1.00, and from zone D £1.25. These points may be plotted to form the final demand curve for the site (Figure 19.3).

4.   On this final demand curve the economic value of the recreation site is represented by the consumer surplus (i.e. the total area between the demand curve and the prevailing price line). This sum gives an indication of the consumer value of a recreation site, even though no price or value was registered for the site within the market mechanism (Ferguson and Greig 1973; Smith 1971; Curry 1980). The demand curves calculated by Clawson and Knetsch (1966) for four national parks are shown in Figure 19.4.

Although Clawson's method has been used with modifications more regularly than any other demand curve formulation, it is not free from criticism. (Daiute 1966; Gum and Martin 1975). Flegg (1976) and Mercer (1979) have drawn attention to the limited assumptions of such models; for example:

(a)   That recreation site value is best measured in terms of numbers of visitors. Clearly, for some areas such as wilderness regions, value is more a function of nonuse or limited use.

(b)   That distance travelled is a reliable indicator of site value. A problem arises if recreationists make multiple destination journeys, including a mix of recreation and nonrecreation visits. Furthermore, in many cases the journey to the site is not perceived as a 'cost' but as an important part of the recreation experience.

(c)   That clearly defined 'visitors' are the only people who derive benefits from a given recreation site. Many people gain a kind of 'psychic income' from the knowledge that certain sites exist should they ever wish to visit them.

(d)   That the recreational value of an area is solely attributable to one form of land use alone. This ignores the potential of multiple land use schemes (Ross and Marts 1975; Peterson 1973; Priddle 1976).

The restricted viewpoint afforded by reliance on economic criteria alone has been highlighted by the general social indicators movement (Pacione 1982) which advocates the inclusion of relevant social variables in the assessment of consumer surplus. A number of researchers have tried to improve the specification of Clawson's initial demand curve by introducing the effects of other independent variables in addition to

Figure 19.3 The Clawson method of recreation demand curve analysis.

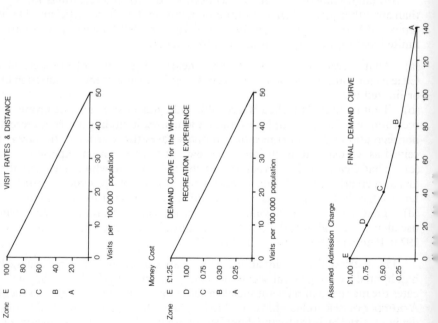

DATA FOR THE DERIVATION OF A FINAL DEMAND CURVE

DISTANCE ZONE	DISTANCE (MILES)	POPULATION	COST PER VISIT (£)	NUMBER OF VISITS	VISITS PER 100 000 POPULATION
ZONE A	20	200 000	0.25	80	40
ZONE B	40	50 000	0.50	15	30
ZONE C	60	100 000	0.75	20	20
ZONE D	80	200 000	1.00	20	10
ZONE E	100	200 000	1.25	0	0

ABSOLUTE NUMBER OF VISITS UNDER A VARIABLE ADMISSION CHARGE PRICE REGIME

PRICE	£0.00	£0.25	£0.50	£0.75	£1.00
ZONE A	80	60	40	20	0
ZONE B	15	10	5	0	0
ZONE C	20	10	0	0	0
ZONE D	20	0	0	0	0
ZONE E	0	0	0	0	0
	135	80	45	20	0
POINT ON FINAL DEMAND CURVE	A	B	C	D	E

Source: adapted from Curry (1980)

Figure 19.4 Estimated visits to four USA national parks under various entrance fee schedules.

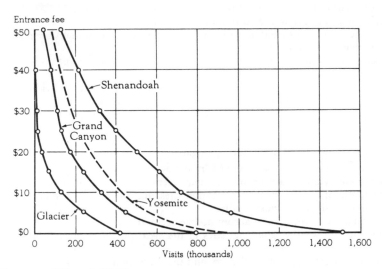

Source: Clawson and Knetsch (1966)

cost (Smith 1977). Several have attempted to include socio-economic factors such as age and family composition (Gillespie and Brewer 1968), sex (Gardner 1967), place of residence (Boyett and Tolley 1966), income (Brown et al. 1964), occupation (Johnston and Pankey 1968), education (Merewitz 1966), and race (Weisbrod 1967). Other variables that influence the choice and use of recreation sites includes tastes and preferences (Sinden 1974), site quality (Stevens 1966, 1967) and the presence of alternative locations (Knetsch 1963). There are, however, serious computational difficulties (e.g. problems arising from multicollinearity) in trying to incorporate a large number of variables into a single demand curve. Experience suggests the need to quantify these variables outwith the demand curve framework, with inclusion only of those exhibiting a high degree of significance for the site and activity under review. Clawson and Knetsch (1966), for example, provide a lengthy list of factors that affect demand for a particular recreation area (Table 19.3) but include only four (population; leisure time; travel mileage, time and costs; and per capita real incomes) in their own estimation of future total national demand for outdoor recreation.

Subsequent tests suggest that 'in general the sensitivity of the results of the Clawson method to the various assumptions which one has to make implies that the method should be used with care rather than not used at all' (Smith 1971, p. 101). There is also evidence to suggest that whereas in North America the travel cost approach is 'perhaps the best method for estimating recreational value of a resource' (Finsterbusch 1980, p. 254), it may be less appropriate 'in a geographically compact country like Britain, where intervening and competitive recreation opportunities abound' (Mansfield 1971, p. 69), or in urban fringe locations where travel costs form a low proportion of total costs (Colenutt 1969; McConnell 1977).

Table 19.3   *Factors affecting demand for a recreation site*

(1) Factors relating to the potential recreation users, as individuals:
    (a) their total number in the surrounding tributary area;
    (b) their geographic distribution within this tributary area – how many are relatively near, how many relatively far, etc.;
    (c) their socio-economic characteristics, such as age, sex, occupation, family size and composition, educational status, and race;
    (d) their average incomes, and the distribution of income among individuals;
    (e) their average leisure, and the time distribution of that leisure;
    (f) their specific education, their past experiences, and present knowledge relating to outdoor recreation;
    (g) their tastes for outdoor recreation.
(2) Factors relating to the recreation area itself:
    (a) its innate attractiveness, as judged by the average user;
    (b) the intensity and character of its management as a recreation area;
    (c) the availability of alternative recreation sites, and the degree to which they are substitutes for the area under study;
    (d) the capacity of the area to accommodate recreationists;
    (e) climatic and weather characteristics of the area, the latter during the period under study.
(3) Relationships between potential users and the recreation area:
    (a) the time required to travel from home to the area, and return;
    (b) the comfort or discomfort of the travel;
    (c) the monetary costs involved in a recreation visit to the area;
    (d) the extent to which demand has been stimulated by advertising.

Source: Clawson and Knetsch (1966)

Several studies have developed demand curve analyses to suggest that charging for countryside recreation may be not only a useful means of raising revenue but also a means of providing detailed information on consumer preferences, and a management tool capable of regulating demand (McCallum and Adams 1980). In particular it has been suggested that the introduction of appropriately designed differential charging structures may be used to direct demand from overvisited sites to environmentally less sensitive areas, and to reduce recreational pressures at peak periods. The pricing mechanism may therefore be one means of spreading recreational demands in both time and space and thus ensuring a better fit between demand and site capacity. In practice the effectiveness of charging will depend on the reaction of visitors to the level and structure of charges imposed. Despite the large volume of literature dealing with recreational demand there is still insufficient knowledge about the effects of alternative charging strategies on patterns of visitor use. The most important gap relates to the lack of knowledge on the elasticity of demand. Information on demand elasticities for a range of outdoor recreation facilities (Shucksmith 1979) is a prerequisite to forecast user numbers and revenue at given locations at different prices.

Complementing aggregate models of recreation demand, recent research has given detailed consideration to the individual recreationist's motivations and satisfactions (Baxter et al. 1977) and to questions such as the degree of substitutability among recreation activities and locales (Hogg 1977). Clearly, if the researcher can ascertain the nature of the specific resource requirements for a range of outdoor pursuits, together with the factors resulting in conflict between activities, then potentially the recreation planner is in a position to maximize user satisfaction and substitutability and minimize recreational conflicts.

Land carrying capacity

The concept of carrying capacity has generated considerable research yet investigators have experienced great difficulty in defining the term. According to Barkham (1973, p. 218) carrying capacity is 'a phrase delightful in its simplicity, complex in its meaning, and difficult to define, as in different situations and to different people it is understood in different ways'. Brotherton (1973) identifies four broad types of capacity:

(1)   Economic capacity relates to situations of multiple use of resources, and is concerned with identifying the intensities of different land uses at which the maximum economic benefit will be gained from the site.

(2)   Physical capacity refers to the maximum number a site can physically accommodate for a given activity, e.g. the number of car parking spaces available.

(3)   Ecological capacity refers to the maximum level of recreational use that a particular ecosystem can undergo before irreversible changes begin to take place. Problems include the trampling effect of hiking on paths or of skiing on mountain slopes (Bayfield 1971; Liddle 1975), and user impact on parks, campsites and picnic areas (Merriam and Smith 1974).

(4)   Perceptual capacity, like ecological capacity, varies depending on the locality and nature of the recreation experience. Wilderness, for example, will have a low perceptual carrying capacity. One of the first empirical studies on this theme was undertaken by Lucas (1964) in the Boundary Waters Canoe Area in Minnesota where he discovered clear differences among the views of resource managers and user-groups on questions of the importance of wilderness, area of wilderness, and essential wilderness qualities.

Carrying capacity is a multidimensional and dynamic concept. Lime and Stankey (1979, p. 106) define recreational carrying capacity as 'the character of use that can be supported over a specified time by an area developed at a certain level without causing excessive damage to either the physical environment or the experience for the visitor'. Recreational carrying capacity is affected by the kind of use, the time of year, and the duration and intensity of the activity and can be modified by management techniques, consequently 'it is impossible to assign to a site a simple figure for its capacity' (Goldsmith 1974, p. 227). In practice, therefore, recreation managers tend to aim for the more attainable objective of surveying certain heavily used sites in order to assess the degree of deterioration and to apply management techniques appropriate to the objectives of the site.

Outdoor recreation management

The primary aim of outdoor recreation management is to balance demand and capacity so that conflicts are minimized and the countryside is exploited to the full potential without a deterioration in its resources. A model of the recreation management process is shown in Figure 19.5. The first step is the establishment of broad management objectives based on the capabilities of the resource base, user preferences and institutional constraints (e.g. budgetary restrictions or overlapping jurisdictions with different views on recreation provision). The next stage, determination of carrying capacities consistent with the management objectives adopted, should be related to the structure of the area (e.g. physical configuration and distribution of facilities). The third step requires the selection of specific management procedures. Finally, following implementation of the selected procedures, evaluation of the system based on monitoring of its operation by managers and feedback from users may lead to modifications being made.

There are basically three types of management procedures available: (a) site management, (b) modification of visitor behaviour through direct regulation, and (c) modification of visitor behaviour by means of indirect measures. Table 19.4 indicates a range of specific strategies within each broad type. The optimum technique or combination of techniques depends on the particular recreational opportunity the area is meant to provide. Two rural areas in which recreation management is currently of particular importance are (a) national parks and (b) the urban fringe.

Figure 19.5 A model of the recreation management process.

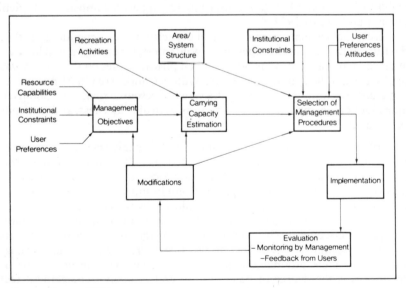

Source: Pigram (1983)

Table 19.4 *Some measures to control the character and intensity of recreational use to meet desired management objectives*

Type of control	Method	Specific control techniques
Site management (emphasis on site design, landscaping and engineering)	Harden site	Install durable surfaces (native, nonnative, synthetic) Irrigate Fertilize Revegetate Convert to more hardy species Thin ground cover and overstory
	Channel use	Erect barriers (rocks, logs, posts, fences, guardrails) Construct paths, roads, trails, walkways, bridges, etc. Landscape (vegetation patterns)
	Develop facilities	Provide access to underused and/or unused areas Provide sanitation facilities Provide overnight accommodations Provide concessionaire facilities Provide activity-oriented facilities (camping, picnicking, boating, docks, and other platforms, playground equipment, etc.) Provide interpretive facilities
Direct regulation of use (emphasis on regulation of behaviour, individual choice restricted, high degree of control)	Increase policy enforcement	Impose fines Increase surveillance of area
	Zone use	Zone incompatible uses spatially (hiker-only zones, prohibit motor use, etc.) Limit camping in some campsites to one night, or some other limit
	Restrict use intensity	Rotate use (open or close roads, access points, trails, campsites, etc.) Require reservations Assign campsites and/or travel routes to each camper group in backcountry Limit usage via access points Limit size of groups, number of horses, vehicles, etc. Limit camping to designated campsites only Limit length of stay in area (max/min)
	Restrict activities	Restrict building campfires Restrict fishing or hunting
Indirect regulation of use emphasis on influencing or modifying behaviour; individual retains freedom to choose; control less complete, more variation in use possible)	Alter physical facilities	Improve (or not) access roads, trails Improve (or not) campsites and other concentrated use areas Improve (or not) fish or wildlife populations (stock, allow to die out, etc.)
	Inform users	Advertise specific attributes of the area Identify the range of recreation opportunities in surrounding area Educate users to basic concepts of ecology Advertise underused areas and general patterns of use
	Set eligibility requirements	Charge constant entrance fee Charge differential fees by trail, zone, season, etc. Require proof of ecological knowledge and recreational activity skills

Source: Mercer (1979) *In* T. O'Riordan and R. C. D'Arge (1979) *Progress in Resource Management and Environmental Planning* Vol. 1. Reprinted by permission of John Wiley and Sons Ltd.

National park systems

The evolution of the modern national parks, which are now found in all continents and under all economic and political systems, began with the American park movement of the nineteenth century; the dominant themes in which were the preservation and protection of the resources of nature and the opening up of these resources for the recreational needs of the nation. This movement culminated in the reservation of the first extensive area of wild land primarily for public recreation in the United States, the Yosemite Grant, in 1864 (Brockman et al. 1973). This was followed by Yellowstone National Park in 1872 and the Niagara Falls Reservation in 1885.

The present parks system of the USA encompasses nearly 300 different areas of diverse sizes and types totalling some 13 million hectares; and in addition to national parks includes national monuments, national recreation areas, and national historic sites. In 1979 there were 37 national parks in USA with a total area of 6.5 million hectares nearly all of which is Federal land. As Figure 19.6 reveals, they are strongly concentrated in the west where the scenic and biotic resources are most valued and where competition from other land uses is less intense. Unlike the siting of lower-level recreation areas the distribution of national parks is not related to population concentration.

The development of the US national parks can be viewed in three phases:

(1)   The period prior to 1940 was a development phase in which efforts were made to popularize the parks, to boost attendance and justify the continued existence of the programme.

(2)   The post-1945 boom in outdoor recreation brought increased pressure to bear on existing park facilities and infrastructure. The main response of the park service was a 10-year (1956–66) programme entitled 'Mission 66' to open up more of the parks and enlarge visitor facilities. As Simmons (1974, p. 399) comments, 'this was a self-feeding spiral because more development led inevitably to increased numbers of visitors'.

(3)   During the 1960s concern over the environmental impact of visitor pressure led to a redirection of aims more in favour of restoration and preservation of the resource base. In order to achieve a balance between the interests of visitors and the maintenance of resource qualities, the National Park Service developed the use of master plans, usually based on a zoning system, and this approach has been widely adopted elsewhere (Yapp and Barrow 1979; Richez 1973; Hookway 1978). De-development is being undertaken so that, for example, private motor vehicles have been excluded from some park areas to be replaced by shuttle buses and mini trains; and speed restrictions, one-way traffic systems and limited parking facilities have been introduced. Visitor transportation systems now operate in 35 park areas in the United States. Similar transport experiments have taken place in England and Wales (Moyes 1977). Public recreational use of the Grand Canyon has been curtailed because of environmental damage and user conflicts, and access to Mount McKinley National Park in Alaska is restricted.

As in the USA, the principal objective of the park system in Canada is 'to protect for all time representative natural areas of Canadian significance in a system of

Figure 19.6 National parks in the USA.

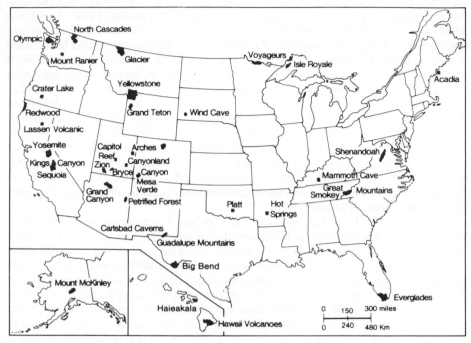

Source: Pigram (1983)

national parks and to encourage public understanding, appreciation and enjoyment of this natural heritage so as to leave it unimpaired for future generations' (Parks Canada 1979, p. 38). The first Canadian national park was the 67 km² Banff National Park established in 1887 and there are currently 29 national parks in the system which also includes more than 20 national historic parks and sites. Development trends echo those south of the 49th parallel with a prewar emphasis on visitor satisfaction being countered in the postwar era by priority for preservation and protection of park landscapes. In proposals for new national parks and reserves in the Yukon and North West Territories particular attention is given to maintaining a balance between the need to protect wilderness values and the rights of local native people to continue traditional extractive activities such as hunting, fishing and trapping in areas like Baffin Island (Gardner and Nelson 1980).

Prior human habitation is also a characteristic of national park areas in Britain where a long history of human settlement meant that there were no great reserves of unoccupied land by the time moves were made to establish national parks at the end of the Second World War. Since widespread acquisition of private land for park purposes would have been prohibitively expensive and politically unacceptable, areas designated as national parks remain almost entirely in private ownership and productive use.

The development of national park systems in the Netherlands, New Zealand, Australia and in developing countries is discussed by Pigram (1983) while the situation in Japan, Sweden and France is examined by Simmons (1974), Lundgren (1980) and Blacksell (1976) respectively. A review of individual national policies and practices reveals both the diversity of approaches and a recurrent theme in the need to achieve a balance between preservation and use of the national resource. This is well illustrated in Ironside's (1970) study of private residential and commercial facilities in North American national parks. More generally, McMichael (1970) has distinguished between park management problems which are externally generated and internal problems arising essentially from visitor usage. Examples of the former include pollution from urban-industrial wastes or from agricultural chemicals entering the park ecosystem; while the latter are a function of visitor numbers and the level and sophistication of facilities provided. Roads, parking areas, toilets, accommodation sites, food outlets, refuse and litter, and off-road vehicles are just some of the ramifications of outdoor recreation that can place pressure on ecological quality and park resources (Pigram 1983).

In Britain the 1968 Countryside Act marked a significant development in national recreation planning by proposing the creation of a new system of Country Parks which would be established and administered by local authorities with grant aid from central government. These country parks would provide outdoor recreational opportunities in a rural setting and would be located so that they could act as 'honey pots' by absorbing some of the recreational pressures that might otherwise fall on the national parks and other areas of vulnerable countryside. The 1968 Act also extended the principles of multiple use to State woodlands and to water catchments thus giving the Forestry Commission and Regional Water Authorities clearly defined recreational responsibilities (Patmore 1983). Between 1968 and 1977 approximately 125 country parks were designated and 155 new picnic sites provided; while many other public and private agencies opened land (e.g. safari parks) and buildings (e.g. stately homes) to the public (Davidson and Wibberley 1977).

According to Tanner (1983) in future the emphasis is likely to be increasingly on the provision of intensive-use areas, like the British Country Parks or the American National Recreation Areas, designed to cater for the immediate recreational needs of a predominantly urban population. There is also growing recognition of the value of trails and footpaths in providing access to rural areas without heavy investment in land acquisition and management. Particular attention has been focused on the recreation potential of land on the edge of urban areas.

Recreation in the urban fringe

It may be argued that concern over the fate of the best scenic areas of a country, as characterized by national parks and similar areas, has blinded people to the possibilities for recreation that exist in most periurban environments. Reasons which have been cited in support of the urban fringe as a recreation locale include:

(a)   the likelihood of a continued growth in leisure demand, much of which could fall on fringe areas;

(b)   proximity to areas of high demand gives the fringe greatest potential for providing recreation opportunities to the whole population, including those without cars and with limited financial resources (i.e. latent demand);

(c)   urban fringe recreation provision can perform an interceptor function and relieve pressure on national parks and other pressured areas;

(d)   fringe provision can make good shortfalls in public open space found in major cities;

(e)   recreation developments can provide the raison d'être for many land uses in the fringe with an indeterminate present or future function;

(f)   provision and effective management of recreation facilities can reduce conflict between fringe land uses;

(g)   the fringe location offers an opportunity to provide innovatory blends of urban and rural recreation experiences;

(h)   recreation schemes in the fringe can involve environmental improvement by transforming derelict and unsightly landscapes.

As yet there is insufficient information on the levels of recreation provision in urban fringes (Elson 1979). The area and distribution of land devoted to leisure use in London's green belt has been estimated at between 6.0 percent (Ferguson and Munton 1979) and 8.0 percent (Standing Conference on London and South East Regional Planning 1976). These figures led Ferguson and Munton (1979, p. 202) to conclude that the supply problem exists less in the total area and number of sites in the green belt and more in 'the spatial distribution of sites, the objectives and practices of the bodies who own and manage them and in the character of, and access to, the facilities offered'. They found little to suggest that sectoral spatial disparities in levels of provision will be reduced significantly in the near future. Since the pattern of provision is essentially inherited, relatively few new sites have been developed in recent years; and the distribution of Country Parks designated since the 1968 Countryside Act 'bears little relation to the pattern of scarcity or to the availability of existing informal recreation sites' (Ibid., p. 203). Harrison (1981) also working in the metropolitan green belt found evidence against the view that recreation sites in the urban fringe act as substitutes for the deeper countryside or as outlets for the residents of innerurban areas. This supports earlier work which found that fringe and deep countryside locations rarely provide interchangeable recreational experiences, and that the urban fringe attracts predominantly local use. Arnott et al. (1978), for example, found that 50 percent of visitors to Strathclyde Regional Park on the southeastern fringe of Glasgow had walked from the adjoining areas of Hamilton and Motherwell. The inaccessibility of many urban fringes by public transport at evenings and weekends also undermines the areas' recreation potential. These findings suggest that the present case for provision of recreation facilities in the fringe may best be argued based on the needs of those who live in the immediate area, the reduction of land use uncertainties, and the beneficial effect that such developments can have on the environment.

A number of different types of recreation provision may be appropriate in the urban fringe, including regional parks, linear and small-scale facilities, and leisure parks.

Regional parks   These 'near-urban' parks (Bryant et al. 1982) are normally located within the half-day use hinterland of an urban area, and offer a variety of out-door recreation opportunities. An example is provided by the metroparks of the Huron-Clinton Metropolitan Authority serving the greater Detroit area (Figure 19.7). The Authority was created in 1940 purely to provide recreational facilities on a regional scale to complement those already available in city and state parks. There is no entrance fee to the parks, although individual activities (e.g. golf or sailing) have to be self-financing; the principal source of income being a local tax levy amounting to one-sixtieth of the county property tax. The location of the parks is related to three factors: (1) they were conceived entirely as day-use facilities and are within 45 minutes' drive of the conurbation centre; (2) they are directly related to the freeway network so that each sector of the conurbation has a park within easy reach; (3) maximum use is made of the presence of the Huron and Clinton rivers – at Kensington and Stony Creek, for example, artificial lakes have been created. Facilities vary widely but the overall aim was to provide 'large, easy-to-get-to picnic type facilities' and ample scope for water-based activities. As Patmore (1972, p. 286) observed, 'the system has real lessons to teach – planned provision, careful location and adequate

Figure 19.7   The metroparks of the Huron-Clinton metropolitan authority.

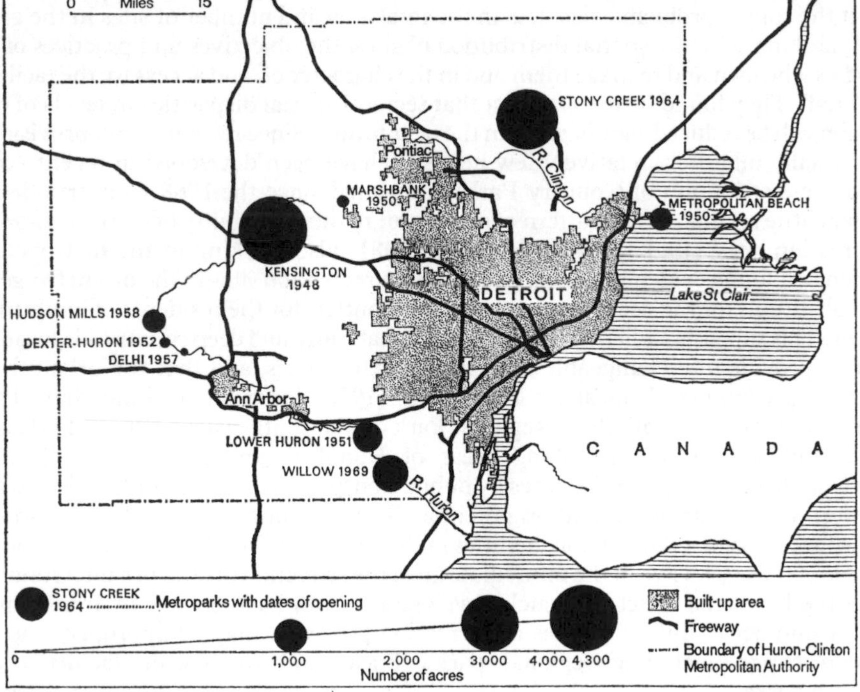

Source: Patmore (1972)

financing give a variety of recreational opportunities for intensive use close to the built-up area of the conurbation'. In the UK the Colne and Lee Valley regional parks, which in size terms lie between national and country parks, are smaller-scale variations on this theme.

Linear and small-scale facilities   There is a wide range of small-scale potential recreation infrastructure in the urban fringe. This includes old footpaths and bridleways often blocked or no longer maintained by local authorities. Nature trails and farm trails can also be laid out close to urban areas (Beynon 1975). Disused canals and towpaths, as provided by the Chesapeake and Ohio networks in the eastern USA as well as several hundred miles in England, are also a potential resource. Flooded sand and gravel pits can become pleasure lakes, and the contracting rural rail network is ideally suited to the creation of walkways and cycleways. The Greenways System in Stoke on Trent connects six towns, links public open spaces and brings green wedges into built-up areas. There is also a system of Blueways along river valley corridors and canal towpaths (Rettig 1976). At Druridge Bay in Northumberland a park has been created from an open-cast mining site and in Lubbock, Texas a recreation zone based on a linked system of lakes was developed from a municipal dumping ground and caliche mining site (Knack 1981).

Leisure parks   This kind of development would be out of place in attractive countryside but requires more space than could be made available in the built-up area and is dependent upon surroundings of parkland and woods which are positively linked with the more formal facilities. The leisure park contains elements of both an urban sports complex and a rural country park bringing together a variety of covered and open air facilities including swimming pools, theatres, zoos, children's farms, boating lakes, and traditional craft activities. Various examples exist including Amsterdamse Bos, the Ruhr Freizeit parks, the Tivoli Gardens of Copenhagen, Ontario Palace, Toronto, as well as theme parks like Sea World in Florida and the Disneyland developments in urban fringe locations in California and Florida. Two problems which hinder the transfer of such schemes to Britain are finance, where a combination of private and public capital may be required; and the rigid separation of town and country planning giving the fringe an indeterminate position in the structure.

References

ARNOTT, A., BEST, J., COPPOCK, J. and DUFFIELD, B. (1978) *Strathclyde Park 1977: Monitoring the Use of a Country Park* Research Report No. 39. Edinburgh: University Tourism and Recreation Research Unit.

BARKHAM, J. (1973) Recreational carrying capacity: a problem of perception, *Area* 5, 218–22.

BAXTER, M., DUFFIELD, B., and BLACKIE, J. (1977) *A Research Study into Recreation Activity Substitution in Scotland* Research Report No. 32. Edinburgh: University Tourism and Recreation Research Unit.

BAYFIELD, N. (1971) Some effects of walking and skiing on vegetation at Cairngorm. *In* E. Duffey and A. Watt *The Scientific Management of Animal and Plant Communities for Conservation.* Oxford: Blackwell, 469–85.

BEYNON, J. (1975) Farm trails in the countryside, *The Planner* 61(2), 52–6.

BLACKSELL, M. (1976) The role of le parc naturel et régional, *Town and Country Planning* 44(3), 165–70.

BOYETT, W. and TOLLEY, G. (1966) Recreation projection based on demand analysis, *Journal of Farm Economics* 48, 985–1001.

BROCKMAN, C., MERRIAM, L., CATTON, W. and DOWDLE, B. (1973) *Recreational Use of Wild Lands.* New York: McGraw Hill.

BROTHERTON, D. (1973) The concept of carrying capacity of countryside recreation areas, *Recreation News Supplement* 9, 6–11.

BROWN, W., SINGH, A., and CASTLE, E. (1964) *An Economic Appraisal of the Oregon Salmon and Steelhead Sport Fishery* Technical Bulletin No. 78. Oregon State University.

BRYANT, C. R., RUSSWURM, L. H. and McLELLAN, A. G. (1982) *The City's Countryside.* London: Longman.

CANADA LAND INVENTORY (1969) *Land Capability Classification for Outdoor Recreation* Report No. 6. Ottawa: Department of Regional Economic Expansion.

CLAWSON, M. (1959) *Methods of Measuring the Demand for and Value of Outdoor Recreation* Reprint No. 10. Washington DC: Resources for the Future.

CLAWSON, M. and KNETSCH, J. (1966) *Economics of Outdoor Recreation.* Baltimore: Johns Hopkins.

CLAWSON, M., HELD, R. and STODDARD, C. (1960) *Land For The Future.* Baltimore: Johns Hopkins.

COBHAM COMMITTEE (1974) *Report of House of Lords on Sport and Leisure.* London: HMSO.

COLENUTT, R. (1969) Modelling travel patterns of day-visitors to the countryside, *Area* 2, 43–7.

COUNTRYSIDE COMMISSION (1974) *Planning for Informal Recreation at the Sub-Regional Scale.* Cheltenham: The Author.

CURRY, N. (1980) *A Review of Cost–Benefit Techniques in Rural Recreation Planning* Gloucestershire Papers in Local and Rural Planning No. 7. Gloucestershire: Institute of Higher Education.

DAIUTE, R. (1966) Methods for the determination of demands for outdoor recreation, *Land Economics* 42(3), 327–38.

DAVIDSON, J. and WIBBERLEY, G. (1977) *Planning and the Rural Environment.* Oxford: Pergamon.

DOWER, M. (1965) *The Challenge of Leisure.* London: Civic Trust.

ELSON, M. J. (1979) *The Leisure Use of Green Belts and Urban Fringes.* London: Sports Council and Social Science Research Council.

FERGUSON, I. and GREIG, P. (1973) What price recreation? *Australian Forestry* 36, 80–90.

FERGUSON, M. J. and MUNTON, R. J. (1979) Informal recreation sites in London's green belt, *Area* 11(3), 196–204.

FINSTERBUSCH, K. (1980) *Understanding Social Impacts*. London: Sage.

FITTON, M. (1976) The urban fringe and the less privileged, *Countryside Recreation Review* 1, 25–34.

FLEGG, A. (1976) Methodological problems in estimating recreational demand functions and evaluating recreational benefits, *Regional Studies* 10, 353–62.

GARDNER, B. (1967) Discussion: analytical issues in demand analysis for outdoor recreation, *American Journal of Agricultural Economics* 49, 1304–6.

GARDNER, J. and NELSON, J. (1980) Comparing national park and related reserve policy in hinterland areas: Alaska, Northern Canada, and Northern Australia, *Environmental Conservation* 7 (1), 43–50.

GILLESPIE, G. and BREWER, D. (1968) Effects of non-price variables upon participation in water oriented outdoor recreation, *American Journal of Agricultural Economics* 50, 82–90.

GOLD, S. (1980) *Recreation Planning and Design*. New York: McGraw-Hill.

GOLDSMITH, F. (1974) Ecological effects of visitors in the countryside. *In* A. Warren and F. Goldsmith *Conservation in Practice*. London: Wiley, 217–32.

GUM, R. and MARTIN, W. (1975) Problems and solutions in estimating the demand for and value of rural outdoor recreation, *American Journal of Agricultural Economics* 57, 588–75.

HARRISON, C. (1981) A playground for whom? Informal recreation in London's green belt, *Area* 13(2), 109–14.

HOGG, D. (1977) The evolution of recreational resources. *In* D. Mercer *Leisure and Recreation in Australia*. Melbourne: Sorrett, 101–10.

HOOKWAY, R. J. (1978) National park plans: a milestone in the development of planning, *The Planner* 64, 20–2.

IRONSIDE, R. G. (1970) Private development in national parks, *Town Planning Review* 41, 305–16.

JOHNSTON, W. and PANKEY, V. (1968) Some considerations affecting empirical studies of recreational use, *American Journal of Agricultural Economics* 50, 1739–44.

KNACK, R. (1981) Canyon lakes: Texas-size success, *Planning* 47(2), 11–17.

KNETSCH, J. (1963) Outdoor recreation demands and benefits, *Land Economics* 39, 387–96.

KNETSCH, J. (1972) Interpreting demands for outdoor recreation, *Economic Record* 48, 429–32.

LAVERY, P. (1975) The demand for recreation, *Town Planning Review* 46(2), 185–200.

LIDDLE, M. J. (1975) A selective review of the ecological effects of human trampling on nature ecosystems, *Biological Conservation* 7, 17–36.

LIME, D. and STANKEY, G. (1979) Carrying capacity. *In* C. S. Van Doren, G. Priddle and J. Lewis *Land and Leisure.* London: Methuen, 105–18.

LUCAS, R. C. (1964) Wilderness perception and use: the example of the Boundary Waters Canoe Area, *Natural Resources Journal* 3, 394–411.

LUNDGREN, J. (1980) The land component in national recreational planning, *Canadian Geographer* 24(1), 22–31.

McCALLUM, J. and ADAMS, J. (1980) Charging for countryside recreation, *Transactions of the Institution of British Geographers* N.S. 5(3), 350–68.

McCONNELL, K. E. (1977) Congestion and willingness to pay, *Land Economics* 53, 185–95.

McMICHAEL, D. (1970) Problems in the management of a national park resource, *Proceedings of the Ecological Society of Australia* 5, 99–112.

MANSFIELD, N. (1971) The estimation of benefits from recreation sites and the provision of a new recreation facility, *Regional Studies* 5, 55–69.

MERCER, D. (1979) Outdoor recreation. *In* T. O'Riordan and R. C. D'Arge *Progress in Resource Management and Environmental Planning* Vol. 1. Wiley: Chichester, 87–142.

MEREWITZ, L. (1966) Recreation benefits from water resource development, *Water Resources Research* 2 (4), 625–40.

MERRIAM, L. and SMITH, C. (1974) Visitor impact on newly developed camp-sites in the Boundary Waters Canoe Area, *Journal of Forestry* 72, 627–30.

MOYES, A. (1977) Recreational transport in England and Wales, *Geography* 62(3), 209–12.

NORTON, G. (1970) Public outdoor recreation and resource allocation: a welfare approach, *Land Economics* 46(4), 414–22.

OUTDOOR RECREATION RESOURCES REVIEW COMMISSION (1962) *Outdoor Recreation for America.* Washington DC: US Government Printing Office.

OWEN, M., DOWERS, S. and DUFFIELD, B. (1974) *TRIP Series No. 1 System Description.* Edinburgh: University Tourism and Recreation Research Unit.

PACIONE, M. (1982) The use of objective and subjective measures of life quality in human geography, *Progress in Human Geography* 6 (4), 495–514.

PARKS CANADA (1979) *Parks Canada Policy.* Hull: The Author.

PATMORE, J. A. (1972) *Land and Leisure.* Harmondsworth: Penguin

PATMORE, J. A. (1983) *Recreation and Resources.* Oxford: Blackwell.

PETERSON, J. A. (1973) Rape of a wilderness lake, *Geographical Magazine* 45, 371–6.

PIGRAM, J. (1983) *Outdoor Recreation and Resource Management.* London: Croom Helm.

PRIDDLE, G. (1976) The revised Ontario provincial park classification system, *Geographical Inter-University Resource Management Seminar* Vol. 6. Waterloo: University Department of Geography, 48–71.

RETTIG, S. (1976) An investigation into the problems of urban fringe agriculture in a green-belt situation, *Planning Outlook* 19, 56–74.

RICHEZ, G. (1973) Les parcs naturels dans le Sud-Est de la France, *Méditerranée* 12, 119–35.

ROBERTS, K. (1978) *Contemporary Society and the Growth of Leisure*. London: Longman.

ROSS, W. and MARTS, M. (1975) The High Ross Dam project, *Canadian Geographer* 9, 221–34.

SHUCKSMITH, D. (1979) The demand for angling at Derwent reservoir, 1970 to 1976, *Journal of Agricultural Economics* 30, 25–37.

SIMMONS, I. G. (1974) National parks in developed countries. *In* A. Warren and F. Goldsmith *Conservation in Practice*. London: Wiley, 393–407.

SINDEN, J. (1974) A utility approach to the valuation of recreational and aesthetic experiences, *American Journal of Agricultural Economics* 56, 61–72.

SMITH, R. (1971) The evaluation of recreation benefits: the Clawson method in practice, *Urban Studies* 8 (2), 89–102.

SMITH, V. (1977) Re-examining an old problem: the identification of demand curves in out-door recreation, *Journal of Leisure Research* 9 (4), 313–5.

STANDING CONFERENCE ON LONDON AND SOUTH EAST REGIONAL PLAN-NING (1976) *The Improvement of London's Green Belt* SC 620. London: The Author.

STATHAM, D. (1972) Natural resources in the uplands, *Journal of the Royal Town Planning Institute* 58, 468–77.

STEIN, T. and SESSOMS, H. (1977) *Recreation and Special Populations*. Boston: Holbrook.

STEVENS, J. (1966) Recreation benefits from water pollution control, *Water Resources Research* 2 (2), 167–82.

STEVENS, J. (1967) Recreation benefits from water pollution control: a further note on benefit measurement, *Water Resources Research* 3 (1), 63–4.

TANNER, M. (1983) Recreation. *In* M. Pacione *Progress in Rural Geography*. London: Croom Helm, 173–97.

WEISBROD, B. (1967) Income redistribution effects in benefit–cost analysis. *In* S. B. Chase *Problems in Public Expenditure Analysis*. Washington: Brookings Institute, 177–209.

WILENSKY, H. (1961) The uneven distribution of leisure: the impact of economic growth on free time, *Social Problems* 9, 32–56.

YAPP, G. and BARROW, G. (1979) Zonation and carrying capacity estimates in Canadian park planning, *Biological Conservation* 15, 191–206.

ZETTER, J. (1974) The application of potential surface analysis to rural planning, *The Planner* 60 (2), 544–9.

20   Power and decision-making

To fully comprehend rural society it is necessary to examine the locus and exercise of power. According to Marx there are two kinds of power: 'the power of property, that is of property owners, on the one hand, and political power, the might of the State, on the other' (Jordan 1972, p. 145).

Landownership

In Britain the importance of land as a factor of production in agriculture and the significance of agriculture in rural society mean that even though, since the Industrial Revolution, the main sources of wealth have shifted elsewhere, landownership has continued to represent an important basis of power. Until the First World War the principal institution of landownership in the United Kingdom was the private estate belonging to an élite group which, despite its declining importance as a source of the nation's wealth, still controlled most of the levers of political power. 'Owning land was then quite distinct from farming land' (Newby et al. 1978, p. 32) and this distinction was reflected in the rural social structure of landowners, tenant farmers, and landless agricultural labourers. The dismantling of the landed estates commenced in the last third of the nineteenth century, with the declining fortunes of agriculture (Perry 1974) and accelerated after the First World War. Within three years, one-quarter of the land surface of the UK changed hands, and by 1927 one-third of the land used by farmers was owned by them. Since the Second World War there has been a consistent rise in the level of owner-occupation in agriculture as large estates have continued to be broken up. The immediate consequence of these ownership changes for rural society is that 'particularly in the lowland arable areas of England, a two class structure of owner-occupying farms and landless farm workers has begun to predominate' (Newby et al. 1978, p. 37). In many areas the social, economic and political leadership of rural society has passed into the hands of farmers rather than the traditional landed aristocracy.

Land, as well as being a factor of agricultural production, is also capital (Massey and Catalano 1978), and represents a secure long-term investment particularly in times of inflation. Thus, in addition to private owners who account for about 90.0 percent of agricultural land in England and Wales, there are also institutional landowners (Munton 1977; Clark 1981; Steel and Byrne 1983) of which there are three broad types: (1) traditional institutional landowners such as the Church, universities and the Monarchy; (2) public landowners such as nationalized industries, departments of state, and the National Trust; (3) financial institutions consisting of insurance companies, public and private pension funds, and property unit trusts. Wormell (1978) provides a detailed discussion of representatives of each of these groups, while estimates of the proportion of agricultural land owned by each are given in Table 20.1.

Table 20.1 *Agricultural landownership by public and semipublic bodies in Great Britain, 1971*

	Hectares	% of total
Monarchy	163,924	10.6
Church land	63,866	4.1
Universities and colleges	77,234	5.0
Forestry Commission	173,800	11.3
Government departments	243,673	15.8
Nationalized industries and public services	246,171	16.0
Local authorities	381,651	24.8
Agricultural Research Council and other experimental farms	7,329	0.5
'Conservation' authorities (National Trust, NCC, etc.)	133,955	8.7
Financial institutions	48,563	3.2
TOTAL	1,540,166	100.0

Source: Munton (1977)

An important distinction exists between landownership and land (use) control, that is between ownership rights and development rights. In the UK these two rights are effectively separated between the landowner and the State. All land, with the exception of that in agricultural use, woodland and much of that in government ownership, is subject to development control. This is in marked contrast to the situation in the USA where the rights of private ownership are paramount. The social and value system which supports private landownership in the United States is also at the core of resistance to formal land use planning. Conflict thus exists between the private decision oriented land market system and the view of public rights groups who maintain that land is a basic resource requiring development largely under public control. Resolution of this debate is of fundamental importance for the distribution of power in the country since 'change in who controls the land will result in major alterations in local power structures, involving a shift from the current land market system, which now often has dominant influence over local government land-use decisions toward increased power for land planners and local, state, and federal government decision-makers' (Lassey 1977, p. 89).

Public control over land in the USA stems from two sources:

(1)   Federal land holdings (Culhane 1981). About one-third of the 2.3 billion acres that constitute the US land area is under Federal control, with the proportion of Federally owned land being over 40.0 percent in states such as Nevada, Utah, Idaho, Wyoming, Arizona, and California.

(2)   Legal rights of eminent domain, police power, and taxation. Eminent domain (compulsory purchase) is the right to acquire property for public use on payment of just compensation to the owner. The police power is the right of the public to restrict or prevent certain land uses which may be detrimental to health, safety or welfare.

Finally, the right of taxation is, in effect, a public right to a share of the product from land through ad valorem and severance taxes. It may be regarded as a sort of 'public rent' paid by landowners to the public for the right to manage the land for their private gain and for the public's protection of their property interest.

Government structure

The allocation and exercise of power within most States is organized according to a hierarchical principle with a major division occurring between central and local government. In the United Kingdom central government sets the legislative framework for local government, imposes certain mandatory levels of service to be provided, and regulates expenditure through the allocation of the Rate Support Grant. Through white papers, circulars and other forms of communication central government departments attempt to establish policy guidelines which they expect local authorities to follow. Following a major reorganization in 1973, local government is carried out in England by an upper tier of 39 counties, 6 metropolitan counties and the Greater London Council, and a lower tier of 296 districts, 36 metropolitan districts and 33 London boroughs; in Wales by 8 counties and 36 districts; and in Scotland by 9 regions, 53 districts and 3 all-purpose island authorities. An integral part of this political-administrative structure is the planning system which operates according to a similar hierarchical arrangement. The new development plan system introduced in the Town and Country Planning Act of 1968 was intended to reduce the degree of central control by devolving greater responsibility to the local level. Central government's function, in theory, is confined to the approval of strategic development plans (structure plans) with local authorities preparing and adopting the local plans which elaborate strategic policies into land use proposals. Central government's policy interest in matters of detail is assumed to be covered by the formal requirement that local plans conform to the policies approved in structure plans. It should be noted, however, that the individual's right of appeal against a local planning decision means that in some cases the Secretary of State is the final arbitrator.

In the USA, the states play a crucial role in government, intermediate between the Federal and local or county levels. Each of the 50 states has its own constitution, legislature and statutes, and is responsible for a wide range of functions many of which it delegates to local jurisdictions. Some of these jurisdictions are independent, in others the local government acts within guidelines laid down by the state, while others have no discretionary power and act simply as an administrative agency for the state. Four kinds of substate local government are typical (Johnston 1982). The most basic of these is the county (which is present in every state except Rhode Island). In rural areas counties are administrative arms of the state providing the minimum services necessary for the dispersed population, for example law enforcement, supervision of public health, road maintenance, and administration of public welfare programmes. Within the counties 21 states (mostly in the northeast) have a subsidiary network of townships whose functions vary considerably from state to state but are generally few. More important areas within counties are the municipalities, densely populated areas that have been legally incorporated to govern defined areas. Incorporation generally follows a petition to the state legislature from the residents of particular areas and a referendum of all voters. The functions and powers of the municipal government are specified in its charter. The final type comprises special districts, most of which are ad hoc bodies created for a specific function. These operate in a complex overlapping set of territories many covering all or part of several municipalities. The most common form of special district is the school district; others cover a wide range of functions of which fire protection, drainage, and the provision and maintenance of parks are the most common. Special districts are created for a variety of reasons, including: (a) constitutional limitations on municipal revenue-raising which make separate districts the only way of financing desired services; (b) to overcome the constitutional prohibition of differential taxing within a local government territory so that the needs of different subareas can be accommodated; (c) a desire to finance services through particular user charges rather than general taxation; and (d) a requirement of some Federal grant-aid offers that particular functions, such as regional scale planning, be undertaken. The popularity of this device means that the number of special districts has increased from 8,299 in 1942 to 25,962 in 1977 (Johnston 1983). Overall, in 1977 there was a total of 79,862 local government units in the USA or '37 separate local government units for every 100 000 Americans' (Johnston 1982, p. 229).

In both the UK and North America, and elsewhere, central government exercises control over the actions of local government in two main ways – through its financial disbursements, and via legislation and the planning system.

Finance

In Britain the bulk of a local authority's finance derives from the Rate Support Grant provided by central government. Until 1979 the Rate Support Grant consisted of three parts: the domestic element, the resources element, and the needs element. The domestic element was paid to district councils to enable them to reduce the level of rates (local taxes) levied on householders. The resources element was paid to compensate those authorities whose rateable value per head of population was below a datum line determined annually by the government. This enabled those authorities with lower tax bases to maintain a similar standard of service to that elsewhere. The largest part of the Rate Support Grant was distributed through the needs element, and clearly the criteria adopted by central government for the calculation and distribution of this component had a significant impact on the effective power of local government. The policy of the Labour government between 1974 and 1979, in response to the emergence of urban deprivation as a readily identifiable problem, was to switch part of the Exchequer aid from rural to urban areas by altering the formula used to distribute the needs element of the Rate Support Grant. As Table 20.2 shows, in financial terms this had the effect of reducing the 1979/80 grant to nonmetropolitan authorities in England and Wales by 6.0 percent (£278 million) from its 1974/75 level, £212 million of this being transferred to the London boroughs and £66 million to other metropolitan districts. Clearly, since 'a 1 per cent change in the total size, or the urban/rural allocation of the Rate Support Grant far outweighs the entire budget of the Development Commission and similar rural development agencies'

Table 20.2 *Percentage share of needs element of rate support grant by type of local authority in England and Wales, 1974–1980*

Groups of authorities	1974/75	1975/76	1976/77	1977/78	1978/79	1979/80
Nonmetropolitan counties	57.5	57.4	55.4	53.8	51.9	51.6
Metropolitan districts	24.9	25.9	25.7	26.9	26.5	26.3
London boroughs	17.6	16.7	18.9	19.3	21.6	22.1

Source: Association of County Councils (1979)

(Moseley 1981, p. 586), such a policy redirection was strongly opposed by non-metropolitan authorities (Association of County Councils 1979). Following the introduction of a Conservative government in 1979 the different elements of the Rate Support Grant have been subsumed into a new block grant and a formula adopted which enables central government to control local expenditure by withdrawal of all or part of the grant from local authorities who ignore government spending guidelines. Thus, through the medium of the Rate Support Grant, the State is able to dictate levels of spending within local units and to direct central funding where it will. The scale of funds involved in this process ensures that any government decision has a significant redistributive impact in terms of both finance and power.

In the USA there are three basic ways of financing local government: taxes, user fees, and intergovernmental transfers. Historically, the backbone of local government finance has been the real property tax which, even with the growth of sales taxes, income taxes and intergovernmental transfer of funds, still accounted for 37.0 percent of all local revenues in 1971. However, as the tax-cutting Proposition 13 in California revealed, the real estate tax is reaching its economic and political limits as a source of local revenue. State and Federal assistance are now necessary to sustain public programmes in rural areas. Accordingly, the most significant development of the last two decades has been in the role of intergovernmental transfers, reflecting the growing importance of Federal grant-in-aid payments as well as state payments to localities (Rainey and Rainey 1978).

The framework for local government finance (as well as for its functions) is established by state constitution and statute law. State governments use three techniques to assist the localities: (1) they directly operate local programmes; (2) they provide grants for local government's operating programmes; and (3) they permit the localities a variety of tax and revenue raising methods. State financial aid to local government in 1974 made up 35.0 percent of county, 21.0 percent of municipal, 11.0 percent of township and 45.0 percent of school district general revenue. Federal involvement in local government finance has also increased to the extent that now 'scores of federal agencies provide money, services, and technical aid for non-metropolitan development' (Fuguitt et al. 1979, p. 69). The multifaceted Federal assistance does not come without cost to recipient states and localities. The costs include conformance to regulations, requirements, mandated programmes, and goals; the necessity of raising 'match' money; and sometimes supporting an unwanted project after Federal funds have run out. In order to offset some of the Federal-dominance problems of grants-in-aid a revenue-sharing programme was initiated by the State and Local Assistance Act 1972, which was reviewed and expanded in 1976. Under this, funds are distributed annually to state and local governments who have some discretion over their use. The amounts received by individual localities, however, are often small and can really be seen as 'topping-up' funds obtained from traditional grant-aid or other revenue-raising programmes.

Clearly under the Federal system of government individual American states have greater autonomy than the English and Welsh counties and Scottish regions, but in both countries central government continues to exercise considerable financial power over activity at the lower levels.

Planning

The organization of planning in England (Figure 20.1) may be taken as a broad representation of the British system, although Wales, Scotland and Northern Ireland differ in points of detail. The planning system has five levels – national advice, regional advisory plans, structure plans, local plans, and development control. The first three may be described as strategic, the latter two as concerned with implementation (Elson 1979). National and regional advice emanates from ministerial statements and from various central and regional offices of government departments. A major operational problem is that government policy itself changes over time. Earlier policy guidance from national government may be working its way down the levels of the planning system only to be overtaken at the development control stage by a policy change. One result of such policy changes overtaking development plan preparation is that government circulars become important considerations in development control. For example, circulars of the early 1970s calling for the release of more urban fringe development land were cited by many developers who appealed successfully against refusal of planning permission on green belt grounds (Langton 1976, 1978). More recently, developers have successfully used Circular 22/80, and its predecessor 9/80, to support their arguments over local authority delay in releasing land for house building (Herington 1982). Although government advice can bring about modifications at a late stage in structure plan preparation to bring it into line with changed national policy, the problem of development plans which are overtaken by national policy changes cannot be removed since plan preparation procedures can take several years.

Structure plans are prepared by the higher-tier local authority (counties in England and Wales, regions in Scotland). The primary purpose is to establish policy and general proposals for development and land use in the plan area. It also provides a framework for detailed local plans. Central government's main functions at this level are to direct that a local authority prepares a plan, and to examine, modify and approve the plan when submitted. Two debate and consultation stages are built into the procedure (Figure 20.2). The first is initiated by the county council through

Figure 20.1 The organization of planning in England.

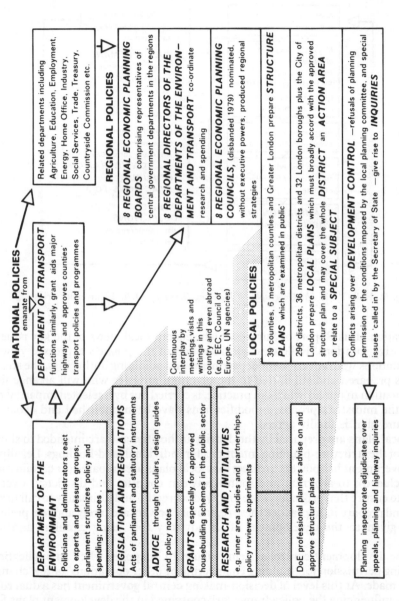

Source: J. M. Hall (1982) *The Geography of Planning Decisions*. Oxford University Press.

Figure 20.2 Public involvement in structure planning in England and Wales.

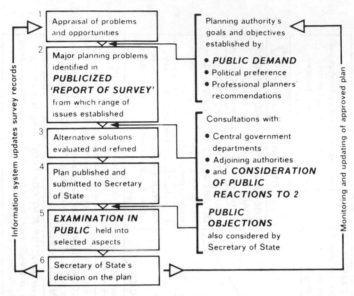

Source: J. M. Hall (1982) *The Geography of Planning Decisions.* Oxford University Press.

publication of its Report of Survey which sets out local views of the key issues and alternative solutions. Following consideration of the public's expressed views and consultations with government departments and adjoining authorities, the structure plan is prepared and submitted to the planning minister who will arrange for the 'examination in public' which, in practice, is carried out by a selected impartial panel. After the minister's proposed modifications have been published and debated the structure plan is finally agreed.

Local plans are prepared by the district authorities and are intended to show the effect of the structure-planning intentions for individual land-holdings. Legally, central government has powers to direct that local plans are prepared (or certain matters are included); to arbitrate in disputes between counties and districts; to vet local plans to ensure that procedures are followed correctly; and ultimately to call in a local plan and prepare it. In practice these regulatory powers are rarely applied, preference being given to the development of an advisory role using circulars and advice notes.

The development control system (Figure 20.3) applies when an application for planning permission for 'building engineering or other operations' or for 'changes of use' is made. At this level of decision-making central government has a dual role. As well as influencing the policy framework contained in the development plans for the area it also acts as arbitrator on appeals. Appeal decisions can thus serve as useful policy indicators for local authorities (Elson 1979).

Figure 20.3 The sequence of development control under the Town and Country Planning Acts.

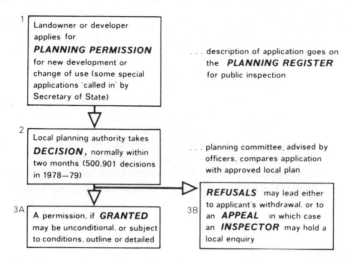

Source: J. M. Hall (1982) *The Geography of Planning Decisions.* Oxford University Press.

The formal planning system in North America is less well developed than in the United Kingdom and local governments have a greater degree of freedom with respect to legislation and environmental decision-making. The prevalent philosophy in the USA is summed up in Lassey's (1977, p. 1) statement that 'until very recently, systematic planning to deal with the potential negative consequences of change in most rural areas has somehow seemed unnecessary and inappropriate'. An ideology favouring private property rights and local autonomy has meant that planning for rural regions has been slow to evolve. As Lassey (Ibid., p. 7) observes 'there is relatively little experience with planning as a formal governmental process, and no widely acceptable institutional structure exists to support systematic public approaches to problem solving and preparation for the future'. The requirement of compulsory plans for each level of governmental region, as is the case in many European and most socialist countries, is not generally understood nor accepted, although it is now required for many Federally supported programmes.

The primary responsibility for planning in rural USA lies with the small town and rural constituency in which the decision-makers are elected county commissioners or supervisors. As Sundquist (1969, p. 226) put it, 'such tiny jurisdictions lack expertise; their elected officials are part-time amateurs and the communities lack the resources individually to employ professional personnel . . . They are deficient in capacity to conceive, plan, design and expedite projects.' The formation of multi-county districts can aid rural government and planning in several ways, for instance by providing areawide public services beyond the ability of individual jurisdictions, and offering a forum where local officials can resolve differences, hire and share professional managers and staff (circuit riders). Increasingly, however, because of the inadequacies of local jurisdictions state and Federal government have assumed the initiative for many former local government functions, including the more advanced approaches to planning.

Formalized planning is essentially ineffective without political and legal sanction. The USA lacks the legislative and legal framework for rural planning that exists in many European countries, such as the UK and the Netherlands. The common approach is the reactive one of ameliorative problem-solving which 'proceeds by studying problems, setting standards for acceptable levels of tolerance of the dysfunctions, and devising means of scaling the problems back down to acceptable proportions' (Berry 1973, p. 178). The implied goal is the preservation of the mainstream values of the past by smoothing out the problems that arise along the way. Whereas in Britain, Sweden, France and the Netherlands private profit oriented development is welcomed only to the extent that it conforms to the public plan, in the USA the favoured approach supports a private development style that incorporates bargaining among major interest groups relatively unfettered by national controls or guidelines.

Pressure groups

Groups formed to actively represent particular interests play a powerful role in the decision-making process. In a rural context in the UK, particularly important pressure groups are those pursuing the interests of farmers (National Farmers Union), landowners (Country Landowners Association) and 'environmentalists' (e.g. the Council for the Protection of Rural England, the Ramblers Association, and local conservation societies).

The National Farmers Union (NFU) was founded in 1908, represents approximately 80.0 percent of all farmers, and is recognized as one of the best-organized pressure groups in Britain, and one of the most successful agricultural organizations in Western Europe (Self and Storing 1962; Beresford 1975). The political character of modern agriculture has meant that the profitability of many, if not most, farmers has depended to a large extent on the NFU's negotiating ability and its efficiency as a parliamentary lobby in what virtually amounts to the collective bargaining of its members' incomes (Newby 1980). The NFU has considerable political influence. It 'makes representations, whenever necessary, to the general public, the food trade, Parliament, the Treasury and any other relevant Whitehall department. Above all it negotiates closely and almost unceasingly with the Ministry of Agriculture' (Green 1975, p. 136). Through the MAFF the NFU has a direct channel of influence into the Cabinet, and is normally consulted on farm price policy as well as on other legislation affecting rural land use at both national and local levels.

The Country Landowners Association (CLA) covers 60.0 percent of the land in England and Wales, and is smaller and less powerful than the NFU. While the CLA has gained the right to be consulted on all matters concerning landownership and is represented on many official committees, it does not enjoy the symbiotic relationship with the government that characterizes the NFU. Nevertheless it has considerable influence, particularly in the House of Lords, and maintains vital unofficial contacts with decision-makers.

The National Union of Agricultural and Allied Workers (NUAAW) is the weakest of the agricultural trinity representing less than 50.0 percent of full-time farm workers. The main problem that confronts agricultural trade unionism is the scale of the task involved in recruiting, organizing, and servicing the membership in the face of a declining labour force scattered in small groups across the countryside. From 1966 the NUAAW attempted to broaden its popular base by recruiting workers in food-processing industries but the powerful Transport and General Workers Union (TGWU) also has an agricultural workers section (which includes farm workers in Scotland). Compared with its urban-industrial counterparts the NUAAW remained weak and financially under strength. As a result of declining membership and falling income, since 1981 the NUAAW has been merged with the TGWU as the Agricultural Trade Group. Clearly, standing alone the NUAAW had neither the power nor the resources to counter the pressure exerted by the farmers' lobby, nor is the level of unionization in agriculture sufficiently high to permit widespread militant action. Indeed, in presenting a case for higher agricultural wages (which must inevitably bring higher food prices) the NUAAW found an ally in the NFU.

The proliferation of environmental organization has been one of the most significant postwar political developments in the countryside (Lowe and Goyder 1983). The emergence of a large and vociferous environmental lobby has helped to establish a frame of reference for public debate over conservation and amenity matters and has had undoubted influence upon official attitudes and policies. In part 'the growth of this lobby has represented a spontaneous grass-roots movement, with amenity societies and other environmental groups being formed locally to pursue some particular interest and only later joining one of the nationally based umbrella associations, which could put them in touch with other like-minded groups' (Newby 1980, p. 250). Buller and Lowe (1982) offer a case study of one local preservation society in Suffolk while Lowe and Goyder (1983) examine five others. The influence of the environmental lobby has increased greatly in recent years, and at the local level consultations usually take place between planning officers (who may even be members) and amenity societies.

Given the variety of interests pursued by pressure groups it would be surprising if conflicts did not occur. There are innumerable examples of local disputes, for example between farmers and conservationists over the removal of hedgerows, or between landowners and ramblers over rights of way. Conflicts can also often generate national interest as in the case of the successful proposal by the Tees Valley and Cleveland Water Board to construct a reservoir at Cow Green to supply the ICI chemical works at Billingham in the face of opposition from botanists and environmentalists concerned to protect arctic-alpine plant communities on Widdybank Fell (Whitby and Willis 1978). Other examples include the more recent controversies over the schemes to extend drainage of wetlands in the Somerset Levels and at Halvergate in Norfolk, and to construct Britain's first pressurized water nuclear power station at Sizewell in Suffolk (O'Riordan 1982).

The local level

Power and decision-making at the local level is, most immediately, in the hands of local politicians, bureaucrats, and planners. Although constrained by the financial and legislative mechanisms of central government these groups have considerable latitude within the overall framework. Many national policies, for example, are permissive rather than mandatory and many others leave considerable scope for local interpretation of how they are to be applied. Blowers (1980) provides an insight into the distribution and utilization of power within Bedfordshire County Council. In this he emphasizes the relationship between planning and politics and illustrates that while the power to make policy and to attempt to implement it is formally in the hands of the elected representatives who constitute a planning committee, in reality this power is confined to a small group of politicians and officials. Overall, 'planning policy-making is conducted within the rules of a game which inevitably reflects the interests of those who possess the information and skill to exploit the process' (Ibid., p. 7). This current of self-interest which underlies many planning policy-decisions may be either individual- or group-motivated, with the resultant actions often legitimized as being in the 'public interest' – a concept which is exceedingly difficult to define. This may be illustrated with reference to the exercise of power in East Anglia, a predominantly agricultural region where, according to Rose et al. (1979, p. 11), 'farmers and landowners dominate rural local government as effectively as they did in the past'. For example, a study of the composition of Suffolk County Council in 1975 found that farmers or landowners held the strategic positions of chairman, vice-chairman, leader of the council, and the chairmanship of all the key committees (i.e. planning, education, social services, finance, and policy and resources). Rose et al. conclude that 'not withstanding the fact that farmers and landowners on local councils claim to be concerned with performing a service for the community, and with discharging the obligations which they see as attached to their privileged position in rural society . . . what farmers and landowners perceive as being in the public interest more generally reflects *their* values, *their* beliefs and *their* ideologies, and thus indirectly furthers their interests to the detriment of less powerful and less prosperous groups' (Ibid.).

Newby et al. (1978) illustrate the effects of the decision-making élite on housing and employment policy in Suffolk where an underlying conservative ethic has tended to perpetuate the status quo. In the case of housing, restrictions placed on new residential development have increased inflationary pressures on private house prices with the result that some of the indigenous population may be priced out of the housing market in their local village through competition with middle class newcomers. Equally, the low-rate policies that have long been pursued by politicians throughout Suffolk (Saunders et al. 1978) have resulted in a particularly low level of council house building despite lengthy waiting lists, meaning that low-paid local workers must either find existing tied or scarce rented accommodation in their home area, or else emigrate. Such restrictive policies, therefore, have had a redistributive effect. This is also evident in employment and income terms. Despite the fact that agricultural wage levels in East Anglia are low and that industrial development might reasonably be expected to raise earned income levels (Lemon 1975), opportunities for attracting new industry into predominantly rural areas have consistently been rejected by Suffolk County Council, on the grounds of environmental conservation. Fuguitt et al. (1979, p. 76) in a parallel example note the activity of 'no growth coalitions' in rural USA 'able to use a variety of state and federal laws and regulations concerning the environment in frustrating development plans unacceptable to them'. Buchanan (1982) in a study of the preparation of the Suffolk county structure plan illustrates the power of a small élite in Suffolk County Council to order the contents of the plan and control the involvement of councillors, officers, nongovernmental organizations and the public through various 'non-decision-making' processes (Bachrach and Baratz 1970). The general argument advanced is *not* that the power of economically and socially dominant groups is necessarily used by them in a cynical way to pursue their own interests but that the effects of the routine use of power are redistributive and are often socially regressive.

Among the constraints on the power of leading members of local authorities are the electorate, political parties, special interest groups, other authorities and central government, existing processes and policies, available resources, and the problems of implementation (Blowers 1980). Consideration of these introduces a further perspective on power and decision-making in rural areas. This refers to the crucial difference between plan making and plan implementation. As Boulding (1974, p. 8) noted, 'the world moves into the future as a result of decisions, not as a result of plans. Plans are significant only insofar as they affect decisions.' Resources represent one of the keys to the ability of a local council to implement its policies. In planning especially, resources are often in the hands of other public authorities with which the local authority must liaise. An indication of the plethora of public sector agencies involved in rural decision-making in Britain is provided in Figure 20.4. Such division and, to some extent, duplication of responsibilities impedes the formulation and execution of plans as each agency operates according to unique terms of reference; and in the view of Leach (1980, p. 293) 'will only co-operate when it suits them, or when they have to, and then very much on their own terms, and in line with their own interests'. For example, the necessity that all modern homes have a main water supply and are connected to a water-borne sewage system gives the Regional Water Authority almost a power of veto over new development. Glyn-Jones (1979) documents the shortfall of housing development in the mid-Devon village of Hatherleigh due to the limited capacity of the sewage disposal system despite its key settlement status in the county plan. Private sector investment decisions also affect the feasibility of local authority plans. In the housing sector, for example, local authority planners have a negative power to refuse permission for any proposed residential development but it is the private sector landowning and development agencies and their financial supporters who decide on the number, type and purpose of proposals (Barrett and Fudge 1981; Cloke 1983). In Devon Blacksell and Gilg (1981) have demonstrated that despite officially stated intentions to impose strict planning controls, new residential development is not necessarily resisted in pressured rural areas when developers decline to intitiate building programmes in places preferred by the local authorities and opt instead for sites from which they would normally be debarred.

The distribution of power in rural society is a multifaceted and complex phenomenon. In both the UK and the USA the power to make decisions affecting

Figure 20.4 Central and local government responsibilities in rural areas.

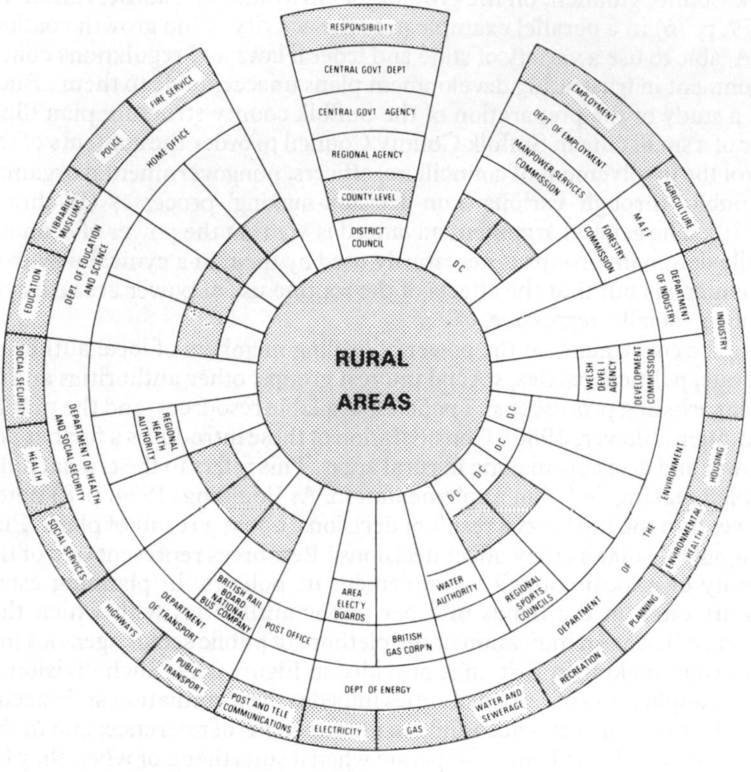

Source: Association of County Councils (1979)

conditions in rural areas is spread across several levels of government and diffused among a host of different individuals, agencies and interest groups. Despite fundamentally different administrative and planning structures an underlying problem in both countries is the lack of coordination among the various decision-makers. In the UK this has led to calls for corporate planning at the county and district level and for a single agency or 'Ministry of Rural Affairs' to coordinate government policies for rural areas. In the USA progress could be based on improving the efficiency and effectiveness of the smaller rural administrations, an extension of the multicounty boards concept, and a move towards a more future-oriented rather than problem-solving form of planning.

References

ASSOCIATION OF COUNTY COUNCILS (1979) *Rural Deprivation.* London: The Author.

BACHRACH, P. and BARATZ, M. (1970) *Power and Poverty.* Oxford: Blackwell.

BARRETT, S. and FUDGE, C. (1981) *Policy and Action*. London: Methuen.

BERESFORD, T. (1975) *We Plough the Fields*. Harmondsworth: Penguin.

BERRY, B. J. L. (1973) *The Human Consequences of Urbanisation*. London: Macmillan.

BLACKSELL, M. and GILG, A. (1981) *The Countryside: Planning and Change*. London: Allen and Unwin.

BLOWERS, A. (1980) *The Limits of Power*. Oxford: Pergamon.

BOULDING, K. (1974) Reflections on planning: the value of uncertainty, *Technology Review* 77 (1), 8.

BUCHANAN, S. (1982) Power and planning in rural areas. *In* M. J. Moseley *Power Planning and People in East Anglia*. Norwich: University of East Anglia, Centre of East Anglian Studies, 1–20.

BULLER, H. and LOWE, P. (1982) Politics and class in rural preservation: a study of the Suffolk Preservation Society. *In* M. J. Moseley *Power Planning and People in East Anglia*. Norwich: University of East Anglia, Centre of East Anglian Studies, 21–41.

CLARK, G. (1981) Public ownership of land in Scotland, *Scottish Geographical Magazine* 97(3), 140–6.

CLOKE, P. J. (1983) Rural resource evaluation and management. *In* M. Pacione *Progress in Rural Geography*. London: Croom Helm, 198–225.

CULHANE, P. (1981) *Public Lands Politics*. Baltimore: Johns Hopkins University Press.

ELSON, M. (1979) *Perspectives on Green Belt Local Plans* Working Paper No. 38. Oxford: Polytechnic Department of Town Planning.

FUGUITT, G., VOSS, P. and DOHERTY, J. (1979) *Growth and Change in Rural America*. Washington DC: Urban Land Institute.

GLYN-JONES, A. (1979) *Rural Recovery: Has it Begun?* Exeter: Devon County Council and University of Exeter.

GREEN, D. (1975) *Politics of Food*. London: Cremonesi.

HALL, J. M. (1982) *The Geography of Planning Decisions*. Oxford: The University Press.

HERINGTON, J. (1982) Circular 22/80 – the demise of settlement planning? *Area* 14(2), 157–66.

JOHNSTON, R. J. (1982) *The American Urban System*. London: Longman.

JOHNSTON, R. J. (1983) Urban government and finance. *In* M. Pacione *Progress in Urban Geography*. London: Croom Helm, 128–47.

JORDAN, Z. (1972) *Karl Marx*. London: Nelson.

LANGTON, T. (1976) *Planning Appeals* Vol. 1. London: Ambit.

LANGTON, T. (1978) *Planning Appeals* Vol. 2. London: Ambit.

LASSEY, W. (1977) *Planning in Rural Environments*. New York: McGraw-Hill.

LEACH, S. (1980) Organisational interests and inter-organisational behaviour in town planning, *Town Planning Review* 51, 286–99.

LEMON, A. (1975) *Post-War Industrial Growth in East Anglian Small Towns: A Study of Migrant Firms 1945–70* Research Paper No. 12. Oxford: University School of Geography.

LOWE, P. and GOYDER, J. (1983) *Environmental Groups in Politics*. London: Allen and Unwin.

MASSEY, D. and CATALANO, A. (1978) *Capital and Land: landownership by capital in Great Britain*. London: Arnold.

MOSELEY, M. (1981) Changing values in the British countryside, *Geographical Magazine* 53 (9), 581–6.

MOSELEY, M. (1982) *Power Planning and People in East Anglia*. Norwich: University of East Anglia Centre of East Anglian Studies.

MUNTON, R. (1977) Financial institutions: their ownership of agricultural land in Great Britain, *Area* 9 (1), 29–37.

NEWBY, H. (1980) *Green and Pleasant Land*. Harmondsworth: Penguin.

NEWBY, H., BELL, C., ROSE, D. and SAUNDERS, P. (1978) *Property, Paternalism and Power*. London: Hutchinson.

O'RIORDAN, T. (1982) Environmental issues, *Progress in Human Geography* 6(3), 409–24.

PERRY, P. J. (1974) *British Agriculture, 1875–1914*. London: Methuen.

RAINEY, K. D. and RAINEY, K. G. (1978) Rural government and local public services. *In* T. R. Ford *Rural USA: Persistence and Change*. Ames: Iowa State University Press, 126–44.

ROSE, D., SAUNDERS, P., NEWBY, H. and BELL, C. (1979) The economic and political basis of rural deprivation. *In* J. M. Shaw *Rural Deprivation and Planning*. Norwich: Geo Books, 11–20.

SAUNDERS, P., NEWBY, H., BELL, C. and ROSE, D. (1978) Rural community and rural community power. *In* H. Newby *International Perspectives in Rural Sociology*. Chichester: Wiley, 55–85.

SELF, P. and STORING, H. (1962) *The State and the Farmer*. London: Allen and Unwin.

STEEL, A. and BYRNE, P. (1983) *Financial Institutions: their investments and agricultural land ownership* Working Paper No. 1. Reading: University Department of Land Management.

SUNDQUIST, J. (1969) *Making Federalism Work*. Washington DC: Brookings Institute.

WHITBY, M. and WILLIS, K. (1978) *Rural Resource Development*. London: Methuen.

WORMELL, P. (1978) *Anatomy of Agriculture*. London: Harrap.

Index